The Deepest South

The Deepest South

The United States, Brazil, and the African Slave Trade

Gerald Horne

NEW YORK UNIVERSITY PRESS
New York and London

NEW YORK UNIVERSITY PRESS
New York and London
www.nyupress.org

Library of Congress Cataloging-in-Publication Data
Horne, Gerald.
The deepest south : the United States, Brazil, and the African slave
trade / Gerald Horne.
p. cm.
Includes bibliographical references and index.
ISBN-13: 978-0-8147-3688-3 (cloth : alk. paper)
ISBN-10: 0-8147-3688-2 (cloth : alk. paper)
ISBN-13: 978-0-8147-3689-0 (pbk. : alk. paper)
ISBN-10: 0-8147-3689-0 (pbk. : alk. paper)
1. Slave-trade—America—History—19th century. 2. Slavery—
United States—History—19th century. 3. Slavery—Brazil—
History—19th century. I. Title.
HT1048.H67 2006
306.3'62—dc22   2006029836

New York University Press books are printed on acid-free paper,
and their binding materials are chosen for strength and durability.

Manufactured in the United States of America

c 10 9 8 7 6 5 4 3 2 1
p 10 9 8 7 6 5 4 3 2 1

Contents

Introduction

This book is about the relationship between the two great slave empires of the 19th century—the U.S. and Brazil—in the context of the African Slave Trade, with the accent decidedly on North America. This is *not* a book about slavery in Brazil; though the narrative engages four continents, the primary focus is on the U.S., more specifically, the role of U.S. nationals as slave traders and sojourners in Brazil; i.e., this book is also a social history about the impact of Brazil on the U.S. It is very much a story that involves Brazil (and Africa) in the eyes of the U.S.—and not vice versa,[1] and it is very much a story about the role of U.S. nationals in the African Slave Trade. It is also a story about the continuing rivalry between London and Washington that had exploded in war in 1812 and then festered as the U.K. abolished slavery in the Empire in the 1830s.

This book argues that U.S. slavery is better understood in hemispheric terms—the Slave South saw in an alliance with Brazil a formidable hedge against a future relationship with the North and, for that matter, a hedge against continuing pressure from London to abolish slavery, a hedge that could mean triumph in a Civil War, if need be.

Two leading characters in these pages are former Virginia Governor, Henry Wise—John Brown's executioner—and Matthew Fontaine Maury, a Virginian of a stature comparable to Robert E. Lee and Stonewall Jackson. As Minister to Brazil, Wise crusaded vigorously against the illicit slave trade to Brazil, while Maury advocated strongly for deporting enslaved U.S. Negroes to the Amazon for the purpose of developing this region; he was also part of a cabal that had designs on seizing the Amazon from Brazil: their ostensibly separate initiatives are best comprehended in unison, i.e., if Brazil could draw upon the labor of enslaved African-Americans, there would be no need to draw upon the illicit trade, which was dominated by forces in the U.S. Northeast and their lust for Brazilian territory was of a piece with their boundless expansion westward in North America. This was one more source of regional tension that was to explode in Civil War. Likewise, the flood of U.S. nationals who arrived in Brazil on their way to the California gold-fields got a glimpse of a brutal slavery that enhanced abolitionist sentiment and also exacerbated regional tensions. This relationship with Brazil was an aspect of a larger phenomenon: the blurring of citizenship boundaries as slavers changed flags in midocean routinely; those who sought to profit from the slave trade often thought that U.S. nationality provided protection and altered citizenship accordingly; diplomats in foreign capitals often acted on behalf of more than one nation; at times it seemed that slave trading was the prime preoccupation of certain diplomats, notably—though not exclusively—those of Portugal serving in New York, who advocated kidnapping Africans and compelling them to be "American," albeit enslaved. This frayed idea of citizenship contributed to thinking in the Slave South that was evolving away from allegiance to Washington and toward a firmer relationship with Brazil.

Contours of the African Slave Trade

Between 1500 and 1800, more Africans than Europeans arrived in the Americas,[2] while recent research suggests that between 12 million and 20 million Africans were shipped against their will by Europeans and European colonists to the New World up to the latter stages of the 19th century.[3] By one estimate 100 million Africans lost their lives as a result of the maritime slave trades.[4] Between 1600 and 1850, "approximately 4.5 million enslaved Africans went to Brazil, ten times as many as went to North America and indeed more than the total number of Africans who went to all of the Caribbean and North America combined."[5] Luanda, Angola offered a shorter sea passage to Brazilian ports than most slave-hunting grounds—35 days to Pernambuco; thus, after 1575, Angolans predominated in the Black Brazilian population.[6]

Yet despite the length and breadth of the era of the African Slave Trade, more than 40 percent made this perilous voyage in the ninety years prior to "final suppression in 1867,"[7] and it was during the 1840s that "the transatlantic slave trade probably reached an all-time peak." Brazil imported well over one million slaves (half of them illegally) during the first half of the nineteenth century compared with an estimated three million slaves during the previous 300 years.[8] From 1835 to 1855 alone, 500,000 Africans were smuggled to Brazil, an essential element of what has been termed "the largest forced emigration in history."[9]

Hence, historians estimate the Brazilian slave population around 1820 to be two million, i.e., two-thirds of the country's total population.[10] In the following decades, U.S. nationals played a key role in skewing further the population of Brazil with their avid smuggling of the enslaved and allowing their flag to be deployed for the same function. In a sense this was appropriate since by 1825, according to Robert Fogel and Stanley Engerman, these two nations contained 67 percent of the total enslaved population in the Americas.[11] Thus, to gain a fuller understanding of "American" slavery, we must examine the U.S. and Brazil tie, particularly since the latter nation provided succor for slavery in the former.

As W. E. B. Du Bois observed, the "American slave trade"—i.e., that of the western hemisphere—during its busiest and most profitable stage "came to be carried on principally by United States capital, in United States ships, officered by United States citizens, and under the United States flag."[12] More precisely, as this illicit business rose in the 1840s, enslaved Africans were transported disproportionately on ships made and/or registered in the U.S. and flying the U.S. flag and, as time passed, increasingly these ships carried U.S. crews and were financed by U.S. capital.[13] The Stars and Stripes began to appear regularly in the foreign slave trade when it was introduced into the Cuban trade following the signing of the comprehensive Anglo-Spanish treaty of 1835. From 1838 there were reports of its appearance in the Brazilian trade and its use increased rapidly during the years 1840–51. Despite federal laws prohibiting the participation of U.S. citizens and U.S. vessels in the slave trade, U.S.-built ships left Baltimore, New York, Providence, Boston, Salem, and other New England ports for Brazil, where they were either sold to U.S. nationals acting as front men for slave dealers or sold directly to dealers. Moreover, "a great many of the slave traders (Portuguese, Brazilians, and others) who chose to seek a safe alternative to the Portuguese flag found it in the Stars and Stripes."[14] The provision of vessels was critical, as this industry was major in the U.S., and the staunch refusal of the U.S. to allow its flagged ships to be searched by the Royal Navy of London was similarly important. As time passed and particularly as the Civil War approached, these U.S. nationals' role became even more prominent in this business.[15]

This Brazilian slave trade as a whole was more profitable than that of any other national slave trade; it was a "veritable El Dorado."[16] During the pivotal 1840s, "there were probably more slaves traded at the Valongo market in Rio de Janeiro than all the New Orleans markets put together."[17] Yet, the importance of this African Slave Trade to Brazil has not been sufficiently recognized in the nation that was one of its principal beneficiaries—the U.S. Not least, this historical amnesia elides the profound point that this odious commerce "constituted a sort of unsuspected and, very often, deliberately concealed genocide,"[18] contributing to the sad fact that "the African population declined significantly as a proportion of the world's population between 1700 and 1900, a decline that can be attributed in large part to the effects of slavery and the slave trade."[19] This occurred as simultaneously much of the wealth of the major nations of Europe and North America was built on the labor and suffering of millions of Africans.[20]

Deport U.S. Negroes to Brazil?

Those in the U.S. in the 19th century who advocated on behalf of an African Slave Trade that was illegal represented the most disunionist and pro-slavery faction of secessionists; indeed, a significant percentage of secessionists in the Lower South actively promoted or sympathized with the slave trade cause on the eve of disunion. This trend lay at the forefront of slavery expansionism and southern nationalism.[21] These notorious "fire-eaters" placed Brazil near the center of their dream of a transcontinental empire of slavery,[22] particularly in the 1850s, when it seemed that slavery was encountering a roadblock in its westward expansion.[23] Thus, lamented the key abolitionist, William Lloyd Garrison, in 1854, "Brother [Wendell] Phillips was right: 'the future seems to unfold a vast slave empire united with Brazil, and darkening the whole west.'"[24] That very same year a group of men with "grandiose ideas" created the "Knights of the Golden Circle" who plotted to realize Garrison's worst nightmare—forging a "great slave empire" that blanketed the hemisphere.[25]

The most articulate and influential advocate of a Brazil strategy was the celebrated Virginian, Matthew Fontaine Maury—renowned scientist and powerful Confederate, who ranks in the state's annals alongside Robert E. Lee. He saw the Amazon famously as the "safety-valve of the Union" and envisioned deporting U.S. Negroes (accompanied by slave masters, of course) to this still relatively underdeveloped region as an advance guard of Dixie colonialism.[26] "It is easier and quicker," argued Maury, "for sailing vessels from the Amazon to make the voyage to New York, than to Rio; and a vessel can make the passage quicker from New York to Rio, than she can from the Amazon to Rio." Thus, he concluded, it would be "wise to transfer the slaves of the Mississippi Valley to the valley of the Amazon"—an analysis that was taken quite seriously at the time in the Brazilian Foreign Ministry, as Maury's provocative words were translated and discussed.[27] In a carefully worded response, replete with loopholes and ambiguities—a classic "non-denial denial"—U.S. Secretary of State William Marcy assured his Brazilian counterpart that he should not take seriously "certain newspaper articles" which "created the [impression] on the mind of [Brazilians]" that a "steamer of the United States is in the Amazon."[28]

Maury was among many in the U.S. who cast a ravenous eye on Brazilian territory. There was a continuity of interest among those who wanted to seize land in South America and those who wanted to ship enslaved Africans from the U.S. to this continent—with the former accompanying the latter as this aggression was being consummated. Strikingly, as thousands of U.S. nationals traveled by ship to Rio on their way to California during the 1848–50 "Gold Rush," a number of them scrutinized carefully the military defenses of this South American giant.[29] W. Grayson Mann, who had served recently as secretary to the U.S. Minister in Brazil, urged the infamous soldier-of-fortune, William Walker, in mid-1857 to "change his focus" from seizing the minnow that was Nicaragua and turn his attention to the whale that was Brazil, claiming that he would then join Walker to help prevent "the fairest portion of God's Creation rotting away in the hands of a decrepit race incapable of developing its resources.'"[30] Mark Twain was among those in the U.S. who "'was fired with a longing to ascend the Amazon'" and "'tried to contrive ways to get to Para'" there. He left Keokuk, floating down the Mississippi heading for this town, though—in a journey that may have been more fanciful than real—"he never got any further than New Orleans."[31] Not surprisingly, the articulate African American, J. H. Banks, agreed with the not uncommon opinion on the eve of the Civil War that the "aim of the slave power is to unite with Brazil and extend the disunion of slavery to the Pacific."[32]

The idea of deporting U.S. Negroes to the Amazon—championed by Maury—was gaining traction, even as the Civil War proceeded. In

1862, a committee of the House of Representatives on "Emancipation and Colonization" considered this notion, arguing that "no one can have failed to observe the power and influence which Great Britain has exercised and the substantial advantages she has obtained in all the countries around the Gulf of Mexico, through the instrumentality of Jamaica Negroes, who are to be found scattered in small settlements through these regions."[33]

A few years earlier, in 1858, a "group of Republican leaders from the border states and the West introduced legislation to subsidize black colonization in Latin America" in an "attempt to rebut the Democratic image of the Republicans as proponents of 'Africanization' of the territories. . . . in the border states especially, they added, espousing colonization was essential to building a Republican Party base among poor whites."[34] This scheme was revived with a vengeance by Washington's Civil War ambassador to Brazil, James Watson Webb, a comrade of South Carolina's pro-slavery leader, John C. Calhoun. But the Brazilian Minister of Foreign Affairs, though finding Webb's plan "highly interesting" that deserved to be "seriously pondered" rejected this mass deportation since "nothing of that sort may possibly be tried in our country, as we have a positive law which expressly interdicts the admittance of any freed Negroes within our limits."[35]

Undeterred, Washington queried a number of Latin American nations within Spain's sphere of influence about accepting deported U.S. Negroes. But Madrid's man in Haiti warned sternly that their presence would be a danger to those of European descent in Santo Domingo and could foment countless local and global conflicts.[36] On the day the Emancipation Proclamation took effect, the U.S. legation in Brazil's neighbor, Ecuador, briskly informed Washington that "in accordance" with instructions from his government, he had queried "the Ecuadorean government on the subject of Negro Colonization. I find them entirely averse to it," this after he had "a conversation with the President at his house" where in line with certain hemispheric norms he "expressed strong antipathies against the Negro race. He regretted that there are so many of them in and about Guayaquil and added that it would be very fortunate for the white race in America if it could rid itself of the Negro element either by transferring it back to Africa or in some other way."[37] Even after the "Emancipation Proclamation," London's man in Washington reported that the "President of the United States sent for me" and "told me that he had been for some time anxious to speak to me in an informal unofficial manner on the subject of promoting the emigration of coloured people from this country to the British colonies."[38]

Certainly the inability of Washington to secure a foreign destination for Negroes aided in compelling U.S. leaders to accept a black presence on these shores. On the other hand, London's reluctance to accept this precursor of "ethnic cleansing" was not necessarily motivated by humane considerations but was more of a reluctance to embrace a stigmatized group or to do any favors for a nation, i.e., the U.S., it had already warred with and with which it endured a continual conflict.

In the run-up to this deportation scheme, sharp conflicts had emerged between London and Washington, not least because of the former's efforts to enforce the ban on the illegal slave trade, which had Brazil as its foremost destination. J. H. Banks spoke for many of his fellow African-Americans when he chose to "look upon [Britain] as the friend of the coloured race. It is a common opinion among the slaves that slavery will be terminated by a war between England and the United States." Like a number of U.S. Negroes, he chose exile in Britain.[39] Would more U.S. Negroes defect to the venerable foe that was the U.K., if plans accelerated to ship them out of the country?

From the other shore, as John C. Calhoun saw it, London's prosecution of anti–slave trade regulations was hypocritical and self-interested, intended to " 'destroy the peace and prosperity of both' " Brazil and the U.S. and " 'transfer the production of rice, cotton, sugar and coffee' " from these two nations to London's " 'possessions beyond the Cape of Good Hope.' "[40] When the legislature in Texas, a state that was long a site for illegal smuggling of enslaved Africans, moved in 1857 toward the legal reopening of the trade, the solons of the Lone Star State argued that abolitionist pressure from London was compelling this conclusion.[41]

Accordingly, the U.S. Minister to Spain, Washington Irving, informed Secretary of State John C. Calhoun about conversations he had engaged in concerning "prosecuting the scheme of organizing a coalition between the French and Spanish colonies, Brazil and the Southern parts of the United States to protect themselves from the Abolition intrigues and the machinations of England."[42] Washington "had refused" to "participate in the new [global abolitionist] initiatives and continually refused to countenance the idea of an antislavery league," while steadfastly refusing to grant the British Navy authority to search suspected slavers bearing the U.S. flag, which encouraged pirates of various nationalities to hoist this banner.[43] Then, during the Crimean War the British, who had the "largest" anti–slave trade "force on the coast" of Africa, "were obliged to reduce it very materially," which was like a dream-come-true for U.S. slavers.[44]

Consequently, as the Civil War approached, Washington was informed by London that "the slave trade continues to be carried on, on the African coast, and almost exclusively by vessels sailing under the American flag, and provided with genuine American papers. . . . American citizens engage in it almost with impunity."[45] Of "170 slave-trading expeditions fitted out in little more than three years preceding 1862"— a time when the trade was reaching new heights in its centuries' long history—"no fewer than 74 were known to or believed to have sailed from New York, 43 from other American ports, 40 from ports in Cuba, and the rest from European ports."[46] Relations between London—the prime enforcer of strictures against the slave trade—and Washington, whose nationals were the prime scofflaws, had deteriorated to the point that even during the midst of the Civil War officials in Cape Town, a major listening post for the monitoring of this illicit commerce, were informed that the U.K. "may shortly be engaged in a war with the United States."[47]

The U.S. and the Slave Trade to Brazil

The U.S. was the principal market for Brazilian coffee during the 1820s and early 1830s, suggesting that North Americans were a beneficiary in a major crop of an economy driven by slave labor.[48] It was not surprising when in early 1826 the President of Baltimore's Chamber of Commerce spoke warmly of "the great magnitude of our Commerce with the rich and extensive Empire of Brazil and with the provinces of Rio de la Plata." This region was absorbing a "larger proportion of the produce of our Country than any other branch of our South American trade."[49] As the flag followed commerce—and vice versa—the U.S. legation in Brazil often was studded with self-interested businessmen. William Wright of Maryland—whose family was prominent in Brazil's economy—also represented the U.S. in this giant nation. His connections to the slave trade caused some abolitionists to fret that such diplomats would be less than aggressive in enforcing the bar against this evil commerce.[50] Manuel Pinto de Fonseca of Rio de Janeiro, a major figure in the unlawful slave trade, "had business connections with the U.S. firm of Maxwell, Wright and Co., also located in Rio de Janeiro"—which, of course, was the prize jewel of the Wright family of Maryland. This company "facilitated the financing of U.S. slavers by Brazilian entrepreneurs and the sale of newly imported Africans to plantations. Wright and Company was the largest U.S. merchant firm in Rio de Janeiro from the 1820s through the 1840s" and also had extensive interests in Cuba, the West Indies, and Europe.[51]

Though they literally wrote the book on U.S. trade with Brazil,[52] Wright and Company were not singular as there were other U.S. firms jousting for influence in this enormously profitable business.[53] Interestingly, Wright was not unique in being a diplomat tied to slave traders[54]: this was a pattern that was not uncommon and given the official capacities of these men, this tie obviously facilitated the continuation of the illicit trade.[55] Though a consensus has emerged that the illegal trade to Brazil had dropped off sharply by the early 1850s, that decade continued to witness human shipments by those with U.S. ties, particularly the Portuguese Company [Companhia Portuguesa] in New York.[56] Certainly, the powerful U.S. was quite lax in monitoring the slaving inclinations of those whose ships carried their flag and whose "citizens" carried their passports.[57]

As Salem, Massachusetts lost out to Boston and New York City for regional prominence in the 1820s, it pushed into new markets, particularly in East Africa, where "some American vessels were engaged in the [slave] trade, buying the slaves at Mozambique principally and transporting them to Brazil and South America."[58] There was "an overwhelming predominance of American influence in Zanzibar during the latter half of the nineteenth century," as slave sales increased in prominence.[59] U.S. influence in East Africa had increased to the point that "Britain had already shown herself desirous of thwarting American rivalry in the East and lent ready credence to rumors of a possible American annexation of Delagoa Bay, which Portugal had practically abandoned for the convenience of our [U.S.] whalers."[60]

The question of whalers and their intersection with the latter stages of the African Slave Trade is not insignificant. In New England, whaling peaked during the 1835–45 decade, then went into a steady decline. At the same time, the crews, which formerly had been comprised "'almost entirely of Americans,'" began to change; there was a "steady replacement of African-Americans and Afro-Indians" by "European immigrants, chiefly Portuguese." This was "the stimulus for the first wave" of "[Lusophone] immigrants in the 1850s, most of them destined for New Bedford."[61] This replacement occurred as the whaling fleet was being converted into a slaving one; whalers "often engaged in the slave trade. Sometimes they would fit out in New Bedford or Long Island Sound ostensibly for the nobler game but, quite, unbeknown to the crew" would become a slaving expedition.[62] Jettisoning African-American mariners facilitated this process.[63]

Disguising slavers as whalers was a prominent tactic deployed to deceive the British Navy. As for the U.S. Navy, which was sworn to disrupt the trade as well, it was often not up to the task. Until 1857, the "U.S. squadron never consisted of more than seven ships and the average was less than five. The British squadron . . . never numbered less than 12 and averaged 18. Furthermore, the U.S. squadron was based on the Cape Verde Islands, which were almost 3000 miles and at least a month's sail from the southern slave trading area."[64] This was notably unfortunate as time passed since "the trade was never so flourishing as in the five years preceding the Civil War."[65] Even the Spanish Foreign Ministry—sited in a nation where slave trading, particularly to Cuba, was rampant—took note of the "sudden and increased activity in the slave trade" in 1859, and the "well established fact that nearly the whole of the fleet is fitted out in Boston, Portland, New Bedford and other eastern ports."[66]

Was U.S. Slavery Influenced by Hemispheric and Global Trends?

The eminent Dixie diplomat, Duff Green, was among the many in his region who had a firm "belief that foreign relations were important to strengthening the South's political position."[67] As slavery came under sharper attack from abolitionists in the 1840s—coincidentally as the slave trade enjoyed a rebirth—pro-slavery forces banded together across borders. Thomas Jollivet of France, a pro-bondage advocate, "made contact" with Green, "an apostle of American slavery, when the latter was in Paris in 1842" and went on to rely on the "slavery apologist John C. Calhoun in his writings, suggesting a community of interests between the French and American plantocracies."[68]

Furthermore, there was a transnational recognition that prices of crops produced by slave labor were significantly influenced by transnational forces. As U.S. nationals accelerated the smuggling of enslaved Africans to Brazil in the 1840s, they were able to increase the crops that were grown there, which ultimately provided a challenge to U.S. hemispheric dominance, which in turn increased pressure in this nation to reopen the African Slave Trade (just as it energized those in the Slave South who opposed the illicit slave trade to Brazil).[69] High sugar prices during this era, which were driven in no small part by a decline in English staple production, were causing more slaves to be imported into Cuba and Brazil from Africa, thereby stimulating the slave trade—and the bank accounts of some U.S. nationals.[70]

In Buenos Ayres [Aires] one Briton opined giddily that the U.S. Civil War would "transfer the production of cotton from America to British India and other countries which are much more under our influence than America was or ever could be."[71] A U.S. diplomat in Brazil disagreed, though this was of small comfort to Washington; Secretary of State William Seward was informed, as the Civil War raged, that "a great development has been given to the resources of this province by the rebellion now so unhappily [occurring] in our country. If 'cotton is king'—his throne promises to be removed to Brazil. The stimulus given to the culture of that staple, if not soon withdrawn will give to this Empire the monopoly which we formerly possessed." Prices of this crop had increased a staggering fourfold.[72]

Consequently, defenders of slavery recognized that the peculiar institution was heavily dependent on currents from abroad. For example, Brazil's legation in Washington analyzed extensively Nat Turner's slave revolt in Virginia, seeking signs of whether this contagion might spread.[73] Even in faraway Buenos Aires, where slavery was hardly prominent, note was taken of this chilling revolt.[74]

Likewise, a few years later the U.S. legation in Bahia, Brazil analyzed extensively a slave revolt in this province, seeking signs of whether this contagion might spread. The U.S. Consul reported on a "most serious insurrection of the black population . . . had it not been discovered a few hours before, the consequences might have been dreadful." A U.S. merchant there spoke of the "great state of alarm and fear that he would continue to have" as a result and was elated that "men from the American Corvette Erie which Captain Percival had kindly lent him [aid] to protect his house as he did not consider himself safe. I heard that Capt. Percival has landed detachments to protect the American Consul and other merchants had offered his assistance and protection to the Consuls of other nations."[75] Brazilian elites could not be indifferent to slave revolts in the U.S., just as U.S. elites could be affected by slave revolts in Brazil.[76]

Just as Liberia was seen in Washington as a convenient dumping ground for free Negroes, thought to be inherently subversive of slavery, there was a similar sentiment in Brazil.[77] Similarly, Madrid monitored carefully the rebellion led by John Brown, no doubt worried about what it meant for Cuba—still languishing in human bondage.[78] In short, proslavery forces in the Americas recognized that the viability of the peculiar institution was deeply influenced by hemispheric and transatlantic currents.

"Africanization," or the fear of growing numbers of Africans in Brazil, also deeply influenced segments of U.S. opinion about the feasibility of reopening the slave trade in their own nation. The influence, as an outgrowth of their numbers, of those deemed to be "black" in Brazil—notably their role in the military—was also frightening to some in North America. One U.S. emissary cautioned his superiors about undue interference in the internal affairs of Brazil. "We should cautiously abstain in this country above all others, from lending the smallest breath of encouragement to insurrection" he warned nervously, since "the physical force of the country is out of all proportion black or colored; no insurrection can be of long continuance without ending in a servile war." This was a "tragedy," potentially "fatal." The "catastrophe I [envision]," he added apocalyptically, "is that Brazil may become a black military despotism," a "disastrous" outcome, he thought. Hence, the "palpable conclusion" he outlined was that "our interests, commercial, political & domestic, lead us to further the repose, the political harmony & the general prosperity of the entire Brazilian Empire."[79] Would smuggling more Africans into the U.S. similarly increase the possibility of "servile war"?

As opinion was souring in certain circles in the U.S. about the viability of slavery, the U.S. Consul in Pernambuco, Brazil thought he espied a similar sentiment in Brazil. "I believe," he announced that "the most intelligent men in this Province are satisfied that the solution of the labor question lies in the abolition of slavery."[80] Hence, the "ratification of the Thirteenth Amendment to the American Constitution was an act of great importance not only in the United States, but also in Cuba, Puerto Rico and Brazil."[81] It was a blow in the long run to slavery in the hemisphere and, most of all, to the clandestine and illegal African Slave Trade to Brazil which had enriched a number of U.S. nationals.

The California Gold Rush and the African Slave Trade to Brazil

As the illegal slave trade to Brazil was increasing, another sizeable movement—albeit voluntary—was taking place. The "discovery of gold in California was to trigger the greatest mass migration in the history of the young Republic up to that time, 80,000 in 1849 alone and probably 300,000 by 1854."[82] The preferred route west was around Cape Horn with a stop in Rio de Janeiro. Hence, in "the first three months of 1849, eighty-six California ships put into the harbor" there; "sometimes a dozen arrived in a single day, bearing as many as a thousand passengers."[83] Their distinctive presence allowed U.S. slavers not to stand out so boldly, thus, helping them to avoid detection. On the other hand, many from beyond the confines of the U.S. South had no specific knowledge of the horrors of African slavery and, thus, Rio was shocking to many, helping to spark abolitionist sentiment. "Slave markets horrified visitors, especially those from New England" according to the scholar, Rhoda Blumberg. "Unlike southern slaveholders, they had never witnessed humans for sale."[84] Nor had many previously witnessed some of the surreal scenes that greeted them in Rio. As enslaved Africans flooded into Brazil and the ships carrying them were hounded by the British Navy, some of the more unscrupulous skippers decided to dispose of the evidence by throwing their cargo overboard, while other Negroes sought to escape by diving into inky waters. As one U.S. national put it, "the harbor is constantly covered with the bodies of blacks," who "are known to [have] thrown themselves in to escape. . . . I have seen them myself left by the tide on the strand."[85]

Strikingly, as these Euro-Americans were repulsed by the dreadfulness of Brazilian slavery, a number of African-Americans viewed this nation differently, using this South American example as a means to discredit the awfulness in North America they were compelled to endure. Brazil, thought Frederick Douglass, was the "only country where the Negro could rise to a high position in society, even to that of judge or major general, if he were possessed of character and talent."[86] His fellow black abolitionist, Martin Delany, concurred.[87] Ironically, both of these sentiments—Brazil as "racial" horror and Brazil as "racial" paradise—served to undermine slavery in the U.S.

Yet neither school of thought seemed to grasp the point that the infrastructure of the illegal trade captained by U.S. nationals and serving Brazil probably had a spillover effect in the U.S., increasing the number of enslaved Africans brought to the U.S., particularly as this commerce increased as the Civil War approached; that is, as Africans were dragged across the Atlantic and Britain sought to foil their landing in Brazil, it made sense for these slavers to head northward to Cuba and New Orleans. Following Du Bois, the scholar Robert Hall estimates that "between 1808 and 1860" about "250,000 Africans" were "imported into the United States," which is probably on the high end but provides a glimpse of the dimension of the problem.[88] In 1859, the U.S. Department of Interior dispatched an agent to the "southern states" to investigate the "extent of importation of Negroes direct from Africa." After "widely conversing with a number of gentlemen of intelligence" and traveling to Wilmington, North Carolina, Charleston, Florida, and elsewhere he emerged with a mixed view, receiving credible reports of hundreds of recent imports to northern Florida.[89] British emissaries in Texas provided numerous reports over the years of enslaved Africans being smuggled into this nation, then state.[90] Certainly the momentum provided by the clandestine trade to Brazil—spearheaded by U.S. nationals —contributed mightily to the flouting of law that led to Africans being brought forcibly to North America. Just as cracking down on the sale of illicit drugs in one neighborhood often drives it into adjacent neighborhoods, something similar was happening with the illicit slave trade.

Likewise, when the Slave South decided to secede from the U.S., many wondered how and why they thought they could prevail against a more populous and more industrialized North, but this thinking elides the reality that the Deep South had sound cause to think that it could rely on the Deepest South—i.e.. an alliance with Brazil—along with its former patron, Portugal, and Spanish Cuba and could thus prevail and ensure that slavery in the hemisphere would triumph.

Confederate Exiles in Brazil

After the Civil War, some U.S. nationals—particularly from Dixie—reluctant to reside under the rule of the government they had just sought to overthrow and unwilling to relinquish their fondness for slavery, migrated to Brazil, where this institution continued until 1888. In 1867, the **New York Times** noticed one "Southern gentleman," who "thinks that in Brazil he can own slaves, can do as he pleases, go where he likes and retain his old views of the inferiority of the Negro."[91] He was among the thousands who made this journey southward, a number of whom tried to bring enslaved Africans with them. This capital flight too was noticed by a British diplomat in Puerto Rico, who was informed of a "cargo of slaves shipped off the coast of Florida" that "had called off Vieques for the purpose of obtaining provisions in order to continue her voyage to the coast of Brazil." He moaned that this "traffic may be carried on with success, a traffic which is even more barbarous than the African slave trade, from the fact that these poor Negroes of the southern states who have received the one great benefit of the late American civil war . . . should again so treacherously be driven into bondage." Like the illegal trade to Brazil and the U.S., one can only speculate about the number of erstwhile U.S. Negroes who were kidnapped and taken to Brazil after the Civil War.[92] The conclusion of this terrible war ultimately was a devastating—though, intriguingly, not necessarily a fatal[93]—blow to this criminality of illicit slave trade.

In sum, this book is an account of the diplomatic history of the U.S.–Brazil relationship—with an accent on North America—in the context of the acceleration of the African Slave Trade. But lurking above both of these nations is Great Britain, whose intervention slowed down the attempt to bring even more enslaved Africans across the Southern Atlantic. In highlighting the role of such figures as Matthew Fontaine Maury, I seek to underscore the pivotal role played by Brazil in the mind of certain leaders of the Slave South to the point where not only it bolstered their idea that they could prevail in the Civil War but also served as a refuge once that conflict ended so disastrously for them.

In this 1830 engraving, black people, including women and children, are in chains and shackles in the foreground, with the U.S. Capitol in the background. An influential corps of U.S. nationals, particularly in New England, New York, and New Orleans avidly backed the African Slave Trade. Courtesy Library of Congress.

1

Toward the Empire of Brazil

Brazil, which borders every nation in South America except Chile and Ecuador, has only a tiny portion of its territory, in the far south, in the temperate zone. Its shoreline stretches for 4600 miles, and it is as near to Africa as to the United States—a connection which inevitably attracted nationals of the latter who were interested in perpetuating the slave trade.[1] This chapter will explore early connections between the U.S. (and the thirteen colonies) in the context of the slave trade to Brazil and before its post-1840 expansion.

The slavery tie between the nation that was to become the U.S. and Brazil stretches back at least to the early 17th century, when the Dutch controlled New Netherlands—i.e., "New York"—and a Brazilian colony and were transporting enslaved Africans from there to North America.[2] Even after the Dutch were ousted from control of Brazil and Portugal extended its domination, this collaboration on the slave trade between North and South America continued. In the early 18th century, Thomas Amory of Charleston, who traded regularly in West Africa, "pointed to the ease with which he could send slaves to Brazil" for "Negroes sell as well at [South] Carolina as at Brazil."[3] Still, Northeastern merchants dominated the slave trade to Brazil.[4] The family of Mary Robinson Hunter, whose spouse served as a diplomat in Rio de Janeiro beginning in the 1830s, was preeminent in this commerce.[5]

The early relationship between the North American colonists and Brazil was facilitated by the relationship between Britain and Portugal. The alliance between London and Lisbon was long-standing—a trend that was evident at the surrender at Yorktown, where the man who presented Cornwallis's sword was Charles O'Hara, the "bastard son of Lord Tyrawley, English Ambassador to Portugal" and "his mistress, Anna, a Portuguese lady." This was reflective of the fact that "many English, because of old social ties and economic trading positions, did business with and lived in both Brazil and Portugal."[6] This London-Lisbon alliance, in turn, facilitated ties between North America and Brazil.[7] The relationship did not cease after the Revolution, as U.S. businessmen were prominent in the slave trade to Montevideo in the late 18th century.[8]

The young republic's continuing interest in South America was palpable.[9] Early on Thomas Jefferson instructed John Jay about the prospects for the ousting of Portugal from Brazil; his opinion that "the slaves will take the side of their masters"[10] seemed like self-interested wishful thinking on his part. Anticipating his fellow Virginian, Matthew Fontaine Maury, Jefferson also asserted that " 'it is impossible not to look forward to distant times . . . [when the U.S. would] cover the whole northern, if not the southern continent.' "[11] According to legal historian, A. Leon Higginbotham, there is "much reason to believe that [Thomas] Jefferson was not truly troubled about the international slave trade,"[12] which suggests that this Founding Father similarly anticipated the most aggressive "fire-eaters" of the 1850s who too envisioned an empire for slavery that encompassed the Americas.

Like revolutionaries past and present, those in North America were not averse to spreading their influence beyond their borders, a trend eased when Brazilian intellectuals "secretly sought out Jefferson in France for confidential advice," just as "overseas [Brazilian] students at the University of Coimbra devoured accounts of the American revolution and of its constitutional innovations." The "martyr of Brazil's aborted revolution of 1789" in Minas Gerais "kept in his pocket a copy of the French translations of the American state constitutions, though knowing no French he had to ask others to translate it for him."[13] Jefferson, the founder who may have paid more attention to his South American neighbor than his counterparts, remarked in his later days that he would " 'rejoice to see the fleets of Brazil and the United States riding together as between of the same family and having the same interest.' "[14]

It is unclear if Jefferson, a slaveholder, had this peculiar institution in mind when he envisioned such an alliance between Brazil and the U.S. since this was the overriding characteristic held in common between these two vast nations.[15] The split in U.S. ranks on the question of the African Slave Trade may have assisted the proliferation of these U.S. dealers in the South American market. Though over the decades the Dutch had been supplanted by the Portuguese in Brazil, slave traders from North America remained a consistent presence in South America. "Ironically," the trade "in fact became more profitable after the ratification of the U.S. Constitution," given the infamous proviso that has been interpreted to suggest that this business would be curtailed after 1808; "three years before the expiration of the clause the demand for slaves increased so dramatically that traders were barely able to keep up with the market. Indeed, the busiest year in the history of the trade for Rhode Island slavers was 1805." Hence, "from 1804 to 1807 state and federal orders to prosecute and fine slave traders were ignored at Bristol; the number of ships leaving that port for Africa soared."[16] These ships were constantly visiting the fertile slave hunting ground that was Mozambique[17]—and Brazil,[18] where business was lucrative and varied.[19] So many Negroes were pouring into Rio de Janeiro that the idea was broached in Cape Town of "purchasing slaves" in Brazil and "liberating them on certain conditions at the Cape."[20]

Likewise, in the early 19th century, a considerable number of "East African Negroes, chiefly" from the Portuguese colony that was Mozambique were "among the cargoes brought to Charleston," South Carolina,[21] just as the Portuguese colony of Angola had supplied a considerable percentage of Virginia's Negroes.[22] There was a continuity of interest in the slave trade between the U.S., on the one hand, and Portugal and its colonies—in Africa and South America, in particular—on the other hand.

Actually, a federal law in 1794 made illegal participation of U.S. nationals in the African Slave Trade—beyond the confines of the U.S. itself—though like most measures of this type it was hardly enforced; it was strengthened in 1800 and in 1808 another such bill was passed, then after the War of 1812, similar laws were passed.[23] Despite these laws, there was no cessation of the participation of U.S. nationals in the African Slave Trade.

For these laws notwithstanding, it was estimated that thousands of Negroes per year were being brought illegally to North America by the first quarter of the 19th century,[24] with Africans being smuggled to these shores from across the Atlantic and points south, e.g., Cuba, Jamaica, and South America.[25] Again, this estimate appears to be extravagant, though it did signal a trend that was ongoing until the end of the Civil War marked the official closure of the trade: when Africans were being traded in the hemisphere with the abandon of pork bellies in today's Chicago, this was accompanied by the kidnapping of ostensibly free Negroes north of the Mason-Dixon line, who were sold south into slavery—perhaps to "The Deepest South," i.e., Brazil, in what amounted to an anarchistic free market.[26] Indeed, some of the more doctrinaire of the free traders argued that "no artificial barriers whatsoever should be erected against the free movement of goods, including slaves."[27]

Washington was officially hostile to the African Slave Trade, though the African Society of London had reason to disbelieve this and in 1816 pointed to the "sudden substitution of the Spanish for the American flag" on ships involved in this commerce. Thus, "the slave trade, which now for the first time assumed a Spanish dress, was in reality only the trade of other nations in disguise." By 1817, the Governor of Sierra Leone thought there was a "greater number of vessels employed in that [slave] traffic than at any former period." Washington was hesitant to join efforts at suppression on the grounds of upholding sovereignty.[28] Thus, even before Britain banned slavery, it was pressuring the U.S. to bow out of the slave trade.[29]

In 1817, Portugal signed a treaty that stipulated that their slave trade on the coast of Africa "should entirely cease to the northward of the equator" and "that it should be unlawful for her subjects to purchase or trade in slaves except to the southward of the line." Among other things, this was a virtual declaration that Angola should be a prime hunting ground for enslaved Africans.[30] In 1818, Washington was approached about cooperating with London on suppressing the slave trade, which in "Article 10 of the Treaty of Ghent (1814)," this new nation had agreed to do; but in the U.S. Senate "the question of an anti-slave trade treaty became entangled with the issue of domestic slavery and the Convention of 1824 was never ratified."[31] London's aggressive approach was not embraced in Washington, nor Lisbon, with the latter taking particular umbrage since it had backed the U.K. repeatedly and thought it deserved better.[32]

London brusquely told Secretary of State John Quincy Adams what he should have known: The "United States have maintained at no time, a greater number of cruisers than two, rarely more than one, and latterly, during several months together, no ship of war, whatever, on the African station. As late as the 14th of January 1822, it was stated, officially by the Governor of Sierra Leone 'that the fine rivers Nunez and Pongas, were entirely under the control of renegade European and American slave traders.' " Adams, in turn, nixed London's proposals to rein in this outlawry, though he acknowledged the slave trade as "piracy" and took a swipe at "Portugal" as "the only maritime power of Europe, which has not yet declared the African slave trade, without exception, unlawful."[33] Meanwhile, vessels out of Mobile and New Orleans were captured with scores of enslaved Africans aboard,[34] while repeated complaints were made about Galveston and Brunswick, Georgia as sieves for the smuggling of Africans.[35] Indeed, in calculating the number of Africans brought illicitly into the U.S. after 1808, one should include the significant numbers brought from territories—e.g., Florida and Texas—that did not fall under Washington's sway until much later.[36]

Given this bent in the U.S., it was inevitable that attention would turn to what was becoming the biggest slave market of all: Brazil. Portugal was seen as a relatively weak power that controlled this huge colony and was, therefore, ripe for dislodgement: In 1817, there was an attempted filibustering effort in Brazil, that implicated U.S. nationals, which was designed to attack Brazil in an effort to "shake the newly elected throne of Braganza [*sic*] to its foundation."[37] Subsequently, relations between Lisbon and Washington were harmed with the "arrival" of "two American vessels clandestinely carrying weapons" to those in Pernambuco leading this "revolt." Simultaneously, "Baltimore gained a notorious reputation as the chief rendezvous for privateers operating in Brazilian waters against Portuguese commerce," which was "worsening diplomatic and naval relations."[38] The U.S. Consul in Pernambuco, Joseph Ray, confessed to John Quincy Adams in 1818 that local authorities "here have since the late Revolution looked on the Americans as suspicious persons who came here for the sole purpose of aiding the patriotic cause in this country."[39] There was concern in Rio de Janeiro that Washington was seeking to take advantage of the fissiparous tendencies that were fomenting various separatist revolts in their nation.

This was occurring as Latin America was plunged into turmoil as nations strained to free themselves from Spanish colonialism. Though John Quincy Adams instructed his Buenos Ayres counterpart that the U.S. was bound to "observe between the parties an impartial neutrality," this did not stop him from coming to the U.S. in an effort to obtain "a number of vessels of war for the Governments of Buenos Ayres and Chile."[40]

Washington may have desired closer relations with B.A., not least since ties with Portuguese Brazil were fraying. When John Graham, the U.S. emissary arrived in Rio de Janeiro in August 1819, he encountered various problems. After a "pleasant passage of forty seven days," he had "difficulty" in "finding accommodation" for his "family"; finally, he met with "the King" but he "spoke however very low and in Portuguese a language," said Graham, "with which I am not as yet very little acquainted." So, he said, "I spoke to him in Spanish," which may have been the least of his growing problems. For when he sought to discuss "commercial intercourse" with the "Minister of Foreign Affairs," he was informed "rather abruptly" that "this was not the time" to "talk of commercial arrangements when two countries were almost in a state of actual war," not least given the "harsh measures understood to have been adopted in the ports" of Brazil "against some vessels of the United States and their crews," including jailing and "putting them in hard labour in chains when they had committed no serious offense."[41] Rumors of filibustering expeditions from the U.S.—or armed attempts at regime change—could not have helped either, while Washington was still smarting since "during the last war between the United States and Great Britain, Portuguese subjects were found on board captured British vessels of war."[42]

U.S. Negroes, often at odds with the government that oppressed them, often were similarly critical of Lisbon. **Freedom's Journal,** the pioneering Negro periodical, denounced Portugal for having "refused to abandon this [slave] trade," specifically noting Lisbon's "claim to carry it on for the supply of her African islands, the Cape de Verds [*sic*] . . . whence it is easy to take slaves to Brazil."[43] In turn, "news of how blacks fared in the United States horrified Brazilians when they read travel accounts, or listened to relatives who had visited Virginia or Mississippi."[44] Their opinions may have been influenced further since "slaves from the United States, Cuba, Northern South America, Uruguay and Argentina had also come to live in Rio."[45] Being valuable commodities, enslaved Africans were as likely to be transported with a master from North to South America as a favored horse—and probably more so.

Fleeing Napoleon, the besieged Portuguese monarch fled to Brazil, where in 1815 these nations were declared one kingdom; by 1820, he had been recalled to Europe by the outbreak of turmoil in his homeland. Taking advantage of this disorder and similar revolts erupting in Latin America as a whole, Brazil proclaimed independence in 1822—a development which was not displeasing to some in Washington who sought to weaken the influence of European powers in the hemisphere.

Moreover, "one important reason why the Brazilian landowners and slaveholders had given their support to an independent monarchy in Brazil was precisely because they saw independence as a means of escaping from Britain's unrelenting pressure on Portugal for the complete and immediate abolition of the slave trade"—a factor also found appealing in certain pro-slavery precincts in Washington.[46] "Recognition of Brasil," said the U.S. representative in Brazil, Condy Raguet, that is "the consummation of such an act before any other nation would give us an influence which otherwise we never can [have]" [emphasis-original].[47]

As Brazil was surging to independence, it was undergoing a remarkable transformation in its makeup; from 1790 to the end of the legal Atlantic slave trade in 1830, Rio de Janeiro saw nearly 700,000 Africans offloaded at its port. This number represents two-thirds of all imports into Brazil during the same time period, with 80 percent arriving from West Central Africa alone.[48] Even at this early stage, U.S. nationals were implicated. In 1821, R. S. Long was under sentence of five years imprisonment in Angola; he was an "American . . . engaged in the slave trade . . . under the Portuguese flag. . . . I understood," said the U.S. Consul, James Bennett, "that he was a pilot but now it appears that he was owner."[49]

This influx of Africans to Brazil was accompanied by a dramatic price increase, as slave prices doubled between 1820 and 1850, an increase well in excess of that recorded in the United States in the same period, which ineluctably captured the attention—and initiative—of U.S. slavers.[50] The presence of these Africans allowed for a dramatic rise in agricultural production, as it was the slow collapse of the Saint Domingue coffee producers after 1790 and the eventual collapse of Cuban coffee production after a series of devastating hurricanes in the 1830s that finally gave Brazil undisputed mastery over New World production.[51]

Ironically, 1830—which roughly marks the year when the African Slave Trade to Brazil was to be halted—actually marked the time when it increased spectacularly. As London saw it, one factor in this process was that "slaves in Africa" were incredibly cheap and wages of ship crews were likewise. Thus, "factories were established on the coast of Africa" and "the slave trade greatly increased under cover of a pretended colonization for Monte Video [*sic*]."[52] In a pattern that was to occur repeatedly, "one Rafael Antonio de Carvalho, a Portuguese, acting as

American Vice Consul at Mozambique" was a prominent slave dealer. It was reported that "the bays of Sofala, Mocambo and Fernando Vellozo" were "much frequented by American whalers. In last July there were as many as five in the bay of Mocambo" while "scarcely any British vessel touches at these ports." Though Lisbon was leery about losing Mozambique, just as it had lost Brazil, this sprawling region was "in fact supplied with every [necessity] by slavers from Rio de Janeiro, Cuba and occasionally by Americans," while "not a single merchant vessel went from the mother country to the province of Mozambique in the whole year of 1838."[53]

By picking on Lisbon, the U.S. had selected, perhaps, the weakest of the major colonial powers. More than this, their erstwhile patron and frequent rival—London—had its navy mostly in West Africa to monitor slave trade depredations, which meant that East Africa was a wide open back door. By the 1830s, the U.S. "had already set up a practical monopoly" in this region and "were extremely jealous of their position."[54] An elongated triangular trade emerged that linked East Africa with Brazil and the U.S.—particularly Salem, Massachusetts.[55] In fact, it was reported, "when the untutored African heard the United States, or New York, or Boston mentioned he thought it some small port in Salem—or so the Salemites averred." Not surprisingly, one of the more commodious dining rooms in the famed Hawthorne Hotel in Salem was named the "Zanzibar Room," homage to the infamous slave entrepot.[56]

U.S. nationals purchased vessels then would rent them to Brazilian and Portuguese slave traders in Brazil. They in turn used these ships, protected by the United States flag and manned by U.S. crews, for the roundtrip voyages to Africa; shipbuilders in eastern ports, including Beverly and Salem, constructed vessels especially for the Brazil-Africa trade.[57] Zanzibar long had developed a well-merited reputation as a chief site for the African Slave Trade and from September 1832 to May 1834 of the 41 vessels recorded as arriving there were 7 from England "(and one each from France and Spain) while 32 were American."[58] Writing from Rio de Janeiro, one Salem merchant observed, "many vessels are leaving daily for the coast of Africa for slaves. The business is increasing very rapidly. . . . the American schooner Carolina has been sold, for a slaver without doubt . . . she is a clipper built from 80 to 90 tons & several years old."[59]

The resultant economic growth in Brazil attracted visitors from the U.S., a trend that was to reach its apex during the California Gold

Rush. But even before Brazilian independence, North American visitors were arriving in the Deepest South and in a trend that was to occur repeatedly, were not overly impressed by what they saw; striking was the fact that "until the 1830s, blacks constituted 63 per cent of the population, whites 16 per cent and mixed-race people 21 per cent"—a ratio that could be chilling to those familiar with Gabriel in Virginia and Stono's Revolt in South Carolina.[60] The writer, H. M. Brackenridge, as did many of his compatriots, was struck that "the Portuguese are generally of a very dark complexion" and "the number of Negroes and of the mixed race was such, as to give a different cast in the general appearance of the population, from that of any town I have ever seen." Writing in 1820, again like many others, this New Orleans resident was taken by the sight of slaves pulling carts like horses and making unimaginable sounds, "all screaming in the same style, producing a general effect, of which I can convey no idea."[61]

Sailing from Philadelphia, Henry Bradley came there in 1821 and was repulsed when he saw "Negroes, Indians and whites bathe in the same water, near its source, which was afterwards to supply the town"; "two-thirds of the inhabitants of Rio are said to be people of colour," which he found startling. There were "hundreds of slaves in the street" with "nothing more to cover their nakedness, than a piece of cloth around the waist. They take the places of horses in this city, as nearly all the burdens, slung upon their poles, are borne to their destination by these oppressed people." While Bradley "resided at Rio, several large ships came in, filled with Negroes" where they were offloaded "like so many sheep." The "buyers examine their teeth and every part of their bodies, as they were purchasing horses. The price of these wretched human beings varied, as the markets were, or were not glutted—200 dollars was the average sum paid for a black woman; 500 for a man." This booming metropolis was afflicted with chaos; "I frequently saw dead bodies in the street," said Bradley.[62]

Like most U.S. visitors, Bradley was struck by the ubiquity of African slavery, though he was not as incensed as others about Lusophone culture which often was viewed as a hotbed of "great miscegenationists" and a sink of Catholic biases. Indeed, the alleged "absence of racial prejudice in Brazil and of a color line struck every American visitor with wonder."[63]

Still, the message that was increasingly transmitted to the U.S. about Brazil was that it was booming, fueled by enslaved Africans[64]—a message that was bound to attract the attention of legions of slave dealers and a growing number of abolitionists. As a result of British pressure, by 1830, Brazil was being compelled to bar the legal slave trade, and slave dealers saw the time leading up to this year as an opportunity to deluge Rio de Janeiro with Africans. "The black population has latterly enormously increased," wrote Thomas Bennett, arriving after Bradley's departure. "As the period approached for the total abolition of the slave trade, capital has been everywhere embarked in the purchase of Negroes. . . . my eye really was so familiarized to black visages, that the occurrence of a white face in the streets of some parts of the town, struck me as a novelty." He found this trend "alarming" though he was struck by the "improved implements of every kind which they use, the machinery they set in motion, the expertness in manual dexterity at which they arrive, and the abridgement of labor which they effect" were "lessons of the greatest value."[65]

In a perception that was to be shared over the years by countless visitors from the U.S., Revered Robert Walsh harbored "serious apprehensions" since there were 2.5 million Africans and "but 850,000" whites; he suspected that the former "will discover their own strength" and "Brazil [will] become a second St. Domingo. This is particularly the case at Bahia and Pernambuco, where almost all the Negroes are brought from the same part of Africa," though "at Rio the case is different. The Negro population consists of eight or nine different castes, having no common language and actuated by no sympathetic tie" and "this animosity the whites cherish and endeavor to keep alive." Like other visitors he was similarly taken by "the horror" of slavery, which was of such magnitude that its victims "not only kill themselves but their children" and was astounded when he ascertained that the slave owners "endeavor to restore" the "darkness" of Africans "by obliging the fair slaves to intermarry with those [that] are blacker than themselves; the good fathers being alarmed at the prospect of keeping, in a state of slavery, human faces as fair as their own." This came to him when he encountered a slave with "soft fair face, light curling hair, blue eyes and a skin as that of a European" who he was "shocked and incredulous" to find that his own father had sold him into slavery.

Walsh was disgusted by the state of Brazilian slaves. "The state in which they appear is revolting to humanity. . . . entirely naked, with the exception of a covering of dirty rags tied about their waists. Their skins, from constant exposure to the weather, had become hard, crusty and seamed, resembling the coarse black covering of some beast, or like that of an elephant. . . . their foreheads retiring, having exactly the head and legs of the baboon tribe"; even "the horses and mules" who "were seen in the same streets" were "pampered, spirited and richly caparisoned, enjoying a state far superior to the Negroes." However, in a pattern that was to be repeated, this disgust translated into abolitionism. Instead, he offered that "the first impression of all this on my mind, was to shake the conviction I had always felt, of the wrong and hardship inflicted on our black fellow-creatures, and they were only in that state which God and nature had assigned them; that they were the lowest grade of human existence"; however, after more sober reflection he "came, therefore, to the irresistible conclusion in my mind, that color was an accident affecting the surface of a man and having no more to do with his qualities than his clothes."

Reverend Robert Walsh also thought slave labor handcuffed Brazil (though a number of his contemporaries hotly disagreed): "the wealth of Rio is vested in this property and slaves form the income and support of a vast number of individuals, who hire them out, as people in Europe do horses and mules. This is one great cause, that prevents the adoption of machinery."[66]

Even in the southernmost cone of the continent, apprehension was mounting about the growing presence of Africans in the hemisphere. In Buenos Ayres, which a century earlier had "some 24,000 inhabitants, of whom at least one-third [were] African Negro slaves"—and also had a considerable population of U.S. nationals[67]—not only was the increasingly "Africanized" Brazil monitored carefully, but, as well, "disturbances . . . among the blacks in the Southern States" of the U.S.,[68] Cuba,[69] and Jamaica.[70] The perception was that enslavement was hemispheric and could hardly survive in one region if under assault in another.

Such perceptions were not foreign to U.S. emissaries in Rio de Janeiro and what they were seeing could not be encouraging to a nation similarly based on African slavery. "Sir Charles Stuart told me," said the U.S. Minister in Rio in 1825, that "abolition" of the "slave trade . . . could only be brought about indirectly for that an open abandonment of it would produce as he thought a revolution."[71] Yet "the demand for vessels for the slave trade is at this time very brisk," John Quincy Adams was told; "the prices of slaves are from about 150 to 180 dollars" and "profits are said to be very great" with "the number imported at this port," i.e., Rio, "for several years is estimated at about 20,000 per annum."[72] Continuation of slavery carried its own perils, it was thought: "15,000 cartridges had been found in the home of one & 5000 in that of another of the officers" in Brazil's multi-colored military who were "conspirators" against their government, and "members of that society . . . had intended to put arms into the hands of five hundred blacks" who hailed from "perhaps the most robust, active and resolute of the African race."[73]

"All seems quiet here, as well as in other quarters of the Empire," it was said months earlier; however, "some apprehensions . . . still exist in regard to the blacks."[74] The "Male revolt" in 1835—which impacted Brazil in a way similar to how the Nat Turner revolt impacted the Slave South—"further heightened the fear of seeing Brazil dominated by blacks,"[75] an apprehension of grave concern in Washington as well. A few years later, the U.S. Consul in Pernambuco was writing nervously about yet another revolt, this time in Bahia: "from one to two hundred of the most valuable houses were burnt, but I am happy to say no property of any citizen of the United States was injured. The destruction of property has been very great. . . . nearly 2000 persons were apprehended on suspicion of having taken an active part against the Imperial Government," as these rebels were bent on "destroying the city entirely in fulfillment of the published threat of Sabino the Secretary of Foreign Affairs and Chief of the Mulatto Party."[76]

This insight was even more noteworthy since U.S. diplomats complained continually of the "difficulty of procuring information relating to events, immediately or even remotely connected with politics. This difficulty in Brazil is probably greater than in any other part of the civilized world."[77] "I have reason to think that my dwelling house has been placed under the especial espionage of the police and that the names of all the Brasileans who visit me, and perhaps of others are furnished to the government,"[78] said the U.S.'s chief emissary [emphasis-original].

Moreover, there was an undercurrent of tension between U.S. emissaries and Brazilian elites, not least since—according to a leading U.S. diplomat—"Brasil in imitation of Portugal has completely thrown herself into the arms of England and, to a certain extent, has transferred her colonial allegiance from one country to another."[79] There was also "reason for . . . forbearance from all agitation here," said one of these diplomats, "inasmuch as all the separatists, nullifiers & revolutionists" —of which Rio had more than its share—"refer to our history without understanding it," which "leads to a suspicion by the loyal Brazilians of our countrymen." Thus, "in the recent discussion of Bahia, our country, its systems & institutions have been referred to by the Republican Party so called as models for imitation; by the loyalists for the purpose of exhibiting the comparative superiority of their . . . system & institutions. In all such discussions," he lamented, "we are mistakenly praised & blamed."[80] Of course, as Brazilian diplomats scrutinized the U.S., they did not necessarily emerge with an elevated view either.[81]

Yet even the prospect of slave-assisted military revolts and increasingly disgruntled Brazilian elites could not distract U.S. diplomats from what seemed to be their primary purpose—profit. Chief among these was William Wright of Maryland, scion of a fabulously wealthy merchant house that just happened to have major interests in the slave trade and the crops they produced. He became Chargés des Affaires in Rio de Janeiro in 1830, just as the slave trade was skyrocketing.[82] There were "some houses in Rio that will do business for less commissions [than] our House," it was said of Maxwell Wright, but, it was added confidently, "no House offers more advantages than ours and very few offers as many in the transaction of American business."[83] Yes, gushed Wright, " 'we have now agencies in all the principal ports. . . . we have the best and most influential, we could possibly have and with my own exertions I expect a considerable increase of our business.' "[84] Given William Wright's strategic location with access to intelligence and the ability to slash red tape on behalf of his firm, this was not puffery. Thus, in 1835 Wright had reason to fret about "the probabilities of a war with France" which had "greatly increased," fomenting "much more anxiety" of those "connected with commerce." In that event, "every ocean will be pervaded by national and private armed vessels"; now it was "unimportant to the ship owners of the [U.S.] as to whose flag may have the carrying of our imports & exports. But it will be deeply important to all the other interests of the country that such carrying trade be conducted by a nation capable of defending her merchant vessels."[85] Wright's portfolio in Rio included intimate knowledge of shipping and its regulations, which was not irrelevant to the slave trade.[86] Wright was positioned nicely at the intersection where politics met economics and was able to use both to leverage his special interests.

Yet even one so blessed as Wright had to recognize that his empire was resting shakily on an unsteady foundation, a fact that came clear after "the late insurrection of the Blacks in Virginia and a still later one in North Carolina" in 1831. When this news reached Maxwell, Wright in Rio de Janeiro, it was not comforting; it was "of a nature to engage deeply the attention of every landholder in a slave holding state. The evil long feared has now commenced; when it is to run we know not. A civil war is bad enough," it was said morosely, but a "servile war" would only "extend . . . atrocities"; "ramifications of this . . . extend, but it is reasonably to be feared that they reach at least to Georgia. Not even in Maryland is our position" secure, it was thought, though "on this shore, the whites outnumber the blacks." The firm had hard questions to answer: "is it to effect tremendously the value of all real property in the state?" And if Negroes could rise up in the U.S. South where they were greatly outnumbered, what did this mean for the security of the firm's investments in Brazil where, generally, the reverse was the case?[87]

As if that were not sufficient bad news, Maxwell, Wright had to contend with "commercial difficulties" in the U.S. engendered by the Panic of 1837, which seemed to get "worse and worse"; "if possible, failure of large houses" would be "occurring daily in N. York & New Orleans, some in Boston." The message to Rio was "do not take any new risks for the present."[88]

Yet if Maxwell, Wright could have espied the activities of one of its competitors, it would have encouraged them, perhaps, to become more deeply involved in the African Slave Trade. "Messrs. Farnham & Fry of Salem, Massachusetts" had ships sailing from New York where "these gentlemen" were "engaged in commerce under the firm of P.J. Farnham & Co." They controlled a "factory, or storehouse, for some years past on the [African] coast at a place called Ambrise [sic], about sixty miles north of Angola and have had vessels engaged in trade there"; "Ambrise" or "Ambriz" was "becoming quite a commercial place—the English having many factories there."[89] But "Ambrise" was also rapidly becoming a major site for the operation of the African Slave Trade and the Royal Navy had "reasons to suppose" that a ship owned by Farnham was "engaged in the slave traffic."[90]

So how could Maxwell, Wright in a thriving Rio de Janeiro, with Africans flooding in from the Atlantic and Indian Ocean basins, put up a stop sign? If they were to do so, it would only serve to increase profit opportunities for competitors. The possibility of deploying legions of slave laborers was too precious to resist. Moreover, Washington itself was resisting stoutly pressure from London to curtail the African Slave

Trade. Quite literally, the nation's capital had become a regional center for this business. One Congressman in 1829 was splenetic in denouncing "slave dealers, gaining confidence from impunity" who "have made the seat of the Federal Government their headquarters," not to mention the "public prisons" and "officers of the Federal Government" who "have been employed and derived emoluments from carrying on this traffic."[91] Though the U.S. was reluctant to send its ships to monitor or halt the slave trade to Brazil, a House Resolution "directed" the Secretary of the Navy to "report if there are a sufficient number of vessels now in commission . . . to enable him to extend adequate protection to our commerce to the Empire of Brazils [*sic*] and to the Republic of Buenos Ayres."[92] William Wright in Rio may have been violating the instructions of his government if he had resisted the temptation of the African Slave Trade.

Still, the pre-1840s era, with its stories of U.S. nationals streaming into Brazil, hardly prepared this South American nation for what was soon to follow.

SLAVE MARKET OF AMERICA.

THE WORD OF GOD.

THE DECLARATION OF AMERICAN INDEPENDENCE.

THE CONSTITUTION OF THE UNITED STATES.

CONSTITUTIONS OF THE STATES.

DISTRICT OF COLUMBIA.

THE RESIDENCE OF 7000 SLAVES

"THE LAND OF THE FREE." "THE HOME OF THE OPPRESSED."

RIGHT TO INTERFERE.

PUBLIC PRISONS IN THE DISTRICT.

Broadside, circa 1835–36, condemning the sale and keeping of slaves in the District of Columbia. The internal slave trade in the U.S. literally sold Africans "down the river," from places like Washington in the Upper South to the Lower South. Courtesy Library of Congress.

2

Into Africa

U.S. nationals were leaders in fomenting the illicit slave trade and, as a result, permanently transformed Brazil for all time. In doing so, these U.S. nationals—and some from Europe and Brazil—"acting alone or in conjunction with the bandits, intervened in the affairs of these [African] chiefdoms to provoke conflicts that generated export captives."[1] The "Igbo example clearly shows that slavery and the slave trade were the primary cause of violence in the West African sub-region for over three centuries."[2] John C. Lawrence of the U.S.'s African Squadron confided to his diary in December 1844 that slavers "foment brawls among Chiefs. . . . it answers a double purpose, that of furnishing the slave market . . . as well as affording protection to themselves as the attention of these savages are diverted from the white residents."[3]

The African Slave Trade reached new heights of destruction as it was coming to a close, particularly in terms of violence, as a result of improvements in weaponry. As early as 1837, one Brooklynite had noticed the central role of Brazil in this late stage of the trade, for "the proximity of this coast to the shores of Africa renders the importation of Negroes to this country extremely easy; with constant and favorable winds, they are enabled to perform the passage in ten or fifteen days, and dispose of their slaves at reasonable prices."[4] Fifteen years later, the famed jurist, Joseph Story, pointed to the role of U.S. nationals as being central to the African Slave Trade. "American citizens are steeped up to their very mouths (I scarcely use too bold a figure) in this stream of iniquity"; they "throng to the coasts of Africa under the stained flags of Spain and Portugal, sometimes selling abroad their 'cargoes of despair' and sometimes bringing them into some of our Southern ports. . . . I wish I could say that New England and New England men were free of this deep pollution"—but he could not.[5] One of his compatriots acknowledged that because Brazil was "much nearer to Africa" than Cuba, "slavers [could] reach this market much easier and dispose of their human chattels at less risk"—and, of course, Brazil was a larger market as well.[6] In particular, the troubled combination of U.S. nationals, Brazilian slavery, and a struggling Africa made for a dreadful combination for the latter especially, while fabulously enriching those involved in this unclean enterprise.[7]

So, what was Washington doing as its nationals were wreaking havoc in Africa and drastically altering the demographic makeup of Brazil? An African Squadron, which like its Brazilian counterpart, was supposed to arrest this seamy traffic across the ocean. However, "between 1843 and 1861, the squadron captured only eleven slavers and these were released on nominal bail or were tried and let off with negligible fines. . . . [few] conviction[s] [were] ever handed down by . . . American court[s] as a result of the activities of the African Squadron. This was in striking contrast to the British Squadron, which between the years 1839 and 1850 alone seized over seven hundred ships, a number that surpassed the entire merchant marine of many nations." In contrast to the U.S., "the British were energetic in their attempts to suppress the slave trade. Between 1814 and 1850, British naval units seized 169 Bahian ships alone, the vast majority in West African waters."[8]

Increased involvement of U.S. citizens in illegal slave trading to Brazil and Cuba[9] came "particularly after 1839 when Great Britain authorized its warships to seize slave vessels flying the Brazilian, Spanish and Portuguese flags, thus making the United States the last major Western nation unwilling to permit the boarding and searching of its ships at sea. . . . U.S. citizens [therefore] offered a wide variety of advantages and services to slave traders. These included swift Baltimore clippers with American crews."[10] And then there was the U.S. flag, which was hoisted by pirates of various nationalities, as it proved to be kryptonite as far as a wary London was concerned.[11] By early 1851, one British representative in Philadelphia was moaning that "two thirds of the slavers which reach Brazil or Cuba, may be said to owe their safety" to the U.S. flag, while "fast sailing vessels"—some constructed with British capital in "New York, Baltimore, Philadelphia"—were similarly de rigueur in this nasty business.[12]

It was not as if this soiled commerce was unknown to the authorities. For example, in May 1857, a newspaper in the ship-building center of Bath, Maine reported blandly that "the schooner Evangeline, now in New York, built in Prospect [Maine], in 1855 and owned by Captain Pittman of Brewer [Maine], who commands her, is strongly suspected of being a slaver."[13] Before that, the U.S. brig "Excellent" sailed into Rio de Janeiro in March 1850. "William Temple, the first mate, was a known slaver"; he and the "master Bruce McKinney . . . swore that the 'Excellent' was bound for California, obtained the ship's papers necessary to clear Rio" but, typically, went to Ambriz on the west coast of Africa instead. "Slave traders took an average of 40,000 slaves from Africa each year for 420 years," says the writer, Pegram Harrison. "The magnitude of these numbers place in perspective the lack of commitment of the United States Government and the Navy Department to suppress the African slave trade and ultimately bring it to an end."[14]

As early as 1828, the premier African-American periodical, **Freedom's Journal** had found that "this horrible traffic in human flesh" was borne by "sharp built brigs or schooners, constructed in the United States and sent out to Brazil and sold for that purpose. . . . it made my heart sick to behold this miserable spectacle."[15] Frederick Douglass was one among many who held in contempt his nation's attempt to halt the illegal trade to Brazil. He denounced the "inefficiency of our preventive squadrons and the impunity with which the nefarious traffic is prosecuted under our flag." The U.S. Minister, he said in 1853, had "sent nearly thirty dispatches to the State Department without receiving an answer to one of them" about this pressing matter. There was a trade in "horses and cattle," said Douglass, from the "Cape of Good Hope to Rio" but after they "clear at the Cape for Brazil. . . . they tumble overboard the less valuable animals, and proceed to convenient points to secure bipeds."[16] His newspaper published a story by Horace Greeley reporting from Bahia, observing that the "slave trade . . . is carried on here extensively, from the Coast of Africa"; "we hear," said the New York–based writer, "that the Baltimorean-built pilot boat 'Henry Clay' is now gone on her eleventh voyage to the coast of Africa for slaves in four years she has been owned here, and that she made in that time over $300,000 for her owners. . . . some 10 or 12 vessels are engaged in the business from this place alone and probably four times as many more from different ports of this very extensive Empire."[17]

Two of the key Brazilians who spearheaded the illegal slave trade— Manuel Pinto da Fonseca and Bernardino de Sa—"were known partially to have financed U.S. slave ships and to have sold slaves brought to Brazil by U.S. slavers. U.S. diplomats in Rio de Janeiro in the 1840s considered these two men the most notorious slave dealers in the city at the time."[18] Surely during the critical decade of the 1840s, when the unlawful trade was reaching new heights in Brazil, U.S. nationals seemed to be ubiquitous. With a crafty ingenuity, these nationals employed devious tactics to smuggle Africans to Brazil. " 'The Sooy,' " for example, was of "American build" and had "on her stern the 'eagle' carved and painted large letters 'Sooy of Newport.' " She had "sailed from the port of Bahia under the American flag, with an American crew on board, for a port on the coast of Africa, the master and crew should leave her; which they did, and she was surrendered to the captain and crew of a slave-dealer there, who landed on the coast of Brazil" with hundreds of enslaved Africans. Another dizzying switch involved the "Sea Eagle" and the "Agnes" which arrived in Cabinda simultaneously. "Brazilian passengers who were taken out" in the former were transferred to the latter, then "Negro slaves were berthed" on the renamed "Agnes" though it lacked "any regular slave deck," so they were "berthed on these mats." The "American flag" was "hauled down and papers taken off and [its] name erased or painted over" and "she sailed on or about the 7th of September 1844, with about 500 slaves, and landed them on the coast of Brazil, near Cape Frio." The U.S. crew "were transferred to the 'Sea Eagle,' which vessel remained at Cabinda until after the arrival" of the renamed "Agnes."[19]

Often during this era, U.S. crews would sail ships to Africa, then turn the ship over to Brazilians—or Portuguese or Spaniards—after the vessel was loaded down with Africans. At times U.S. whalers would engage in freelance slave trading, grabbing whatever Africans that were in reach, when dropping anchor in Cape Verde, for example.[20]

In 1847, the British diplomat in Rio de Janeiro, Lord Howden, complained about such tactics observing that "it is the custom to ship the [U.S.] crew which brought this vessel to Africa, aboard some other [U.S.] vessel not intended to take slaves back to Brazil, and which may thus be searched without risk by a [U.S.] cruiser; this confederate vessel often serving also as a decoy to lead these cruisers astray. The first of these vessels lands its cargo of slaves somewhere on the Brazilian coast and then returns to Rio in ballast, while the second vessel enters there direct with the former crew ready for another passage and with the very few articles of commerce afforded by the slave districts in Africa." Ships often had "two owners and two nationalities" and "two sets of papers. . . . she will be American while going to the coast of Africa and Brazilian when returning from it."[21]

At other times, U.S. slavers were disguised as whalers, on one occasion in 1849 in conjunction with Manuel Pinto da Fonseca, a New Bedford–based vessel brought *"eleven hundred and fifty Negroes"* [emphasis-original] in various voyages to Brazil; "in the event of falling in with an American cruiser, [she] would hoist the Brazilian flag—if an English cruiser, the American flag and thus avoid capture." The captain hailed from "Dartmouth near New Bedford."[22] As the Civil War approached, Britain took note of the U.S. ship " 'Atlantic,' " another slaver disguised as a whaler. Naturalized U.S. citizens from New Bedford of Portuguese origin were the owners; their firm was "Abranches, Almeida and Co." It was "suspected . . . she would proceed to the Mozambique Channel," though it "next turned up [in] the Bahamas as the 'America' " where it was wrecked in an attempt to send Africans to Cuba.[23]

It was hard for legitimate commerce to compete with the banned trade. One commander of the African Squadron complained that in Luanda, Angola, "wealth and prosperity" were dependent on the slave trade. In 1848, the amount of goods entered for the legal trade, amounted to about ninety thousand dollars; and at the same time, there were smuggled goods for the purposes of the slave trade, "amounting to the sum of eight hundred thousand dollars."[24]

The authorities complained constantly about the deviousness of the slavers. As the leading Washington official, Abel P. Upshur, put it, their "cunning" was astonishing; they were "constantly devising new disguises and schemes of deception, by which he may elude detection and escape the consequences of his crimes. . . . they take especial care to put on the appearance of honest traders, and to be always prepared as if engaged in pursuits of lawful commerce." They paid sailors more than, say, whalers, or the merchant marine. Upshur, however, conceded that his country did "not regard the success of their efforts as their paramount interest nor as their paramount duty," which was as explanatory of the success of these slavers as their craftiness.[25]

This guile was aided immeasurably by natural factors. "Pursuit" of slavers "could only occur eight out of twenty-four hours, somewhere between dawn and 2 P.M. Darkness thwarted all efforts at capture; the culprits were fully aware that cruisers would not commence chase after midafternoon. Thus, the remaining sixteen hours belonged to them."[26] Some U.S. vessels in West Africa would light a "triangular fire lit on a height, two fires apart at the base and one on the top of the hill, forming the triangle. The meaning was slaves are ready with canoes on beach: a number of flashes, of which six were counted, indicated the number 600 slaves. The slaver's signal on arrival at night on the date appointed for shipping, consists of a triangular blue, white and green light hoisted in the rigging. There are numerous distant signals for communicating with the offing."[27]

By dint of such measures, Africans were pouring into Brazil in the 1840s, often transported on ships bearing U.S. flags. Things had gotten so bad that the U.S. missionary, the Reverend J. Leighton Wilson, who was posted to Gabon during this time lost hope that this traffic in human beings would ever end. "The opinion has long been entertained by many sincere friends of Africa," he said despairingly, "that so long as the demand for slaves in Brazil is so great, it will be impossible to break up the slave-trade by any forcible measures." The only solution he could conjure up was a radical free trade in Africans: "the most certain and effectual way of breaking it up [i.e., the slave trade] will be to let the Brazilians have unlimited access to the coast of Africa, and so glut their own markets that slaves will become comparatively useless."[28]

For a while, it seemed that the Reverend Wilson's musing was becoming reality. A member of the Royal Navy discovered to his dismay that "slaves were sold on the coast of Africa in 1847 for a mere song— an old musket was considered too much—while in the Brazils they realized 50 [pounds] a-piece." Hence, "owing to the great demand for slaves in the Brazils, the speculators are fitting out large steamers capable, it is said, of carrying three thousand slaves. These vessels are armed, and two only have as yet been captured," concluded Lieutenant Forbes in 1849. "Slave merchants employ boats to a distance of forty out at sea, to watch the cruisers, and, incredible as it may appear, yet it is no less a fact, that one of [Britain's] ships was actually reported to that distance daily by whale-boats."[29] "The number of these slave depots on the coast between the Isle Sherbro and Gaboon [sic]," said John C. Lawrence of the U.S. African Squadron in 1844, "is really incredible when we consider how well it is scoured by vessels of war"; rather brazenly, "there was not the least concealment made."[30]

Understandably, there was considerable focus on Angola, the chief Portuguese colony in West Africa, which was a fertile source of enslaved Africans for Brazil.[31] British and, at times, U.S. vessels sailed southward to monitor this vast land, along with the adjoining region of Cabinda and the mouth of the Congo River. But often ignored was Portugal's colony in East Africa, Mozambique, which increasingly was being raided for slaves as the attention of the anti-bondage authorities was directed westward. Scholar, Abdul Sheriff, attests that "the Trans-Atlantic slave trade from Mozambique to Brazil revived after the shift of the Portuguese court to Rio de Janeiro" and "especially in the 1820s when up to 16,000 slaves were exported in a single year."[32] "We have little knowledge of the details respecting the slave trade on the Eastern Coast of Africa," U.S. Secretary of State, Daniel Webster, was informed in 1842; "the field of operations to carry on the slave trade is so extensive, the profits so great and the obstacles in the path so many, so various, so difficult" to scrutinize that the authorities complained that they were at a loss when the slavers turned eastward.[33] Five years later, a British emissary in South Africa was complaining that "the Slave Trade has recently increased on the east side of the coast. . . . some of the speculations of that nature which were carried on on the west coast of Africa have been transferred to the Mozambique Channel," allowing "vessels, almost all of which go to Rio [de] Janeiro escape without capture."[34] In 1848, London's man in Rio, James Hudson conceded that "at no period during the history of the Brazilian Slave Trade have so many dealers left Brazil as of late for Africa to purchase slaves; at no time have so many vessels been employed in this traffic." So, where were the vessels obtaining enslaved Africans? "The larger share of orders for slaves," he said, "has been sent to the Mozambique coast, because the Rio slave-traders have learnt that that part of Africa is less guarded than the Western Coast."[35] Characteristically, "the vessels" arrived in Mozambique "with American colors, under which they remain until the slave cargo is prepared and other arrangements for receiving the same completed. . . . when all is ready the American colours are hauled down" and "Brazilian colours or . . . none at all" were displayed.[36] Facilitating East Africa's path toward becoming a major preserve for the hunting of Africans, was the fact that "the Governors of Ibo and Quillimane" were "notoriously engaged in aiding and assisting in the traffic and further" it was "more than suspected that the Governor-General of Mozambique is himself in collusion with slave-dealers and that he has received large sums of money on several occasions for contriving at the dereliction of duty on the part of his subordinates."[37]

One of the most infamous episodes that implicated eastern Africa was only exposed when the slaver in question landed in Brazil and was detained: The man who became Pedro Parris was born of "full blooded native African parents somewhere on the eastern coast of Africa" in "about 1833." When he was "about ten years old" a "terrible uproar arose in the night and as his father stepped out of the hut to learn the cause[,] he was struck down. The terrified family scattered, attempting to escape as best they could in the confusion and darkness." But Parris was "taken. The last he saw of his family that night was his grandmother screaming on a large rock on which she had sought refuge as he was being hurried away." The captives were kept on a forced march that entire night and in the morning he found that his three brothers also had been seized. He never saw or heard of the rest of his family again, however. With other captives, he was on the march for several weeks before being taken to the island of Zanzibar. Unclear as to what had befallen him, he—along with some of the other captives—felt "they were to be eaten." Here he "first saw a white man," who was quite "harsh" "beating" him and others in order to "hasten" his acquisition of the Portuguese language, which "would bring a higher price." Finally, he was "sold" to a "Captain Paulo who bought a full cargo of slaves and shipped them" to Rio de Janeiro, Brazil "on the vessel of Captain Libby of Portland, Maine." In Zanzibar he "had been named Pedro."

However, "the sailors on Libby's vessel had not shipped as slavers, and were much enraged when they discovered what [traffic] they had been drawn into." Hence, in Rio the U.S. Consul discovered what had happened and the captors and "Pedro" "were taken" to "Portland by an American warship then at Rio under charge of slaving," where they were "indicted." "Pedro" was a chief witness against the defendants and, along with a number of other young African boys, was taken in by families in Maine, a state that was to become his home. Thus, in 1856, when George Gordon—who had served as Consul in Rio—ran for Governor of Massachusetts as a "Know-Nothing," he "needed something to check the trend of abolitionists" toward the recently formed Republican Party; he "sought out Pedro and employed him for six weeks making campaign speeches for Gordon"; so inspired, "Pedro Parris" sought to become a "ventriloquist."[38]

The trial of the perpetrators of this kidnapping masquerading as commerce was revelatory. The man who became "Pedro Parris"[39] had been brought from East Africa on a ship owned by George Richardson of New Orleans and financed in part by Maxwell, Wright of Baltimore and Brazil and Manuel Pinto da Fonseca of Rio de Janeiro. There was also a New England connection as the Captain, Cyrus Libby, hailed from "Scarborough in the County of Cumberland" in Maine, as did the vessel's owner, Richardson, who formerly resided there. Another owner of this vessel, the "Porpoise," was Adams Bailey, Jr., a Boston merchant.

Questioned in 1845, Libby was incredulous, arguing that "the first I knew of the boys being on board was when we were about half way . . . from [Mozambique] . . . when I saw the said boy on deck, at play with other boys, unconfined and at perfect liberty," playing "with the son of the pilot," who too was a "black man"; the Captain was not overly disturbed, since he "then believed and now believes that said boy was the son of said pilot and free and not a slave." "I do suppose and believe," he swore, "that these boys were free & not held by any person as slaves, that they went over to Rio Janeiro to be educated and then to be sent back to the coast, as is customary." "I was entirely deceived and defrauded," he charged. But his incredulity was hard to accept in light of the prominent role in his enterprise of Maxwell, Wright, known to be involved in the banned trade, which instructed him in Rio that "after leaving this port, you will please follow the instructions of Mr. Antonio de Luis da Cunha, on board, as far as your charter party will permit you to do so." The latter was the agent of Fonseca and it was clear that his role on board ship was major.[40]

On the other hand, Libby's story was not entirely unbelievable. There were Negro crew members on board his vessel, which could bolster his alibi that he thought "Pedro Parris" was not a slave. Mark Tanner, a self-described "colored man," was 24 and born in Bristol, Rhode Island. But he would not substantiate Libby's tale, asserting that when they arrived from New England in Brazil before heading for East Africa, he "asked for his discharge but Captain Libby would not give it to him."[41]

But then there was another "colored man" on board, Peter Johnson, who was the "cook and steward." Born in Kingston, New York and 29 at the time of his 1845 deposition, he joined the vessel in Rio in early 1844. Unlike Tanner, he could "understand" and "speak" Portuguese "imperfectly," to the point that he could comprehend "common conversation." Ashore in Mozambique, while at the so-called slave "factory," some of the slaves were walking about and some sitting down; others were standing up. . . . males were chained together; the women with chains around their necks." However, Johnson had other things on his mind that did not necessarily include the chief witness against Libby, i.e., "Pedro Parris." "Deponent asked one of the Portuguese crew about a large good looking woman[,] he said that she was one that Paulo had just bought." Johnson did notice, however, that "all the Negroes . . . had been branded, either upon the breast or the back of the shoulder and the brand wounds were then raw." Evidently Johnson did not choose to remark on the irony of his being now enmeshed in the most fetid and squalid of slave raiding while being part of a group—U.S. Negroes—that were largely the product of a similar process.[42]

Of course, the crew was hardly comprised wholly of U.S. Negroes, though like Tanner and Johnson, most hailed from the Northeast, especially New York, Rhode Island, and Maine. There was Charles Hendricks, for example, who was born in Sweden—but had "never been naturalized"—and had sailed from the U.S. for nine years before being detained by the authorities for slaving. He placed Libby at the scene of the crime and added for good measure that "Manoel Pinto of Rio" was likewise involved.[43] His countryman, John Williams, 24, was also a "native of Sweden" but was considerably less garrulous.[44]

But the most damaging testimony came from another African boy, known as "Guilheme" or "George Williams." He was "colored or mulatto" and thought to be 14 (his mother, he said, was a "white woman" and his "father was black"). Born near "Inhambane" in Mozambique, he was sold and wound up on the "Porpoise" where the crew "threatened us at sea—that if we did not do everything well we should be flogged on shore at Rio." Many of his relatives were "murdered" in the process of capturing him—including his "father and mother"—but still he "did not want to go" but was compelled. "Captain Libby named him George Williams" and took him on a journey from eastern Africa to São Tomé, then to "Cabinda" and from there to Brazil. A crew member "threatened to sell him" all the while, though Libby himself never "called him his slave." He witnessed the buying of slaves in Mozambique. Like "Parris," "George Williams" was inclined to return to Africa but he added poignantly, "I'm afraid of being made a slave again. I would rather go in this very ship," speaking of the U.S. naval vessel that was to take him to New England to testify against Libby, "to the United States."[45]

"Pedro Parris" also did not help Libby's case. He was told after being captured and enslaved that "when any person should ask me, to answer that I was free. . . . I was branded on the breast" to sanctify this reality. Like, "George Williams," he too expressed a fervent "wish to be a free man and go to the United States."[46]

"The whole experience of the trials," Captain Libby cried out, "will not fall short of $2500." This would involve "stripping him of every farthing he had on earth and even taking," said the sympathetic reporter, "the old homestead from his aged and widowed mother"—and this was not to mention the accompanying "ten seamen, government witnesses" who were "confined in jail."[47]

Unfortunately, many Africans did not have the kind of happy ending endured by "Pedro Parris"—rescued and sent to a new life in the U.S. Such was the fate of another U.S. flagged slaver, the "Kentucky," which in 1845 also found itself in Mozambique with 500 potential African slaves aboard. Resisting the fate that awaited them, these Africans "rose upon the officer and crew; a majority of the men, all of whom were in irons, got their irons off, broke through the bulkhead in the females department. . . . the Captain armed the crew with cutlasses and got all the muskets and pistols and loaded them and crew were firing down amongst the slaves for half an hour or more. . . . in about half an hour they were subdued." Retaliating, some of the rebels were then "hung," as a "rope was put around their necks and they were drawn up to the yard-arm clear, of the sail. This did not kill them, but only choked or strangled them. They were then shot in the breast and the bodies thrown overboard," while "the legs of about a dozen were chopped off"; "when the feet fell on deck, they were picked up by the Brazilian crew and thrown overboard, irons and all. When the woman was hung up and shot, the ball did not take effect, and she was thrown overboard living, and was seen to struggle some time in the water before she sunk"; then "they brought up and flogged about 20 men and six women" in a fashion described as "very severe," to the point where the floggers "got tired." The "flesh of some of them where they were flogged . . . putrified and came off" as the Africans writhed in the "most intense agony. They were a shocking a horrible sight during the whole passage," said an eyewitness, a member of the crew; unsurprisingly, "there was no disturbance on board after this" on the part of the survivors, mostly "Negroes . . . from nine or 10 up to 30 years." This ship, the "Kentucky," was seen as a companion of the "Porpoise."[48]

The horrible conditions that characterized slave ships sheds light on the level of African resistance. A British emissary in Bahia, a presumed destination for those to be held in bondage, inferentially indicated why when he observed that "it appears incredible, but it is nevertheless a fact that a ship's long boat manned by three persons and measuring twenty-four feet extreme length, seven feet breadth and only three feet nine inches depth, has arrived here from the coast of Africa, in which fifty miserable children had actually been stowed and thirty-five conducted hither, fifteen having died on the passage. It is more than probable," he concluded sadly, "that every soul on board would have perished for want of water and provisions, had they not been relieved by a merchant vessel when reduced to the last extremity."[49] This trade was extraordinarily cruel. A British representative observed that "for many years" he had the "habit of asking the different [enslaved] Africans with whom I have conversed the circumstances under which they were brought; and they, with scarcely any exception, state that they were kidnapped or taken in what they call their wars." Many were brought from the continent's interior, marching "one, two or three months to the coast."[50]

Many Africans did not take kindly to the presence of ships flying the U.S. flag in their vicinity. The U.S. brig "Mary Adeline" discovered this to its dismay. In the summer of 1852, this vessel was nearing the "Shark Point, in the River Congo," when suddenly it was "attacked by the Natives." These "savages" were "coming down the river in great numbers for the purpose of plundering my vessel," said the master of this vessel; "many of them [were] armed with muskets," about "fifteen hundred of them" in this category with weapons, including "spears and cutlasses." Some of them were "furnished with hooks and poles by which to scale the side. I had six muskets and two rifles only on board," he continued; "they suddenly set up a fiendish yell and leveled their muskets at us. We had barely time to cover ourselves before a large volley was fired which fortunately did no other damage than to sails and rigging." Riding to the rescue was a British ship that ultimately prevailed; yet, the "savages with great cunning took advantage of this and again approached in greater numbers than before for another combined attack. . . . I fired a charge of grape into them," he recalled, "and fortunately killed and wounded a considerable number which had the desired effect of inducing them to retreat." Still, but for the serendipitous arrival of a British vessel, "not one who was on board of my vessel," he assured, "would ever have been heard of again."[51] Yes, confirmed the commander of the intervening vessel from Britain, "[we] defended your vessel from the murderous attack of at least 3000 Natives," reminding him that this part of the River Congo was "always attended with great risk."[52]

As this incident and the perilous voyage of Pedro Parris suggests, there was a considerable traffic in Africans traversing the Atlantic westward and northward. In 1836, the abolitionist David Ruggles was among a group involved "in an attempt to rescue slaves from a Brazilian ship docked in New York."[53]

Mahommah Gardo Baquaqua was kidnapped in Africa, brought to Brazil as a slave, then transported to New York City. In Manhattan "at the dock at the foot of Roosevelt Street, on the East River, local abolitionists, organized loosely as the New York Vigilance Society, approached" the ship, "initiating a legal tug-of-war over the fate" of Baquaqua. He managed to escape bondage but "by the latter half of 1853 . . . it seems that Baquaqua was increasingly disillusioned with United States society. . . . 'I did not like to stay in this country,' " he said.[54]

Born in Central Africa, Baquaqua—a Muslim—was the slavers' nightmare, proudly proclaiming in 1854 that he was "stirring up the colored population and agitating for the abolition of slavery all over the world." What had led him to this revolutionary posture was his experience, enticed to drink an intoxicating beverage in Africa, before being taken prisoner and taken to Pernambuco. He was forced into a form of alien worship—"we all had to kneel before them," i.e., slave-owners; "whilst worshipping," he said, "my master held a whip in his hand and those who showed signs of inattention or drowsiness were immediately brought to consciousness by a smart application of the whip. This mostly fell to the lot of the female slave." Taken to Rio de Janeiro, he was almost sold to a "colored man." "I merely mention this fact," said Baquaqua, "to illustrate that slaveholding is generated in power . . . and that the colored man would as soon enslave his fellow man as the white man, had he the power." He worked on a ship and reinforced there was what "we all had learned," i.e., that "at New York there was no slavery; that it was a free country," where he finally attained a form of freedom.[55]

The Tucker Family of South Carolina was engaged heavily in shipping goods to California via Brazil; so it may not have been surprising in the summer of 1848 when a "Negro runaway," a "well dressed" slave with "plenty of clothes and some money" was found on one of these voyages; the captain's "first impulse was to turn back, in hopes of finding some vessel bound to Carolina or Georgia to put him on board" but decided to continue; it was unclear if this stowaway made it to California—or Brazil.[56]

Nevertheless, the enormous profits of this trade guaranteed that the slavers would continue their dirty business. Speaking from Rio in 1848, one British diplomat declared awestruck that "the profits are enormous. . . . Portuguese in this city who arrived here a pauper and [were] now worth half a million sterling at least, all made in the Slave Trade"; this "army of slave dealers never wants recruits." It fed corruption, bribing of officials, not to mention "many thousands of white men [who] must be employed in watching" slaves; "the more valuable labour of a certain number of whites must be abstracted from the service of the country," providing further basis for the potent idea that the African Slave Trade was suffocating Brazil in the long-term.[57]

Yet attempts to seize Africans for slavery continued. In the late spring of 1847, the Royal Navy, which concentrated mostly in western Africa, found the time to send "four boats up the River Angazha [*sic*]" in Mozambique to "take or destroy such . . . vessels as may be there found, engaged in the traffic and commerce of slaves." Their intelligence was timely and actionable for on the "approach" of their vessels, "a slave brig was set on fire by the persons on board—the 'Lucy Penniman,' an American barque was also at anchor here: on the officer boarding her, the remaining (she having lost a boat's crew a few days before) crew came forward and stated that they had been illegally employed in the Slave Trade against their will."[58] Another time the British were not as lucky for as they approached the slaver in the waters of eastern Africa, they "were fired upon by a number of persons from the bushes, which were not more than thirty yards off. . . . the Captain claimed the protection of the American flag" while "the crew had come forward to ask our protection, they being in fear of their lives."[59]

Even Lisbon, lax in the best of times, was becoming concerned about the increasing encroachments of U.S. slavers in what they deemed to be their territory. Cases proliferated of U.S. flagged vessels "not having cleared from Rio de Janeiro for any certain and definite port on the eastern or western coast of Portuguese Africa" and suspected of being involved in the "contraband trade and in the illicit traffic in slaves."[60]

Washington's representative in Lisbon was displeased with Portugal's displeasure. "Her crew and passengers were thrown into prison," said J. B. Clay, U.S. Chargés d'Affaires in Lisbon, referring to U.S. nationals,

Black female slaves in Brazil, circa 1830s, from various ethnic groups, reflecting different styles of dress and adornment. U.S. slave dealers ventured not only to western Africa but also to eastern areas such as Mozambique. Courtesy Library of Congress.

and "remained some eleven months" incarcerated where "her captain and first mate died as is believed from starvation." This was an outrage: "no nation has a right," he said accusingly, "to seize and condemn them if they be taken on the high seas, although brim full of slaves from neck to kelson, save their own. The general law of nations does not condemn the slave trade," he insisted. Anyway, the ship was not engaged in the slave trade and, besides, Portuguese law in Mozambique could not apply to the U.S., not least since this vessel was actually in the waters under the jurisdiction of the "Moorish Sultan," closer to Zanzibar than Mozambique.[61]

It was not as if Lisbon was that concerned with the buying and kid-napping of Africans—after all, they had done more than their share in this grimy realm; there was a graver concern that Washington, even then considerably larger and more powerful than this Iberian nation, had designs on their closed markets and spheres of influence, from South America to Africa.

Lisbon was livid about the routine snatching of Africans from Cape Verde by U.S. whalers, compelling the U.S. Secretary of State to apolo-

gize.[62] Then there was the irksome "case of the slave brig 'Susan'"
which led to a Portuguese claim of "$22,701.24 in behalf of the 'Por-
tuguese passengers' captured . . . in that brig and brought into the port
of New York." This was "'an American built brig with a crew of Portuguese and Brazilians'" that was "'bound directly to the slave coast of
Africa'" then, presumably, to Brazil. The son of Portugal's "Consul
General" in New York represented "'some of the parties, passengers of
the Susan,'" which raised questions about Lisbon's official posture
about slaving—a nagging question that Lisbon also had about Washington.[63] Like an old married couple that desperately needed counseling,
Lisbon began dredging up past grievances to fling in Washington's face,
such as incidents that occurred years earlier during the time of Brazil's
struggle for independence when ships "owned" by U.S. nationals captured Portuguese ships. Lisbon remained angry about this. In so many
words, Washington replied that this was too bad.[64]

In a sense this was a phony conflict, for on the larger question of the
criminal slave trade, Lisbon may have been more unenthusiastic than
Washington in seeing this enterprise end.[65] In 1847, as the raids in Portuguese East Africa increased tremendously, London complained that
the "Portuguese government had instructed the Governor-General of
Mozambique to revoke the permission which he had granted Her Majesty's ships employed in the Mozambique Channel" in order to "act
against that [slave] traffic." Since "great facilities exist towards carrying
on the Slave Trade on the east coast of Africa," this would "give great
encouragement to the Slave Trade."[66] The Mixed Commission at the
Cape of Good Hope, which was designed by London to crackdown on
this unlawful commerce, should have been overworked in the late
1840s if Portugal had desired to cooperate in seizing slavers. Instead, it
was found that "no case has been brought before them for adjudication
during the year ending December 31, 1848 and that no Negroes have
been emancipated by Decree of this Mixed Commission since its establishment."[67] Typically, in 1851, when Francisco dos Santos Tavares was
a "prisoner of the Mixed Commission Court," apparently on charges of
slave trading, this Lusophone national managed to "escape," as he
"deceived the Mixed Commission as to the departure of the said Tavares in the American vessel 'Sacramento.'"[68]

It was left to the South African press to ascertain that it was "evident
that a flourishing slave-trade is now being carried on in this quarter, not

directly from Delagoa Bay or Inhambane [East Africa] but chiefly from points on the coast, between the Portuguese settlements and undoubtedly with the connivance of the authorities there. Cape Corrientes, between Delagoa Bay and Inhambane is the chief seat of the trade" and there was "not a sign of an English cruiser upon the whole northeast coast."[69]

But what about U.S. "cruisers"? The record is mixed: basically there were some conscientious U.S. Navy men operating within the confines of a fatally flawed policy. For example, in 1850, George Stoner of the Brazil Squadron told the Secretary of the Navy, "I have uniformly used every means in my power to obtain information" about the "slave trade" but the "British Minister" in Rio said that the "authorities of the United States in Brazil have not continued to exert the same degree of vigilance as before"—though he thought this was "entirely destitute of foundation of truth." No, he insisted, the problem actually was "the want of small steamers and sailing vessels capable of overhauling at sea and of pursuing" slavers, not to mention the "numerous smaller ports" slavers could draw upon. "Vessels suitable to operate against them have been withdrawn from the station and not replaced, notwithstanding my repeated representations to the Department." This led to "prostitution of our flag."[70]

William Graham, Secretary of the Navy, comrade of Matthew Maury and fan of his plans for the Amazon, did not demur, though Stoner had to realize, Graham thought, that there were other issues beyond chasing down slavers. Relations between Brazil and Buenos Ayres had "assumed a more threatening appearance . . . war seems inevitable" and the navy had to think about protecting U.S. interests in this vital region—yet "the present naval force here will prove very inadequate to the proper protection of our interests," so a "small steamer would under such circumstances prove a most efficient addition to the squadron."[71]

So, Graham with one hand endorsed Stoner's goal for small steamers and with the upper hand suggested that ships could be put to better use than tracking down slave vessels.[72] Rather than cooperating with London on handcuffing the unlawful slave trade, there was an instinct in Washington to act, instead, as a counterweight to this power.[73]

Other U.S. Navy men were not as conscientious as Stoner. Andrew Boyd Cummings, for example, took a fancy to "Negro dance houses" of São Tomé, West Africa, and mused about recruiting musicians there for similar establishments back home—"what a glorious speculation it would [be]," he enthused, "to hire this whole party & to transport them to New Orleans"[74]—and had a penchant for becoming embroiled in untidy disputes in Angola involving U.S. nationals, as opposed to halting the trade in human beings. He was exultant about the "prospect of bombardment" of Benguela, as a result of this matter, "it would have been a little excitement for us"—though no such aggression seemed to be generated by the African Slave Trade.[75]

Likewise, in Angola, Britain's representative there thought he had detected an "alteration" in the "tone" of U.S. "Commodore Lavallette" when he spoke with him as the fall of 1851 approached. "On the subject of the slave trade and the prevalent feeling in the United States respecting it," it was indicated that "this would be their [U.S.] last appearance in this latitude and that the Squadron was to be withdrawn; trusting to other measures such as Colonization and the establishment of a line of steamers between the United States and Liberia for the accomplishment of the desired end. . . . this end, however, seemed to be less the suppression of the Traffic, or even the Prevention of the abuse of the American flag than the relieving [of] the United States of their free black population, which, whether, voluntarily or otherwise, must, it was said, be got rid of."[76]

By this juncture, Britain had escalated its tactics against the African Slave Trade. "We have captured and burnt Brazilian ships in sight almost of this capital," said a British emissary in 1850 and, surprisingly, he added, "we have one half of the daily newspapers in this capital in our favor." Things had gotten so bad that "American holders of vessels built for [the] Slave Trade and brought here for speculation, cannot find purchasers for them."[77] "The number of Africans imported as slaves into Brazil had greatly diminished," said this same emissary, James Hudson, one year later; this was accompanied by the "arrival of white artisans," whose numbers had "greatly increased." Moreover, a number of Africans, 400 free "men" from "the interior of Congo even to Mozambique on the south" wanted to leave Brazil and "settle at or near Ambriz."[78] The "appearance" in Brazil of "yellow fever in 1849–50 was attributed to the arrival of slaves from East Africa. A public outcry against their import resulted in a radical drop in the number of slaves brought in by slave vessels. An annual figure of [imports] of 60,000 at 1850 was soon reduced to a few thousands by 1853."[79] London was placing so much pressure on Brazil in 1850, that the visiting U.S.

midshipman, Andrew Boyd Cummings, found "there was quite an excitement here for a while against the English, so great indeed that it was even dangerous for an Englishman to be seen in the street for a while."[80]

This woodcut, which originally appeared in the U.S. abolitionist organ, *The Liberator*, accompanied an article written in 1832 protesting the African Slave Trade to Brazil. Slaves were occasionally thrown overboard by slave dealers who wished to escape payment of an importation tax, or who wished to get rid of evidence of illegal slaving. Courtesy Library of Congress.

3

Buying and Kidnapping Africans

Coffee was the driving force behind the stunning growth of the enslaved population of Brazil in the 19th century and U.S. nationals were a prime motor pushing Africans across the Atlantic from the late 18th century through the late 1840s.[1] As the taste for this beverage grew among refined palates in Europe and North America, the demand for slaves grew accordingly, particularly among the coffee planters of the Paraiba Valley.[2] Factors were at play limiting import of slaves in other regions; thus, 1848 "marked the beginning of an extended lull. That year, slave revolts in Martinique, St. Croix and Puerto Rico along with the appointment of Puerto Rico's first abolitionist governor (after the revolts), combined to discourage further importation of slaves."[3] This served to augment the importance of Brazil as a market for enslaved Africans and, correspondingly, was keeping certain U.S. nationals quite busy.[4] Yet this unity of interest between and among certain forces in the U.S., Brazil, and Africa was contested, particularly in North America which created strains that eventuated in Civil War. It was also contested by the U.K., which by seeking to half the illicit slave trade was also interrupting a profitable commerce in agricultural commodities —to the benefit of London, alleged its critics. This chapter will detail the extensive involvement of U.S. nationals in the African Slave Trade to Brazil, particularly in the 1840s, along with the ineffectual efforts by Washington to halt it. As the decade wore on, this trafficking in human beings was becoming a big business that was enticing foreign nationals to adopt U.S. citizenship so that they could better take advantage of the immense profitability that was being generated. Meanwhile, London vainly sought to stem what seemed to be an inexorable tide.

One British emissary had "received authentic information that upwards of twenty thousand slaves had been surreptitiously landed in the Brazilian territories within the last four months of the year 1842" alone and this was just the beginning of a decade-long trend.[5] Some U.S. nationals were smuggling Africans to Brazil to produce coffee that was then exported in substantial amounts to the U.S. Ships in turn would return to Rio de Janeiro with finished goods, also lumber and candles. This was a virtuous circle—for some—and a nightmare for others, principally Africans.[6]

But for British pressure, the number of Africans flooding into Brazil may have been substantially larger. It was the weight of London that led in 1835 to a so-called equipment clause in a global treaty; that is, "on the basis of chains, excessive rations, superfluous shelves in the hold, and other indications, the clause permitted the capture and adjudication of slave ships without slaves on board."[7] Similar pressure from London led to the Webster-Ashburton Treaty of 1842, whereby Washington was obliged to station a naval squadron on the West African coast. Of course, Salem merchants had long since established a base in the open back door that was East Africa—and, in any event, this team was sited in Cape Verde, "far from the most important slave trading areas; few American cruisers ever ventured as far as the Congo or Angola." This was a "'sham patrol.'"[8]

Furthermore, those actually caught in the act had little to worry about. "Of 96 prosecutions between 1839 and 1862 executed under the pretext of the slave trade acts only 12 (12.5 percent) returned guilty verdicts where the convicted slaver was given a judicial punishment . . . of 95 slave ships seized for suspected engagement in the slave trade between 1837 and 1862, in only 56 (58.9 percent) cases were the craft condemned (found guilty) and the master forced to face some sort of adjudication." U.S. courts and the U.S. Navy "were notoriously soft on the international slave trade.[9]

London was not the only force pushing for the end of this horrible traffic. In 1839, the Massachusetts Senate pressed the U.S. Congress to adopt more stringent measures against this business, not least since the ships carrying these human cargoes were almost all of U.S. construction, it was reported. Stricter laws were needed since "the several acts of Congress" were "if not actually a mere dead letter, at any rate, almost entirely ineffectual"; "several years have elapsed since a single armed ship of the United States, with instructions to cruise for and capture such vessels . . . have ever been known to have made even a transient visit to the western coat of Africa."[10]

Yet even these paltry efforts inflamed certain elements among the slaveholding elite in the U.S. John C. Calhoun "exerted a decisive influence over the foreign policy of the United States" for "forty years"; his son was "married to the daughter of Duff Green," another power at Foggy Bottom, which magnified the influence of both families.[11] Calhoun, a renowned son of the South Carolina slaveholder class, had long thought that Brazil was "a most important section of our [*sic*] Continent, in the condition of which every one, who looks to the future must take a lively interest," and he was not happy when London began to lean on the U.S., compelling this nation to do something about its slave pirates.[12] "Next to the United States," considered the powerful politician, "Brazil is the most wealthy, the greatest and most firmly established of all the American powers. Between her and us there is a strict identity of interest on almost all subjects, without conflict, or even competition, on scarcely one." Calhoun thought that "to destroy" slavery in either "would facilitate its destruction in the other. Hence our mutual interest in resisting [London's] interference with the relation in either country." He advocated a staunch and strict international solidarity with Brazil—not least since this was in the self-interest of the Slave South. To be sure, his defense of Brazil was mostly on the basis of slavery, more so than the slave trade, but in context this often amounted to a distinction without a difference.[13]

Calhoun also felt that the defense of slavery and the slave trade would forestall something akin to a "race war." If London prevailed, "we must look not to Jamaica but to St. Domingo for an example. The change would be followed by unforgiving hate between the two races & end in a bloody & deadly struggle between them for the superiority. One or the other would have to be subjugated," it "would be calamitous beyond description." The fates of the U.S., Brazil, and Cuba were linked inextricably as a result, for a setback in one could lead to catastrophes in the others.[14] Calhoun repeatedly referred to these three nations as if they were one unit.[15]

As he saw it, London's pressure on both Brazil and the U.S. was just part of an elaborate plot to "maintain its preeminence" by undermining its rivals. London was contemplating "force" and this "blow" would "first be struck at the [U.S.], Brazil and other slaveholding countries"—and the "reason" was "obvious," i.e., "to give her a monopoly of the great staples they produce, and through them, a monopoly of the trade of the world." Since its abolitionist measures of the 1830s, London could not compete with slave labor and, thus, was compelled to extinguish human bondage altogether—or so thought Calhoun.[16] "Let England succeed with Brazil" with its anti-bondage pressure and next "she will coerce emancipation in Cuba," then the U.S, thought the Dixie diplomat, Duff Green. Their ideological counteroffensive "should raise the banner of free trade," even then the trump card of economic arguments.[17]

"Now is the time," Green exhorted, "to make common cause with Brazil & Cuba," the other recipient of human contraband. He instructed Secretary of State Abel P. Upshur that the "position which England has assumed toward Brazil" was "conclusive argument why the United States and Brazil should act together against" England.[18] Simple survival was at stake since Brazil and the Slave South "were producing cotton, sugar and other staples cheaper than the British West Indian colonies," which impelled the U.K. to destroy both.[19] Green was not content with issuing spirited exhortations, as he lobbied vigorously against global treaties against the slave trade, particularly in France where his influence was greatest, and invoked Brazil as the reason.[20] He was outraged by London's effort in pushing the so-called Quintuple Treaty of 1841, designed to hamper the illicit trade and went further to urge Abel P. Upshur to "prepare for war" with Britain and pressed President Tyler to whip up public sentiment similarly.[21] The U.S. legation in Rio de Janeiro echoed these claims, arguing that London's representatives there were "what would be termed [in] the United States 'abolitionists'"—then a hated term—which, it was said, "has made the very name of an Englishman odious to the people of this country."[22]

White Southerners were not the only U.S. nationals opposed to London's efforts to halt slave traffic between Africa and Brazil. Lewis Cass of the State Department was a Michigander and he too took exception to these multilateral treaties cooked up in London, though his motivation was less sympathy for bondage than concern about sovereignty in the face of the entreaties of a former colonizer,[23] or so he suggested.

Meanwhile, U.S. ships were inundating Brazil, some engaged in ordinary trade—some of which was of strategic importance to North America—and many others depositing enslaved Africans on the shore, while others were being sold for this same illegal purpose. "The United States trade with Rio de Janeiro is considerable," concluded one analyst in

1838. At that juncture, goods from Richmond exceeded those from New York by a factor of four and actually doubled that from Lisbon. Similarly goods from Richmond far exceeded those from Baltimore and Boston (of course, if profits from the illegal slave trade had been factored in along with questionable transfers of vessels, trade with the Northern U.S. would have been much more substantial).[24]

Margaret Lockhard Davis, writing from Pernambuco, was happy to tell her "dear father" in 1843 that "we have had a number of Salem men here within a few months. . . . it makes it very pleasant for us to see people from our own native spot."[25] Similarly satisfying was her residence, "about two & half miles from the city, a delightful spot surrounded by pleasant fields" with "an English family side of us."[26] In 1849, Chaplin Conway of Massachusetts had only been in Bahia for "30 days" before concluding that this was "the worst place that I have seen . . . in all my going to Brazils [sic]"; one reason was clear: "they say that there is [sic] 20 Negroes to one white person" and "there has arrived since I have been here two or three Cargoes of Negroes from the coast of Africa."[27]

The torrent of Africans streaming into Brazil was hard to ignore, which could make the reverie of a Ms. Davis less pleasant if they were ever moved to revolt. This human flood captured the attention of Reverend Pasco G. Hill, who had spent almost two months in Mozambique before arriving in Rio de Janeiro in the early 1840s. "I attended one of the slave auctions," he wrote morosely speaking of this boomtown; there were "about twenty five of both sexes . . . seated on benches behind a long table, which as each in turn ascended to be better viewed by the bidders, a sullenness of look seemed to express their feeling of degradation in being thus put up to sale."[28]

The presence of these U.S. nationals reflected the fact—as U.S. Secretary of State, Abel P. Upshur, was informed—that by 1843, "the American arrivals" of vessels in Rio "have been greater than ever known"[29] and from 1840 to 1845, the number of U.S. ships sold in this thriving metropolis increased sixteenfold, with most having been registered previously in New York, Baltimore, and Nantucket and with many intended for the slave trade.[30] This steady traffic of U.S. vessels south was thought by London to be impelled by purposes less than benign. Concern was raised about the "practice . . . adopted by the United States

Consul at Rio de Janeiro of granting 'sea letters' to American vessels, which as was clearly pointed out . . . affords such great facilities to the operations of Slave Traders."[31]

Interestingly, the number of U.S. ships departing Rio for Africa was also increasing sharply,[32] along with the number of U.S. ships arriving in Rio from Africa, particularly from the rich slave-hunting grounds that were the Portuguese colonies of Angola and Mozambique.[33] The U.S. emissary in Rio, George Gordon, confessed in 1845 that "a man could not be in Rio de Janeiro two days without knowing that all trade between Brazil and the coast of Africa was either directly or indirectly in aid or abetment of the slave trade [and] consequently unlawful"[34] and this was not taking account of U.S. ships arriving further south which were also thought to be smuggling Africans into Brazil.[35]

The very construction of ships in itself was bringing handsome profits to the U.S. Hundreds of persons were required to construct and prepare a vessel for a voyage to the African coast, including countless numbers of carpenters, chandlers, coopers, sparmakers, and sailmakers. The U.S. "became the world leader in the construction and use of fast-sailing vessels in the illicit slave trade. . . . Baltimore shipyards led the United States in construction of fast-sailing vessels for the international slave trade," while "the true masters of the construction of slave trading craft were located in the most northern state in New England, Maine." Shipbuilders in this latter state "constructed more vessels for use in the international slave trade than did Chesapeake shipyards." U.S. nationals "earned enormous profits from the sale of both new and used U.S. craft to slave traders." Thus, in June 1845, a "Brazilian slave trader offered Sammuel [*sic*] Dewing, captain of the U.S. merchant ship *Leader* from Boston, $9000 for the craft. Another slave trader in Rio de Janeiro offered him $12,000 to sell the *Leader* into the slave trade." James Potter of Providence "offered to sell his 407 ton *Panther* to the Brazilian Manuel Fonseca in Rio de Janeiro for $25,000. . . . in 1843 the U.S. Brig *Agnes* sailed to Rio de Janeiro and a British broker named Mr. Wetman chartered the craft to the notorious Brazilian slave trader" Fonseca. Numerous such transactions occurred.[36]

The open and notorious involvement of those from the U.S. North in the African Slave Trade—though the most vigorous defense of enslavement itself emerged from those from the South, like Calhoun and Green —made it difficult for the international community to make crucial distinctions between these two regions, which complicated further Washington's attempt to bar secession. An Irish member of the British Parliament summarized the feelings of many when he said that " 'it was notorious that the real traffickers in the flesh and blood of their fellow men were citizens of the Northern States. It was in Yankee ships, floated by Yankee capital, commanded by Yankee skippers, sailing forth on their abominable errand with the connivance of bribed Yankee authorities that this work of the devil was carried on.' "[37]

It was understandable that such heated remarks would be made in London for British diplomats were carefully scrutinizing the role of U.S. nationals in the African Slave Trade and they were displeased with what they saw. Their Consul in Rio de Janeiro, Robert Hesketh, observed in 1847 that "American vessels adapted for the slave trade are continually brought to this port and sold to the slave traders" which was why "the influx of African slaves was so great during the latter part of 1846 that it occasioned a glut in the market." In fact, "every succeeding year more plainly shows than at Rio Janeiro [*sic*] and its vicinity, the head-quarters of Brazilian slave trade are established"—the city was "one large slave market." This was skewing the economy since "the agricultural class continues its ruinous system of paying more for slave labour than the net produce of their crops can bear."[38] His colleague, J. J. C. Westwood was of like mind, asserting that the U.S. "flag affords in every way the greatest protection of the Slave Trade" with record numbers of Africans arriving which led to a "decline in the price. . . . as the planters are seldom able to pay ready money, slave dealers supply them with slaves to work their estates at much higher rates, at one, two, and even four years credit, taking as security for ultimate payment, mortgages on the estates; and in this manner the slave-traders hold the agricultural proprietary body at their mercy and under their control"—which was also enriching mortgage-holders, who often were U.S. nationals or tied to them.[39]

Some U.S. diplomats in Rio de Janeiro knew that their countrymen were spearheading this bloody trade in the 1840s when it was escalating. " 'I regret to say this,' " exclaimed David Tod, " 'but it is a fact not to be disguised or denied, that the slave trade is almost entirely carried on under our flag, in American-built vessels, sold to slave traders here, chartered for the coast of Africa, and there sold, or sold here, delivered on the coast.' " The " 'entire trade carried on in American vessels between Brazil and Africa, is directly or indirectly connected with the slave traffic.' "[40]

There was a U.S. naval squadron patrolling off the coast of Brazil but it was a maritime version of the Keystone Kops, totally ineffectual, wracked with problems of various sorts. Hence, "the proportion of slaves landed in Brazil in vessels which were or had been or were pretending to be American rose steadily during the late forties from 20% in 1848 (itself a remarkable figure) to almost 50% in 1850."[41] Indeed, "it seems certain that the volume of slave trade to Brazil, Cuba and the United States was far greater during the period of the Anti-Slavery Squadron than before 1807."[42]

A typical event occurred when "midshipman Edward Henshaw was admitted on the Sick Report of this ship with mental derangement" and "threatening violence to himself and to those about him." It was recommended that he be sent back home because of his "feeble health."[43] His colleague, "Midshipman Edward Hopkins" wanted to return home "on [the] first vessel" and needed "sufficient funds" to "pay to settle my debts honorably." The "amount" was "nearly four months pay, say $150.00."[44] An emblematic maritime roustabout, Hopkins was accused of "using personal violence" against those around him and other forms of "conduct" that were "outrageous."[45] He was not alone. There was, for example, "a seaman of the name of Thomas Williams," a "notorious thief and in other respects a man of infamous character." His commanding officer "refused to take him back" and wanted to "return" him to the U.S. or "discharge" him.[46]

One time, according to the U.S. Minister in Rio, a boatload of Africans arrived in Liberia on a navy ship led by a captain "so unfit for duty from drunkenness" he was hardly coherent. "There was no proper authority exercised to prevent the hungry & thirsty wretches from eating the raw beef & beans on board; thus for several days there was nothing cooked for them & they were totally neglected. No less than about 150 died in the course of about 14 days." It was "better to have allowed them to be enslaved in Brazil," he concluded ruefully: this was "disgraceful to our naval service."[47]

There was a "number of cases of smallpox" aboard ship, which did not improve the demeanor of the seamen or their willingness to stay the rocky course.[48] "Illness" was said to be spread if not caused by "the confinement of a small vessel" in this often insalubrious "climate"; this commander wanted Washington to "relieve me from the command of this vessel" so he could "return to the United States."[49] Illness, in fact,

was evidently a factor in explaining the often demented madness of seamen and slave ship crews alike.[50] The U.S. military at this time was not
attracting the most wholesome of recruits[51] and this certainly hindered
their ability to execute a difficult task under the best of circumstances—
halting a fleet of devious, at times well-armed, slave ships.

Besides, the U.S. Navy also had to spend a considerable amount of
time defending U.S. business interests in a region wracked with turmoil
in the best of times,[52] not to mention dodging all manner of hazards
while ashore—sometimes from angry Negroes:[53] this too complicated
their ability to monitor slavers.[54] There were thousands of miles of
coastline to cover, in any case; thus, in the slave center of Pernambuco
where "political intrigues" had "led to violent animosities" with "much
bloodshed and destruction of property," by mid-1845, it had been
"more than a year since any American ship of war" had been there; in
fact, for the longest they had seen "no armed vessel of any nation . . .
on this part of the coast,"[55] which was unusual in a region festooned
with "men-of-war" from Britain, France, and elsewhere.[56] Furthermore,
it was hard to develop intelligence sources among the locals; thus, in
Bahia there was a "very strong prejudice against" the U.S. Consul, because of his "opposition to the views these people have in regards to the
slave trade."[57] A goodly number of U.S. nationals in Bahia were likewise opposed to this abolitionist-minded diplomat.[58] Similarly, in Rio de
Janeiro, a beleaguered U.S. diplomat complained that "in a city like this
where the slave trade interest has a powerful ascendancy over all, it is
apparent that any valuable information I receive must be received by me
confidentially or not at all."[59] The environment was so unforgiving that
the legation and the naval squadron faced severe problems in "the conveyance of correspondence and letters," which was "unsafe. The usual
channels of communication having been dishonored: letters having been
taken out and others delayed."[60]

Occasionally, amid the chaos, the "Brazil Squadron" of the U.S.
Navy had the opportunity to keep an eye on slavers,[61] which were cir-
cling from the Indian Ocean and navigating the Atlantic—or at times
traversing the Pacific to reach Brazil.

In 1840, Sandwith Drinker was in faraway Zanzibar, yet he "expressed surprise" that "none others but Salem vessels had visited" this
island slave mart off the coast of southeast Africa. Naturally, he visited
the local slave bazaar to inspect the merchandise.[62] The U.S. Consul

there, Charles Ward, also had Salem roots—but diplomacy was not his only capacity there as he was also a "merchant conducting business" who often approached the ruling "His Highness, the Sultan of Muscat . . . not in my official capacity" but as a businessman, a development that could spawn conflicts of interest just as it could spawn opportunities.[63] Cotton grown in the Slave South was sold there, "bought by the natives for the coast trade and in return all the ivory, gum, copal, hides, etc. are brought to Zanzibar"; though "the natives [were] treacherous," Zanzibar was an "important place of trade."[64]

In the same year that Sandwith Drinker made it to Zanzibar, Thomas Nalle of a leading slaveholding family of Virginia was with the U.S. brig "Dolphin" in West Africa, near Cape Mesurado. "There are more than two hundred thousand slaves carried annually from this coast to the West Indies and South America," he alleged. "I have no doubt that many are smuggled into the United States," he added, not least since this business was so profitable: "a noted slave dealer on this coast by the name of Pedro Blanco, a Spaniard, has lately retired from his Occupation with a capital of four millions of dollars."[65] Joel Abbot of the U.S. ship "Decatur," writing from Port Praya, could not help but notice "the many cases of American vessels bringing out slave cargoes on freight to slave merchants at slave marts, and some with evident previous arrangements for the sale of their vessels, having brought out as passengers the officers that were to take charge after the change of national character and who would, if nothing occurred to prevent, carry away a cargo of slaves under another flag and ownership." "If they succeed in landing in the West Indies or Brazil one cargo of slaves in three that may be embarked from the coast," it was said, "their gains are sufficient to induce them to persevere."[66] This profit was encouraging U.S. nationals to move from simply supplying ships to captaining them. "The slave trade . . . has increased within a year or two to a great extent," said the U.S. Consul in Rio de Janeiro glumly, and "in some cases it has been carried on by Americans in American vessels." There was "John Miller of New York," for example: "I have no faith," he added, "that the government here will aid me in bringing Miller or any other slaver to justice." There was "the 'Fame,'" a "whaler from New London," which "came into this port from the Pacific Ocean." The Consul "afterwards learned that" this ship "landed over seven hundred slaves to the eastward of Cape Frio" and had "cleared about 40,000 dollars by the voyage." But the U.S. had only "one frigate and one brig" to patrol a huge area and was unable to respond effectively.

A number of these U.S. citizens involved in the African Slave Trade were newly naturalized, e.g., the "Frenchman by birth," Lewis Krafft, who gained his citizenship in March 1847—before being accused of slave trading in 1848. Born in Paris in 1811, he arrived in Manhattan in 1826 where he became a sailor, traveling frequently to Cuba and Louisiana, before arriving in Rio as the illegal slave trade was heating up in 1843. He had been a "clerk in a slave factory on the coast of Africa" and now had "connexions [sic]" in Brazil "wholly with slave dealers, such as Bernardino de Sa, who ranks second only to Manoel Pinto da Fonseca in this country and perhaps the world." His travels were dizzying, going from Havana to New Orleans and back routinely and "from Havana to Cape de Verd[e]; thence to Sierra Leone; thence to Maxumbia; thence to Loango; thence to Cabinda; thence to Ambriz; thence to Loanda; thence back to Ambriz [sic]"—then to Brazil.[67]

As Britain cracked down, slave trading became more and more a " 'big business' "—a transnational business, in fact, that demanded heavy travel—with "large firms owning fleets of vessels and secretly condoned by their governments." The Royal Navy's labors "gradually weeded out the law-abiding and the faint-hearted. It left the business to tough and desperate men, those who were prepared to fight their way through the navy patrol"—or dodge them through dizzying travels; these were "ne'er-do-wells, thugs, and impoverished multinationals."[68]

Yet, with all their ministrations, the Royal Navy—limited in its right to board and search ships flying the Stars and Stripes—often seemed like a besieged team of firefighters in a town beset by expert arsonists. "A very great portion of the Slave Trade, particularly from Cabinda, is now carried on under the protection of the American flag, with impunity," it was said in 1845.[69] Where were these enslaved Africans arriving? "At no period," said London, "has the Brazilian Slave Trade been so extensively carried on as it is at the present moment in Rio de Janeiro itself,"[70] while "United States vessels and crew have of late been made subservient to the purposes of the Brazilian slave dealers."[71] Moreover, even Spanish ships and vessels of other nations were sailing out of U.S. ports because of the extreme laxity in enforcing laws against the trade[72] and, perhaps inevitably, there was a spillover of this commerce into North America itself,[73] a process facilitated by, e.g., the "formation of a secret society in Galveston for the express purpose of upholding slavery and putting down its opponents," led by chiefs of "slave trading transactions."[74]

Also in 1845, "nefarious practices of American vessels" were denounced by one British official: "this evil has much increased since . . . last year, as many more vessels, protected by American papers, have sailed with slaves from the coast this year than last, and [we] fear, if not checked by our squadron, it must still further increase to an enormous extent, as it is under the American flag alone that they can now carry on this trade with impunity and but few of the United States Squadron have ever visited the south coast; and those that have, appear to have studiously avoided touching at Cabinda, the chief port where these practices are carried. Besides the American vessels bought by the Spanish and Brazilians, as slave vessels, there are many other American vessels, that are chartered exclusively to bring a full cargo of slave goods from Rio Janeiro [*sic*] to Cabinda." These were mostly from Baltimore, Philadelphia, and Boston.[75]

But what seemed to particularly gall these U.S. captains, besides the indignity of being boarded and searched by the Royal Navy, was *who* was involved. The U.S. flagged ship "Cyrus" out of New Orleans was detained by the British "five miles off Cabinda." It was a "slaving vessel . . . filled with slaves" according to London's officer. But what seemed to particularly grate on the nerves of Captain P. C. Dumas of the detained vessel—"the American flag has been insulted," he charged hotly —was that "four Negro sailors" from Britain were involved. The "British Captain, officer and Negroes had trampled on the American flag, broke my trunk open and took away my papers," which supposedly left the crew "exposed to be robbed by the natives of Cabinda."[76] Apparently Dumas's destination was Rio de Janeiro.[77] But London had reason to be aggressive in its approach for like filings to a magnet, U.S. slavers were flocking to the beleaguered continent in the mid-1840s to buy and kidnap Africans.[78]

The illicit slave trade to Brazil that was being engineered significantly by U.S. nationals was taking on the earmarks of big business and, consequently, was also attracting European men who sought to engage in this lucrative commerce and were not adverse to taking on U.S. citizenship as a result. The U.S. nationals in the navy whose task was to crackdown on this business were notably inept, which was not surprising given the influence of men like John C. Calhoun in Washington. Yet, there was no unanimity of opinion among U.S. elite circles on the necessity of this odious trafficking in humans. Certainly, the eminent Henry Wise of Virginia, the tormenter of John Brown, was a stern critic of this business.

Henry Alexander Wise. Before serving as governor of Virginia from 1856 to 1860 (a tenure that included the authorization of John Brown's execution), Wise was the chief U.S. diplomat in Brazil during the 1840s when the illicit slave trade there was escalating. Courtesy Library of Congress.

4

Wise?

The illicit slave trade to Brazil did not easily coexist with simple notions of a rapacious Slave South hell-bent on dragging more Africans across the Atlantic into slavery and a pious abolitionist North determined to thwart their schemes. Such an analysis hardly explains the activities of the Virginian, Henry Wise, during his tenure as a U.S. diplomat in Brazil. Still, he was one of a number of U.S. nationals who resided in this South American nation during a time when enslaved Africans were arriving in enormous numbers and their reaction to this phenomenon inevitably had an impact on how the peculiar institution itself was received in the U.S.

Henry A. Wise was no abolitionist—though he was influential, having considered a race for the presidency in 1856.[1] As a Congressman, he avowed that if Washington "began to discuss ending slavery in the District [of Columbia] he would 'go home . . . never to return.' " Slavery, he thought, was " 'interwoven with our very political existence, is guaranteed by our Constitution, and its consequences must be borne by our northern brethren as resulting from our system of government, and they cannot attack the system of slavery without attacking the institutions of our country, our safety and our welfare.' " John Quincy Adams was among the many northerners Wise despised, in this case because he felt this patrician was not sufficiently hostile to Haiti.[2] He occasionally described Negroes as " 'wooly headed,' 'splay footed' and 'odiferous,' " while "his slaveholdings expanded during the 1840s." He was a fervent advocate of the supposed benefits of slavery, declaring that " 'whenever black existed . . . there was found at least equality among the white population.' "[3]

If Wise is recalled at all today, it is as the man responsible, as Governor of Virginia, for executing John Brown in 1859, viewed widely among Euro-Americans as a criminal for leading a bloody revolt against slavery at Harper's Ferry. Wise was single-minded about what should befall the captured Brown, not least since he was gravely concerned about what signal to slavery his uprising wrought. "The very sympathy with John Brown," exclaimed Governor Wise, "so general, so fanatical, so regardless of social safety, & so irreverent of the reign of law, demands his execution, if sentenced by the courts. The law he insulted & outraged are now protecting all his rights of defence and all his claims to mercy." So moved, the last act of his administration was the hanging of Brown and his followers.[4] Wise went on to join secession and become a "General in the Confederate army."[5] Unsurprisingly, this "swashbuckling defender of slavery's interests" was "one of those present at Appomatox Courthouse when Lee surrendered to Grant."[6]

Yet, scholar Mary Catherine Karasch is no doubt correct in suggesting that Wise's "consular reports," while serving as Minister to Brazil, "provide the best . . . descriptions"[7] of slave trading to South America. Historian Don E. Fehrenbacher concurs, noting that Wise "antagonized . . . the American business community in Rio" with his fervor against the slave trade.[8] His fiery denunciations of slavers could be seen as self-interested, in that many in Virginia saw this state as a prime source for slave exporters to the point where his compatriot, Matthew Fontaine Maury, envisioned sending Afro-Virginians all the way down the river to settle and develop the Amazon region of Brazil. After all, there was an analytical distinction between slavery and the slave trade—the latter could in certain instances reduce the value of existing slaveholdings by increasing supply.

It was Wise who deemed abolitionism to be "sedition" and agreed with placing "abolitionists in a position of embarrassment, from which they cannot easily escape."[9] It was Wise who in campaigning for James Buchanan in his race for the presidency chortled that in Virginia "we now get a thousand dollars for a sound slave" and "we would then have gotten from three to five thousand dollars for an operative in the gold mines of California." "War" with Britain, he thought, would be "dangerous to the slave breeding states" of which his dominion was paramount, as it might disrupt this profitable business; "it would be an act of folly or crime, or a blunder worse than crime." Thus, Buchanan was "the choice of the Virginia Slave Breeders," whose champion Wise was.[10] Nevertheless, it was Henry Wise who hailed from an affluent family—his father was a lawyer[11]—that raised a clarion call against the invasion of slavers from his homeland at a time when some of his countrymen in both the U.S. and the Slave South would have preferred that he had done otherwise. In detailing Wise's tenure in Brazil in the 1840s when enslaved Africans were arriving in significant numbers, this chapter seeks to suggest not only that pro-slavery and anti–slave trade postures could coexist in one person but, by inference, this also underscores the importance of Maury's plan to ship enslaved U.S. Negroes to Brazil, which obviated the need for the illicit slave trade that Wise railed so vehemently against.[12]

Wise took particular umbrage at London's pressure on the illicit slave trade, assuming—perhaps correctly—that it was a short step from there to objecting to slavery itself. Moreover, Wise's attempt to deflect anger about the slave trade to London and the wider U.S. concern that increasing the number of Africans in Brazil could reproduce a Haiti—except on a much wider scale—also points to how transatlantic and hemispheric concerns influenced the discourse on slavery and the slave trade in the U.S. Wise's recall from Brazil reflected a hardening of the posture of the Slave South, which theretofore had tolerated anti–slave trade views that created openings, it came to be seen, for abolitionist views. In this sense, the end of Wise's quixotic and flailing tenure in Brazil represented yet another step toward Civil War.

Wise was not an intimidating physical presence. He was "remarkably lean"—5'11" and a mere 130 pounds—and was "originally fair skinned" but probably because of exposure to the piercing sun rays during Virginia summers became progressively "swarthy." His hair was a "light auburn"—and "when young, almost flaxen"—which he "generally" wore "long and behind his ears." His head was "large with great depth between the temples," his "forehead" low but "broad" and his "eyes large, gray and deep set, arched by a heavy and remarkably expressive brown"; his nose was "large and prominent," his mouth "capacious," his lips "rather thick," his jaws "lank and florid," his chin "broad and prominent" with a furrow "from the center downwards." He possessed "manly and defiant features" that were accentuated by the fact that he was an "excessive chewer of tobacco," though he "never" smoked and "rarely" drank "anything of an alcoholic character." He was "remarkably abstemious." As he grew older he had begun to "stoop a little" and since "upon the whole" he was "not a handsome man," this latter characteristic became more pronounced during his dotage. Politically, besides being a leading Confederate, in the antebellum era he was fiercely opposed to the Know-Nothing Party. He was more qualified than most for his post in Brazil, since "he read French and understood a smattering of Spanish"—but, typically, "no Portuguese."[13] He was also feisty, at one point "Richmond friends" of his were "suffering great anxiety for a day or two on your account occasioned by rumours of differences between yourself and another gentleman which might possibly end in a duel!"[14]

Politically, he was also well connected, although when his name was sent to the United States Senate in 1842 for the "mission to France," a "Whig Senate rejected him." He obtained a congressional seat nonetheless in 1843, then "it was discovered" that the health of the frail Wise "was giving away rapidly from the constant excitement of about ten years. Consequently, his friends sent his name again to the Senate for the court of Rio Janeiro" [*sic*]. He was approved this time and in May 1844 sailed southward and did not return until October 1847. It turned out that he found just about all the excitement he needed in monitoring and combating the incursion of U.S. slavers.[15]

Wise, who was "one of [President] Tyler's best friends," apparently "was not instructed at all" about the African Slave Trade in Brazil before departing. And even though he was a stern critic of this business "he did not call on Congress for more severe legislation"; instead and in tune with prevailing mores, he "blamed the British for their share in the traffic" and "reiterated Calhoun's accusation" that London's "apprenticeship system imposed on freed slaves," along with Africans heading for slavery but captured on the open seas, "was nothing but a perpetuation of the slave trade in another form." Still, despite his toeing the ideological line, his patron, John C. Calhoun of the fire-eating state of South Carolina, was "highly dissatisfied with the Minister's reports" from Rio de Janeiro though Wise "had been instrumental in making him Secretary of State." Yet, since Wise was a major player in Virginia and national politics and "could become important in the race for the presidency in 1848," Calhoun "recommended to the new administration that Wise be maintained as Minister to Brazil."[16]

This was not as difficult a decision for the White House as it may appear since Wise did stress, quite fashionably, hostility to London's stopping and detaining U.S. ships—"Great Britain had no right to exercise any authority" in this sphere, he thought—and sought at least verbally to stress Brazil's supposed "partiality to the U.S.," which was "apparent" and "no less manifest in their distrust of Great Britain."[17]

Nevertheless, one of his initial maneuvers was seeking to break the long-standing link between serving as a U.S. diplomat while engaging in slave trading: he pushed the "revocation of the appointment of a Brazilian citizen named Souto as Vice Consul of the U.S. at Victoria for the Province of Espirito Santo" since "this man, it seems, is a very prince of slave-dealers and has actually. . . . been using his pretended office under the U. States [*sic*] for the purpose of aiding and abetting the slave-trade."[18] His colleague in Brazil, George Gordon, a Massachusetts politician, reflected this biregional approach when he pursued slavers with equal vigor, finding their "manner of prosecuting the Slave Trade upon the coast of Africa . . . truly astonishing . . . particularly in regard to the connection of American citizens therewith, and the use and prostitution of the American flag in furtherance thereof."[19]

But this repetitively expressed anger aside, the Wise-led legation in Rio de Janeiro stressed with similar repetition, "interference by Great Britain," not only with "this subject of the slave trade" but also with the more sensitive issue of "domestic slavery in the U. States [*sic*]." London's crusade ineluctably had led it to consider the spillover of this global business into the U.S. itself, which impelled it to look at what was thought to be the major prop of this commerce, i.e., slavery in the U.S. But for Wise this was "our most delicate of domestic institutions, the most sensitive to foreign intrusion." "Now what can this mean?" he asked Calhoun imploringly. Why was the British Consul in Mobile saying, " 'there is <u>no known party</u>' " of abolition [emphasis-original]. Was "this a permissible [function] of a British legation in the U.S.?"[20] This was outrageous, he thought. "They pry into *the treatment of the slaves by their private owners, into the food and raiment, into the disposition of masters to manumit them*" [emphasis-original]. "Ought this to be suffered," he asked, "at a time when insurrection and massacre are set on foot in the neighboring island of Cuba"—not to mention Brazil where the contagion could also spread. Thoughtfully, Wise attached a letter from the British Foreign Office asking pointed questions about slavery in the U.S. itself—including the sensitive inquiry of details about imports of slaves from Africa itself.[21]

Burnishing his fashionable anti-London credentials, Wise told Calhoun that "to some my letter may appear to partake of the tone of the partisan against Great Britain"; well, he said, "I am willing that it should so appear." As for a U.S. national detained by the British for involvement in the trade, Wise was "fully convinced that the case was one of great outrage upon the flag & commerce of the U. States, in any & every aspect in which it can be viewed. . . . Great Britain had no right," he insisted fervently, "to exercise any authority whatever over him or his vessel." In fact, he continued, "the attempt on the part of Great Britain to subject our vessels to her acts of visit or search, was among other causes an obstacle to any successful suppression of the African slave trade." He was willing to propose a compromise with London in that the U.S. would "waive all claim to their right of search of U. States vessels; and would no longer pay bounties of so many pound sterling per capita for every recaptured African to the officers of her cruisers," if "the British government would cease itself to partake in some sense of the slave trade" by "carrying every captured slave into her colonies." Like many in the Slave South, Wise was worried that London's seizing of slave ships and diverting Africans to their colonies as apprentices was little more than warfare against slavery as practiced in the troika of the U.S., Brazil, and Cuba and a boost for their own colonies in the global competition to dominate the production of key agricultural crops. "Is it not in fact a part of the slave trade to take them away from their own country, without their consent, to bind them out under a system of apprenticeship?"—since "they may be lawfully held in bondage for a term of 5 or 10 years, why not for 50 or 100 years or any period beyond the duration of human life?" Instead, Wise "urged that moral means were much preferable to physical force" in handling the trade.[22] The U.S. was banking on Brazil reacting similarly to British meddling, which "gives the impression at least of a foreign government overruling the domestic concern & interfering ostentatiously with matters purely local or municipal."[23]

But it would be unwise to stress unduly this questionable aspect of the U.S. Minister's mission in Brazil. For he did have the gumption to tell Calhoun bluntly that "the African slave trade 'thickens around us' and we are trading on its dragon teeth." The "only effectual mode of carrying on that trade between Africa and Brazil, at present," he stressed, "involves *our laws and our moral responsibilities* as directly and fully as it does those of this country itself," meaning Brazil [emphasis-original]. In fact, he emphasized, "without the aid of our citizens and our flag, it could not be carried on with success at all." This "trade between Africa and Brazil" was "almost the only trade of the world left in which our citizens and vessels can now violate our laws for the suppression of the foreign slave trade." The "number of slaves imported from Africa into Brazil during 1844, was at least 64,000," he claimed.[24]

Not only was Wise willing to cross swords with powerful forces back home who were displeased with his hostility to the trade, but he also managed to incur the hostility of some Brazilians. One of the chief slave-dealers, Manuel Pinto da Fonseca, was according to Wise, "said to be actually engaged to be married to a daughter of one of the Ministers and he is also the intimate friend of the most influential person in the government"[25]—none of whom were happy with Wise's demarches. The " 'secretaria' " of the "court police," Joaquim Jose Moreira Maia, for example, was upset with Wise's "irregular conduct" in detaining U.S. nationals on Brazilian soil then sending them back home for trial.[26] There was repeated "abuse" of him in the "newspapers" in Brazil, and "petty slights of not inviting me to court," he added, which was not an imposition since "the only reward for going . . . on a hot day in a hot uniform is to make three bows forward and three bows backward and then 'bob out [of the] Imperial presence.' My Republican heart was glad to be relieved from this *only* court duty which I have ever seen here prescribed or followed" [emphasis-original].[27]

There were a number of reasons for Wise to be so confrontational. His critics thought that Virginians generally had a material basis for their self-righteousness about the trade, given this state's own role as an exporter of Africans. Flooding the hemisphere with Africans—particularly when they were growing crops that could be equally grown in the Slave South, e.g., sugar in Louisiana—could drive down the price of African sales and, perhaps, crop sales also in the U.S. itself. There was also concern that Brazil could become a second Haiti, only bigger and more dangerous, if the number of Africans there increased—and this could have potentially devastating impact on the long-term viability of the Slave South.

While Wise ran the risk of harming relations with Brazil, simple diplomatic statecraft suggested that this nation's conflicts with Britain should be tailor-made for an alliance with the U.S. "It was but yesterday," said Wise, that he "had to dispatch . . . a cutter to look out for an American barque which had the night before landed 450 slaves within cannonshot of this harbor!" i.e., Rio de Janeiro. "The Minister and Counsellors of state and Senators and delegates in the legislative chambers" were "undoubtedly engaged in this bold . . . horrid traffic" and the "principal capitalists" involved were "the owners of the newspapers

. . . in this city"[28]—and they were hardly pleased with his opposition to this dirty business. In the sunset of his life, Wise recalled ruefully that "almost every one (excluding the Emperor . . . and a few honorable men) was interested in the trade. Cabinet Ministers, Judges and minor authorities of every kind were guilty of participation or connivance" and he "had disturbed a hornet's nest" with his angry lobbying against slavers. "He soon became the most unpopular man in Rio de Janeiro and every possible annoyance was received by him from both Government and people" and "finally the Government ceased all diplomatic relations with him." President Polk would not relieve him but the isolated Wise was obliged to leave his post nonetheless.[29]

Yet this baring of fangs in Brazil hardly compared to the hostility that Wise faced back home. "I know very well," he admitted, "the very strong representations from certain parties against me." These were "the slave-trade vessel owners of the Northern cities. I have exposed their abominable traffic here and have severely shocked its profits if not its conscience. Out of 22 vessels of our merchant marine engaged in the African trade between the coast & Brazil since 1845," he charged, "but four hail south of Philadelphia" and these "were from Baltimore. The Agnes, which was sold on the coast and brought over about [600] slaves was owned by a Quaker of Delaware who would not even eat slave sugar," while "the owner of the 'Herschel,' a vessel which has made several trips to the coast under the charter party of notorious slave-traders here, is also an owner of an abolition newspaper in Bangor, Maine. His name is Dow. In public I am told he rebuked his [captain] for engaging in such a charter, and in private told him to do so again, as it was very profitable. He is the owner of the 'Amelia' . . . & gave instructions . . . to charter her also lately for the coast." As Wise saw it, history was repeating itself. These damned Yankees were "now doing for Brazil" what they "did for Virginia and the other Southern states in N. America"—"carrying the slave cargoes from Africa under the protection of the U. States flag; with the additional evil to us at this day that they are thus affording the only good cause upon earth to the English to search our vessels" which "at the very moment they would plunge us into a war with Gt. Britain under the expectation of compelling emancipation in the southern states by the treaty-making power & by the black regiment of Jamaica. This actual & potential interest has been secretly exerting all its influence to cause my recall," he complained. "It won't show its own face in the attempt but avails itself of every collateral pretext & agency in its reach." The "miserable ex-Consul here [George] Gordon," a Massachusetts member of the party he despised, the "Know-Nothings," was "induced" by his "neighbors and friends in Boston and by the hope that a quarrel with me would be acceptable to [President] Polk" and also with the powerful "Prince of slave-dealers in Rio, Manoel Pinto da Fonseca & his company," to "forward a regular budget of slander against" Wise to Washington. "He got many of the merchant captains, I am told, to sign affidavits that I was bent on destroying all American trade to Africa," he asserted, "and he sent on a mass of such matter & its proof, of which I have never yet read." The "vessel owners and vessel captains desirous to engage in the African trade" and "their friends" were "conspirators against me," said Wise. "They find a number no doubt in the U. States who are my foes of old, and they find more who desire the place I hold, and these united, and their friends, make a pretty formidable host. Can it be expected that these," he asked rhetorically, "will release their combinations & efforts against me?" He felt "grateful to [President] Polk for his magnanimity toward me personally," thought Wise but was otherwise convinced that Northern pro-slave trade antagonists were after his scalp.[30]

This was something of an overstatement. Just as Wise's enmity toward London[31] clouded the point that they were as hostile to the trade —if not more so—as himself, his unfriendliness toward the U.S. North, clouded his view of similarly anti-slaver colleagues, such as George Gordon.[32] Nevertheless, Gordon, like Wise's other detractors, had a hard time quarreling with the Minister's aggressive approach to the role of U.S. nationals in the African Slave Trade to Brazil. It had "grown so bold and so bad," Wise declared shortly after arriving in Rio, "as no longer to wear a mask even to those who reside here" and was "unblushingly carried on by our citizens under our flag." However, he did decry Gordon's approach as the "crying injustice of punishing the poor ignorant officers and crews of merchant ships for high misdemeanors and felonies, when the ship-owners in the United States, and their *American consignees, factors, and agents* abroad are left almost entirely untouched by penalties" [emphasis-original].[33] The latter were disproportionately from the U.S. North, he thought.

Why were they attracted to this inhuman business? Wise thought he knew. "The profit of the slave trade, then, may be put down safely at from 600 to 1200 percent," he offered. "This accounts for the enormous prices they pay for vessels and their charters to 'the coast' and for the risks which they can afford to dare in the traffic. The worst of it is, too," he added with the air of a man who knew of what he spoke, "that they import so few females in comparison with the number of males, that the annual increase by propagation in Brazil is not likely, for a long period, to diminish the necessity for additional slaves."[34]

This assumption did not spare him from further scrutiny of the illicit slave trade. Wise was pushed to ask rhetorically of the powerful Baltimore–Rio de Janeiro firm, "Maxwell, Wright & Co.," which was suspected of collaborating with slavers, "Why I, an American slaveholder, manifest such extraordinary zeal in this subject? The only answer I shall deign to give is, that the fact of my being a slaveholder is itself a pledge and guarantee that I am no *fanatic*" [emphasis-original]. Repeatedly he averred that "I find the same old interest at work here, and now, to fasten American slavery on Brazil, which, in our early history, fastened its condition of a Slave State on Virginia: vessels and capital from precisely the same quarter bring the slaves to this country in this age, which carried them to that country in times past." His words dripping with acerbic sarcasm he exclaimed, "the very lands in the old and new worlds, where 'world conventions' are held, and whence abolition petitions flow, are the lands where there are manufacturers of goods 'fit for the coast,'" yet they " 'will not eat slave sugar!' "[35]

Wise's Brazilian counterparts in Washington kept a careful eye on his activities.[36] During Wise's tenure, the U.S. was involved in a delicate diplomatic minuet, seeking to win over Brazil as an ally in its ongoing conflict with Britain—but these two nations though at odds about slavery and the slave trade were similarly skeptical of Washington, notably the annexation of Texas and war with Mexico. Hence, Wise's forthrightness about illegal slaving in Brazil was not tailored to appeal to the elites he was lambasting, though this South American nation continued to look to Washington—and not unsuccessfully—for diplomatic support in its conflict with London over the slave trade.[37] Since some powerful U.S. elites were seeking to expand their domestic slave empire by "establishing a cotton factory in Rio de Janeiro," impetus was added to the U.S.-Brazil relationship—Wise's denunciations notwithstanding.[38] This is why during the height of Wise's stay in Rio, one visiting U.S. national found that "an Englishman is despised in this place. But Americans are beloved & have much attention paid them. Some of our officers having been taken for Englishmen are stoned."[39]

But it was more than Wise that was complicating U.S.-Brazil ties.

During the summer of 1847, Jose da Cosat de Rocha arrived in New York City from Rio de Janeiro, accompanied by three enslaved Africans, including "Maria," a "servant and nurse" to his "wife and family." Somehow they managed to escape and their case wound up in the Court of Common Pleas where Brazil's Consul, Luis Henrique Ferreira Aguiar argued forcefully that the "said slaves were brought to this country under the firm faith and assurance that the rights of property of foreign subjects are held sacred in the United States." Apparently, this property was not recovered satisfactorily, which could only inflame relations between the two hemispheric behemoths.[40]

Fracases in Manhattan set aside, Wise remained ensnared in a maze of contradictions, seeking to flay Northern slavers while embracing those who ultimately were financing them, not to mention slaveholders as a class. The Brazilian Foreign Ministry took note of a bitter complaint from the **Salem Register**—a newspaper in a town that included citizens that benefited handsomely from the African Slave Trade: The "difficulties which unfortunately now exist between this vast country" (Brazil) "and our government may soon be brought to an amicable conclusion," despite the "high handed conduct of our late Minister of that Court," meaning Wise. His conduct, it was said, "threatens to involve our country in another war," as if fighting Mexico were not enough. "Our fellow citizens are deeply interested in the lucrative and advantageous commerce carried on between this city and various ports of Brazil. Our East India commerce too, passes within a few hundred leagues of the Brazilian coast and would be exposed to the utmost danger in case of a war." Wise should be reined in, it was thought, as "the Brazilian Court has already recalled its Minister and the public feeling throughout that country is decidedly against that and would need but little fanning to break into a flame in which the lives and fortunes of many of our fellow countrymen would be consumed."[41] "Documents relative to Mr. Wise's difficulty with the Brazilian government" were "published from which it appears that Mr. Lisboa, the Brazilian Minister at Washington called at the Department of State and requested the recall of Mr. Wise." The "Emperor had determined he should never again be invited to Court." It was expected that Washington would acquiescence, being reluctant to confront Brazil while it was fighting Mexico.[42]

The days of the besieged Wise were numbered. He complained to William Wright of Maxwell, Wright that his "greatest annoyance" was the African Slave Trade, which had "become outrageous under the U. States flag" to "the disgrace of our nation." "I was confident," he told him for whatever reason, "you would approve of my motives & action in suppressing this nefarious traffic"; "it is impossible," he added, "to carry on what is called the <u>lawful</u> trade to Africa from Brazil without becoming involved more or less in the <u>reputation</u> if not in the actual guilt of the <u>unlawful</u> traffic between these two countries [*sic*]"—which was an implicit rebuke of Wright's firm [emphasis-original].

Nonetheless, Wise continued to hold Wright close, accepting his "very respectable present of a round of beef" which was "in excellent order" for "our palates, if not our hearts" for which he was "grateful."[43] He sought to "invite" Wright to his "house" in Rio "immediately" when this financial baron showed up in Rio.[44] Perhaps Wise's growing isolation as a result of his uncompromising rhetorical hostility toward slavers prompted him to at least welcome Wright, a man of no mean influence. Or, quite possibly, his inflammatory diplomatic messages aside, the opposition to the African Slave Trade by Wise, the slaveowner, could not transcend the rhetorical.

Rio was "not like home," Wise told Wright, yet he had "met so much kindness from every American and from all, in fact, especially from your nephew that I am conditioned to remain here a few years, if permitted to do so," though the "climate" was "rather enervating and somewhat insidious I think."[45]

"Enervating" was another way to describe Wise's recurrent condition in Rio de Janeiro's often unwholesome climate. Wright was told by a colleague that "when I arrived here yesterday" in Rio "I found Mr. Wise much worse [than] I expected, he complained of soreness in his side & was very restless. He asked me to remain all night as he feared he might be attacked with sudden spasms—which I of course did. He suffered much pain during the night."[46] "The state of my health will not permit me to be with you," Wise told colleagues in Brazil. "For the last two or three days my system has been quite disordered. . . . I have been compelled to resort to copious doses of medicine."[47]

Perhaps because of his difficulty in adjusting to Rio's climate and the concomitant political isolation he suffered, Wise—though a rhetorical lion in opposing slavers—was the main man in charge when slavers were streaming into Brazil and unloading their human cargoes. Certainly his outspokenness was not shared universally among Washington's power elite, which no doubt reduced his effectiveness. When the

Department of State was queried by Wright during the height of Wise's tenure in 1845 about the questionable practice of U.S. nationals selling their ships in Rio—which were then promptly dispatched to pick up enslaved Africans on a strained and stressed continent—the response was something less than ringing in condemnation.[48]

Yet, how could it be otherwise given the political situation in the U.S., where some Northerners were profiting from the slave trade while many Southerners were reluctant to tamper with this commerce for fear that it might compromise their jealously held peculiar institution? The fact that Wright had been posted to Rio de Janeiro was suggestive of Washington's true feelings about fighting the trade, as his firm had been implicated in this business. His "long residence at Rio de Janeiro and the experience necessarily acquired in the performance of your office there," recommended him to both business and government, Wright was informed.[49]

Maxwell, Wright was a transnational firm with major interests along the eastern seaboard of the U.S., not to mention trading in all major capitals, including Antwerp, Amsterdam, Malta, Naples, Venice, Stockholm, Hamburg, Bombay, and the continent of Africa—especially Brazil's major slave labor products: sugar and coffee.[50] This firm was engaged in "very large quantities" of commodities in Brazil, while Wright for a while was a well-respected diplomat.[51]

But one thing Wright did have in common with Wise was conflict with elites in Rio de Janeiro. He too was obliged to carp about "having been removed from the Consulate of the United States" in Rio " 'by request of the Brazilian Government,' " though he had "filled" that job "for . . . six years." His problem was not with slavers but the alleged "many acts of injustice having been practiced upon our commerce, in the ports of this Empire" and, said Wright, "it was my duty to complain."[52] Washington, thus, had to "annul" his "commission" though his "conduct" was "perfectly satisfactory to our government."[53]

Wright still remained central to Maxwell, Wright's business in Brazil and was angling for escalating his presence as Wise was arriving. His nephew sought to remind him of Rio's "privations and disagreeables [*sic*] to which a residence here subjects a family and recollect only the more agreeable occurrences of your time." But the firm was attracted to the handsome profits that only a slave labor economy could supply. "I do not know how it is," said Robert Wright, "that having made as you have done a great deal of money in this country, you have so little to show for it. . . . you were spending too much money"—and now needed more.[54] He had a point for at that time a fellow Baltimorean, Joshua Cohen, was profiting nicely from various commercial dealings in Brazil, particularly the importation of sugar.[55]

William Hunter was, like Wright, a U.S. diplomat in Brazil whose family was implicated in the slave trade. His spouse—Mary Robinson Hunter—unlike Wise, arrived in Brazil with mild sympathies toward slaves but in the hothouse environment that was Rio de Janeiro, she was transformed—albeit in a manner unlike Wise's rhetorical crusade against the slave trade. Born in New York City to a wealthy landowning family that had made a small fortune in the African Slave Trade, she married the scion of an equally prominent Rhode Island family that also had profited from this vile business. In 1834, her spouse—William, a lawyer who was to become a U.S. Senator—accepted a diplomatic post in Brazil where both resided until 1848. "In the beginning" of her stay abroad, "Mary sympathized with the plight of slaves" in Brazil, but as "time passed and her difficulties in managing her other household servants increased, she had a change of heart regarding their treatment and on occasion whipped them and slapped them, something she previously deplored. Mary's initial compassion toward slaves, however, was also tempered by her fear of them" for the "1830s" in Brazil were "rife with slave insurrections" and "given the large numbers of slaves in Rio de Janeiro, Mary dreaded a slave revolt and feared its consequences for the white population."[56]

Over and over again in her lengthy stay in Rio, which ended in 1848, "she expressed concern about being left home alone with her household servants and she avoided going shopping in Rio because she disliked being jostled in the streets by Negroes." Her fears were comprehensible. In 1841, she recounted how a "female slave" had "mingled some poisonous root (which is known only to the blacks) in some chamomile tea her master had ordered her to make for him." He found out somehow, then got some "thumb screws to make her confess." She apparently did so and implicated others in the plot and "they were all severely whipped for three days in succession and they are now about selling the girl." Then a Brazilian "merchant" was "murdered by his Cook on his return from the theatre," which made her "shudder." He "very imprudently bought his black, knowing him to be [a] bad one, because he was a good cook" but the slave was "angry with his master, it is said, for making him go out on Sundays and holidays"—and retaliated. He "had

long been watching an opportunity of revenge." Appropriately, the
"night was dark and rainy" when he struck. "He had sent the footman
up to the house for an umbrella" for his spouse to "walk up the hill.
While she sat in the carriage, the black came out of the stable, passed
the two sons and ran a knife into his master who just said: 'He has
murdered me' and fell dead." Then another master was murdered "by
some . . . young blacks." They "overtook him on the road and killed
him with clubs. They have confessed the act but no reason can be assigned for their conduct," she concluded sadly. They "did it for frolic,"
apparently; "one of the boys was only 14, born to the estate."

Then there was an attempted insurrection in Rio in the 1840s.
"These reports alarm me very much," she cried. "It seems to be the beginning of a retributive justice mercifully delayed, the distant but certain
precursor of the thunder which must break on this benighted land. A
few days ago there was another insurrection in preparation up the bay
at the foot of the Organ Mountains. On Christmas day they were to
march down to the city, secure both arsenals and murder all the whites.
People here feel perfect security from the circumstances of the slaves
coming from various parts of Africa," she said uncertainly, "and are not
as in Bahia, Para, and Rio Grande all of one or two tribes. They speak
different languages and are in a state of hostility towards each other at
home. The whites believe that they would not cooperate against them,"
she sighed, "but I think this is a false security. The blacks of different
tribes and interests when at home have been here long enough to feel
deeply the oppression and cruelty of the whites towards all of that
colour. They will one day join heart in hand to avenge it," she predicted. "It will be black against white and the difference is fearfully in
their favour as to numbers. The computation is 20 black to one white
and daily increasing in the same ratio is ships load of these poor
wretches are constantly landed on the coast near Rio and marched
down to the market." This "increases my fears," she cried, "and my
sleep is often disturbed . . . I lay watching for daylight to dispel the
gloom and fears of night." Was it wise to continue such reckless importation of Africans? Wise—and many others who were not necessarily
opposed to slavery itself—thought not.

Her diary is studded with references to Rio being "in a state of excitement," "conspiracies have been detected, a great many persons of
high standing and great fears were entertained that insurrection would
break out." Though she was turning against the slave trade, she was

turning against slaves too. "I have not as much sympathy for this class of beings," i.e., slaves "as on my arrival here. I hope my heart is not harder," she added unconvincingly, "but I have experienced so much of their ingratitude, treachery and the basest qualities of human beings that I feel they deserve punishment." Thus, when her "patience" was "much tried by the black girl's quarrel & loud talk in the kitchen" of her house and "finding she would not be quiet," Robinson said furiously, "I whipped her." Another time, she "gave" a "sound slap" to another slave, though this corporal punishment seemed to be coarsening her; "you might as well slap an elephant as a black; they are proof against such assaults." While in Brazil, she was preoccupied with beatings, aborted uprisings, and conspiracies, unpleasant encounters with Negroes, and a series of health issues that may have been psychosomatic and intimately connected to her experience with slavery. Her domestic experience sheds light on Wise's campaign against the slave trade, while at the same time he remained a firm advocate of slavery itself. Even when thousands of miles away from the U.S. South, pro-slavery advocates were straddling the back of an African lion that was both dangerous to ride and dangerous to dismount.[57]

London's representative in Rio de Janeiro was thinking along the lines of Mrs. Hunter—and became similarly disillusioned. In 1847, he declared that "before arriving in Brazil I had heard it averred that there was a great feeling of disquietude pervading the white inhabitants as to the growing disproportion between them and the black races held in bondage and I had counted upon this fear of the future as an element which might be turned to advantage"—but, sadly he concluded, "this is not the case."[58] The powerful William Marcy, U.S. Secretary of War from 1846 to 1849 and Secretary of State from 1853 to 1857, was similarly opposed to the slave trade due to "anxiety over 'Africanization,' "[59] while earlier **Freedom's Journal** pointed to the growing enslaved population of Brazil—and concomitant growing unrest—as a loud warning to Washington: the " 'triumphant reveling in white blood' " in the Deepest South and the "daring movement of the slaves, while they were in possession of arms, have caused no small excitement among the white population [there]."[60]

This tangled web produced similarly contradictory responses from Washington. In March 1845, John C. Calhoun told Wise's comrade, future U.S. President, James Buchanan, "I express the hope that Mr.

[Henry] Wise may be continued at Brazil. I am sure one better qualified cannot be selected to take his place."[61] But, evidently, as the significance of Wise's campaign became clear, Calhoun changed his tune. "I fear with you," he told Thomas G. Clemson, then in Brussels, "that Wise is pursuing an injudicious course in reference to the slave trade. My instructions to him were full & pointed on the necessity of preserving the most friendly relations with Brazil in every respect. It would be greatly to be regretted, if he has taken any step, calculated to have a contrary effect."[62] Wise was running afoul of a powerful faction in Dixie, who clamored for reopening the African Slave Trade—not only in Brazil but also in the U.S. itself. Wise was "influential" but also "opportunistic" and "distrusted" it was said. "De Bow in Louisiana, Wigfall in Texas, Yancey in Alabama, Ruffin in Virginia and Governor John H. Adams and Maxcy Gregg in South Carolina noisily threw in with the idea" of "Leonidas W. Spratt," who "proposed reopening the African slave trade." It was felt that "more Negroes would reduce prohibitively high prices and allow a wider participation in slave ownership." Virginians were "being selfish," it was thought, "by opposing the trade so that Virginian slave-breeding would continue to enjoy high prices within the domestic trade."[63] "We have no right to interfere with the slave trade in other countries," said the future secessionist, Jefferson Davis; he was equally "opposed to the African squadron" which monitored this commerce. "What would we say," he asked querulously, "if any other country should take such position towards the United States? . . . Our laws should be confined to our own country," he insisted. That "ships of American construction will probably be found in the slave trade," received no objection from him.[64]

On the other hand, African-Americans were not as sympathetic to Wise as might have been imagined. He was a "Virginia Bragadocio [*sic*]," and "foolish" besides said Frederick Douglass at a time when Wise was clashing with slave dealers,[65] a view not universally shared.[66]

Despite his connections at the highest levels, Wise was becoming a liability. "The business of chief interest before the Cabinet today," President James K. Polk noted in early 1847, "were our relations with Brazil, which from those of amity had recently been disturbed by an unfortunate occurrence at Rio [de] Janeiro. A riot had taken place among some Americans on shore."[67] Instructively and disturbingly, though the U.S. was then enmeshed in a war of aggression against Mexico that would result in the seizing of a quarter of that nation's territory, President Polk was expending valuable time soothing the frazzled nerves of another southern neighbor who feared Washington's territorial designs.

Wright clashed with Brazil on financial matters, just as Wise had clashes with this nation about the African Slave Trade—though the two were intertwined. For there were various "American claims" that "Brazil refused to pay," which made Wise's complaints even more hard to swallow. Wise was "an old friend and confidant" of James Buchanan, with whom he communicated frequently and at length, which put the White House in a sticky position when Lisboa, the Brazilian Minister in Washington "requested that Wise be recalled." Initially, the White House refused; instead, upset over its unresolved financial claims it appeared that gunboat diplomacy "threatened." Shortly thereafter, Wise "asked for home leave and it was granted. It was a gentle exit and saved face all around" when the vehement anti–slave trade advocate—and slaveholder—sailed northward back home to Virginia, leaving in shambles the struggle against the massive importation of enslaved Africans to Brazil.[68]

Wise's odyssey in Brazil suggested how tensions were rising both within the Slave South and beyond this region's borders as Civil War loomed, for at times it seemed that he was angrier with slave traders in the U.S. Northeast than slave-owners themselves. Moreover, his critique of Brazil complicated his region's ability to gain adherents in South America for this titanic conflict—a prospect that was made more difficult, in any case, due to Brazil's apprehension about the U.S. seizing Mexican territory. This meant that Wise's hostility to London, which otherwise might have received a favorable hearing in Brazil, was vitiated. Brazil had further reason for nervousness about U.S. policies when the California Gold Rush led to the arrival on their shores of tens of thousands of visitors from their North American neighbor.

5

Crisis

Charlotte Gardner of Nantucket was one of many U.S. nationals who made her way by ship to California from the eastern U.S. around Cape Horn with a stop in Brazil. Whiling away the weeks on board, she began reading the bestseller, **Uncle Tom's Cabin.** "Speaking of the effect of reading 'Uncle Tom's Cabin,'" she confided to her diary in 1852 a story that "recounts a similar circumstance which occurred," i.e., a "lady whose nervous temperament was so highly excited by the perusal of that now fashionable production gave birth to two young babies of fine physical conformation but whose skin was of the color prevailing in the dominion of the King of Congo. Investigations established the pleasing fact that there had not been a color[ed] person seen in that quarter of the country for three years previously." Though she was deeply interested in slavery and Africa, it is unclear if her approaching a site known to be in the process of being swamped with enslaved Africans particularly from Congo influenced her fevered accounts; she did note mordantly that "yesterday we passed near a vessel which we supposed was a slaver from Rio de Janeiro. She did not show her colors."[1] A few years earlier, the U.S. naval officer, Captain William H. Parker, arrived in Rio. "One of our midshipmen . . . (an oldster) told me that the slaves were brought into Rio; but they could not be seen in consequence of their being painted air color, which of course rendered them invisible! He said that the slaves were landed and taken to a pond outside the city; and the air-colored paint being washed off, they became visible."[2]

Though Brazil was thousands of miles away from the U.S., the nature of travel by ship meant that Rio de Janeiro was a necessary stop in the journey from the U.S. Northeast to California, just as Dallas is a necessary stop in flying today from Raleigh to San Francisco. This meant that thousands of U.S. nationals were regularly arriving in Brazil, well on its way to becoming the most formidable slave society on the planet. For many who had never seen this peculiar institution up close, Brazil stirred abolitionist sentiments that contributed to rising national tensions. For others, it reinforced the idea of the normalcy of slavery, thus calcifying existing biases. And for others—like Gardner and Parker—it stirred imaginative fantasies that reflected a terrible crisis induced by slavery and the African Slave Trade.

There is no precise agreement on the number of U.S. nationals who arrived by sea to California during the Gold Rush, which was ignited in the late 1840s just as the illicit slave trade was booming.[3] "For the period from April to the end of the year [1849]," "tabulations run as high as 91,000, as low as 30,000" and "of this number, about 20,000 evidently took the Horn route," and "roughly 70 percent of these were Americans." Just as it is highly possible that there was more altering of nationalities in the antebellum era than today between U.S. Negroes and Afro-Brazilians—e.g., the transition of "Pedro Parris" from "African" to "Afro-Brazilian" to "African American"—"it is a historical paradox that a hundred [and fifty] years ago Cape Horn was less remote than it is today." "Seventeen thousand miles of ocean, more or less roll between New England, Cape Horn and California" and this protracted journey was traversed not in hours in a supersonic jet but in weeks on a listing vessel—with a stop in Brazil.[4]

There was a "great change" in Rio after the Gold Rush; "last year," said one U.S. observer, "the American vessels of war were put down after <u>all</u> others—English, French, Sardinian, Danish, Belgian, Austrian —everything was put down before our 'vasos de guerra' or vessels of war," but "now, all that is changed—we are the favorites—the great people of the moment," he said.[5]

Many of these U.S. nationals had had no direct personal experience with the quotidian horrors of slavery.[6] Brazil, as a result, became a cracked mirror by which many interpreted the rising controversy over bondage in their homeland, often invigorating or engendering abolitionist sentiments[7] or hardening pro-slavery feelings or fears about the implications of "racial ratios" favoring Africans.[8]

Certainly, the critical role played on U.S. vessels by African-Americans was not conducive to enlightenment for some of these southward bound visitors.[9] Sailing from Boston to California via Brazil, John Duchow watched as "one of the colored waiters in the cabin, named Dennis, struck one of the other waiters and the captain put him in irons a

short time."[10] "A Negro is not to be trusted," was the moral drawn by
one Euro-American sojourner after his encounter on board ship,[11] while
sailing "from Boston to San Francisco around Cape Horn" one national
became more sensitive to matters of color.[12]

Interestingly, as this migration westward continued, some Dixie propagandists mused about the "applicability of slave labor to the soil of
Southern California," which was "becoming a theme of discussion in
that region, and it is probable that the experiment will one day be
tried."[13] In August 1850, a ship set sail from Charleston to California
with white Southerners and their slaves aboard, bent on establishing a
slave colony in the state that would work the gold mines.[14] Like the
illicit slave trade itself, where Northerners were prevalent, it was hard
to discern angels and devils in this story since the Democrats backed
slavery's extension on white supremacist grounds and the nascent Republicans often opposed extension on similar principles, wary of the
very presence of the darker-skinned.[15]

The trip to California via Brazil hardened regional differences in the
U.S., further paving the way to Civil War. "Slavery was a subject that
most Forty-Niners avoided," concludes the scholar, Donald Jackson,
"but the ardent abolitionists among them were offended by the Rio
slave market."[16] "One of the black marks against the land, in the opinion of those from the abolitionist strongholds at home," said the writer
Oscar Lewis referring to Brazil during the Gold Rush, "was the open
trading in slaves to be seen both at Preia Grande across the harbor . . .
and in the great central market in Rio itself."[17]

Writing from Rio in early 1849, the '49er, John H. Beeckman, told
his "dearest wife" that the "most unpleasant feature" of this city "and
the one which strikes a northerner with strong feelings of disgust and
compassion is slavery," as the Africans were "treated much worse than
brutes" and "at the caprice of master or overseer beaten over the head."
"It completely sickens me," he said, "and hereafter I am an abolitionist
of the deepest dye," said a man previously without strong convictions
on this subject. He did not shrink from seeing Africans rise up, which
may have lubricated the path for similar thinking in his homeland: "if
there is to be a revolution," he ruminated, "I hope it will take place
while I am here as I feel quite desirous of seeing how these poor miserable Portuguese and Brazilian soldiers, most of whom are black will
fight."[18] Ruth Nash of Maine also on her way to California noticed
at the same time that "the great and distinctive characteristics of the

Brazilians are its slaves and slavery, and one cannot help but shudder to have such sights before his mind, so degrading to humanity, to obtain human beings down to bondage."[19] C. S. Stewart, who hailed from the Northern U.S., was irate about the presence in Brazil of U.S. nationals, "entitled by birth and citizenship to stand beneath the protecting folds of the stripes and stars of our country, who till now have been active agents in, and have shared largely in the emoluments of this wicked outrage," meaning slavery.[20]

Of course, there were U.S. nationals in Stewart's homeland who accepted willingly the same "emoluments"—a conclusion which arrived at could help to tear asunder the fabric of the nation.

Moreover, it seems that for those "from the New England and Middle states the Cape Horn route was generally preferred," while those "from the Southern states" favored "the Isthmus of Panama or Nicaragua or Mexico" (which suggests that there were factors inherent in the route west designed to induce an intriguing encounter with slavery from those least likely to have done so previously).[21] Thus, "the Cape Horn voyage of '49 produced a profound impact on all social levels among the Argonauts, something they never forgot to their dying days."[22]

The influx of these North American '49ers apparently had an impact on Brazil as well.[23] Salvador Ramirez arrived in Rio de Janeiro in March 1849 en route to the Golden West and noticed "California ships—a dozen—are anchored or dropping their anchors around us." A routine followed that many travelers took note of: "we were . . . boarded by two men-of-war, commanded by midshipmen. . . . They said the people were terribly alarmed at the great influx of Yankees and that the Emperor had ordered a double guard to be placed for the protection of the city and preservation of order." The Brazilians, he thought, were "frightened at the appearance of so many Americans and are much more lenient with them, in fact they dare not molest them at all." This was not an easy task to accomplish since Ramirez was "sorry to say that a great many of the Americans here have disgraced the name outrageously by getting up rows at the hotels both among ourselves and the natives."[24]

Such rowdy behavior may have derived from what Julius Howard Pratt detected when he stopped in Rio de Janeiro during the same era;

"the world has never witnessed so motley and promiscuous a throng in pursuit of a common object as sprang into life simultaneously in the winter of '48 and '49. . . . adventurers, thieves, gamblers, murderers and criminals jostled each other." This was bound to induce "great social upheaval," he thought.[25]

These U.S. citizens were cascading into Brazil at a time when the national anthem veritably was "Manifest Destiny" and filibustering expeditions—or armed assaults by a freelance band of U.S. nationals on foreign lands—were all the rage. As such, many of these visitors sized up Brazil,[26] gauging what it would take to take over, oust the regime, and plant the "stars and stripes"—a disposition fueled by their contempt for the inhabitants. William L. Carshaw of the U.S. Navy had participated in the war against Mexico in "lower California and Sonora, Mexico" and passed through Rio on his way there. Arriving in July 1846, he took detailed notes on "forts," including pointed remarks "on several hundred large guns . . . mounted" to defend the city.[27] When the U.S. Navy visited Santa Catarina in Brazil, it was noted carefully that the "harbour is defended by three forts."[28]

Many Brazilians did not take kindly to such attitudes.[29] Mary Smith, on her way to California in 1853, stopped in Rio de Janeiro and was stunned. "I have heard several . . . Americans say there's not a place on the face of the earth where American vessels have put, where they have so much trouble and vexation as at Rio." She visited the "English Cemetery" where she saw "the graves of a number of [New] Englanders"—though it was unclear if their being buried in Brazil was a direct result of their own "trouble and vexation at Rio."[30]

When future Californians poured into Brazil, many in this South American nation nervously compared themselves to recently subdued Mexicans and wondered if a similar fate awaited them.[31] As there were "something like thirty five hundred Americans perambulating the streets of Rio at all hours bidding defiance to all law and order," their fears were not necessarily irrational.[32] A. H. Cazzam, was associated with Peter Remsen, a noted cotton factor, cattle breeder—and slaveholder—from Mobile. He was not upset when in 1849 "Rosas" of the Argentine was discussing "making war with Brazil. If France & England will only let him alone he will wallop Brazil in no time & take Rio Grande do Sul from her—most of the Rio Grande people want to get rid of the Brazilians—they are the most troublesome & rebellious subjects in the

Brazilian Empire & altogether the most warlike." But this was not just a curious spectator—"I would . . . join Rosas if he marched into the province," he added belligerently.[33]

When 23-year-old Horatio Chapman of Connecticut arrived in Rio in 1849, he was suitably impressed—though his positive descriptions seemed to have been influenced by the language of military reconnaissance. " 'It was a fine bay,' " he thought, " 'surrounded on all sides, except at the entrance by rocks and higher hills; and it was thus strongly fortified by nature as well as by art. Had it been in the hands of the government of the United States,' " he added, " 'it would have been almost impregnable to any other nation. But as it is owned by the Portuguese, an ignorant and superstitious people, military discipline not being understood by them, notwithstanding there were a great many forts in and around the harbor, yet an intelligent people understanding the art of war might with very little exertion compel them to surrender.' "[34]

A few years later Henry Beckett arrived in Brazil on his way to the Pacific Northwest; "speaking of soldiers," he said reflectively later, "their system looked very odd to us. Some regiments are made up of blacks and whites, all colors and all heights. Their crack regiment was picked men, all blacks," while the "city gendarmes, with their short swords, were very officious and mean"; "they never missed an opportunity of snatching your pocket knife out of your hand and striking it on a wall and breaking it. Their annoyance and the natural prejudice of Americans with any colored race put in official position over them, brought on quite a number of collisions, our boys generally coming out best."[35]

"There is so many California vessels arrived here lately that the Brazilians are frightened," said Joseph Hamilton of South Carolina in March 1849. "They think they are going to annex Brazil to the U.S. and have posted three times the regular guards all over the place."[36] "There are enough Yankees in port now to take the fort, city and adjacent country and drive every yellow-skinned Braziliano into the mountains," thought the visiting Edward Brown in December 1849.[37] "All the defense that Rio can boast of for the present," thought Roger Conant traveling via Rio to the territory of Washington after the Gold Rush, "is a miserable fort, which a Yankee gun boat could batter down in a[n] hour."[38] After noting that some of his fellow U.S. nationals in Rio— "sorry to say"—had "performed acts that would not be permitted in their own country," one unnamed visitor who spent 25 days there, observed that "the city is protected by armed police night and day but they do not give the appearance of being very formidable antagonists." Some of his countrymen were told to disperse by these police; yet even though the former were "unarmed," they "drew up in the order of a charge of cavalry & all being ready the word 'charge' was given and all dashed into the midst of the soldiers [*sic*] dispersing them in every direction."[39]

The complexions of these police and soldiers and those they were sworn to protect seemed to influence how they were perceived by these U.S. visitors and how much force they thought it would take to oust the regime.[40] George Coggeshall was in Rio in 1837 buying coffee bound for New Orleans and concluded quickly that "it cannot . . . be expected that such [Negro] men will fight, except by compulsion. If their army is as badly organized as their navy, I should think they would make but a feeble resistance in defending their metropolis against any powerful maritime nation." Now he held "no prejudice against them" but found Brazilians generally "so deeply imbued with ignorance and superstition, and so firmly wedded to obsolete religious mummeries, that it will take a great many years to transform them to a great people."[41] Thomas Williams of Boston arrived in Rio in 1849 and noticed the "standing army" which "was the greatest sight of all," as "they were actually . . . slaves though they looked tolerable [*sic*] well but they seemed to me as though five hundred of Yankees [could] whip the whole of them" since "they don't seem to have that life or spirit" "that the Americans have," he thought. This lack of "spirit" was unsurprising since "they get no pay"—"nothing"—and "poor living and the worst treatment"; they were "nearly all blacks," though "now and then [an] officer with tolerable light complexion but not real white for the white people do nothing at all."[42] Another visitor in 1849 noticed that "in the city & at every village in its vicinity can be found a standing army, mostly all blacks commanded by whites or half breeds, rather weak appearing army on the whole."[43]

W. S. W. Ruschenberger in 1848 found the "standing army of Brazil" to be "so small as scarcely to merit the name," while the "navy is not effective . . . and there is no prospect of improvement."[44] One anonymous U.S. visitor noted that "soldiers" in Rio were "all colors from white to black, all young men and some mere boys"; "they do not appear to be well-disciplined" to the point where a "troop of Yankees would make sad havoc among them."[45]

A number of these sojourners thought there were inherent reasons that explained why Brazil was supposedly substandard when compared to the U.S.[46] Thomas Ewbank observed that on the Iberian peninsula "Moorish customs are inherited with Moorish blood and traceable in their colonies," e.g., Brazil. This made for "traits decidedly Oriental" and "peculiarly Asiatic," especially "in their tools and processes." The "first tool I recognized at once," he said, was "Roman and Egyptian" and certainly not on a par with what he knew at home.[47] "The people are inferior to the Americans," opined Milton Stevens in May 1849, "they are very small in size and swarthy."[48] One visitor in 1849 averred that "the whites are rather dark complection [sic] & amalgamating with the Negroes make a population of divers [sic] colors" and lesser stock.[49] C. S. Stewart was repulsed by the "fearfully mongrel aspect of much of the population, claiming to be white"; the "almost unlimited extent of mixed blood" was horrid, he thought, and "cannot fail to be revolting."[50]

John Callbreath noticed that " 'you cannot find a white man doing any kind of work and I do believe if it was not for the Yankees . . . and English the race would run out.' "[51] Rather astonished, James Orton was dumbfounded to discover that " 'it is generally considered bad taste in Brazil to boast purity of descent.' "[52] James Lamoureaux Pangburn arrived in Rio in April 1849 and was horrified at the sight of the "great number of Negroes that everywhere met me. These, to one accustomed to civilized life are truly objects of disgust and I am told compose two thirds of the population."[53] Mary Smith a New Englander en route to California was similarly horrified at what she saw. "The lower class are real Africans," she said. "No one ever need be frightened at homely ugly looking faces at home—they don't know what an ugly face is— positively I would not think possible for any <u>human</u> being to look as ugly as some of the boatmen and slaves here. . . . the idea of remaining three months—it is very unpleasant" [emphasis-original].[54]

At the same time, the presence of armed soldiers of darker complexions seemed to send a frisson of apprehension coursing through the veins of some of these visitors, as if—once again—they were witnessing a Haiti magnified or the rise of a darker power or a glimpse of their own futures, none of which were viewed as being particularly appetizing. John Stone arrived in Rio during the rush westward for gold. He found the place "disgusting" and "filthy" while "many of the Negroes who make up the chief population live in a state of nature and nudity."

But what was noticeably striking, he thought, was "the military display in this great Brazilian capital," which "inspired much dread, the soldiery being made up of coal black Negroes, who at their country's solemn call were ready to risk their lives, their fortunes and their sacred honour . . . and a contact with whom would fill with dismay and horror, all persons with delicate olfactories." Worse, these men who were "armed with muskets and gleaming bayonets" acted to "drive any white people who innocently saunter by, from the sidewalks into the muddy streets by rude assault and at the point of bayonet."[55] When Samuel Upham "visited the Emperor's church" during the Gold Rush era, he was stunned: "as I crossed the threshold," he recalled later, "the first object that met my eye was one of the Emperor's guards, whose complexion was a shade lighter than the ace of spades, with a musket at his shoulder and stationed near the altar" as "worshipers of all ages, complexions and conditions were kneeling about the church."[56] L. M. Schaeffer was part of the 1849 Gold Rush and stopped in Rio in May and was stunned similarly.[57]

These guests from the U.S. at times tested the limits of tolerance of their hosts, leading to confrontations with which U.S. nationals were not accustomed: spats with armed African men. In 1846, sailors from the USS Saratoga were on leave in Rio and, typically, were "rather inebriated and creating a noise in the streets," when they were "violently assaulted by the police of that city," who "rushed them with drawn swords" and detained them forcibly. Minister Henry Wise "informed" the authorities that if they were "not released," he "would open the batteries of the U.S. frigate Columbia on the town." The sailors were released but that did not halt the repetitive friction between the two nations as Washington was "continually complaining of insults offered to our flag, continued annoyances in the Custom-House and fines, not lawful, imposed upon them." As the U.S. saw it, their visitors were pouring money into Brazil's economy, not to mention the "importation of millions of bags of coffee annually" from that nation and the vessels "bound to California with passengers" which "touched at that port for supplies." The Brazilians should recognize, it was said, that the U.S. had "the power of resenting insults"—and they could have added that they were not pleased by being "insulted" by darker authorities.[58]

Violent confrontations between U.S. nationals and Brazilians were not uncommon; in 1849, two of the former were murdered after a particularly brutal encounter in Santa Catarina, Brazil.[59] On another occasion in Rio two U.S. nationals were slain, "whereupon the Argonauts armed themselves and drove all the [Brazilian] soldiers into the mountains and took possession of the place."[60] Passing through Rio in 1850, John R. McFalan spoke of the famed "Sugar Loaf" mountain where "it is said . . . a daring Californian got access to its summit and placed there the American flag; with a telescope," he added.[61]

The fascination of these visitors [62] with their hosts' complexions—even those presumably in the elite—was palpable.[63] John Esaias Warren made it to the Amazon as the Gold Rush was unfolding and found it worthy of note that "in the selection of officials no regard whatever is paid to color. The president himself was a woolly-headed mulatto, and, not only that, but he was reputed to be the son of a padre; and as the padres are excluded from matrimony by the statutes, his genealogy certainly cannot be of the most honorable character."[64]

Richard Morton of Virginia was not as dispassionate about this same phenomenon. "This morning I breakfasted with a black man," he said a few years after the Gold Rush's height; it was "no uncommon thing for a free <u>black</u> man to be invited to the table with white persons," he added, "but I had hoped never to make one of the number, but this morning one as black as the <u>ace of spades</u> sat opposite me at the table." He was not happy about this. "<u>I felt really mean</u>, I could not object however without offence to my very kind host, gratitude & politeness both bade me <u>endure</u> it." Morton seemed to be undergoing a kind of racial crisis, simultaneously befuddled and outraged by what he was experiencing. His attitude did not improve as he was ambling along a road "on foot & was attacked by <u>three large boys</u>" and, he said, "had to use my stick dexterously to keep them off & have now only one regret on the subject viz: that [I did] not <u>whip</u> the <u>black</u> to whom [they] belonged." Later after finishing dinner at the home of a friend, his travail continued as a "dance commenced & there not being ladies sufficient for the <u>men</u>, the mulatto girls were brought in to <u>fill up</u> & some three or four of them occupied the floor during the whole evening (there always about the large fazendas [plantations] a number of bright mulattos, generally the <u>whitest</u> & best looking members of the establishment, who stay about the house as <u>companions</u>. . . . for they do <u>no work</u>)." Yet Morton refused to take advantage of this titillating situation—or so he said. "I was never tempted to take part in the dance," he sniffed, "& never except to oblige others." He did deign to cross gender borders, however, as he was "importuned by a 'fellow of <u>my height</u>' to dance as

---

his 'vis-à-vis'" and the gracious Morton was "in the act of consenting when he led me across the room & took one mulatto girl & told me to take another just be her side for my partner, but I could not 'go that' & declined on the spot most emphatically much to his discomfiture" though "no one else [there] seemed to have much preference."

Morton was continually taken by surprise at the patterns he was witnessing that were so unlike his native Virginia. He "saw" a "young lady with a naked black child in her arms . . . hugging & kissing it [*sic*]." He had "no disposition to get any 'closer' to her than was necessary as a result." He was taken to meet an upstanding member of society and, "to my utter astonishment he turned out to be Chinese, he stands very high in the community—is said to be the best man about here; I never before heard of a Chinese rising to respectability anywhere." Then he discovered this gentleman was "not a Chinese but a native of Bombay, India & his parents are Brahmins, he was educated for a priest but at 21 he declined taking orders & came to Mozambique . . . where he had an uncle" then to Rio "where [he] had a relative." He studied medicine, became a doctor, and "made a little fortune"; despite Morton's astonishment at his presence "he was extremely kind to me," he felt, "I never met with more kindness anywhere" [emphases-original].[65] Morton's continuously stunned reaction was reflective of a larger "racial crisis" in an encounter with a nation whose "race rules" seemed to differ from his own, thus casting doubt on whether the U.S. course was universal or "natural"—or could be dislodged ultimately.

Still, some of these U.S. nationals were taken by the horrible spectacle that was human bondage. Those not familiar with this practice were noticeably repulsed and revolted. J. L. Ackerman was making his way to California from Boston via Brazil during the Gold Rush when he found himself in Rio. It was "as great a slave market as there is in the world. I was astonished," he said using a word that frequently peppers narratives of U.S. visitors to Brazil, "at the vast number of slaves to be seen in the square and about the landing, they have to perform all kinds of drudgery, you will see no trucks and drays for hauling goods here as you will in the States, all is done by slaves." The sight of these "poor slaves" touched his heart. "The first thing that drew my attention on landing," he asserted, was a "poor slave, a brute in human shape was applying a raw hide to his back with all his might. It made my blood chill within me at the sight. I thought to myself that I should like to have my will of the brute for a short time. I would give him slavery to his heart's content," he warned. This trip "was the first time I ever had slaves under my authority," he said, "but I did not abuse that authority"—unlike what he had witnessed, as his abolitionist sentiments flowered.[66]

Samuel Adams had managed a drugstore in Brooklyn before pulling up stakes and heading for California gold in December 1849. Arriving in Rio he found that "one of the most unpleasant things I saw . . . was a gang of tall straight able-bodied blacks chained together round their neck, there were sixteen in all." This too sparked abolitionist sentiments within him: "the great slaveholder," he thought, "is fastening around the souls and bodies of our young men and women too, their disregard of everything relating to their best and most precious interests."[67] Milton Stevens cried to his "Dear Mother" that in Brazil "they have slaves by the thousands and treat them very cruel. I have seen them whip[ped] . . . some of them chained together. . . . they are all marked like sheep and some of them are naked."[68]

While in Rio, Samuel Upham "saw a Negro who was afflicted with the elephantiasis, one of the most loathsome diseases imaginable, but quite common in this country. His left leg was swollen to nearly the size of his body, and from the knee downward protruded excrescences as large as English walnuts. The skin of the diseased limb appeared rough and scaly and several of the toes had dropped off the foot. I saw others," he recalled with disgust, "afflicted with this disease who had lost their lips and noses."[69]

James Woods arrived in Rio in August 1849 and was greatly displeased by what he saw. "Not infrequently when a slaver is chased by a man-of-war," he noted with horror, "they throw the slaves overboard to prevent detection. . . . A tale was related last night which was truly horrible," he observed. "A slaver was pursued by a man-of-war lest he should be found in possession of slaves and be declared and treated as a pirate; he had all the slaves brought out and fastened by means of a rope extending around the vessel, on the outside of the vessel, so that with one blow of the axe they could all be dropped in the ocean. Slavery is an awful terrible curse. But language cannot describe the horrors of the slave trade. . . . the poor Africans!" he moaned, "the whole world is against him. . . . very justly have the United States and Great Britain declared the slave trade piracy. . . . oh what a terrible cause is slavery and the slave trade how supremely horrible."[70] The mundane sights of oppression seemed to numb. "Saw a dead Negress on the beach," said one visitor blandly in 1849, "saw dead nigger [*sic*] towed by canoe toward shore caulkers."[71] On his way from the eastern U.S. to California, James Woods sailed through Rio; "soon after breakfast," he observed, "the dead body of a poor Negro came floating past the vessel. It was a dreadful sight. The remarks of some of the passengers on the occasion were light and trifling" in response.[72]

Salvador Ramirez was taken by the sight of a "great number of aged slaves, who being of no further use are turned out to die gradually, I saw hundreds of [such] hideous spectacles."[73] "Loafers," which were "such a nuisance in the United States," were "here entirely unknown, no collections of people are seen here on the corners of the streets," said one U.S. visitor.[74] Put simply, said James T. Jones visiting Rio in 1844, a "Brazilian slave is a <u>real</u> slave. An American slave, no slave at all" [emphasis-original].[75]

Visitors from the North were also moved by the labor that slaves were compelled to perform. "One finds among them all sorts of mechanics," said C. B. Richard in the late 1840s; "they are almost the only carriers of burdens one finds in Rio. . . . half of them sing the refrain, frequently the word 'coffee' or the name of the article they happen to be carrying . . . the other half renders the accompaniment with a monotonous boom, boom." In the "long but very narrow and dirty streets" there were "large, bare and neglected public squares" dotted with "shackled slaves . . . having run away a few times are now forced to carry a fetter that they cannot remove—usually an iron ring around the neck with iron horns . . . thus they are recognizable to the police." Other slaves chose to "roam the streets half-naked in quest of a livelihood" which was "not an agreeable sight to a stranger."[76]

Salvador Ramirez wondrously declared that "what strikes the stranger in this country is the immense number of slaves." They were "at every corner"—"you are constantly surrounded by them, groups of slaves of all sizes, who make quite an income for their masters by carrying water to the city and supplying the inhabitants. . . . I noticed that their heads as a general thing are bare of hair upon the top on account of this constant friction" from carrying loads on their heads.[77] One visitor heard of a "Negro who carried a barrel of flour 20 miles on his head!"—which was not uncommon since "a large portion of the transporting of goods from one part of the city to the other is done by Negroes. They have a kind of dray which is drawn by Negroes, generally about 5 to a dray, one at the pole, two at the wheels and two to push behind." Instead of "oxen" or "mules," Brazilians used Africans.[78] C. H. Keefe in 1849 observed something similar. "Having but very few horses," in Rio, the enslaved "actually have to work harder than most of our horses at home. I have seen them go in squads of 20 or 30 with all the furniture of a house on their heads, some with tables, others with sofas and chairs, on a kind of dog trot singing 2 or 3 words which one sings and the rest join in a chorus of 'yam yah' or 'wol wor' or something similar."[79]

Albert Lyman did not miss the "great excess of the slave over the white population in Rio. . . . the former are nearly five times more numerous than the latter" and "usually go in gangs of from twelve to thirty, sometimes yoked together with heavy necklaces of iron and attended by a driver. . . . they move along at a slow trot, humming a monotonous refrain the words of which are often changed."[80]

Another unidentified visitor in 1849 noticed that these "poor, degraded & oppressed beings" were involved in tasks that "would seem incredible if not related by those who are entitled to full belief," "such as carrying a single umbrella, a cup of coffee, a small vase of flowers and the like on their heads" or pulling a "water cart, similar to the water carts of New York except being pushed and pulled along by Negroes instead of drawn by a horse."[81] M. J. Randall observed that "the ladies, who can afford it, are carried about in palanquins, by two or four Negroes."[82] Visiting Rio in 1858, the Virginian, Richard Morton, found that it was not appropriate for Euro-Brazilians "to carry [any] bundle; no matter how small, in your hand, through the streets; you must have a <u>black</u> to carry it for you" [emphasis-original].[83]

On his way to California from Boston, Thomas Williams arrived in Rio in 1849 and immediately observed that "the boatmen were all black and they were a ragged set of beings, the most they had on was a coarse piece of cloth around their loins without hats or shoes or anything in the shape of a garment for it appears that the whites do no labour at all," which was "disgraceful" as "the Negroes are their cattle to do all labour." He visited a slaughter house and found it "disgusting" that "no white man [was] to be seen at any kind of labour," while the Africans were a sight, "blood running down the faces and over the shoulders and back to their heels, of all such sights this was the most filthy." Dumbfounded, he wrote, "I have seen a slave with three bags of coffee on his head at one time and close at his heels . . . another with a barrel of flour on his head." There were "no privies in the houses" and in his hotel, "he was shown to a room and in a few minutes a slave entered with a tub and actually [stayed] in the room while [he] eased himself," then carted the night soil away. "The poor slave . . . dare not murmur nor complain, or the lash is laid on his back which is always bare." Slavery, he concluded, was "the curse of curses" and, thus, said Williams, "I was happy to leave Rio with all its beauties and splendor."[84]

A nameless visitor concurred, mourning that a "stranger here whose affections are far away with those he loves, cannot but sympathize with these poor fellow creatures who have been taken by violence from their homes, their wives and their children, and enslaved in a foreign country, where hope cannot befriend them!"[85] "I would rather, a thousand times, be a sheep, pig, or ox, have freedom, food and rest for a season, and then be knocked on the head," observed Thomas Ewbank of Brazil, "then be a serf on some plantations." "Here are slave dealers," he lamented, "who weep over the legendary sufferings of a saint, and laugh at worse tortures they themselves inflict."[86] Like animals, slaves "at night" were "locked up in cells," but unlike animals, this was "done to keep their slaves from any outbreak or insurrection which is constantly feared."[87]

Of course, there were other U.S. nationals, including non-Virginians, who were not angered by the slavery they saw but, instead, quickly adjusted to it.[88] There was a famous "Captain Cathcart," who was "well known to Americans calling at Santa Catarina," Brazil. He was an "American whaling captain who, upon returning to Nantucket after a long voyage, learned that his wife had been unfaithful during his absence. He divorced her and immediately set sail. At a stop in Santa Catarina he fell in love with the daughter of the local governor, sold his ship and cargo (which did not belong to him) and set himself up as a plantation owner" and rather rapidly "gained a great ascendancy over the simple people" there; he owned a "large plantation and several Negro slaves."[89] Typical of that time was the fact that Cathcart for a while acted as a U.S. diplomat there.[90]

But whether budding abolitionists or flame-throwing advocates of bondage, U.S. travelers in Brazil were generally unenthusiastic about this nation. **Godey's Lady Book,** published in Philadelphia, was not known to have a significant Negro readership; yet, their correspondent, just back from Petropolis, "where the Emperor has a palace" was at one of that region's "very poor hotels. At one of these I was staying recently," it was said, "when there arrived a family, consisting of a young gentleman with his wife, his wife's sister, a young lady of sixteen years of age, a black nurse, and a baby. *They all occupied the same bedroom!* And this not from necessity. . . . these were *highly respectable* people, of the best families of the place"—"this fact speaks volumes," it was concluded triumphantly [emphasis-original].[91] "A more miserable dirty place I never saw," said Daniel S. Hayden, who stopped there on his way from Maine to California. "The houses are low & the streets narrow & full of blacks of all conditions from the officer in power to the beggar with no finger or toes"; besides "yellow fever" abounded.[92] Another unidentified sojourner arriving in May 1850 also detected the "prevalence of the yellow fever," with "about thirty thousand persons [having] fallen victims to it since January." The "filthiness of the inhabitants" was revolting.[93] The inadequate plumbing system was an abomination to one U.S. visitor; "at night these tubs [carrying human waste] are carried off on the heads of Negroes and emptied into the harbor"; "this is done after nine o'clock at night, at which time the streets are filled with Negroes, with these tubs on their heads, which creates often a very unpleasant odor!"[94] Ruth Nash of Maine declared that Rio was a "very filthy city," with "streets" being "narrow and dirty. The gutters are in the middle of the street where a stream of water runs which emits a very disagreeable smell." There were "dead bodies . . . laid out in the green house. Those of the poorer classes and slaves are thrown into a trench where they are sprinkled with lime, placing one layer on another until the trench is filled. The crowded state of the place of internment [sic] is evident from the numbers of skulls and bones laying about, some still with the flesh adhering to them."[95]

U.S. visitors often tended to view Brazil as a sewer of iniquity and corruption, a situation that some also tied to enslavement. " 'A married man is excusable so far from [home],' " said one U.S. husband in search of prostitutes in the "Deepest South," " 'and the prices were reasonable in Rio.' " One wrote a "poem to 'The Slave Girl at Rio,' " drooling about " 'her bosom's swelling outlines' to her 'dark and lustrous eye' and then came his penultimate admission: 'I should I knew see naught on earth / So beautiful again,' " before adding tellingly, " 'but 'twas no use to figger in setting up a wail; for she's the blackest nigger that I saw out of jail.' " Also driven to verse, another would-be Whitman spoke of " 'where rivers of liquor are flowing[,] where each step in the street dark damsels we meet, tempting us to buy their bananas to buy-o; we cannot begin to set forth our chagrin at leaving thee; City of Rio.' "[96]

The mason and farmer, Samuel Whiting of Rhode Island—who fought with the North during the Civil War—perceived an "intemperance and licentiousness" that "seem to abound here," speaking of Rio. "What is still more disgraceful," he groused, was that "more or less of nearly every California company that stops here helps to swell the tide of this iniquity," as "there were some who drank to excess."[97] Henry Beckett, though he was on his way to the Pacific Northwest and not California, may have been the kind of man conjured up by Whiting; approaching Brazil he rhapsodized since "in viewing Rio from the sea it makes one think of the Elysian fields of a Mohammedan paradise with the beautiful girls, which, they say, were made to tempt the youth and torment the men."[98]

Thomas Williams of Boston found "some very handsome black women" in Brazil, adding "but for their colour they would be very handsome and as good looking as most women but it makes every heart sick to see their degradation but it is and likely to remain."[99] Albert Lyman saw "Negro women . . . lounging about the fountain near where we landed, chattering away in a strange gibberish like monkeys."[100] Thomas Ewbank observed that in Brazil "neither age nor sex is free from iron shackles. I met this morning a very handsome Mozambique girl with a double-pronged collar on; she could not have been over sixteen."[101] Richard Morton of Virginia, after being in Brazil for over a month, bewailed that the "only pretty Brazilian woman" he had "yet seen" was his host's wife—and she was "<u>white</u> too" [emphasis-original]. "I have for two months been in a country," he complained, "where there are scarcely any pretty women."[102] Levi Holden was in Brazil a few years earlier and "did not see any pretty women. They had the sallow complexions of Indians without the healthy glow in the cheeks & lips, these latter being of a leaden and healthy hue."[103] "The ladies here, as a general rule," were "very dark," said one Philadelphia-based periodical, and "very ugly. In no part of the world can so much ugliness and so few good looks be met . . . nowhere does the female sex possess so little attraction." This supposed trait was tied to morals since "at a very early age, sometimes at twelve years old, she is married" and "conversation, of course, these ladies have none. What can they talk about?"[104]

"Father & daughter, brother & sister dwell together as man & wife, among both higher and lower classes," thus the "moral desolation which pervades the whole country," concluded one Virginian.[105]

Most of these visitors were men and their reactions to Brazilian women were striking. But their reactions may have been skewed because "another feature of Brazilian society," as Reverend L. J. Hall put it, was "the exclusion of females from the public gaze."[106] J. D. B. Stillman concurred, declaring "there is no animation in Brazil—no social sound, no voice of mirth," one reason being "woman is a slave! She is illiterate and suspected. Women are not allowed to frequent the streets, day or night." He did not "see any females, except [those that] are blacks!"[107] This too may have pushed these numerous visitors in a perverted cycle of revulsion and attraction into the "bosom's swelling outlines" of poor African women. Slavers preferred men to women, in any event, then—according to one U.S. visitor—discouraged their slaves from having children, as they can get them from Africa with less expense than they can "raise them at home"; thus, he "saw very few children."[108]

A. H. Cazzam of the U.S. was unimpressed with the southernmost part of South America generally. He found those of Buenos Ayres to be a "very healthy & handsome race of people—much handsomer than the Brazilians," who, of course, had a larger African population. Yet, like Brazil, he found there a "laxity in their morals" too "that might shock you at first sight. . . . for instance, a great many respectable people received into society & who visit all the parties & balls have had children before they were married. . . . such as the husband being a priest or the wife a nun." He struggled toward moral relativism—"it is impossible to do justice to judge one nation by any standard of conventional morals that belong to another nation"—but still he had much to object to among his hemispheric neighbors.[109]

U.S. nationals were flowing into Rio at a time when anti-Catholicism was proliferating back home and this too marked their presence there, making them feel that the residents were not worthy of this vast land and, perhaps, those from the North should substitute for them. "I could not conceive why any mortal man can be so very superstitious as to believe in a religion like this," said Ralph Cross Pendleton, speaking of Catholicism in Brazil during his 1852 visit from New York.[110] One U.S. visitor met a "gentleman" in Brazil in 1852, who "had once resided in Virginia," who expressed "unqualified disgust of the Roman Catholic religion."[111] James Woods en route to the Gold Rush made his way to Rio and was acidulous in referring to this "great city almost wholly given to idolatry."[112] Others thought that this religion was a profound cofactor in the subordination of enslaved Africans. "A custom is observed here, and I am told in well-regulated families in Brazil, which," said C. S. Stewart in 1856, "were it anything more an unmeaning form would be interesting. It is the asking of a blessing from the master every morning and every evening at the close of the day's work by all the slaves, of both sexes and of every age . . . the slaves as they present themselves merely exclaiming, in all manner of intonations of voice and in every mood of humor—'Jesus Christ!'—while the master, be he talking or laughing, eating or drinking, or in whatever way employed, without any interruption and seemingly without any regard to the import of the salutation, as abruptly replies, 'Siempre!' [*sic*] 'Forever!' "[113]

The irascibly racist Richard Morton of Virginia pointed out "another custom . . . of the blacks, when they first see you in the morning or if they meet you on the road, they hold their hands & say, '. . . Jesus Christo,' & you are expected to reply, 'a dios,' they also do the same thing when they come in from work at night. . . . the expression means 'praised be our Lord Christ Jesus.' "[114]

William Edwards, the former U.S. diplomat in Buenos Ayres, who visited Brazil in 1847, discerned that "every morning and evening the blacks knelt in devotion. Upon certain evenings all of them, and some of the neighbors, would come together and for an hour chant the Portuguese hymn in wild tones, but very pleasing. A lamp was constantly kept burning in this chapel. Similar customs [obtained nationally] and by many of the planters the blacks are trained up rigidly to the performance of these observances."[115]

Hence, though many U.S. visitors viewed Brazil negatively as a morass of enslavement and religious rigor mortis, others thought—when compared to the U.S.—Africans were advantaged and African-Americans in the U.S. were among these. Frederick Douglass frequently evoked the example of Brazil repeatedly to indict U.S. slavery. "Indeed," said his paper, the **North Star** in 1848, "in many countries, where multitudes of Africans and their descendants have been long held slaves, no prejudice against color has ever existed. This is the case in Turkey, Brazil and Perisa. In Brazil there are more than two million of slaves. Yet some of the highest offices of state are filled by black men. . . . hundreds of Roman Catholic clergy are black and colored men, these minister to congregations made up indiscriminately of blacks and whites."[116] "If the colored man can rise from degradation to respectability in Brazil," said Douglass in 1858, "with the same treatment he can rise here. If he can be esteemed as a man by the Portuguese, he can be so esteemed by Anglo-Saxons and Celts."[117] "Take slavery as it existed in Cuba or in the Brazils [*sic*], or anywhere else," said Douglass later, "it was nowhere so destructive of all the rights of humanity as slavery in the United States."[118]

In a perverse way, Richard Morton of Virginia made an argument that dovetailed with Douglass's, otherwise his diametric opposite. "As a <u>general thing</u>," he said with emphasis, "<u>one of our</u> Southern blacks does more work than <u>two blacks in Brazil</u>, I am competent to gauge." Brazilian slaves "cannot compare at all with those of Va. [*sic*] except the blacks 'who work the coffee.' "[119] Accidentally, Morton here also touched on a reason why slavery hampered the development of the productive forces in Brazil, as the proliferation of enslaved Africans, often rebellious, hindered the economy. "The mechanics here are mostly slaves," said Samuel Upham, "a Yankee mechanic would perform as much labor in one day as two slaves in the same length of time."[120] Euro-Brazilians, thought John Beeckman, were "slow of belief and seem rather inclined to risk their capital and credit in the slave trade to the coast of Africa than send their vessels to the Eldorado of America. Every merchant here is either directly or indirectly engaged in slave traffic—at which their government winks."[121]

On the other hand, Thomas Ewbank argued that "here" in Brazil "are many wealthy people of color. I have passed black ladies in silk and jewelry, with male slaves in livery behind them. . . . several have white husbands." Even Brazilian slaves seemed advantaged—"I have now seen slaves working as carpenters, masons, pavers, printers, sign and ornament painters, carriage and cabinet makers, fabricators of military ornaments, lamp-makers, silversmiths, jewelers and lithographers," while "some write Arabic fluently and are vastly superior to most of their masters."[122] "The slaves in this city," said Samuel Upham speaking of Rio, "appear to be well treated and seem happy. I asked several if they would like to return to Africa. Their reply was: 'me no like to go back to Africa among the nigger thieves!' " Free Negroes were thought relatively advantaged compared to their counterparts, not to mention slaves in the hemisphere, not least since there in Rio "they wear shoes; the slaves invariably go barefooted."[123] Yet, whether one were an abolitionist like Douglass or opposed to same, like Morton, Brazil was evoked readily as a basis for either argument. Brazil seemed to harden the sentiments of abolitionists and pro-slavery advocates alike, thus hastening the lurch toward Civil War.[124]

Ironically, the images transmitted about Brazil in the mid-19th century by U.S. visitors may have been more graphic, numerous, and important than any images rendered since by similar sojourners. Slavery in Rio de Janeiro left an indelible impression upon those on their way to California. But their compatriots—particularly Matthew Fontaine Maury of Virginia—had a different view of Brazil; he appreciated this South American nation so much that he thought it would be a good idea to seize some of its territory.

Matthew Fontaine Maury. An eminent Virginian, Maury was a commander
of the Confederate States Navy during the Civil War. He also had designs
on the Amazon, including a plan to deport enslaved African-Americans
there. Courtesy Library of Congress.

6

The U.S. to Seize the Amazon?

A street is named for him in Richmond, an oil portrait of him hangs in the Virginia State Library, a county in Tennessee has been named after him, along with a wing of the Naval Academy at Annapolis and a destroyer, not to mention his prominence at the University of Virginia where his name is inscribed on the frieze of the Rotunda.[1] This "internationally famous man" is credited with the founding of an entirely new science, the "physical geography of the sea," known today as oceanography, which "revolutionized merchant traffic on the high seas."[2] It was he who was substantially responsible for the "impressive performance" of antebellum U.S. vessels with the "publication" of his "charts of ocean winds and currents, which showed that the fastest course under sail was not always the shortest in miles," thereby facilitating the mass migration of the Gold Rush via Brazil and Cape Horn and the illicit mass migration of Africans across the Atlantic.[3] His "fertile brain conceived the Panama Canal" before it was built and "fifteen years before the Pony Express we find him advocating a monthly overland service to Oregon." His works went through 19 editions in Britain and were translated into eight languages.[4]

He received "honors from universities, acclamation from nearly 50 learned societies, and decorations from Emperors, Kings, and Pope Pius IX" and "authorship of a memorial for the free navigation of the Amazon which was endorsed by the 14-state economic congress, the Memphis Convention and presented to the U.S. House of Representatives of 3 March 1854." Tens of thousands of copies of a report on the Amazon he initiated were printed, which was "clear evidence of the intense interest generated by the exploration" there he sponsored.[5]

He is still a celebrated Virginian, comparable to "Stonewall" Jackson or Robert E. Lee. Yet Matthew Fontaine Maury not only devised a scheme to send U.S. Negroes to Brazil, but he also exceeded the most anti-union elements among secessionists in his zeal in collaborating with foreign powers against Washington during the Civil War, a development that was a logical extension of the former proposal, both reflecting his view of national boundaries as impermanent and transitory. For it was Maury who "engaged in a long series of negotiations with the Emperor Napoleon of France and the Archduke Maximilian of Austria concerning the separation of California from the United States and its restoration to Mexico as a reward for French intervention on the side of the South" during the Civil War.[6]

Before this later cartographic scheme, in the 1850s, Maury devised a plan to transfer enslaved Africans in the U.S. from the South to Brazil, the Deepest South. If Brazil could get slaves from the U.S. instead of Africa, the number of slaves in the U.S. would be cut down and the kidnapping and buying of new slaves from Africa would be prevented— hence, the implication of the crusade of his compatriot, Henry Wise. As he saw it, the law of supply and demand would facilitate this massive movement southward, just as it had already supposedly played a role in the Negro transfer from the northern to the southern U.S. He did not believe southern slaveholders would consent to the freedom of their property without being paid and, conveniently, he was of the opinion that the desire of the Brazilians for slaves would meet the desire of a good many of those in the U.S. to dispose of their slaves at the market price: it was the logic of the Virginia slave-breeder, the same mentality that had impelled Wise toward opposing the African Slave Trade so vociferously. Ultimately, this cleansing of the U.S. South of Africans would serve to, at least, reduce slavery—and the number of Negroes— in that nation, just as it would increase it in Brazil.[7] Maury, who was lame as a result of a severe fall from a stagecoach in 1839, which disqualified him for further active service on land or sea, then turned his fecund and mobile intellect to the seas, devising schemes that placed Brazil in the bull's-eye.[8]

Sending U.S. Negroes elsewhere was an idea that was not unique to Maury, as this notion was often seen as complementary to emancipation. There was talk in the 1840s about settling U.S. Negroes in "British Guiana," on the northern coast of South America, close to Brazil.[9] Nor was Maury unique in having designs on the Amazon, as this region was "potentially . . . one of the richest of the globe"; the "entire river system" drained "areas of some 1,722,000 square miles, or over twice the estimated drainage region of the Mississippi and its tributaries."[10] Monroe Edwards of Texas was in and out of Rio de Janeiro in the 1830s, once listening carefully as he was told that because the prices of " 'colonial produce' " were " 'unusually high and that regulates the demand for slaves. The prices will stimulate the planters to enlarge their cultivations extensively. They cannot do this without an increase of slaves, and I should not be surprised if the next year saw seventy thousand wool heads taken from the coast.' " He and his friend then repaired to the U.S. Consul to get papers to facilitate their going to Africa on business; they were worried but "found the Consul remarkably indifferent to everything." Slave trading was nothing new for Edwards, as he had been active in supplying his nation, Texas, and, in the process, had become a "rich man; one of the richest in Texas." He considered establishing an enterprise in the Amazon, "far enough in the interior to be beyond the supervision of any active authority"; these "distant plains though hidden from the eye of nations and beyond the immediate observation of the effeminate power of the Brazilian government" were "nevertheless within a step of the great high roads of the world." As he saw it, if he could get a "thousand men together there . . . no South American state" could "bring sufficient force together to dislodge us."[11] Nevertheless, as a self-confessed "forger and swindler," Edwards's words have to be viewed cautiously, if not suspiciously.

Yet there is little doubt that there were U.S. nationals with grand plans for the Amazon, licit and illicit. This is why in 1856 "plenipotentiaries" representing many South American nations "signed a Treaty of Union at Santiago that among other things" sought to define "filibustering," which was seen as "piracy" and "pledged mutual aid against invasions, and invited all other Latin states to join the alliance."[12]

It appeared that as early as the 1830s, U.S. business was doing a better job of penetrating the Amazon than their French and British competitors.[13] Symptomatic were the plans of the U.S. businessman, Peter Remsen. A cotton factor and cattle breeder from Mobile, he represented a trend that seemed to be growing as the antebellum era was coming to an end—a kind of "slave imperialism," whereby southern entrepreneurs were exporting capital and seeking to continue the existence of human bondage. In 1847, he was involved in planning to operate a "steam boat" on the "River Amazon."[14] High of forehead with blue eyes, an oval face, sandy hair, and short of build—an unimposing 5'7" tall[15]— Remsen had imposing plans, nevertheless, for this vast largely unexplored region.

He was not alone. Even then there was an "American society" in the principal town of that area, Para, that was deemed "rather more sociable and friendly with one another than they are at Rio, perhaps because there is less fashion, less show and less pretense among them"; moreover, on this raw frontier—"this place does not contain over 12,000 inhabitants"—"rents" were "uncommonly low. . . . servants"—i.e., enslaved Africans—"can be purchased low, say from $200 to $250 and hired for three or four dollars a month."[16]

Yet amid such favorable conditions for U.S. nationals in Brazil, there were significant concerns. As some saw it, London—the ubiquitous foe —displayed more "energy & resolution" in "protecting the rights of British subjects" than their U.S. counterparts. "By playing upon the fears of the Brazilians, although they heartily detest her, Great Britain gets all her claims paid promptly; whilst we, who . . . get nothing from them but interminable delay & evasions." For "more than twenty years" this "entreaty and patience" had "been unable to accomplish anything" and a "decent respect for our national rights of honor, demands that other measures should now be tried." What was needed was "authorization to demand immediate settlement, backed by ten or a dozen vessels of war ready to blockade Rio, would accomplish more in twenty four hours than our pacific & affectionate diplomacy has accomplished in as many years."[17]

U.S. business interests, pressuring the U.S. government to engage in gunboat diplomacy on their behalf, was not just limited to the Amazon. During the same period, the same issue arose at Pernambuco, as the commanding officer of the USS Bainbridge was told about "political intrigues" and "violent animosities" that could lead to "much bloodshed and destruction of property." Concern was raised about the impact on "lives or even the property of our fellow countrymen," and an urgent request was made for this ship to "pay a visit as it is now more than a year since any American ship of war has been here"; this "would no doubt have a very salutary influence at present, particularly as no armed vessel of any nation is on this part of the coast."[18]

Yet even in more developed Pernambuco, pressure was building for the influx of more enslaved Africans. "Pernambuco has a population of perhaps one hundred and twenty five thousand," said the U.S. Consul, Walter Stapp; "this exceedingly high price of living has necessarily produced an equally high demand for labor in all departments of Pernambuco life. . . . I am informed by the most respectable merchants in

Pernambuco that the price of living here, is as great in, almost, any other commercial port in the world." Like the Amazon region, the "climate" here was also "fearfully destructive" and "of the foreigners who have located here in the last few years <u>more than seventy five percent have perished</u>" [emphasis-original], to the point "when friends part, for an hour, they shake hands with a warmth that is almost tearful, for they know not that they shall meet again in life!"[19] Were not Africans the only humans who could withstand this withering environment?

Bahia was little different, with U.S. nationals proliferating as the illicit slave trade escalated. " 'Bahia is the only town [*sic*] in Brazil in which there exists an American cemetery . . . belonging to citizens of the United States,' " Secretary of State Daniel Webster was informed.[20] When visiting Bahia in 1841, the South Carolinian John J. Pringle observed that there were "very few Americans in Bahia but a great deal of English society." Of the three major groups there—"whites, mulattoes and blacks," he was happy to note that the "whites have now the supremacy" though he seemed to be concerned with the rapid influx of Africans and what this might mean for the "racial" balance; "during the short time that [we] were there," he wrote, "two vessels sailed for the coast of Africa, one of which had been chased several times by the English men of war but had always succeeded in escaping."[21] Simultaneously, U.S. vessels were flowing into this increasingly "Africanized" province, with a plurality from Richmond, followed by Baltimore and including quite a few from New York City, Boston, and Philadelphia.[22] If history was any guide, some of these ships would be sold for the purpose of seizing people in Africa for the purpose of enslavement in Brazil.

It was such simmering pressure that set the stage for more aggressive U.S. plans for the Amazon, just as it provided a backdrop for Matthew F. Maury's more elaborate arrangement for Brazilian territory. For Washington maintained a special interest in the Amazon, carefully conducting reconnaissance.[23] Washington was also concerned about the "scarcity of labor" in the Amazon, which was "felt more and more each year," a dearth that Negro slaves could have alleviated. This lack "retards the capital advancement of the commercial and agricultural interests of this province," it was said. Brazil made "several attempts to introduce [colonists] from Portugal which have not proved entirely successful" as "hard work and exposure prepared them to become an easy prey to the yellow fever which proved fatal to many."[24] U.S. nationals were arriving regularly in the Amazon in the 1850s; "the capital of our citizens [is] employed in this province [and is] wholly invested in commercial pursuits, almost without exception in the prosecution of direct trade with the United States, the exports of produce exceeding the value of our imports of merchandise, by nearly one-hundred per centum"—this despite the oft criticized "scarcity of labor," which continued to be "felt more and more each year."[25]

Despite—or perhaps because of—this influx of U.S. nationals, they were being treated increasingly harsher by the authorities. "Five men, said to be Americans" were murdered in 1855 near the "Brazilian military post on the Peruvian frontier by order of the commander of that station, a [captain] in the Brazilian army"; when "they were <u>murdered</u>, they were upon their <u>knees</u> begging for their lives," yet were "shot down, like so many sheep" [emphasis-original].[26] "Almost all white foreigners that pass through this part of Peru are called Americans," thought one observer, which at once suggested the suspicion of these visiting U.S. nationals, their growing numbers, and the sharper reaction to them.[27]

Yet as draconian as such responses were, they did not exhaust the warp and woof of the danger involved in venturing into the rough and raw frontier that was the Amazon. In 1855, for example, there was a "fatal epidemic . . . the Asiatic cholera. . . . the number of deaths in this city during the month of June, was 510, of which 420 were of cholera and in many places in the interior, the mortality has been much greater. . . . the disease has been in great measure confined to the colored and Indian population"—yet another factor that cried out for an infusion of more enslaved Africans.[28]

Since the Maury family tree stretched over oceans and continents, perhaps it was not surprising that the most distinguished scion of this clan would devise such grandiose schemes. The "Fontaines and Maurys" could trace their ancestors back to France "in the year 1500," while others "settled in Virginia in 1716 and 1717."[29] In 1825, when he was about 18, Sam Houston himself recommended Maury for an appointment at the Naval Academy, who he deemed to be a "a young man of uncommonly fine talents."[30] His nephew, General Dabney Herndon Maury, who termed him "the most lovable man I ever knew," recalls that his uncle's potential bloomed late as he was " 'twenty-seventh' " at Annapolis and " 'there were only forty in the class.' " But he always had exhibited a resolute autodidacticism having pored over "Scott and other English classics," in his youth: he "was very fond of Shakespeare and all his life he read and studied the Bible," on which he exerted his "wonderful . . . power of concentration."[31] After graduating, in 1829, he was aboard the USS Vincennes in Callao on the western coast of South America, "busy making preparations for a voyage around the globe."[32]

These early ventures marked the coming trajectory of his life, as ocean currents and foreign adventures—especially in Brazil—were the keynotes of his future. It was Maury who debunked "another myth among merchant skippers . . . that the best route south to Rio de Janeiro was well outside Brazil's jutting Cape São Roque. . . . some captains nearly crossed the Atlantic all the way to Africa in order to avoid Brazil's cape. But Maury found—largely from the logs of skippers who had blundered inside Cape São Roque—that there were actually favorable currents that could be ridden out around the Cape and helpful winds close to land to add to a vessel's speed." As a result, "the age of [the] American clipper ship had begun," cutting the time in half to Brazil, i.e., "Baltimore to Rio in 38 days—17 days faster than the usual time." This facilitated, as well, travel to California,[33] as "the clippers' impressive performance were aided by the publication of Matthew Maury's charts of ocean winds and currents, which showed that the fastest course under sail was not always the shortest in miles."[34]

It was in 1850 that he zeroed in on Brazil, noting that "vessels traveling under Canvass from the Mouth of the Amazon to Europe to Rio to Africa, or around either of the Capes, must stand North, and pass not far from the West Indies. This fact . . . makes that river basin nearer to us than Brazil (if we call Rio[,] Brazil) and puts practically the mouth of that river almost as much within the Florida pass and under our control, as is the Mouth of the Mississippi."

Now with the Amazon River basin firmly in view he asked rhetorically, "who shall people the Great Valley of this Mighty Amazon? Shall it be peopled with an imbecile and an indolent people or by a go ahead race that has energy and enterprise equal to subdue the forest and to develop and bring forth the vast resources that lie hidden there?" Rather surreptitiously, Maury assigned William Herndon to explore this area in the early 1850s, putatively in violation of Brazilian sovereignty, to take on a "mission," whose "object" was to "prepare the way for that chain of routes which is to bring this result about"—i.e., to establish the suzerainty of the "race that has energy and enterprise": Euro-Americans. "Your going," he told the young Herndon, "is to be the first link in that chain which is to end in the establishment of the Amazonian Republic."

But what about Brazil? Dismissively, Maury roared that "it cannot no more prevent American citizens from the free, as well as from the slave states, from going there with their goods and chattels to settle and to revolutionize and republicanize and Anglo Saxonize that valley, than it can prevent the magazine from exploding after the firebrand that has been throw into it. That Valley is to [be] the safety valve for our Southern States, when they become over-populated with slaves, the African Slave Trade will be stopped, and they will send their slaves to the Amazon. Just as the Mississippi Valley has been the escape valve for the slaves of the Northern, now free, States, so will the Amazon be to that of the Mississippi." Britain, he thought, was beginning to feel too dependent on the U.S. South for cotton and might want to snatch the Amazon for that purpose—so Maury's initiative was preemptive. "The Valley," he declared, "in a few years will become to be regarded for all commercial purposes as a sort of an American Colony."

This was covert action of the first rank. "*In the first place,*" he insisted, "*the object of your journey should not be talked of*" [emphasis-original]. Maury provided a lengthy list of things Herndon should catalogue, including minerals and indigenous flora and fauna. "What are the able bodied sold at there? Is there any importation from Africa? To what extent and how do the untried slaves just from Africa compare in price with those who have been raised and trained in the country." In sum, "note down and take note of everything that you see, hear, feel or think while on the way down."[35] It was not long before the U.S. Consul in the Amazon "received from Mr. George Manning (agent for Lt. Maury) a letter of enquiry respecting the river Amazon and the Province of Para."[36]

The designated trailblazer, William Lewis Herndon, was peripatetic, having spent 1832 in Lisbon—a frequent port of call for those with dreams of expanding the bounds of bondage—and in 1837 was "anchored in Rio," then "cruising between Rio, Bahia and River Plata."[37] He was a "slight man who wore thin gold spectacles"; he had a "red beard running the edge of his jaw from temple to temple." He had "been at sea since he was fifteen" and had soldiered in the "Mexican War and the Second Seminole War." Like Maury, Herndon too had febrile dreams about Brazil; "the Valley of Amazon and the Valley of

Mississippi are commercial complements of each other—one supplying what the other lacks in the great commercial round. They are sisters which should not be separated"—something that Brazilian sovereignty was preventing. With this thought firmly in mind, he embarked on this perilous expedition to the "Deepest South" in 1851, noting as he crossed onto Brazilian soil that "the Commandant . . . never left me a moment to myself until he saw me safely in bed on board my boat. I did not know, at first, whether this was polite attention or a watch upon me, but I think it was the latter." Quite quickly this unease abated as he bumped into his compatriots—"everywhere on the river," he recounted, "I heard sounded the praises of my countrym[e]n." A bit optimistically he opined, "I presume that the Brazilian government would impose no obstacles to the settlement of this country by any of the citizens of the United States who would choose to go there and carry their slaves; and I know that the thinking people on the Amazon would be glad to see them." Going further, he added, "I am under the impression that, were Brazil to throw off a causeless jealousy, and a puerile fear of our people, and invite settlers to the Valley of the Amazon, there might be found, among our Southern planters, men, who looking with apprehension (if not for themselves, at least for their children) to the state of affairs as regards slavery at home, would, under sufficient guarantees, remove their slaves to that country, cultivate its lands, draw out its resources, and prodigiously augment the power and wealth of Brazil." Like Maury, Herndon was passionately optimistic about this region's prospects. "I have no hesitation in saying," he beamed, "that I believe in fifty years Rio [de] Janeiro, without losing a tittle of her wealth and greatness, will be but a village to Para and Para will be what New Orleans would long ago have been but for the activity of New York and her own fatal climate, the greatest city of the New World; Santarem will be St. Louis and . . . Cincinnati."

Also, like Maury, Herndon had a bold oceanographic vision for this region of Brazil, arguing that "ships sailing from the mouth of the Amazon, for whatever port of the world, are forced to our very doors by the southeast and northeast trade winds; that New York is the half-way house between Para and Europe." And this Herndon-Maury vision was not unique to them, for it was then that the young Mark Twain traveled down the Mississippi, thinking "he would book passage on the next ship out of New Orleans bound for Para, Brazil. Once there, he would work his way up the Amazon into its tributaries." For his part,

Herndon "musingly dropped a bit of green moss, plucked" from this U.S. river and "as it floated along I followed it, in imagination, down through the luxurious climes, the beautiful skies and enchanting scenery of the tropics, to the mouth of the great river; thence across the Caribbean Sea, through the Yucatan pass, into the Gulf of Mexico; thence along the Gulfstream, and so out upon the ocean, off the shores of the 'Land of Flowers.' " Herndon's enchanting analysis captured the imagination of a nation then imbued with the messianic revelation of "Manifest Destiny." Herndon turned their attention southward toward the largest prize of all, a prize that made seizing Cuba seem trivial by comparison. Herndon's report sold 10,000 copies in its first run; "three months later . . . another twenty thousand" were sold and "the book became an international best-seller."[38]

Written in April 1850, Herndon—who happened to be Maury's brother-in-law—spoke dramatically of the " 'universal Yankee Nation' " that was destined to blanket the hemisphere. The "purpose of Herndon's mission was to 'prepare the way for that chain of events . . . which is to end in the establishment of the Amazonian Republic.' " Once Brazil permitted U.S. nationals to "navigate the river, American settlers from the free and slave states would follow inevitably. . . . the Amazon would serve both as a 'safety valve' for excess southern slaves as well as a rich source of cotton for England." Repetitively, Herndon's patron emphasized that the Valley of the Amazon was " 'but a commercial appendage of the Mississippi,' closely connected to it by prevailing currents and winds. . . . according to Maury, a tree cut at the headwaters of the Missouri River and another cut at the headwaters of the Amazon would meet in the 'Straits of Florida' if each was allowed to float freely. The Amazon and Mississippi River basins, then, comprised . . . part of a vast undeveloped commercial empire which could be dominated by southern ports, such as New Orleans and Norfolk. . . . in a climate he believed . . . congenial to cotton, rice, tobacco and sugar cultivation, Maury expected southerners to settle, transplant their institutions, move their slaves, and become a virtual colony of the Mississippi Valley."[39]

But what if Brazil was unwilling to accede to the aggressive overtures of its more populous neighbor? Britain was not a passive witness either as this scheme was unfolding, and their man in Washington heard that Maury's response was " 'we mean to have a fight with her,' " meaning a Brazil unwilling to capitulate. As John Crampton saw it, "there will be one feature in regard to the Amazon which will ensure the popularity of any move in that direction in a great part of the Union—I mean the South—there will be no objection to the Southerners proceeding to that part of the world 'with their property' (that is, their Negroes), as there was in regard to California from which that 'property' was excluded by Congress altho' the country was conquered, as they (the Southerners) said with their blood and treasure as much as with that of the North. They are still indignant at this prohibition"—which could mean bowing to Maury's Brazilian scheme or, alternatively, heightening regional tensions in a giant step toward Civil War: in any case, Brazil was at issue.[40]

Reflecting this tension over Brazil were the words of the radical Southern extremist, Edmund Ruffin. He denounced the "hypocricy [*sic*] of the pretended horrors of slavery," which was supposedly "actuating Northern abolitionists." Why focus on the "Southern states," he wondered querulously and not "Brazil," where slavery was indeed "inhuman & horrible." This led him to dangerous ground: "if our secession & independence were once accomplished," he thought, "& Northern politicians could no longer command votes or power by denouncing slavery, we should be nearly as safe from their anti-slavery action as are Brazil & Cuba now."[41]

Just as Dixie nationalists were coming to intertwine their fate with that of Brazil and Cuba, this prospect was also dawning on others. As the Maury-Herndon project was gaining traction, Congressman David Wilmot observed that "slavery looks forward with exulting confidence" to the "revival of the foreign slave trade, and to an alliance offensive and defensive with Brazil for the protection and aggrandizement of slavery and to enable it to defy the public opinion and power of the world."[42] The recently founded newspaper, the **New York Times,** took careful note of the words of a counterpart journal in South Carolina which called on its readers to follow the " 'true policy,' " i.e., " 'to look to Brazil as the next great slave power. . . . *instead of courting England, we should look to Brazil* [emphasis-original]. . . . The time will come when a treaty of commerce and alliance with Brazil will give us the control over the Gulf of Mexico and its border countries, together with the islands, and the consequence of this will place African Slavery beyond the reach of fanaticism, at home or abroad. These two great Slave Powers now hold more undeveloped territory than any other two governments, and they ought to guard and strengthen their mutual interests by acting together in strict harmony and concert."[43]

The Brazilian Foreign Ministry paid close attention to these plots—for which it had not been consulted—on its territory. It obtained and translated a copy of Maury's message to William Graham, U.S. Secretary of the Navy, and could not have been pleased. The Amazon, rhapsodized Maury, was in a "country that sends its waters from South America into the Caribbean Sea" and was the "grandest and most magnificent water-shed in the world. . . . the Mississippi and its tributaries have been called 'Inland Seas.' The Amazon is an 'Inland Ocean.' . . . the Gulf Stream as it gathers strength to force itself through . . . Florida . . . sweeps by the mouth of the Amazon as it does by the Delta of the Mississippi. . . . from a commercial point of view, the whole of South America is but a peninsula pendent from the North and as dependent upon North America as peninsulas usually are upon the main. . . . were the navigation of the Amazon open to our citizens, much of Equador [*sic*], most of Peru and nearly all of Bolivia might be supplied with articles of American growth and manufacture through it instead of around Cape Horn, and then on the backs of donkeys across the Cordilleras and the Puna, up the Andes and down again. . . . the silver mines of Peru and Bolivia would probably soon receive a new impulse. . . . their produce would flow down the Amazon along the great equatorial and Gulf Stream currents to our very doors and so assist to balance the stream of gold which we are to expect and almost to fear from California." The Amazon region, thought Maury, was a prize waiting to be developed and this idea—repeatedly—was linked to the companion notion of U.S. bondage. "Is the time yet to come when the United States are [too] overpeopled with the black race? And if so, when shall an outlet be found for them? In the Valley of the Amazon."[44]

The Brazilian press also got wind of Maury's plans. It was "feared," said one journalist from Rio de Janeiro, "that the U. States will hasten to arrange . . . for the navigation of some of the tributaries of the Amazon and thus judge themselves authorized to enter the Amazon from within, as its journals of New York & New Orleans already propose. We have been careless on this matter and must now hurry about it," it was said with anxiety. "This nation of pirates," it was said of the U.S., "like those of their race wish to dispossess all the people of America who are not Anglo-Saxons." This article made it to the hands of Maury's comrade, William Graham, who filed it away for future reference.[45]

Graham, whose role as Secretary of the Navy placed him in a strategic position, saw Maury's Amazon plan as part of a larger scheme for South America. He was told in 1852 that "the defeat and expulsion of Rosas from Buenos Ayres will open to the trade of the world the fine countries bordering on the Uruguay and Paraguay Rivers. Our government ought to be among the first to take advantage of that opening."[46] For the longest time, the U.S. had paid insufficient attention to the nation that became Argentina but as "the news of the assembling of a Congress of representatives from the principal Latin American states at Lima, Peru early in 1843, where Mexican–United States relations were to be considered," Washington became "more concerned about [its] prestige in South America." Certainly, the war of aggression against Mexico in 1846 could hardly be ignored by Latin America. Henry Wise had once told John C. Calhoun that " 'the U. States and Brazil are the two elder sisters of North and South America and are in a moral sense responsible for the whole family of states in the New World.' "[47] But even Brazil, admitted to parity with the U.S. in Wise's formulation, was beginning to think that, instead, a fate akin to Mexico was the destiny slotted for it by Washington.

Maury's relationship to Graham showed that his designs on the Amazon were not apparitions, for this North Carolinian was a "unanimous" choice in 1852 as "candidate for the Office of Vice President,"[48] while Millard Fillmore found their "official intercourse" to have "been so intimate and so entirely harmonious."[49] The potent politician from New York told Graham that he had a "vacant room" at his house "at your services" and almost demanded that he "become our guest during the time you remain in the city."[50]

Maury would need these powerful contacts that reached into the inner sanctums of the White House if his ambitious proposals were to become reality. Seeking to outflank a Brazil that was hesitant to open its territory to a nation that some there viewed as piratical, Maury proposed to Graham that the U.S. "negotiate a treaty, guaranteeing to Peru" certain "islands" near "Amazonia," "on condition that she would open one or more of the river towns in her Amazonian provinces to American commerce by making them ports of entry; or whether we might not go further, and in consideration of the guaranty, ask of Peru this right of navigation to be exclusive to the American flag, together with that of the coterminous nations only, as Brazil, Bolivia, etc. Thus, by getting such a right from Bolivia and the other states whose territories are drained by that river and its navigable tributaries, we should exclude France and England with their mischievous abolitionists from those waters and from a participation with us." Like many aggressive men in Washington before and since, he saw the "State Department" as "inefficient"—"nobody there seems to understand South American affairs," he groused, while he was dreamy about the prospects, suggesting that Herndon's report would "show the country [Brazil] to be all you ever imagined of it."[51]

After dispatching Herndon southward, the prolific Maury then picked up his pen and with a pseudonym of South American vintage—"Inca"—in the canonical publication of the Slave South, **De Bow's Review,** began to propagandize further on behalf of his ambitious Amazon plan. "Our commercial transactions with Brazil and the valley of the Rio de la Plata," he insisted, "are already worth more than they were any of the countries of Europe, except Great Britain and France" —and that did not include the illicit slave trade. It was the South that should spearhead this Brazilian initiative, he said, already intimating that he saw this region as a separate nation: "if the South do not make haste soon to take it up and embark in it, we may rest assured the North will not be slow" for "that Valley is a slave country" and should remain that way. "Wherever they are found, the African delights to dwell; and he alone is equal to the task which man has to accomplish with the axe in the valley of the Amazon" for "the settlement of the valley of the Amazon, its relation to this country, its bearings upon our future commerce and withal so potential, that the destiny of the United States seems to be closely connected with, wrapped up in, and concealed by this question." The Amazon was the future: "there will soon be no more Mississippi lands to clear, no more cotton fields to subdue, and unless some means be devised of getting rid of the Negro increase, the time must come—and sooner or later it will come—when there will be an excess in these states of black people."

There was a precedent for this as the "New England states and the Middle states did not emancipate their slaves; they banished them," but the "South could not, if she would, banish her slaves and tell the world that it is emancipation; for she has no place of banishment to send them to." And they could not be expropriated for "did ever any people incur such a tax? History affords no example of any. . . . unless some means of relief be devised, some channel afforded by which the South can, when the time comes, get rid of the excess of her slave population, that she will be ultimately found, with regard to this institution, in the predicament of [those] with the wolf by the ears—too dangerous to hold on any longer, and equally dangerous to let it go." For "sooner or later, come it will, and come it must—when the two races will join in the death struggle for the mastery. The valley of the Amazon is the way; in this view, it is the safety-valve of the Union. It is slave territory and a wilderness." The idea was "the entire suppression of the African slave trade with Brazil"—following Wise—"by a substitution of a slave emigration from the United States."[52]

"We are nearer to the Amazon, or rather to the mouth of it than any other nation," said Maury. "China wants to trade with us, but Japan stands by the way-side and shuts herself up and out of the world. She is not in the fellowship of nations, and we send a fleet there to remind her that she cannot be of the world and live out of it at one and the same time"—Brazil should get the same treatment, he thought. For "the five Spanish-American republics want to trade up and down the Amazon; but Brazil, worse than Japan on the wayside, stands right in the *door-way* and says, 'Nay, I will neither use the Amazon myself nor permit others to use it'" [emphasis-original]. This was little more than a "state of war," this was "their policy." Brazil and "her rulers have had" the Amazon "for three hundred years, and the first practical step towards subduing it and developing its resources, has yet to be taken." This was "the question of the day. The problem of the age is that of the free navigation of the Amazon and the settlement of the Atlantic slopes of South America."[53] "The time will come" he predicted, "when the free navigation of the Amazon will be considered by the people of this country as second in importance, by reason of its conservative effects, to the acquisition of Louisiana"—"if it be *second* at all" [emphasis-original].[54] This explosive message was taken directly to the halls of Congress.[55]

Maury also addressed directly the commanding North Carolinian, William Graham. "When the states of the Union were all on the waters of the Atlantic," he said in October 1850, "we had a seafront of only 2000 miles. But now, our ocean front is more than double that." The expansion into California and the fact that getting there from the East often led to Cape Horn, inevitably made the U.S. vision more capacious. "Then, the shortest way from state to state was within our own borders and by inland channels of communication; now, [it] is through foreign countries, and by a double sea voyage." This meant the "Navy must be challenged or we shall fail properly to provide for the common defense of the Pacific coasts." But on the west coast of the U.S. there

were "no shipyards, public or private, no timber sheds stored with timber, no railroads to fetch it from the forest; & no mechanics, except at
exorbitant rates to build them." Consequently, a "considerable increase
of the Navy is called for on account of our acquisitions & the settlement of our people on the Pacific Coast." Like slavers who looked to
whalers, Maury did the same—but to the navy, looking to "10,000
American seamen employed in the whaling business" to join this U.S.
force, along with "the merchant sailors."[56]

He also spread this message to Brazil. "Now for the last two years I
have been urging upon the government to make a treaty with Brazil,"
he said in 1851, "and to remind her in that treaty that we are her best
customers for coffee; that nearly all she produces is consumed in the
United States, where it is admitted duty free, and of course the con-
sumption is largely increased thereby." There was a condition, however.
"I have urged that we should say to Brazil in that treaty, 'Stop the
African slave trade, or we will put a duty on that coffee, and thus lessen
the demand for the fruits of slave labor.'" This did not mean stop slavery, however. For "the people of Amazonia will have slaves—they are
very near to the coast of Africa, and if they cannot get them in one they
will in another. The alternative is, shall Amazonia be supplied with this
class from the United States or from Africa? In the former case, it will
be a transfer of the place of servitude, but the making of no new slaves.
In the latter, it will be making slaves of free men" and "in the former
it would be relieving our own country of the slaves."[57] As pressure
mounted in the Slave South, Maury saw his plan as the most reasonable
alternative. "I cannot be blind to what I see going on here. It is coming
to be a matter of faith among leading southern men that the time is
rapidly approaching when, in order to prevent this war of the races and
its horrors," the white South "in self-defence" would "be compelled to
conquer parts of Mexico and Central America and make slave territory
of what is now free."[58] Moreover, as Maury saw it, his country had to
strike first in the Amazon as a pre-emption of rivals in London and
Paris. The U.S. had to "exclude France and England, with their mischievous abolitionists, from those waters," i.e., the Amazon River.[59]

Brazil was not standing aside idly as other nations were contemplating its territorial integrity, however. Fearing filibustering, Brazil cut a
deal with Peru restricting navigation of ships in this region and in 1867
the Amazon was finally opened to "world commerce."[60] Brazil's lega-

tion in the U.S. monitored carefully the North American conversation about the prospect of seizing their territory.

Maury's was not a lone voice in the wilderness calling for action in the Amazon and signaling the importance of Brazil, though these voices were not necessarily in accord with every jot of his proposals. The **Southern Standard** of Charleston felt that "instead of courting England, we should look to Brazil and the West Indies. These two great slave powers now hold more undeveloped territory than any other two governments"; thus, if the Slave South and Brazil chose to "act together by treaty we cannot only preserve domestic servitude . . . we can defy the power of the world." The Slave South had "been too long governed by psalm-singing schoolmasters from the North" and the time had long since come for a change. A sort of slave imperialism was proposed, as it was said, "the time will come that all islands and regions suited to African Slavery, between us and Brazil, will fall under the control of those two slave powers." With audacity, it was proposed "to take Cuba. To conquer St. Domingo and reduce its inhabitants to slavery. To unite with Brazil . . . to enter into an alliance with Brazil." Said a nameless abolitionist voice, "it is seldom [one] will find more of what is being called 'letting the cat out of the bag' . . . the [Kansas]-Nebraska bill is but the first," this was the "easy step in this comprehensive plan of Africanizing the whole of the American hemisphere."[61] Said another, the Slave South was looking to an "alliance, offensive and defensive with Brazil,"[62] while another declared, "it was predicted twenty years ago, that if [the Slave South] got Texas, it would not stop until it reached Brazil."[63]

Naturally, this idea of dispatching U.S. Negroes to the "Deepest South" did not evade the attention of the intended victims. Writing from exile in Canada, one editorialist ridiculed the "stupendous scheme of the Slave Power," this attempt to "secure an outlet for their surplus slave population, now staring them in the face like doom. If they could but get a foothold in that rich tropical [Amazon] valley, establish slavery there by arrangement with Brazil, create a commerce between it and the Southern States, direct and institute lines of steamship, slaves could be transported with convenience . . . a great slaveholding empire would arise, fortifying the system at home and removing for centuries the only danger which threatened it."[64] The **Provincial Freeman** reacted sharply to Maury's plan to "memorialize Congress" to "send one or two small naval steamers up the Amazon River for the purpose of exploring its tributaries" and "that the government of Brazil be requested to permit these vessels to make explorations and surveys of the shores of the Amazon belonging to that nation." They sensed the implications of the idea of converting " 'the mouth of the Amazon and the mouth of Mississippi into one' "—this would be a boon for the consolidation of hemispheric slavery. They did not miss the import of the point that " 'ships sailing from the mouth of the Amazon for whatever port of the world, are forced to float to our very doors by the S.E. trade winds; that New York is the half-way house between Para and Europe.' " They recognized that U.S. Negroes would be on the move southward when " 'Southern planters, men, who looking with apprehension . . . to the state of affairs' " of " 'slavery at home, would under sufficient guarantees, remove their slaves' " to Brazil.[65]

Frederick Douglass also was alarmed by these Amazon plans. "We noticed with no small interest," he said, "the published accounts of the large expeditions which the last season sailed out of New York, to explore this father of Rivers and its borders," which were initiated by the "capitalists of our metropolis," along with "other large expeditions which lately sailed from San Francisco to Peru and Equador [*sic*]." It was stated "publicly" that "unsuccessful efforts have been made to engage Brazil in a treaty with the United States for the protection and propagation of slavery on the continent." As Douglass saw it, there was more to fear from "filibustering" in Brazil, more so than Cuba, the U.S.'s immediate neighbor.[66]

On the other hand, because of the rather benign view of Brazil taken by a number of U.S. Negroes, there were other voices that echoed Maury's sentiments about sending this group southward—not for slavery but for freedom. "I am neither a Northern agitating Abolitionist nor an Ebony-line Colonizationist . . . I am . . . a let-alone-ist," said a man identified as "Chr. Reemlin," but compared to the U.S., he saw Brazil as the " 'promised land.' " Looking ahead he foresaw a time "a hundred years" hence "after the abolition of the slave trade" when there "will be a hundred millions of white people within the United States. How proportionally small will then the black population be compared to the white!" What to do? Well, there was "in America a country, a climate and a soil, on which the Negro may yet be free and great," and this was "South America, on the Amazon River, the Orinoco" which was "but half the distance from Africa that Europe is the United States. . . . South

America may become to the Negro what North America is to the European—a freer field for his higher development." Brazil, he thought,
"may yet accept similar offers to those made by the Negro King of
Dahomey in 1796 to Portugal, which were, to bring about a Negro emigration on a large scale, and with it to colonize and overrun the greater
part of Eastern South America." Since Brazil had banned the slave
trade, "it will soon feel the effects of the stoppage of its annual supply
of population and then it will be in the proper humor to try the new
experiment."[67]

Despite the sunny optimism, these sentiments may have been misplaced, because Brazilian elites for good reason and bad were not necessarily open to an influx into their nation of U.S. Negroes. Certainly,
Matthew Maury had a more ramified network of contacts in the Lusophone world than virtually any African-American. He was in particular
close touch with William Figaniere, Portugal's long-time representative
in the U.S., who was suspected of involvement in facilitating the slave
trade. "I regret that I was not in town when you did me the favor to call
at the [Naval] Observatory," Maury told him in the fall of 1856, as he
added thanks for the "documents and parcels which you were kind
enough to leave."[68] Perhaps prompted by Maury, Figaniere contacted
the U.S. Navy telling him that the "Navy Department at Lisbon is desirous of obtaining a copy of the . . . work on 'Boat Armament.' "[69]
J. A. Dahlgren instructed this Portuguese national that "the late operations of our Naval force against the Chinese forts near Canton, have
afforded another evidence of the power of the Howitzer against masses
of men who lack the discipline and nerve of the troops of civilized
nations. And although I trust that your settlement at Macao may not be
molested, yet a due supply of Field Howitzers supported by rifled muskets would afford the best security against any attempt on the part of
the Chinese."[70] Helpfully, Maury forwarded for Lisbon, a "parcel containing six sets of charts of the Japan expedition (Commander Perry)
. . . to transmit the same for the use of the Portuguese Marine."[71]
During this time this Portuguese representative—quite strikingly—was
making repeated requests for detailed maps of the U.S. and was also
"asking for the best published information" held by the U.S. Patent
Office "in respect to the culture and manipulation of the cotton."[72]
As the Civil War approached, Maury's contact with Lisbon increased
sharply and, in turn, Portugal was foisting various awards upon him,[73]
not least because over the years this—then—U.S. national supplied this

pioneering nation of navigation with considerable technical information about the seas.

Appropriately given his knowledge of the oceans, Maury had a truly global network,[74] which allowed him to see more clearly than most the importance of the Amazon for his nation's ambitions. Moreover, such contacts would prove to be useful when he joined with others in the Slave South to secede from the U.S.; for even before secession, Maximilian who seized Mexico when Washington was embroiled in Civil War, told Maury "with affection of a friend," that he was "deeply moved at your generous and flattering proposal to enter my service if I am ever called to ascend the Mexican throne. . . . I hope the day will come when you and I will play a prominent role together."[75] Though skeptical of French abolitionists, Maury was embraced by Paris, even before this nation moved to seize Mexico.[76]

This paid off for France when during the height of the Civil War, Maury announced that "should the enemies of my country," speaking of the Confederate States of America, "attempt to assert their Monroe Doctrine when you ascend your throne, then it may become the policy of Mexico, as it is already the interest of the Confederacy to see California withdrawn from her present political associations. Though never a resident of that state," Maury conceded, "I am not altogether unknown to the people there," not least since so many from the Slave South had migrated there. "I might be of some service in assisting its dismemberment," he added helpfully. "A few good ironclads quietly sent around Cape Horn at an early day would find themselves complete masters of the coast; for the Federals have nothing in the Pacific that could cope with them." A double-dealer of rare skill, Maury was also willing to "tender" his "resignation . . . in the Confederate Navy . . . whenever you may require my services" and swear loyalty to Mexico.[77]

There was also sentiment among Maury's comrades to try to restore slavery in Mexico, which along with Cuba and Brazil, could become a formidable bondage bloc that could ultimately challenge Washington profoundly. But a few weeks after the Civil War ended, an informant in Richmond while conceding that "we are, it is true, in a very unhappy condition; & the prospect before is not bright," was "satisfied" that "we shall fare better here than in a Catholic, Spanish country." Worse, it was "not possible to get the Negroes to go away from here with their former owners. They are all turned loose & are as wild as zebras" [emphasis-original].[78] Thus, Maury was reduced to endorsing a plan to go to "China for labourers,"[79] which—as it turned out—became something of a substitute for enslaved Africans in the wake of the Civil War. Later after reconciling with Washington, he perked up at the idea of "San Domingo annexation. . . . if it be annexed," he told a friend, "there may be a field open there, for the display of your talents. . . . the best of mahogany comes thence and in the olden times the coffee and sugar planters there did splendidly and since emancipation everything has gone to ruin."[80]

Maury, who had a more spacious vision than his comrades from the Slave South—a vision that incorporated Brazil—was a diehard Confederate, "he was one of the last Southerners to despair of the ultimate issue of the Rebellion, which he hoped to see protracted over a dozen or more years."[81] Again, though Maury was emblematic, he was not unique. An "organization familiarly known as the 'Knights of the Golden Circle' was bound under an ironclad oath to uphold the interest of the Southern Confederacy at any cost" and was said to have "numbered 100,000 men."[82] Another Virginian, Edward Bryan, had proclaimed that "he would like to see slavery cover the entire area from Norfolk to Rio de Janeiro."[83] And at that juncture, the Slave South would be following Maury's scheme and exporting Negroes to the Amazon—and feasting on the profits.

Maury's bold schemes were indicative of an era when citizenship was blurred and territories were being seized promiscuously. Most of all, it was a period when huge profits were to be made from buying and selling Africans. However, the official ban of the African Slave Trade, a ban which many Virginians supported, did create an "artificial" blockage in the market. But what if this were to change?

7

Making the Slave Trade Legal?

" 'It is truly lamentable,' " said Abraham Lincoln just before his election as President, " 'that Great Britain and the United States should be obliged to spend such a vast amount of blood and treasure for the suppression of the African slave trade.' "[1] His words reflected a deepening reality: the trade to Brazil had slowed down considerably, not least because of external pressure from London; but, perhaps as a result of this pressure in or about Rio de Janeiro, as Lincoln's victorious election approached, "just one British cruiser went on a slave trade patrol off the coast of Cuba in 1861."[2]

This chapter concerns the spectacular rise in the illicit African Slave Trade in the late 1850s and how the apparent victory of those who profited from this commerce ironically sounded the tocsin for the institution of slavery, as emboldened fire-eaters from Dixie overplayed their hand and pushed the nation toward Civil War.

Just as cracking down on the sale of illegal drugs in one neighborhood can serve to increase this traffic in adjacent areas, the pressure in the "Deepest South" was causing the illegal trade to grow in areas north of Brazil. Moreover, it seemed that "American traders were anxious to ship all the slaves they could before Lincoln's known views could take effect."[3]

At this moment, New York City "was gaining the dubious honor of being 'the greatest slave-trading mart in the world' "; by 1857, this metropolis, perhaps more so than New Orleans, the logical contender for this title, was " 'the commercial center of the slave trade.' During the months from January 1859 to August 1860, it was conservatively estimated, close to one hundred vessels left the city for the slave trade."[4] The trade in Africans had become so commonplace[5] that the press in Gotham began to speak of various ethnic groups from this continent in the same way they might have discussed the merits of a Chablis versus a

Merlot.[6] A formidable infrastructure for the slave trade had developed in this city that included ship fitters, suppliers, attorneys, recruiters of crews, and bribed marshals and custom agents. One longtime federal judge in New York, Samuel Rossiter Betts, later lauded as the father of U.S. maritime law, set a standard of proof so high that slave trade convictions were rare and severe punishment even rarer.[7]

This infrastructure also meant that it was a simpler matter to bring slaves to the U.S. itself.[8] This brought the ugliness of the African Slave Trade that much closer to U.S. shores, thereby exacerbating tensions— and not just between North and South but, as well, between the Upper South of Wise's Virginia, which remained hostile to the trade, and the Lower South. In addition, the prices of enslaved Africans were cheaper in Brazil than in the U.S., which was a further incentive to take the risk of bringing them to the Slave South, where prices were higher.[9]

In fact, as the pivotal decade of the 1850s was drawing to a close, the price of enslaved Africans was rising, giving more incentive to smugglers to tempt fate. One domestic trader's books revealed that prices rose in 1855—generally—from $450 to $810 and a few years later by considerably more.[10] Yet, as one reporter noted during this same period, "slaves of ten to twelve years of age up to an adult can be bought on the Congo River at $25 or $30 per head and landed in New Orleans or Texas for $30 more, making the cost $60; but call it $100."[11] The profits were too handsome to ignore easily.

Thus, in the Deep South the African Slave Trade "cause was increasingly put forward as part and parcel of the southern nationalist agenda." Some "Texas county conventions of the Democratic Party passed resolutions in favor of the slave trade, and Hardin R. Rummels, a secessionist and advocate of the African slave trade, defeated Sam Houston in the gubernatorial elections."[12] In the spring of 1857, the incendiary Southern nationalist, Edmund Ruffin, argued that reopening the slave trade was "obviously impossible so long as the present union with the northern states lasts"—which pointed to secession. "All the southern states suffer greatly from the scarcity & high price of labor," he complained, yet they could "obtain no supply from abroad." Ruffin, who kept a close eye on such matters, also noticed when "a first cousin of President James K. Polk, [Leonidas] Spratt" became an "ardent champion of the slave trade, having presented to the Montgomery Commercial Convention of 1858 a series of resolutions calling for a reopening of the African Slave Trade."[13]

J. D. B. De Bow of New Orleans was elected President of the "African Labor Supply Association," organized at Vicksburg months after Spratt's initiative, with a stated aim of reopening the trade.[14] " 'We must have Africans,' " De Bow insisted with passion.[15] In January 1859, influential South Carolina Congressman, William Porcher Miles, "added his voice to those of James De Bow and the fire-eating Southerner, William L. Yancey, in calling for a repeal of federal laws that prohibited the African slave trade."[16]

There was something in the air. The filibuster, William Walker—a Southerner who happened to be in Europe during the failed revolutions of 1848—had his eyes on hemispheric expansion "intended not only to reestablish slavery, but to revive the African slave trade. . . . slaves would not be carried to Central America from the southern states, because the demand for Negroes in the Lower South was already greater than the supply."[17] Walker, who ruled briefly in Nicaragua, was said by a comrade to have been an "advocate" of this idea "to an extreme degree, and believed in it with the same zeal and fervor that a Christian believes in the truth of the Christian religion."[18] Sober voices were thinking—and debating—the previously unthinkable. The attorney, Robert Harper, was worried about the presence in his country of more "millions of wild Africans," yet he conceded that reopening the trade now had a "degree of importance which no longer admits of its being treated with silence or contempt." Yes, it would heavily profit the Northeast due to their "kidnapping propensities" but Brazil—a "feeble state"—showed that imports could occur despite the "discouragements and harassments of a British squadron."[19]

Harper had a point. The 1850s crackdown by London on the illegal trade to Brazil impelled those in the U.S. who benefited from this commerce to look elsewhere for profit, which was exacerbating tension in the hemisphere and elsewhere. One journal linked the fate of the U.S. with Russia and Turkey, as a result.[20] Spain, a slave trading scofflaw of U.S. dimensions, began to worry that the enthusiasm for bondage in Cuba's northern neighbor was becoming so intense that Madrid would have to worry about further filibustering escapades in its Caribbean territories.[21] Their Consul in Galveston—long a hotbed of slave smuggling —worried that this town was one of the "most active centers of permanent conspiracy against Cuba."[22]

The apotheosis of the illegal slave trade to Brazil came in the 1850s when a severe crackdown there allied with rising prices in the U.S. to create enormous pressure to reopen the African Slave Trade and, barring that, facilitating a torrent of smuggled slaves. While slavery was the prime cause of the Civil War, a closely allied factor was tension arising from the slave trade.

Rather defensively, one pro-slavery ideologue in the U.S. after noting that a "very extensive commerce exists at this time and has long existed between our Northern ports and the empire of Brazil, and the most amicable relations are maintained, notwithstanding the prevalence of slavery in the latter," yet, he wondered waspishly, "we hear of no abductions of slaves from [Brazil]" by the "pious philanthropists of the North." This was just more hypocrisy, it was said. "The Amazon" was "owned by both Brazil and Peru" and "the harmony between the governments of those countries is not disturbed by this fact"—so why couldn't an independent Slave South share the Ohio and Mississippi Rivers with the U.S.? Again, double-standards and rank hypocrisy barred such realism, it was thought.[23]

As time passed, the Virginians—Wise and Maury—were losing ground. This duo were increasingly being viewed as being parochial and selfish, narrowly defending the interests of their slave-exporting state. The illicit slave trade to Brazil had been hampered but the traders themselves had not been run out of business, and the idea of using their infrastructure to bring more enslaved Africans to North America gained traction. In turn, those of the Wise-Maury persuasion echoed the sentiments of a "Georgian secessionist" in opposing the African Slave Trade who "asked the Virginia [secession] convention, 'Why, we would soon be drowned in a black pool; we would be literally overwhelmed with a black pool; we would be literally overwhelmed with a black population.'"[24] In 1858, Wise himself filed away an article that reflected the growing temper of the times: "It is a great loss to the United States and to the commerce of the world," it was said, "to have vast tracts of cotton and sugar lands in the Southwest remain wild and uncultivated for the want of African labor. Without an increase of African labor in the New World its white population, with that of Europe, must have its independence increased on the British possessions in India, and at greatly enhanced prices, which, it is believed, has been the long cherished desire of the East India Company." At this moment, "about three out of every five vessels employed in the slave trade" were "fitted out in the United States and the remainder in Cuba. About two-thirds of those sent from the United States are fitted out in the port of New York." This trade "was carried on almost exclusively on the Congo River, or from neighboring points," particularly northern Angola—then, as now, a region pockmarked by unrest and poor infrastructure.[25]

The New York writer, Henry J. Raymond, was incensed with this developing momentum toward reopening the African Slave Trade and lashed out bitterly at William Yancey, a principal proponent. He was, said Raymond, seeking to "secure the repeal of the laws of Congress" against the trade "in order to extend slavery into the Territories. . . . To use your words, 'We of Alabama want slaves to be cheap—we want to buy them, not to sell them. It is a Virginia idea' "—a Maury and Wise idea—" 'that slaves ought to be high. Virginia wants $1500 each for her Negroes: we want to get them cheaper.' 'Cheap Negroes' is the grand consummation at which you aim." But this was not only designed for exploiting the "territories"; Yancey and his cohorts had coopted Maury's idea of expanding further into the hemisphere. He was, said Raymond, so determined that he would "destroy the Union" to do so. "Why? Because it does not permit the continuance of the African Slave Trade."[26]

This claim was continuously being repeated in the North of the U.S.; in a sense, they were arguing that more than slavery, it was the slave trade that was the locomotive impelling Civil War. Henry Wilson of Massachusetts took to the floor of the U.S. Senate in May 1860 to denounce this trend. The "Republic of the United States," he charged, "which began its existence by the condemnation of the African slave traffic—is the most powerful supporter of that traffic among the nations." What had inflamed his ire was a recent court decision in South Carolina that asserted that "importing Africans who were not free in Africa is no offence against the Act of 1820 and is not therefore punishable as piracy." This was a loophole through which could be driven vessel after vessel filled to the brim with enslaved Africans, in a manner that mimicked what occurred in Brazil in the 1840s—with, most likely, some of the same U.S. nationals who were active there pushing this development. There had been a change in the South since the 1820s when many in that region had applauded the cessation of the trade, he thought, and Wilson did not like what had risen in its place. Wilson also sensed that the Brazil trade had created momentum that ineluctably had created "blowback" on these shores.[27]

Wilson was shrewd to be concerned about developments in the Palmetto State, since a few years before his peroration, a legislative committee deliberated reopening the trade. The "minority" which exhorted that the "epithet 'piracy' is an insult" to the slaveholder, sought to adhere to the Wise-Maury view by arguing that there was a "vast distinction between upholding Slavery and upholding the Slave Trade," for doing the latter would "decrease the value of our slaves." They too were concerned about "rivals to fear," e.g., Brazil but thought this threat could be met without using draconian measures. They dismissed the notion that reopening the trade was "for the advantage of the poor non-slaveholder" and the hint that the "opposition to it springs from a determination on the part of slaveholders to prevent the participation of their poor fellow citizens . . . and to maintain a species of slave aristocracy." This was dangerous reasoning since, a la Brazil, increasing the number of Negroes could make this community more rebellious. Perceptively it was added that there was a "universal opinion abroad, that we retain our authority through the ignorance of our slaves as to their real strength"—an advantage that could be compromised if the numbers of enslaved increased dramatically.[28]

It was "well known," said the legislature, "that the British Government has a predominating influence at the Spanish and Brasilian courts" and wanted to drag Cuba, Brazil, and the Slave South down to the supposed level of their possessions in the West Indies. "Southern civilization & southern resources & prosperity are endangered as well from <u>foreign</u> as from internal influences" [emphasis-original]. Cuba and, more potently, Brazil, were seen as fire walls protecting U.S. slavery, with a breach in that southern wall ultimately imperiling what came to be the Confederacy. Reopening the slave trade was one way of fighting London and augmenting slavery's strength. But even if London succeeded in barring slavery in Brazil and Cuba—which was "not unlikely"—reopening the trade was called for since in that event "an active competition [in] the sugar & tobacco market will spring up between" the Slave South and "the rest of the world. This competition will call for an additional supply of slaves, independent of the demand of the cotton interest, & thus an additional inducement will be held out for the importation of Africans." Moreover, the North received European immigrants to settle new territories on the continent and, thus, the South needed enslaved Africans to compete with this. "No time should be lost," they beseeched, to bring in more Africans.[29] Indeed, if there was no slave trade, it was argued disingenuously, "the effect would be to shut up the population of the Negro countries within their own borders. It is well known that there is not and cannot be any such thing as voluntary emigration from these countries. The slave trade is the only outlet" and if it were blocked, this would be akin to "prohibiting emigration," which would not be done to Europe, so why do it to Africa?[30]

"Free trade" in Africans was the demand, with "low duties" besides. The clause in the Constitution on the slave trade showed that "Congress has no authority to prohibit the slave trade by virtue of its power to regulate commerce. . . . this prohibitory power belongs to the state[s]," it was said.[31]

Further south in Savannah, which had been the initial port of entry for a considerable number of enslaved Africans, stories were proliferating in the press featuring citizens assembling to urge Congress to repeal all laws interdicting the importation of Africans.[32] This occurred as the Georgia Senate debated a bill to strike out a clause in the Constitution barring importation of slaves from abroad,[33] while the Southern Commercial Convention passed a resolution in favor of repeal of federal laws barring the trade.[34] Of course, the press in this Deep South city covered the fact that the trade on the coast of Africa was flourishing,[35] not least due to dozens of vessels owned by U.S. nationals and the goodly number of vessels embarking from New York City.[36] Locally, John Du Bignon was found "not guilty" after being charged with landing enslaved Africans on Jekyl Island.[37]

Further west in 1858, a "committee of the Louisiana legislature approved a bill which would have permitted citizens" of this state "to import slaves from Brazil, Cuba and Africa." In a sense this was simply ratifying practice since "for almost two decades after the Louisiana Purchase, slave smuggling was carried on to such an extent that it was almost common."[38] This idea of reopening the slave trade was linked, as in Louisiana, with the development of other markets, particularly Brazil. This stood to reason as the dream of exploiting the Amazon with its seemingly impenetrable jungle seemed ideal for slave labor and a potential rich field of investment besides. For example, the **Southern Standard** of Charleston, South Carolina counseled that if the Slave South and Brazil sought to "act together by treaty *we cannot only preserve domestic servitude, but we can defy the power of the world. . . . we can* open up the African Slave emigration again" [emphasis-original].[39]

Further west still, in Texas, "the legislature ordered the printing of 10,000 copies of John Henry Brown's report favoring the slave trade," while Sam Houston termed the Democrats a "slave trade party." Senator Stephen Douglas claimed in 1859 that "15,000 Africans had been imported" of late, while newspapers of that era carried "thinly veiled" ads for "newly acquired Africans."[40] That same crucial year, 1859, the "Republican Association of Washington" charged flatly that the "African Slave Trade with the United States [is] now actually reopened . . . the current information of the day leaves no room to doubt that cargoes of slaves are being landed from time to time, in the Gulf States and that preparations are being made to enter upon the traffic in good earnest and upon a large scale. . . . capital enough, ships enough and seamen enough can be found in New York City alone, to supply to the Gulf States one hundred thousand Negroes annually."[41]

Denizens of Manhattan had noticed this development since among them resided some of the major actors in the illegal slave trade. Portugal's representative in this city, who was suspected of being immersed in this unclean commerce, was briefed about this by a local abolitionist. "I think I can throw some light upon the questioning which you put to me," said R. W. Russell, "namely why have not some of the principal parties really engaged in this country in carrying on the prohibited trade been detected and punished?" And, why instead, had the local authorities continued to "persist in insinuating that the Consul General of Portugal is engaged in the illegal traffic?" Why was this occurring when "sailors" could be "hired with impunity in New York" for this business? "There is now a strong party in the South in favor of legalizing the importation of slaves from Africa, so that Texas and other states may be able to get an abundant supply of laborers at low prices, instead of having to pay high prices to Virginia and the other slave raising states." It was "perfectly clear that no effectual obstruction to the foreign slave trade can be raised by any efforts in the city of New York, under the existing laws. Here," it was proclaimed, "the capital can be found for the trade and the sailors, agents, etc. to carry it on." Russell thought the present prosecutor in Manhattan to be a "pro-slavery man," who deflected attention from this fact by targeting "foreigners . . . exclusively," as "it would have been impolitic for him to attack *native American firms*" [emphasis-original]. On the one hand, the prosecutor "really believed from what he had heard that the Consul General was engaged in the foreign slave trade," along with a number of other Brazilians and Portuguese. Yet the focus on these foreigners gave a wide berth for U.S. nationals to encroach upon their markets.[42] On the other hand, the blurring of citizenship boundaries between the U.S. and

Portugal meant that it was becoming increasingly difficult to make meaningful distinctions between the two nations.[43]

Still, the authorities in Manhattan had good reason to be suspicious of some of the Portuguese nationals among them for though some had thought that by 1856 the African Slave Trade to Brazil had been extinguished, that year witnessed the "revolting picture" of "the slaves 370 in number attempted to be introduced into Brazil on board of the schooner 'Mary E. Smith' of New Orleans. . . . captured at the Port of St. Matheos in the province of Espiritu Santo."[44] With "Vincent Cratonick . . . an Austrian by birth but a naturalized citizen of the United States" at the helm—he had "years" of service as "chief officer in one of the Brazilian steam packets running along the coast" and, thus, was familiar with the porous coastline—the "Mary E. Smith" was "fitted out for the slave trade in Boston," "went direct to Africa, took her cargo of slaves and was captured by the Brazilian government. . . . among the papers found on board were several original letters of Manuel Bazilio da Cunha Reis, a partner of Figaniere, Reis & Co., of New York, which disclosed the fact of his one-third ownership of the [vessel] and of his having given her dispatch from Boston."[45] Soon William Figaniere, Portugal's Consul General in New York, still protesting his innocence, was "suspended by his government," as he was "under suspicion" due to "his dealing with those engaged in the traffic."[46]

It was not only Portuguese in New York who were involved in this grubby activity, but there were also New Yorkers in Portugal who were similarly implicated. Nicholas Pike, the U.S. Consul in Oporto, reported in 1857 his "suspicions that many persons engaged in this illegal [slave] trade are connected with merchants doing business in this city." An "American vessel" left New York in May 1856 with "logwood (about 40 tons)" and a "crew of six men, all suspicious characters"; "it was the intention of the consignee to place her in the slave trade." There were "many parties, naturalized Portuguese citizens and others residing in the United States, who are said to be concerned in this vessel. I have been informed that she is really owned by . . . Barboza, merchant, doing business in New York City, and this gentleman is in partnership with persons in this city of Oporto," while "some of the crew confessed . . . that they had resided a long time in the state of Louisiana."[47]

Commander Charles Wise of the Royal Navy had more than an inkling about what all this meant. He was stationed near Cabinda, off the coast of Angola and in the summer of 1858 was observing a dizzying number of slavers bearing the U.S. flags sailing within his purview. There was, he said, a "new and formidable form of conducting the slave trade by Joint-Stock companies, designated 'expeditions to Africa'" and "principally formed by some of the most respectable firms in Havana and also at New York, Boston and New Orleans." Again, playing on blurred citizenship boundaries, "the agent procures naturalized citizens to act as captains of the intended slavers," then "procure[s] a crew, generally composed of foreigners," while the vessel [too] is cleared as *bona fide* American." On board were "cargoes of rum" and "muskets" that were to be exchanged for Africans. "Vessels proceeding to the Bights Division for slaves are generally consigned to one or other of the veteran slave dealers formerly engaged in the Brazilian trade" and "on the South Coast they are consigned in a similar manner." There they deployed "every exertion to put our cruisers on the wrong track; the position or change of each vessel is telegraphed along the coast, and in the neighbourhood of cruisers fires are invariably lit upon the shore, the smoke of which, as a warning of danger, is observable about fourteen miles at sea."

Yet, more than slick tactics, it was the migration of Wall Street tactics that was energizing the slave trade since "joint stock speculations engaging in the slave trade can never experience a loss. The greater the number of vessels dispatched for slaves, the greater the chance of success; for if two vessels out of twelve escape with slaves, the proceeds will pay the expenses of the remaining ten and still leave an immense profit," since "if two vessels out of twelve belonging to a company escape with cargoes of 600 each; the profit realized will amount to about 189,200 [pounds]." Thus, in 1857, "31 vessels . . . proceeded to the West Coast of Africa for slaves . . . capable of conveying 19,200 Negroes and . . . 19 were captured, while 11 or more than one-third escaped with 7400 slaves. The profit . . . must have been immense . . . [about] 1400 percent." This was rending further the fabric of an already distressed continent, as "slave hunts by the people of the King of Dahomey against the inhabitants of Abeokuta and vice versa, have of late been common occurrences. . . . the King of Dahomey demands from 60 to 170 dollars each for his slaves; the consequence is, the majority of slavers proceed to the headquarters of the Slave Trade, the South Coast," where Africans were cheaper. And, yes, he concluded wearily, "the Slave Trade is entirely conducted under the American flag."[48]

Back home, some were increasingly enraged by what U.S. nationals were helping to engender. "Without exception," said one concerned writer in the pro-slavery **De Bow's Review**, "every diplomatist, every speaker in Parliament, every declaimer at the hustings, every contributor to the numerous journals, concurs in attributing the present lamentable condition of the African slave-trade to the inadequacy of our law, the negligence or imbecility of the American government and its officials, or to the persevering activity of our people in opposition to and despite the professed wishes of that government."[49] London in turn was pressuring Washington—which was serving to foment abolitionist sentiment generally, which was impelling the nation toward sharper regional conflict.

Meanwhile, reports continued to proliferate about enslaved Africans flowing into the Slave South as this Civil War approached.[50] Some of these "recaptured Africans" were halted on the high seas and taken to Liberia, which witnessed a "great and unprecedented influx" of these "wild heathen from various tribes."[51] Some of these "nude and emaciated creatures" made it all the way to New York City; "a number of our recaptures," it was said, "have wandered away under the idea of returning to their own country. . . . one man hung himself in a fit of mental despondency and some 40 have died."[52] Still, they kept coming, notably to Key West[53]—"three slave-ships captured lately, & 1700 recaptured Africans are now at Key West," said fire-eater Edmund Ruffin in June 1860[54]—and other desolate parts of Florida.[55] In 1858, Howell Cobb, Secretary of the Treasury, ascertained that a "slaver with a cargo of Africans will attempt to land the same very soon [on] the southwest coast of Louisiana or on the Texas coast—most probably the latter."[56] Cobb was suspicious when "Messrs. E. Lapitt & Co., merchants of Charleston, South Carolina" sought "to clear the American ship 'Richard Cobden' . . . for the coasts of Africa for the purpose of taking on board African emigrants." This was a ruse, he thought.[57]

Others were arriving in Manhattan.[58] A number of "very sprightly young lads" arrived in New York City in "full health and spirits"; "they could soon be taught enough of the English language to become valuable," it was thought, and could be sent to a local orphanage.[59] The U.S. vessel, "San Jacinto," off the coast of Angola in the fall of 1860 captured a "cargo of 750 Africans and have sent her [crew] to Norfolk, Va. for adjudication." This slaver, the "Bonito," had been "cleared in New York on the 16th of July last. . . . the chief mate is Robert Johnson alias Robinson, and the second mate an American from Portsmouth, N.H. named Nathaniel Currier, alias Farrell, alias Bell"; in addition there were a number of Spanish surnamed individuals in the slaver's crew.[60] Like other Africans captured on the high seas, these were "unfortunate creatures"—"two committed suicide" and "neither persuasion nor force could make them take food. Two died of disease, one fell down the hatch and broke his neck and one died in the harbor." Thus, by the time they reached Monrovia, this "immense and overwhelming influx of naked and homeless savages" of 750 had been reduced to 617.[61]

Encouraging to U.S. slavers was the reluctance of U.S. juries to convict them for violating the law. Such was the case of the ship " 'Echo' "; this trial, says historian Ronald Takaki, "showed that African slave traders would not be punished in the South." Just as there was an "underground railroad," some Southerners called for a " 'submarine railroad' from Africa to the South."[62]

This apparent ceaseless tide of Africans flowing across the Atlantic was infuriating to some. Charles W. Thomas, a Georgian, chaplain to the African Squadron from 1855 to 1857, was upset by the "influx in . . . considerable numbers of savage Africans into the southern states"; its continuation "would be dangerous to the institutions of these states, and in portions of them dangerous to the existence of the white race," and the blame rested squarely on the shoulders of "reckless speculators, fitted out at New York and Boston."[63]

The African Squadron was still around as these events were unfolding but was widely viewed as ineffectual. The chaplain of the Squadron, the Reverend Thomas, found that the "African station is not popular with navy officers . . . because of its expensiveness, the long interval of 'news from home' and the monotony of the cruiser's life there." The food was not very good either.[64] This was not an ideal environment for a superb performance. "Of the more than two hundred persons arrested by the United States authorities for involvement in the traffic between 1837 and 1862," says the historian, Robert Conrad, "almost half were never brought to trial, about a third were tried but acquitted, and less than two dozen were convicted and sent to prison, most for short terms that were quickly ended by presidential pardons."[65] On the other hand, the Squadron's performance may have been improving as the pivotal election of 1860 approached—but this may have served the unintended consequence of stoking the fury of Southern extremists, who feared that they could only attain their coveted goal of ever cheaper Africans by secession.[66]

Overall, however, the Squadron's performance left much to be desired, something that perpetually infuriated London. As the crucial election year of 1860 was approaching, Lord Lyons assailed the "apparent apathy of Commander Totten" of the U.S. "in the fulfillment of his duties." "Noted slavers" were "openly cruising under American colors between Ambriz and the Congo," yet Totten and his crew seemed oblivious.[67]

Andrew Boyd Cummings was a sailor on one of these Squadron ships, cruising off the coast of Angola in 1857, and he was decidedly unimpressed with the job he and his comrades were performing. "Our Captain, though one of the pleasantest gentlemen socially," he said "lacks energy & boldness, he is the most timid captain with a single exception I ever sailed with. I believe one or two slavers have slipped through our fingers and now that our whereabouts is known all along the coast, they will keep a double lookout." He heard of "slave traders being up the Congo [River] & loading with slaves but our sanitary regulations prohibit our running up any of the rivers." Anyway, he was not exactly ecstatic to be among so many Africans—"the natives are a miserable squalid looking set of wretches, small slender, entirely different from our Kroomen & the stalwart darkies of the north coast."[68]

He was impressed with the slavers and their tactics of avoiding detection; "our appearance will be telegraphed by means of fires & canoes for a hundred miles in a single night." The Congo River was a "grand emporium" for slaves; "they collect them & keep them in a house or enclosure called a 'barracoon' until a fair chance offers to ship them to Cuba or Brazil."[69] But Cummings was hardly sympathetic and exposed his raw sentiments when he said his experience in Angola "seems to verify the poetical adage (& philosophical too) of 'nigger will be nigger.'"[70]

George Hamilton Perkins, born in 1836 in New England, sailed with the African Squadron and seemed to be a spectator as the Royal Navy swooped down on U.S. slavers. "A week ago," he said in November 1859, "one of the English ships captured an American slaver with five hundred Negroes on board. The English make a good many captures," he added admiringly. In faraway Fernando Po, off Africa's west coast, "we boarded a ship called the 'Firefly' and it was the same one father took me on board of years ago in Boston. She was suspected of being a slaver then and *might* lie under the same suspicion now" [emphasis-original]. This enforcer of anti-slave trade laws added, "if father was in business now and had some vessels here, I could attend to his affairs for him, and might even send him a whole cargo of Negroes if he said so!" Throwing up his hands figuratively, he added, "it is almost useless to try to do anything to stop the slave trade; our cruisers cannot do much under our laws and the English make the principal captures. Slaves are being constantly shipped and the King of Dahomey is now on a slave hunt to supply some ships which he expects from the States."

Perkins was bewildered by "our laws regulating captures" for they were "as inflexible as the Westminster Catechism, and a Captain could not detain a vessel without great risk of civil damages, unless slaves were actually on board. Suspected ships might have all the fittings and infamous equipage for the slave-traffic on board, but if their masters produced correct papers the vessels could not be touched; and our officers not infrequently had the mortification of learning that ships they had overhauled and believed to be slavers, but could not seize under their instructions, got off the coast eventually with large cargoes of ebon humanity on board. Not so with English commanders," whose anger at U.S. nonfeasance led them from being "at first cordial and agreeable" to "cold and indifferent . . . after a few months."[71]

William McBlair of Maryland was also toiling on behalf of the African Squadron and his opinion of what he was seeing was not very lofty either. "The slave trade" was "flourishing in this coast," he said of Angola in 1857. "It is said that five vessels have lately left with slaves. The Congo River and its neighborhood have been the headquarters and American gold is now quite plenty there, having been brought in vessels which clear from New York."[72] Yet he was not sufficiently motivated to attack what he was witnessing. "I wish honest abolitionists could see the degraded & impoverished condition of the natives," he told his wife in late 1857, for "they would find that much unnecessary sympathy had been expanded. When I tell you that fathers sell their children for a bottle of wine you will have a pretty good idea of their moral[s]." "And," he added, "it is supposed that if this season proves as dry [as] the two last that the people will be suffering famine to such an extent that they will be flocking to the coast as they have on a former occasion, requesting to be carried to some other country where they could get something to eat" since "provisions of every kind are now very scarce and although we are daily in sight of the coast, we have to live upon salt"; "it is impossible to get an egg at any price." He observed "Yankee traders" in Luanda, including a "noted slave trader."[73] The beleaguered McBlair reported officially that "I cannot impress too strongly upon the government the inability of the present squadron of sailing vessels to carry out their views and urge the employment of steamers for that purpose." At that point in the fall of 1857 "on the eastern bank of the Congo River," an "American bark was in the neighborhood expecting a load of slaves"; this was one among "several American vessels, one a very fine clipper from New Orleans," all set "to carry off slaves."[74]

Her Majesty's Consul in this same Angolan city, Edmund Gabriel, observed in 1859 that "the traffic under the flag of the United States was prosecuted to an amazing extent and with greater impunity than ever." One of his countrymen, an English commodore, declared in 1857 that the " 'many instances of American slavers leaving ports in the United States fully fitted for the slave trade' " was increasing. " 'New Orleans, being a seaport of slaving celebrity, may be expected to take a leading hand in such expeditions,' " he offered, " 'but I cannot help feeling surprised that New York should be, this year, one of the greatest slave-trading ports.' "[75]

U.S. nationals may have been returning to their wicked ways of slaving in part because traditional trade seemed to be slowing down in the 1850s in key regions of West Africa.[76] The Kimball family of the U.S. Northeast had done quite well over the years in this area, trading in rum, tobacco, ground nuts, and the like. But as early as 1853, their agent writing from Lagos was disconsolate, asserting "where I shall go next is uncertain. I thought some of going to St. Thomas & from there to Gabon but what I have on board won't pay for the trouble. . . . times are not so good in the Bight as I expected."[77] As time passed, things did not seem to improve; "there is nothing doing at this place," it was reported in 1855, referring to Lagos, though trade in oils continued.[78] The goods that were advancing in price were often seen as complements to the slave trade. Thus, writing from the "Gold Coast," Kimball's agent spoke glowingly of the "extraordinary advances in the price of gunpowder which article is now selling here at twenty two cents per pound . . . the price of rum is also advancing."[79] By 1856, he was "sorry to say" that he "had sold all" of this explosive item.[80] Yet by 1859, there were still sour complaints emanating from the Gold Coast that "times are still dull . . . markets are overstocked . . . tobacco unsold. . . . there is some twenty American vessels, that have thrown their cargoes into the market on credit, and like all the rest will have to wait sometime for their pay. . . . times cannot be much worse." This agent tried to buck himself up—"I have always had fair luck before, and I am not quite discouraged yet"—but harsh reality was hard to overcome with bright sentiments.[81] Weeks later there were further complaints that the "trade about Accra is spoilt for sometime [as] an act of late war between government and Bush Niggers [sic]," though this conflict was not said to be tied to the proliferation of gunpowder for which the Kimballs were so responsible.[82]

Further down the coast in Angola, yet another U.S. Northeast family was not celebrating either. "Trade is very dull," Robert Brookhouse was told in the spring of 1856.[83] In 1859, he was informed that his agent near Benguela had been "very ill for the last two months" and, besides, was "not very fluent in Portuguese," which might explain why "trade" was "at a standstill."[84] Intriguingly though "business" was "so poor"[85] in Angola, there did appear to be a demand for the provision of U.S. flags[86]—with the extremely skeptical suspecting that they may have been attached to vessels engaged in shady business. In 1856, Simon Stodder of Salem said that in Luanda there had "been considerable . . . American produce . . . sold here . . . we could have sold more." Interestingly—and perhaps alluding to the slave trade—he added, "we could have sold more if we had it to sell. . . . I am in hopes that those New York merchants that send vessels to the Congo River also for a decoy send [vessels] to Loanda and Benguela."[87]

Though business was not booming, in Luanda, it was reported in 1858, there were "thirty-nine Portuguese firms and two American firms which do more business than all the others put together. There is now not a single English mercantile house," in this sprawling city, which convinced the suspicious that London's crackdown on the slave trade was part of a larger scheme to batter rivals while gaining a toehold in a growing market.[88]

Across the continent, there was a "virtual monopoly for the Americans for the coffee and gums of Aden, for the dates and hides of Muscat and for the ivory of Mozambique. . . . at the same time the English Consul in Zanzibar reported direct trade to England from that island as completely non-existent"[89]—again convincing the suspicious of London's ill motives. George Abbott of the U.S. State Department was told that there was "no doubt the American flag has been violated on the South coast in the Portuguese territory by vessels purchased or chartered in Rio [de] Janeiro" for purposes of "the slave trade." This was no minor matter since "from 8 to 1000 slaves" were "brought from the coast for the yearly supply of the island." All this was occurring as the "American trade has been steadily increasing" and a "formerly . . . large English trade in Zanzibar . . . [was] entirely stopped."[90]

It is virtually impossible to disentangle what aspects of U.S. trade with Africa in the run-up to the Civil War were illicit and which were legitimate. The experience of George Howe suggests why. In 1860, this medical student was residing in New Orleans when a physician friend asked if he were interested in a trip "to the coast of Africa," presumably for the purpose of dispatching U.S. Negroes to Liberia. But once at sea, he discovered that he was on a slave ship with the Congo River as its destination. Soon another shipload of Africans—this one over 1000—was landed at the U.S.'s doorstep, in Cuba.[91] At the same time, London's representative in the U.S. worried that the "American ship 'Thomas Watson' now on her voyage to Liverpool is suspected of having been engaged in the slave trade and that slaves may have been landed from her in the United States." Camels from the Canary Islands were thought to have been brought to the Southwest in this vessel but, it was thought, the "importation was too inconsiderable for the amount of tonnage employed and may have been used as a pretext to conceal slaves."[92] From Cape Verde came the report of the "suspicious nature" of a vessel arriving from New York that had manacles concealed on board with a crew of "American citizens excepting one." "No doubt exists in my mind," said the British Consul, "that this vessel is engaged in a slave trading voyage. . . . her crew, with the exception of two persons, do not speak the English language. There is a Portuguese supercargo on board."[93]

In 1859 in the Azores, Britain's Consul had a strange experience. "An American schooner called 'William'" arrived and made "large orders for provisions and bought an anchor and chain and several spars and employed carpenters on board." The ship's captain, George D. Walker, was asked "to bring his ship's register on shore, but always made some excuse." Owing money for debts run up during this brief interlude, he slipped away, though "in his hurry he left his carpenter on shore who states an oath that the real name of the vessel is the 'Wanderer' of Savannah . . . and that the Captain's real name is Lincoln Patten . . . state of Maine . . . a few days after leaving Savannah the said Captain stated to the crew his intention of going to the east coast of

Africa for a cargo of slaves."[94] "Early in 1861 the United States Navy captured three American slavers, one with as many as nine hundred slaves on board. . . . on the east coast," though it was "commoner to find American slave ships sailing under Spanish colours."[95]

Summing up the state of the illegal slave trade in 1859, London's Foreign Office concluded bluntly that the "slave trade has increased considerably within the last two years" and "will [be] carried on with still greater vigour during the present summer. The vessels engaged in this traffic are almost exclusively American or at any rate they are furnished with American papers and fly the American flag." Washington "of late" had "failed to carry out their treaty engagements," for "within the last two years there have been periods when a United States ship of war has not been seen on the African coast for months" and "this too at a time when every slaver on the coast was furnished with American papers and flying the American flag." Now there had been "no attempt to land slaves in Brazil having been made since . . . 1855" and this traffic was "considered as extinct."[96]

But miles from the shores of Florida, the trade was flourishing and this inevitably was drawing the attention—and ire—of abolitionist forces on both sides of the Atlantic. As the Civil War approached, London's emissary in Havana noticed that the "slave trade continues to be carried on from this island upon the most extensive scale"; the "vessels employed" were "mostly . . . American built." Hence, "the number of Spanish ships has consequently become small that are engaged in the traffic."[97] Correspondingly, the number of U.S. ships was ballooning, with one September 1858 report from Havana listing 59 ships sailing to Africa in recent days—"50 American, 7 Spanish, 1 Peruvian and 1 Norwegian."[98]

1858 also proved to be a banner year for the slave trade in Angola. "This traffic appears to have received a considerable impulse during the last twelve months," said Edmund Gabriel of the U.K., reporting from Luanda. The reason? "Enormous profits," along with the "great facility and security afforded the slave dealers by carrying on their operations under the disguises of the American flag." Effective measures off the coast of Brazil had forced the trade northward toward the U.S. and Cuba so that now an African was worth "400 to 500 dollars" in Havana but could "be bought on this coast for 15 or 20." This was all rather "distressing."[99] Reporting from further north in Sierra Leone, Commander Charles Wise of the Royal Navy concurred with this dismal evaluation, adding that "in all the annals of the Slave Trade the year 1858 will have been the most successful . . . never was the system better organized or more systematically carried out." The U.S. flag continued to "cover this disgraceful traffic and does so more openly than in the year 1857 for in that year the papers in many cases proved to be . . . palpable forgeries, while in 1858 the slavers' registry and principal papers were genuine in, I think, every instance."[100] Spectacular increases in the African Slave Trade continued in 1859, particularly from Angola and especially under the U.S. flag.[101]

Hampered by the crackdown on the trade to Brazil, U.S. slavers concentrated more on Cuba, which allowed for more smuggling of Africans into the U.S. Southeast.[102] One illustrative example was the slaver "'Cora,'" captured off the coast of Angola with "705 slaves on board" but with "neither papers nor flag on board but the words 'Cora, of New York' were on her stern."[103] Thus, between August and October 1860 alone, "3071 Negroes" were "rescued from foreign slavery by the capture of . . . four vessels."[104] Even the Portuguese, somnolent in the best of times about the African Slave Trade, were beginning to notice the activity of U.S. slave traders in or about Luanda.[105] Increasingly, the slave trade was being disguised as a form of voluntary emigration of African "colonists" or "servants," who were being dispatched across the Indian Ocean to Mauritius or Reunion Island[106] or from Angola to St. Thomas—or São Tomé e Principe.[107]

Even Washington's representative in Luanda had detected these trends. In 1856, the Secretary of the Navy was "advised by John G. Willis, the U.S. Commercial agent at St. Paul de Loando that 'the slave trade is still carried on to some extent by vessels sailing from New York.'"[108] The next year Willis continued to complain that "the slave trade on this coast is now flourishing. . . . the Congo River and its neighborhood have been the headquarters and American gold is now quite plenty here, having been brought in these vessels which clear from New York—some for Cape Verde and some for Loando, but which seldom come here."[109] In 1859, Willis had "heard of four or five shipments" of Africans "being made, the last one a few days since, in which one thousand slaves were placed on board one vessel. The 'trade' has now gone in part, from the Congo River to the north of that river."[110]

The crackdown on the slave trade by the British in Brazilian waters contributed to the move northward of this business—closer to the protective embrace of U.S. shores: this and the enthusiasm for the trade expressed by Dixie nationalists fearful of what an ascending Republican Party might bring, combined to give an electric jolt to this commerce globally. The presence of the Royal Navy near the Congo River and Angola provides some indication as to what slavers were doing there, yet their corresponding difficulty in monitoring East Africa means that the depth of the African Slave Trade as it lurched to its conclusion is harder to measure. "It was largely because our Navy was so busily engaged in an endeavour to suppress the West Coast trade . . . that the East Coast was so neglected," said one British analyst.[111] Contemporaneously, in 1858 a British official agreed, asserting that the "materials for a report on the present state of the slave trade on this coast are so scanty, that I can scarcely venture to make one. That slaves have been exported there is no doubt"; even "the late Governor-General of Mozambique" had "been a party to the shipment." Suggesting how and why it was difficult to comprehend the African Slave Trade in isolation from other forces, it was declared that the perilous "state of affairs in India [the Sepoy Revolt] and at the Cape . . . prevented any adequate force being sent to . . . Mozambique, and it has been, with slight exception, entirely unwatched." As a result, it was declared glumly, "the prospect of putting down the slave trade has seldom been less encouraging."[112] "It is only within the last few years," said the British Consul in Zanzibar in January 1861, "that the Slave Trade from Zanzibar has assumed such large proportions."[113] Simultaneously, another report from this east African island noted ominously that "a Spanish slave-agent from Cuba arrived here in an American vessel and took up his abode with notorious Spanish slave-agent Buona Ventura Mas, who has long been carrying on an extensive Traffic in Slaves in the Zanzibar dominions."[114]

Shortly before that Joseph T. Crawford, London's representative in Havana, asserted that "the slave trade, which is being carried on so extensively and successfully, has been revived in . . . Mozambique and the East Coast of Africa"; for an "abundance of Negroes" there, "their cheapness" and "less risk of capture" meant that "numerous expeditions have been fitted out and gone in that direction"—"not infrequently" these journeys did "originate in the United States of America." There were "agents from Boston and New Orleans who are engaged in completing the subscriptions for shares, which have been already in part filled up by American capitalists," as this putrid business had become an easy way to make easy profits. "One of these schemes is for a ship of

900 tons to bring 2000 slaves." Africans were "to be had on the East Coast of Africa for about 28 dollars each; and even so they are paid for in goods, upon which there is at the least 100 percent of profit." Vessels did "proceed from the United States, under American colours, to a port in Madagascar. . . . the victims being brought over from the opposite coast of Africa in Arab vessels." At that moment, said Crawford, "we have none"—meaning "cruisers in these waters."[115] The U.S. was similarly deficient in East Africa.[116]

In the run-up to the Civil War, U.S. slavers had "flooded the zone," carpet-bombing the southern coastline of Africa from Angola to Mozambique with slave ships. Charles Wise of the Royal Navy sensed this from his perch near Cabinda, where these vessels long had honeycombed. In the late spring of 1859 he was typically flummoxed. "Within the last six months upwards of twenty-five slavers have sailed for the coast of Africa; only eight of that number . . . have been captured. What has become of the remaining seventeen vessels, of which we only know four to have escaped, while two more have doubtless shipped ere this. All these vessels, with one exception, were American" and their "profits" were "enormous." "This year the number of vessels escaping will exceed all known annals of [the] Slave Trade and encourage the Americans to enter with all the energies peculiar to them, for the remained of the present and the ensuing year of 1860."[117] Even Washington's man in Angola, John G. Willis, had noticed in late 1859 that that "slave trade has been remarkably active this year and many vessels have left this coast with slaves."[118]

By the summer of 1859, Wise was feverishly apoplectic in his denunciation of U.S. slavers. "105 slavers capable of conveying 71,000 slaves will arrive on the African coast in the course of the twelve months ending March 1860," he declared, and "one fourth of that number will be seized" by the Royal Navy, "still leaving 79 vessels"—and this was "exclusive of slaves shipped from the East Coast of Africa." With enraged sarcasm he proclaimed, "Such is American Law! The captains of slavers ridicule it. They boast openly that money does all things. . . . correct papers will cover almost any amount of slave trading," as the "many instances of American slavers leaving ports in the United States fully fitted for the Slave Trade," indicated. "New Orleans, being a seaport of slaving celebrity" and "New York" being "one of the greatest slave-trading ports" were clearly culpable. It was well known that Lusophone nationals and diplomats involved in "such houses as that of

Cunha Reis, Figaniere and Co. of New York" were "acquiring thousands by a successful traffic in blood" but the U.S. authorities were lethargic. They all were "sacrificing to their idol gold the lives of many thousands of poor, harmless, defenceless wretches."[119]

He was upset for sound reason[120] though top U.S. diplomat, Lewis Cass, pleaded ignorance, asserting blindly in the spring of 1860 that "if there has been any recent increase in that Trade or any employment of American capital in its prosecution, of which employment I have seen no proof."[121] Actually Cass was well aware that in 1858 London had retreated decisively on the right to search U.S. flagged vessels—a feat which the historian Andrew McLaughlin termed "one of the most just and most brilliant triumphs of which to this day our diplomacy can boast."[122] But, ironically, London—which was overburdened in India, the Crimea, and elsewhere—did Washington no great favor in yielding. This may have been a Pyrrhic victory in that the accompanying emboldened conversation about taking advantage of London's yielding by reopening the slave trade to the U.S. itself, contributed to sectional tension. For a great Civil War was to grip the U.S. and, though in its early stages, the increase in the African Slave Trade seemed to dwarf even the extravagant surges that had begun in 1858, this conflict was to place a permanent clamp on this infamous commerce and, in the process, contribute mightily to abolition in what had been the largest market—Brazil.

The late 1850s marked a zenith for the illicit slave trade and the profits to be gained flowed into the pockets of men on both sides of the Mason-Dixon line, particularly those in New York and New Orleans. But as London pushed the trade out of Brazilian waters, it simply moved further north to the doorstep of the U.S. itself and, thus, ironically, the actual rise of this commerce actually marked its death knell, as the apparent successes of fire-eaters from Dixie helped to push the nation into a bloody conflict.

Slave deck of the "Wildfire," brought into Key West from the Congo River on April 30, 1860. Men are on lower deck; women on upper deck. As the Deep South moved toward Civil War, the slave trade to Cuba and Brazil increased with spillover onto U.S. shores. Courtesy Library of Congress.

8

The Civil War Begins /
The Slave Trade Continues

In the antebellum era, slavery and, especially the African Slave Trade, were a "significant factor in the diplomacy of the Western Hemisphere. The influence of the institution on relations with Great Britain, Spain and Mexico"—not to mention Brazil and Portugal and Southern Africa—"has been described as a 'constant orienting factor in the diplomatic history of the United States.'" But ironically, just as the ascendancy of the Republican Party in 1860 marked a spike in regional tensions nationally, the prospect that this organization would be less circumspect toward the illegal slave trade than its predecessors was a harbinger of improved relations internationally, especially with London. If the U.S. was spending less time confronting the U.K. on contentious matters, which, in a sense, were distilled expressions of white Southern nationalism—such as the right to search suspected U.S. slavers—this meant more time and opportunity for North and South to confront each other.[1] And that only served to underscore the importance of an alliance of the Slave South with the slave empire in Brazil in this confrontation; moreover, even if London's pressure was hindering the transport of enslaved Africans to Brazil, this did not signal the end of the trade. How the Civil War influenced the fate of this trade and the Slave South's relation to Brazil are the linked themes of this chapter.

There was much for North and South to confront each other about, particularly concerning the African Slave Trade, which had become an impassioned rallying cry for the most determined secessionists. Even those who were willing to conciliate the South on the question of slavery—acknowledging its reality below the Mason-Dixon line but hesitant about its expansion—found the prospect of reopening the African Slave Trade, de facto or de jure, hard to swallow or ignore. "There is no doubt," concludes one analyst, "that a sharp increase in slave traffic was taking place in 1859 and 1860," accompanied by a "flood of rumors concerning the landing of fresh Congoes along Southern shorelines"[2]—and "geographically, no shoreline could have been better laid out for smuggling than the coasts of South Carolina and Georgia," as "no amount of patrolling by land or sea could have stopped smuggling."[3] Concurrently, ideologues of the Slave South felt that they could build a stronger, more cohesive nation if they could cut ties with the North and formalize relations with, e.g., Brazil.

L. W. Spratt spoke for many of his fellow fire-eating white Southerners when he said bluntly that "in a union of unequal races there is nothing wrong in relations of inequality. . . . if slavery be right, there can be no wrong in the foreign, whatever there may be in the domestic slave trade." This ban against the "foreign" slave trade simply served to "send the slave, that else might come to us, to Cuba and Brazil, and to intensify the sufferings of his transportation. They certainly do not arrest the slave trade." He concurred with the notion that " 'the foreign slave trade will restore political power to the South,' " by increasing her population and congressional representation. As these fire-eaters saw it, when Washington would not yield on this bedrock point, this was little more than rank hypocrisy, worthy of secession.[4] Such unforgiving attitudes led the British writer Thomas Macaulay to conclude during the antebellum era that " 'I do not deem it unlikely that the black population of Brazil will be free and contented within eighty or a hundred years; I do not envision, however, a reasonable likelihood of similar change in the United States.' "[5]

For its part, London was in a bind. There was pressure domestically to press for the end of the slave trade and slavery, just as there was similar pressure to make sure that Cuba did not fall into U.S. hands. The former objective pushed toward abolitionism, while ensuring that Cuba remained Spanish soil empowered a European nation that in many ways was more antithetical to abolitionism than the U.S. itself.[6] Simultaneously, Madrid was seeking to conspire with Washington in legitimizing objections to London's persistent demands to search potential slavers.[7] This was a difficult circle to square.

In February 1859, Congressman J. B. Clary of Kentucky took to the floor of Congress to address these matters. It was Her Majesty's government and the closely linked question of slavery that was at the heart of Washington's foreign policy and, as he saw it, this was unacceptable.

Why should the U.S. be "forced" to "maintain at vast expense on the coast of Africa, a squadron equal to about one-seventh of our whole force." Now, Mr. Clary did not like the African Slave Trade, and this was not because of any charitable attitudes toward Negroes but "on account of the white race, and upon grounds of expediency."[8]

When secession occurred and the so-called Confederate States of America (CSA)[9] were confronted with the question of what was to be done about the African Slave Trade—which by 1861 was reaching ever greater heights—it too found itself entangled in a morass of contradictions. Thus, weeks after the Emancipation Proclamation in 1863, CSA leader Judah Benjamin—whose Jewish origin has been stressed historically but whose Portuguese origin is more relevant to the African Slave Trade, given the preponderance of Portuguese Americans in this illegal commerce[10]—contacted his representative in London about the provisions in this newly formed nation's Constitution concerning the African Slave Trade: " 'Congress shall also have power to prohibit the introduction of any slaves from any State not a member of, or Territory not belonging to, this Confederacy.' " "It is thus seen," said Benjamin, "that while the States were willing to trust Congress with the power to prohibit the introduction of African slaves from the United States, they were not willing to trust it with the power of prohibiting their introduction from any other quarter"—including Brazil, Cuba, and Africa itself.[11] This was a loophole large enough to steer a fully armored slave ship through—and this is precisely what occurred.

Yet it was not done openly, it remained shrouded, though it was hardly a secret that some of the most determined secessionists were ardent advocates of the African Slave Trade. Why? One reason was international public opinion and a fear that major powers would be averse to recognizing diplomatically a nation that would be so audacious as to deal in human flesh. The supposed "intercepted instructions" of Benjamin to his emissary, L. Q. C. Lamar, spoke directly to this matter, reminding him, "you are well aware of how firmly fixed in our Constitution is the policy of this Confederacy against the opening of that trade."[12] Opponents of the CSA were not buying this subterfuge. Delegates to the Maryland Constitutional Convention held during the Civil War were instructed that these rebels "were seeking nothing more nor less than the reopening of the African slave trade. That is what they were for, and they knew they could not have that so long as the Constitution and the laws of the United States were in force." All they wanted was to buy "Negroes for $30 a head," "instead of paying you $1000 for every Negro they bought"—it was just that simple. Seizing Texas was simply the first step in this plot "and here is the beautiful feature of their scheme, they did not intend to stop with the acquisition of Texas." For after that "lay Tamaulipas, Chihuahua and other Mexican states" —and then moving further southward.[13]

When London got its hands on the CSA provisions on slave trading, elation did not reign. There was "abolishing the punishment of death for slave trading," to begin with; then, said Consul Robert Bunch from Charleston, it also provided that " 'Negroes, coolies, mulattoes or other persons of color' who may be found on board of any vessel captured for violating this Act shall in certain cases be sold at public auction for the benefit of the Confederate States and of the informer." Would not this simply transfer the profit from slave trading from the individual to the state, thus providing even further incentive for an acceleration of this foul commerce?[14] London was displeased.

The problem for the CSA was that potentially valued global allies— e.g., slaveholding Spain—seemed to agree, in certain respects, with an abolitionist viewpoint. This was an abrupt turnabout for Spaniards had found a congenial home in Charleston as early as 1816.[15] There was substantial traffic, understandably, between Havana and Charleston— two of the major poles of human bondage in the hemisphere—during the antebellum era.[16] When the CSA was organized, the Spanish Consul in South Carolina was reminded by a rebel official of the "good will and respect which you have created here in the discharge of your official duties."[17]

Thus, when P. J. Rost of the CSA met in Madrid with Spanish Secretary of Foreign Affairs, Calderon Collantes, he was initially satisfied, being "well pleased with the allusion" comparing Spain's earlier struggle against Napoleon to that of the Slave South against Washington. Madrid's man went on to say that "*on the question of right he had no doubt it is clearly with the South*" [emphasis-original]. One can imagine Collantes nodding vigorously when Rost told him that Spain's "interest was that North America should be possessed by two great powers who would balance each other." Spain "was our natural ally and friend," Collantes was told, "with similarity of institutions, ideas and social habits." Then one can imagine Rost frowning when Collantes shifted the discussion by reminding him that the "North had always been friendly"—being the "best customer for the sugar" of Cuba—while the

South was "ever hostile to Spain." "No private expeditions had ever sailed from [Northern] ports for the invasion of Cuba but invariably from those of the South and that if the Confederate States become hereafter a strong government, their first attempt of conquest would be that island." Yes, "the South would . . . deem in its interest that a great country like Spain should continue a slave power. The two, together with Brazil, would have a monopoly of the system of labor which alone can make intertropical America."[18] But that was not enough to win over Madrid wholly for Spain had not forgotten events of a few years earlier involving Southern-inspired filibustering expeditions to Cuba[19] and designs on Spanish territory near Hispaniola.[20]

When one discusses the waxing and waning of the African Slave Trade, at issue by definition are forces external to North America—Africans, in the first place. This is even more the case when it is considered that during the Civil War—and even before—how this institution was propelled by U.S. and CSA nationals heavily dependent on developments in London, Havana, Lisbon, Madrid, Kingston, Port au Prince, and, of course, the twin towers of the African Slave Trade: Luanda and Rio de Janeiro.

When he was asked in the antebellum era if he " 'could conceive of a greater and more atrocious evil than this slave trade?' " John Quincy Adams answered simply, " 'Yes. Admitting the right of search by foreign officers of our vessels upon the seas in time of peace; for that would be making slaves of ourselves.' "[21] Such an attitude brought Washington into a bruising confrontation with London, particularly after the latter moved to ban slavery, then sought to handcuff the illicit slave trade.

As noted, Washington felt that London's attitude was not motivated wholly or solely by humanitarian considerations. Thus, in the summer of 1849, Jamaican planters met to complain about competition from slave grown sugar and other crops in light of the "continuation and great increase of the foreign slave trade." Brazil was mentioned specifically as providing unfair competition, thus motivating London to crackdown on the slave trade there—which brought the U.K. into conflict with U.S. slavers.[22]

The Foreign Office in London was told that "this anti-slave trade movement is now rapidly extending itself over the whole of this island. The Kingston Petitions bear a list of signatures far exceeding the numbers which have been attached to any petition on any subject which has ever been addressed to Parliament from Jamaica."[23] London found it difficult to ignore this pressure from its rich colony and, correspondingly, had to pressure those vessels—many of them bearing U.S. flags—that were bringing enslaved Africans to the shores of its competitors, particularly Brazil. But what was complicating things for these antagonists of U.S. slavers and their transoceanic allies was that there were those who were sharply disagreeing with these Jamaican planters. At Maryland's 1864 Constitutional Convention, one debater argued passionately that "the world furnishes no instances of these products being grown upon a large scale by free labor. The English now acknowledge their failure," while "Brazil, whose slave population nearly equals our own, is the only South American state which has prospered."[24]

Congressman J. B. Clary of Kentucky expressed the sentiments of many when he denounced what he saw as London's hypocrisy in seeking to curtail the African Slave Trade. "It is a fact not known to everyone," he declared, "that for every slave taken by a British cruiser she receives. . . . 5 [pounds] or about twenty four dollars. . . . the slave ships are taken either to Sierra Leone or St. Helena and the slaves . . . are reshipped on board of British transports and sent to Demerara, Berbice and her West India islands and apprenticed." Where was the humanity in that, he wondered.[25]

Humanity, indeed, countered advocates of the British Empire. There increasing doubt was being expressed about the "most abject and hazardous dependence upon the Slave States of America," not least since "England's demand for slave grown cotton" was "the secret of American slavery." There was an alternative, however: "cotton," it was said in 1858, "*can* be grown on the banks of the Indus, by *free labor,* at a less cost, and with a greater profit, than it can be in New Orleans or Mobile or Arkansas" [emphasis-original]. With mercantilist confidence it was announced that "one 10 [pound] note invested in the 'East India Cotton Company' will do more to put an end to the slave trade . . . than double that sum contributed as a mere donation to an 'anti-slavery society.'" "So long as cotton is selling for 500 dollars a bale and Negroes are worth from 1000 to 1500 dollars, all the preaching, and all the entreaty, and all the schemes for the emancipation of the American slave, will be as fruitless as 'the whistling wind' . . . as soon as cotton is grown in sufficient quantities, and at a fair profit, on the banks of the Indus . . . by free adult labor, that moment the 'slavery of the South' will cease to be either a necessity or an expediencey [*sic*] and *America will be free!*"[26] [emphasis-original].[27]

The walls were closing in on the Slave South. Anger was turning to hostility in the U.S. itself as the overflow from the flood of Africans brought to Cuba were arriving in the southern states, providing a wretched picture of inhumanity, while Britain was openly considering reducing sharply its dependence on southern crops, thereby jeopardizing potentially millions in investments. In that context, secession, and a lurch toward closer union with Brazil, seemed less like desperation and more like self-preservation.

There was pressure of a different sort emerging from Jamaica's neighbor, Haiti. David Brion Davis acknowledges that "the destruction of slavery in Saint-Domingue gave an immense stimulus to plantation slavery from neighboring Cuba to far-off Brazil"[28] and, by implication, to the African Slave Trade as well. Though the scholar David Geggus has "seen no evidence to suggest the Haitian Revolution was invoked by leaders of the Male Revolt" in Bahia, he does acknowledge this hemispheric—and, in fact, global—reach of this epoch-shattering Caribbean event.[29]

Certainly there was hemispheric apprehension about the potential reach of Haiti's abolitionism, not least in those nations within Spain's sphere of influence,[30] just as the planters of Kingston were forced to consider the implications of slave unrest in Puerto Rico[31] and Venezuela's move toward abolition was influenced profoundly by Port au Prince.[32] Madrid's representative in Washington kept a close eye on abolitionism in the U.S., wary of its implications for Cuba and Puerto Rico,[33] just as it monitored carefully developments in Haiti, constantly sensitive to the implications for "race" and slavery.[34] Though the number of Africans in the Argentine was considerably less than that of Brazil, there too close attention was paid to developments in Haiti and slavery in the U.S.[35] And just as there were imaginings in the U.S. about shipping certain Africans en masse to Liberia, similar ideas had arisen at the same time in Brazil.[36]

The point is that those who profited from slavery and the slave trade were aware that the existence of this system was not wholly dependent upon domestic events or occurrences in one nation, just as in the late 20th century apartheid rulers realized that the continuation of their system was not unconnected to the fate of Jim Crow.[37] In a similar fashion, the fate of slavery in the hemisphere was heavily dependent on the destiny of this institution in the Slave South—and Brazil. Actually, even those who abjured slavery and the slave trade too had to contend with the stiff competition provided by a nation that deployed laborers who received no wages.

In certain precincts of the Slave South, denizens realized that their collective fate was linked with that of Brazil. "We have common interests and sympathies with the people of Brazil and Cuba," said one Charleston publicist in 1847, who was worried that "our relations" with these slave states were "threatened to be disturbed by" abolitionism. Even at this early date it seemed that the U.S. South felt it held more shared aims with its hemispheric neighbors than the U.S. North, arguing repetitively, "we have common interests and sympathies with the people of Brazil and Cuba" and need to make "more intimate the connection between the ports of the United States in Cuba and Brazil. . . . we afford remunerating markets for coffee, sugar, cocoa . . . and . . . New Orleans, Savannah, Charleston, Norfolk and Baltimore are much nearer to the great West, than are Philadelphia, New York or Boston"— not least since they were closer to Rio de Janeiro. The "slaves and other property" of Brazil and Cuba would "in our harbors be secure from abolitionists and other plunderers and that most if not all of the staples of our country can be supplied [to] them on as favorable terms as any others." Seemingly moving toward secession at this early date, "southern"—not U.S.—"commercial agencies at Havana and Rio de Janeiro" were demanded.[38]

A few years later concern was raised that "when Cuba and Brazil are annexed" to the U.S., the "clamor in favor of continuing the traffic, which already exists in those countries, would be irresistible." Already, the "slave traders have a party in Congress and that they rank distinguished Northern Senators, as well as Southern, among their leaders," which made this merger of slave empires well-nigh inevitable.[39] Minimally, it seemed that the Slave Power was seeking "an alliance, offensive and defensive with Brazil," which could overwhelm any hemispheric abolitionist objections.[40] "It was predicted twenty years ago," said one prominent mainstream newspaper in 1854, "that if the [Slave Power] got Texas, it would not stop until it reached Brazil." In reaction that same year to the Kansas-Nebraska Act, Congressmen Solomon Foot of Vermont, Daniel Mace of Indiana, and Reuben E. Fenton of New York signed a statement that declared this legislation was " 'to be followed up by an alliance with Brazil and the extension of slavery in the valley of the Amazon.' "[41] An antebellum Southerner advocated a " 'treaty of commerce and alliance with Brazil' " which would " 'give us the control over the Gulf of Mexico and its border countries, together with the islands; and the consequence of this will place African slavery beyond the reach of fanaticism at home or abroad. These two great powers . . . ought to guard and strengthen their mutual interests. . . . we can not only preserve domestic servitude but we can defy the power of the world.' "[42]

Even before the Civil War erupted, perceptive analysts had realized that the North's evident advantages in population and industrial plants could be neutralized, if not overwhelmed, by hemispheric alliances that focused on a nation, Brazil, that was larger in territory than the U.S. and contained many more enslaved Africans.[43]

This attitude in Brazil had been nurtured by the U.S. Minister to Brazil at the time of secession. In presenting his credentials before this ominous moment, Richard K. Meade "in a memorable speech expressed his hope that the two nations"—the U.S. and Brazil—"might be brought into the closest alliance. The special motive he assigned, was that the two great slave-holding nations of America needed to combine to resist the anti-slavery pressure of the rest of the world." Secession was not just an event but a process and even before the firing on Fort Sumter, many white Southerners in the employ of Washington were laying the groundwork and busily preparing for the advent of the CSA. Certainly this could be said of Meade who in his pointed remarks asked Brazilian elites what would be the "influence of our extinction of slavery upon the institution in Brazil?" Brazilian "slavery," he declared, "has found the same incentive in coffee to strengthen and perpetuate itself that our own institution did in cotton." Brazil, he proclaimed, was "more like the United States than any other nation in the world."[44]

Later, R. C. Parsons of Cleveland, who arrived in Rio de Janeiro just after Meade had departed, in order to lead the U.S. diplomatic corps, blasted this "doughty fire-eater from Old Virginia," whose activities seemed to "reveal that a persistent effort was then made to induce Brazil, at that early day, to look forward to a time when the 'great rebellion' should be consummated." Meade's son, Richard Kidder Meade, Jr., had been part of the assault on Fort Sumter, which was viewed as more than coincidence.[45] Meade, Sr. was a "well-known politician of the extremist Calhoun school" and as early as 1849 was "openly charged . . . on the floor of Congress . . . with entertaining disunion sentiments and cherishing disunion projects." He was a firm advocate of a "grand Pro-Slavery alliance with the Brazilian Empire."[46] Sending him as Minister to Brazil was not just a boost to the nascent Confederacy, it revealed a stunning naivete on behalf of Washington, akin to appointing Benedict Arnold to be Ambassador to the Court of St. James.

As late as July 1861, Meade was having discussions with the Emperor—while he was serving as Washington's emissary—about CSA prospects. He opined that the war "would perhaps last twenty years"; the "Emperor expressed the kindest feelings of friendship toward Mr. Meade but made no remarks indicative of his views and feelings in regard to the state of our country, to which allusion had been made."[47]

Meade's successor, James Watson Webb, was no abolitionist, far from it, yet even he was outraged by Meade's behavior. This Confederate "asked me in London," said Webb, "for a letter of introduction to the President, assuring me that, although a southern man, he had faithfully discharged the whole duty to the Union. This turns out to have been a deliberate misrepresentation." For while in Rio as "Minister he was openly and offensively a secessionist and traitor and did all in his power to bring the government of our country into disrepute." He was not alone. "Robert G. Scott" the "late Consul" in Rio was also "an open-mouthed traitor and a loud-talker." Webb's abrupt replacement of Meade put the Emperor on the spot; he said he would "be embarrassed in making a reply and equally embarrassed in not replying to what I said in condemnation of slavery" if Webb were to refute Meade's earlier words. "He begged, therefore, that I would not insist upon the exercise of the right to reply publicly. . . . it would relieve the Emperor of all difficulty in regard to the question of slavery, and which is already making itself felt in the phases of party here," suggesting how conflict in the U.S. was rippling outward.[48]

Still, this contemplation of Brazil was a matter for all sides. At the 1864 Constitutional Convention in Maryland, which was rocked with debate about what Emancipation might entail, one delegate sought to reassure with copious references to the Brazilian experience and how this nation exemplified what the dark-skinned could accomplish.[49] Abolitionists argued that "even . . . Brazil with her four million [*sic*] slave gives the free-born colored man and the emancipated slave equal privileges with others, and opens to him every avenue to wealth and fame,"[50] while in July 1860, this same nation was viewed as a negative example by an advocate of human bondage. This nation's alleged predilection toward "amalgamation" means that if an "insurrection" occurred, " 'the whites will be sure to suffer from the savage rapacity of the mixed races, especially those who have African blood in them.' " " 'Aversion to hybridity, then, is the safeguard of the people.' " That the African "enjoys not only the same social but the same political rights as any of the natives of the country" was seen as lunacy and a "fictitious show of civilization."[51] President James Buchanan, perhaps, had the final word in this discourse that looked to Brazil for insight into festering internal tensions within the U.S., when he argued that the North had no more cause to interfere in slavery in the South as they had to do the same in "Russia or Brazil."[52]

In mid-1860, London thought that little had changed since the mid-1850s in Brazil, in that there were "not only no cases, but even no suspicions" of slaving.[53] But it was not as if a wave of abolitionism had washed over South America. Instead the Civil War heightened fears in the hemisphere about slavery's fate. For by December 1861, the **Charleston Mercury** was chortling that "Brazilians [were] sympathizing almost to a man with the secessionists, under the impression that the South was fighting the battle of Brazil—fighting to protect their property in slaves" for there was a nagging fear that "if the North had abolished slavery in the Southern States, she would turn her attention to abolishing slavery in the Brazil Empire."[54] Thus, said the **New York Times,** speaking of Rio de Janeiro, "perhaps in no place or in any other foreign country has the effects of the rebellion . . . been so much felt as in this port."[55] Indeed, said this periodical in words thought sufficiently worthy to be retained by the Brazilian Foreign Ministry, "in the good years before the war we took from $22,000,000 to $25,000,000 worth of Brazilian products annually and sent to Brazil sometimes between $6,000,000 and $7,000,000 a year."[56]

The South Carolinian who penned the above words of warning may have pricked up his ears if he had heard another kind of warning emanating at that moment from Brazil. A Brazilian senator was demanding the reduction of the numbers of slaves in large cities and an increase in farming areas and checking the ongoing deportation of slaves from north to south, which was mimicking similar antebellum trends in the U.S., for "was it the case, gentlemen," he argued, "that when some years ago in the United States the Northern states abolished slavery and it remained in the Southern States, the industrial interests of the

Southern States became entirely opposed to those of the Northern? Was it not after the creation and growth of diversity of interests that the explosion took place which has not yet terminated?"[57]

Profit-hungry slave traders had accelerated the hunting and seizing of Africans in the run-up to the ascension to power of the Republican Party in 1860. After that, with Civil War on the horizon and the allure of handsomely easy profits to be made and stashed away for the foreseeable stormy day, this foul enterprise accelerated further. The African Squadron, inept in the best of times and hardly present in East Africa, in any case, had to become more concerned with CSA privateers raiding U.S. commerce or bombarding north of Baltimore. The U.K. remained on duty but some British elites were not necessarily displeased with the prospect of a CSA victory that could reduce sharply the power of the behemoth that had arisen in North America. Late in 1862, for example, the U.S. Consul in Pernambuco observed that "the British residents on this coast, both official and private are noted for their sympathy with the rebellious part of our people," referring to the CSA.[58] Then there was a powerful "Copperhead" element in the U.S. Northeast that had refused to accept the demise of the African Slave Trade, even when rebels assaulted Fort Sumter in early 1861.

As secessionists began moving relentlessly toward a conflict that many saw as giving a new birth of freedom to the African Slave Trade, it was reported from West Africa that out of 36 slave vessels recently detected, "29" were "under the American flag alone" with six being Spanish; "and as the [U.S.] squadron find there is no use in detaining vessels unless they have slaves on board, although they may be otherwise fully equipped, the difficulty in successfully checking this illegal traffic is at once apparent." The valley of the Congo River down to Luanda tended to "contribute the greatest number of slaves" and "American [slave] vessels fitted as whalers" continued to be active.[59]

Thus, by July 1861, the Royal Navy's reports sounded as if they could have been written in 1858. The "slave trade is at present carried on almost entirely under the American ensign," it was said. The "Congo is, without doubt, the center of the Slave Trade in this part of the coast . . . the value of the slave being only twenty-five dollars on this part of the station; while it is eighty dollars in the Bights"—this was "no doubt the reason why slave-vessels generally come to the South Coast." This trade reached to Luanda, though it was doubted if it took place south of there. Though a Civil War ostensibly over slavery was raging, the refrain had not changed: "as vessels engaged in the Slave Trade almost invariably fly the American flag and our cruisers are prohibited from in any way interfering with them, of course we are to a very serious extent powerless in putting a check to the Slave Trade."[60]

By October 1861, the words from the South Coast seemed even more desperately inflamed. Britain's representatives asserted that "at no period since the establishment of this Commission has the Traffic in Slaves been carried on with greater activity or daring on this part of the coast than during the past year. . . . not less than 6000 slaves have been shipped from the immediate neighborhood of the Congo during the past five months" with "all wearing the American flag." With U.S. monitoring reduced as a result of Civil War, "the slave dealers in the Congo are already exulting in the impunity" resulting.[61]

In the early stages of the Civil War, the U.S. was seeking to detain slavers,[62] which was wise given that the enormous profits from such ventures could only buoy opponents of the Union's ultimate objectives. Yet soon London had "with great regret to report . . . the retirement from the West Coast of Africa of the United States's ships of war" that had been off the coast of northern Angola and at the mouth of the Congo River basin; this placed "additional pressure" on the already besieged Royal Navy.[63] This was a boon to slave dealers. Shortly after this U.S. departure, Secretary of State William Seward was informed that Brazil—which some slave traders continued to lust after as a recipient for their human cargoes—"from its location and sympathies, is destined to supply and furnish ports of security for the privateers of the Southern States."[64] That same year Lord Lyons in Washington observed that "Mr. Seward came to see me" and "asked me to let him speak to me very confidentially." Naturally, Lyons immediately reported this conversation to London, as the Secretary of State "went on to express great apprehension lest *any* Power should recognize the Southern Confederacy. He seemed even to feel alarm lest Brazil or Peru should do so. In fact, the immediate object of his visit appeared to be to endeavour to ascertain through me whether there could be any truth in private information which had reached him that Brazil had determined already to recognize the new Confederacy. Brazil, he said, might perhaps be led to do so by community of feeling on Slavery" [emphasis-original].[65]

In a veritable response, it was not long before there was the "arrival . . . of the American barque 'J. J. Cobb' " in Luanda, which had "been notoriously employed in the Traffic in Slaves between this coast and Cuba during the last two years."[66] Reflecting confidence that either the CSA would prevail or that North American flagged vessels were exempt from international treaty obligations or that even a Washington victory would bring no end to slavery, North American flagged slavers continued to descend on Africa even as the Civil War raged. Commodore Edmonstone of the Royal Navy reported in November 1861 that "the Slave Trade is now, with a few exceptions, entirely carried on under the cover of the American flag." The "withdrawal of the United States Squadron gives additional facility to the slaver," it was said, "they have nothing to dread." Now the "Spanish slave trade to the Havana will be carried on under the American flag more freely and with less risk than ever."[67]

Nathaniel Gordon was raised in a relatively prosperous home in Portland, Maine; it was one of the older residences in this eponymous port city, built in 1740, reflecting the stolid economy of this Northern metropolis that came to benefit from the African Slave Trade. It was a three-story building, one of the largest square-roofed houses of its day and at the time it was built it was called one of the finest in the city, with three chimneys, an abundance of large, deep fireplaces with beautifully carved mantles of mahogany and rosewood. The finish was remarkably fine, reflecting the refinement of Gordon himself who was a "companionable boy of likeable ways and much charm of personality" —even then he was considered a leader. "Quick to learn, he was a keen observer" and early on could hardly ignore "stories of rich silks and jewels, of gold cups and vases found in the house on York Street."[68]

So moved, it was not long before he followed his home state's traditions and became a successful slaver with a dark reputation, a veteran of slave smuggling runs to Cuba and Brazil. In 1853, Gordon landed 500 enslaved Africans near Rio de Janeiro, then burned his ship to escape capture.[69] Early in the morning of 8 August 1860 he "sailed from the Congo."[70] He had a cargo of liquor on board, along with 890 Africans, of which 172 were men, 106 were women, and the rest were boys and girls.[71] He was on his way to offload his human cargo in Cuba when he was detained. His captives were taken to Liberia and Gordon was returned to his homeland to stand trial for violating laws barring the slave trade.

Gordon was indicted in New York City on 29 October 1860 on the charge of "detaining Negroes with intent to make them slaves" and arraigned on 2 November. "With force and arms in the River Congo on the coast of Africa," Gordon "did piratically and feloniously, forcibly confine and detain eight hundred Negroes . . . names . . . unknown." Gordon had good reason to think that despite being caught with hundreds of Africans in hand, he was in a city that was congenial to his offense, so—at least it was thought—he pursued a strategy of delay. His lawyers moved to quash the indictment on 24 December and by June a jury was assigned. By 30 November 1861, the trial opened—but by that time opinions about slave traders had soured, even in Manhattan where they had flourished not so long ago.[72] If Gordon had been scouring the local press, he might have noticed that just before his trial commenced, the U.S. District Attorney in this city had just "secured another condemnation of a vessel for fitting and with intention to proceed upon a slave voyage."[73]

Anxieties were rising as the trial approached. New York, a stronghold of the African Slave Trade, was becoming suffused with the sentiment that this Civil War and the sacrifice it entailed was being done to assist despised U.S. Negroes; thus, as Gordon's fate was being decided, "innocent Negroes" were "hanged to lamp-posts by a New York mob."[74]

E. Delafield Smith, the District Attorney, declared that Gordon "had been in custody for a long period of time, with no apparent effort to prepare the case for trial. Indeed, my eminent predecessor had declared in open court last winter that in his judgment, public opinion would not justify a capital conviction." When the U.S. Navy man who detained Gordon defected to the Confederacy, this opinion was bolstered. Gordon's "counsel had personal friends of his own German Jewish faith on the jury," which was worrisome to the prosecution. Reacting defensively, they "labored to separate the case from all questions as to slavery or slavery extension in this country." Apparently the tactic worked, as "the jury were out thirty minutes and returned with an honest verdict of guilty." Still, "the effect" in New York was "never paralleled by that of any criminal conviction in either the state or U.S. courts. Persons crowded into my office the following morning and asked if it was really so. As Gordon" was "an old offender, having been previously on two of these slave voyages," the prosecution was loath to be lenient with him, not least since the "cruelty exhibited by the evidence in these cases surpasses the common belief in respect to the atrocities of this trade." The prosecutor was "sorry" for Gordon but, it was added, "he should think of the agonies of the dying in his ship's hold." These words were written carefully, as the prosecution was desirous that "this letter should be read" to President Lincoln himself.[75]

Gordon sat impassively in the courtroom as a key witness "presented a heart-rending account of the wailing despair of human beings packed like cattle in the quarters below" deck and when the verdict was returned, he again did not flinch, receiving "the news with no change in the ice-hard cruelty of his eyes." This reflected the fact that Gordon continued to have reason to believe that he would not receive severe punishment, even when convicted. "The slave trading interests" had "left no stone unturned to procure a pardon for him" to the point where the morning "of the scheduled day for the hanging, an informer sped to the District Attorney's office with word that a rescue mob was forming to storm the jail and free the prisoner." Finally breaking down, Gordon sought to poison himself, as strychnine was smuggled into his jail cell with cigars apparently. Now a "raving maniac" he was "pinned to the floor by two husky guards while Dr. Simmons, the prison physician, endeavored to use a stomach pump on him." Gordon was unable to escape the "dubious distinction of being the first man to be hanged for slave running."[76]

Still, his death did not pass uncontested. A "well of sympathy" for him emerged. "The newspapers described the tearful scene when he saw his wife [and] family for the last time."[77] Britain's Consul in New York, took note of his death, observing that despite "the most strenuous efforts on the part of his friends, aided doubtless by the pecuniary influence of the slave trading interest in this city," Gordon was executed, though a "general impression prevailed to the last moment that the sentence would not be carried into effect."[78] Gordon's words as the smuggled poison worked its destruction on his body—" 'I've cheated you! I've cheated you!' "[79]—stood as a compelling verbal metaphor for though his life was taken, the life of the African Slave Trade survived his passing.

For just as Gordon was entering the courtroom, "300 slaves had been shipped on board an American schooner at Whydah [West Africa]. . . . several American vessels had arrived with rum and tobacco which it was expected would all return with slaves. Most of these vessels are from Salem and Boston. The Slave [Trade] has been in such a flourishing condition for years," it was reported, "and is principally carried on by Americans from the Northern States."[80] The African Slave Trade had attained sufficient momentum that London worried that even if Gordon's execution presaged a crackdown in the U.S. Northeast, slaving interests would simply move to "Liverpool . . . Cadiz, Barcelona and Marseilles," just as earlier they had relocated their exports from Brazil to Cuba and points northward.[81] What may have motivated this concern was the case of a vessel "fitted out in Lisbon for the slave trade" that had arrived from New York; it was suspected that the detainees did "intend hereafter to make Lisbon and Cadiz the base of their operations instead of New York." The problem was "the selling of an American vessel in a foreign port to be there fitted out for the slave trade is not forbidden by law."[82] Weeks after Gordon's execution, Secretary of State Seward announced that "the schooner William L. Coggeswell was recently seized at Lisbon by order of Mr. Harvey the United States Minister there upon suspicion by him supposed to be well founded that she had been fitted out for the purpose of prosecuting the African slave trade."[83] Moreover, there were searching allegations, frequently asserted, that there was "corruption" and collusion between the federal authorities and the slaving interests in New York that a mere Civil War had not squashed.[84]

Certainly there was no immediate deterrent effect attached to Gordon's incarceration, for after he was jailed, "the ship 'Nightingale'" arrived in New York from "the west coast of Africa . . . having been captured with 935 Negroes on board." The culprits included Samuel B. Haynes, Bradley Winslow, and Minthone Westervelt—the latter born in Staten Island of a "well-known family," while Haynes—like Gordon—hailed from Maine.[85] Domingo Martinez, a notorious "Brazilian slave dealer" who resided at "Whydah," did not seem to be deterred by what had had happened to Gordon. He was reported to carry on the "Slave Trade extensively with Cuba and the United States; he [was] also engaged in commerce with Brazil, chiefly with Bahia."[86] In fact, new areas of slave hunting seemed to be opening up, especially in East Africa, which in recent years had zoomed in importance as a site for obtaining human cargoes. By September 1862, British sources in South Africa were observing that "American slave vessels are now in the practice of proceeding to some of the west ports of Madagascar for their cargoes, which places are beyond the limits laid down in the treaty and therefore it can be evaded by them with impunity. The ports alluded to are independent of the King of that island, and the slaves are conveyed thither in native vessels from the East Coast of Africa, to be shipped off as opportunities offer."[87] That same year U.S. slavers were said to be operating near the tiny Caribbean island of Anguilla, though it was unclear if Africans from Madagascar were arriving in that vicinity.[88] Still, by May 1862, the U.S. Attorney in New York City reported six recent or ongoing prosecutions for slave trading.[89]

If there had been another city that could have challenged Rio's title of chief CSA sympathizer, it might have been Lisbon or Oporto. Recently naturalized U.S. citizens who only quite recently had resided in Portugal had been instrumental in perpetuating the African Slave Trade from their base of operations in New York City, New Bedford, and other Northeast locales and when it seemed that the Civil War was leading to more scrutiny of their activity, some of them began to move across the Atlantic to the land of their birth, where they resumed their slaving with a renewed gusto.

It would take more than litigation to bring the African Slave Trade to heel for it had already begun to metastasize and assume new forms. In early 1862, reports from Luanda indicated that "upwards of 2000 Negroes have been conveyed hence to St. Thomas since the 1st of January of the past year. . . . these Africans—who are the rudest and most unenlightened," according to a Portuguese official, were "recently brought in from the interior" but were deemed not to be slaves but servants.[90] From that island, long a major entrepot for the slave trade— a kind of West African version of Zanzibar—they could "emigrate" across the Atlantic.

This thought had occurred to at least one official in Lisbon. Such a practice "must have the effect of stimulating the slave trade in the interior of Africa," it was asserted. "Portuguese subjects are largely engaged in the slave trade" and "Portuguese authorities connive at it, if they do not actually participate in that traffic," it was conceded honestly and this was just one more example.[91] In boldly raising a point that had been obvious for decades if not centuries, one can sense the impact of the Civil War on the fate of the African Slave Trade: for even before it became clear that this would become a war of abolition, it was apparent that it might become so and that this transformation would then bring Washington in league with London to crush the recalcitrant and intractable, a category that had long claimed Lisbon. Concern in this sleepy capital began to be expressed about the "extent to which the traffic in slaves is now suffered to be carried on directly or indirectly in His Majesty's African dominions, owing to a want of due care and energy on the part of the local authorities." It was discovered suddenly in early 1862 that "great facilities have been afforded to the operations of the Slave Trade in the vicinity of the River Congo by the numerous small craft employed in the coasting trade . . . sailing under the Portuguese flag and provided with official papers of the Government of Angola," not to mention those transported "from the River Gaboon [*sic*] and adjacent parts of the continent."[92]

Portugal, a relatively small nation with an outsized colonial empire based disproportionately in the rich slave-hunting grounds of Angola and Mozambique, knew that if the Slave South lost the Civil War, Lisbon could possibly suffer more than a Mississippi slaveholder. In the early stages of secession, Portugal "received communications from some of the Vice Consuls in southern states asking if they could clear vessels as heretofore"; their emissary in the U.S. was cautious, noting that CSA "sovereignty" was "not recognized by" the "King of Portugal."[93] Again—like Spain—an ideological soul-mate that the CSA might have thought would stand resolutely by her side, Portugal instead was hedging its bets.

Robert dos Santos, Vice Consul in Norfolk, was not happy with this. He had "[tried] to keep neutral in the present deplorable war," he lamented in the summer of 1862, though he admitted that "of course, I can't help sympathizing with the South as I was born here and as I believe that her cause is a just one." Despite this, he also admitted, "I have taken no part in the war," though he had a "brother who has been an officer in the Confederate Army." He felt oppressed by the U.S. authorities, however, they had "not molested" him because of his brother but insisted that "the Portuguese flag which flies over my property will not be respected" and that "unless" he took an "oath of allegiance to the northern Government that not only will they confiscate my property but I will be required to withdraw beyond their lines." He was adamant in refusal—"The oath of allegiance I will never under any circumstances take. I am a citizen of Virginia and go with her wherever she goes." He requested a "copy of the treaty between the U.S. & Portugal" in search of legal validation of her parlous position.[94] He may have been luckier than his counterpart, Joaquim de Palma, Portugal's Vice Consul in Savannah; both "he and his family suffered when the federal army under the command of General Sherman passed through

Winnsboro in the state of South Carolina where he had removed his family and effects."[95] A sign of the times was the claim that a "fire" that had led to de Palma's setback was "the work of a Negro woman residing in the village."[96] Also telling was when the State Department claimed that they had never recognized da Palma's diplomatic status, indicative of how Lisbon had inserted its nationals throughout the nation, who then proceeded to engage at times in slave dealing.[97]

Portuguese and Portuguese-Americans, whose slave trading activity and other nefarious activities had been overlooked, now found themselves targeted. A. M. da Cunha, who moonlighted as Portugal's Consul in New York, theretofore a lucrative site for transoceanic slave-dealing, complained that his vessel that had "recently arrived from Havana" was "sold without my consent." Then the now chastened diplomat cum businessman was "informed" and "received instructions not to permit the clearance of any Portuguese vessel from the port" of New York "without receiving special permission from Washington and that these instructions apply to vessels of no other country than Portugal"[98]—in earnest of their instrumental role in slaving, a role that had been virtually ignored until Washington concluded that those backing a treasonous rebellion and the resultant dissolution of the U.S. might be the ultimate beneficiary of this traffic.

Finally getting wise, Washington was beginning to squeeze a major generator of the irrepressible conflict—Portugal—and as the prospect began to shrivel for the kind of large-scale slaving that this nation and some Portuguese-Americans had engaged in from the U.S. Northeast and New Orleans, shrinking along with it was the idea that a Confederacy could survive whose secession had been driven in no small part by slave traders. Blandly though pointedly, Secretary of State William Seward informed Lisbon's representative that "with a view to avoid obvious uncertainties and inconveniences, it is deemed indispensable that this Department should be promptly apprised of any appointment of Consular Officers of Foreign Powers in the United States"; he added, almost offhandedly, "information whether the person appointed is a citizen of the United States or a subject of the Government who may appoint him is also desirable."[99] Portugal continued appointing emissaries, taking pains to have them in New Bedford and Bangor, theretofore headquarters for illegal slaving.[100]

Washington was smart to be suspicious of Lisbon and its activities in North America. Portugal's Consul in New York claimed, for example, that "several poor and uneducated subjects of Portugal residing" in the major slave smuggling center that was Galveston, had been subjected to "forced enlistment into the military service of the so-styled Confederate States."[101] U.S. patriots were not so sure about the compulsion involved.

Better late than never. Cutting off Portugal's oxygen supply to the CSA was a major step on the road to curtailing the African Slave Trade, particularly the role in it of U.S. nationals and nationals of Portuguese ancestry. In the 1850s the illicit slave trade to Brazil was curbed, then it was pushed northward to the doorstep of the U.S. where it was squelched. However, this, ironically, gave a new boost to the idea of Matthew Maury of sending U.S. Negroes en masse to the Valley of the Amazon.

9

Deport U.S. Negroes to Brazil?

The Civil War delivered a forceful blow to the solar plexus of the illicit slave trade and transnational slavery itself. Yet the continuation of slavery in Brazil and the unresolved status of U.S. Negroes seemed to lead some to conclude that deporting the latter to the Valley of the Amazon would make for a serendipitous confluence. Brazil, which was quite friendly to the so-called Confederate States of America, was less welcoming to the prospect of opening its doors to a stream of dark-skinned people.

James Watson Webb, who served as U.S. Minister to Brazil during the Civil War, was no abolitionist,[1] a point recognized by his comrades.[2] "One fourth" of abolitionists were "<u>fanatics</u>," thought Webb, and "three fourths" were "<u>knaves</u>" [emphasis-original].[3] The influential politician from Maine, Hannibal Hamlin, had to remind Webb during his tenure as Brazilian Minister, that it was "supreme nonsense to contend that property in slaves, whether in the person or the service has any special immunity, over any other property."[4]

A man of action as well as words, on the evening of 1 October 1833, a group of active colonizationists and their sympathizers—who thought that free Negroes would be better off in Africa—met in Webb's office. Then he was the 31-year-old feisty editor of New York City's influential, pro-Whig Party " 'Courier and Enquirer.' There they planned to pose as 'friends of immediate abolition in the United States' and invade the initial meeting of the New York City Anti-Slavery Society." That evening 1500 showed up "yelling for the blood of Arthur Tappan and [William Lloyd] Garrison." Webb, "an ardent Episcopalian" and "former Army officer," was also a "key figure in the October mob and the North's most vehement anti-abolitionist spokesman to support African colonization."[5] Webb was also an ardent "racist," who "denounced the abolitionists" with full-throated fervor. "In common with many other northerners, Webb believed that abolition was more dangerous than slavery" and also thought that "colonization of slaves in Africa was the only practical remedy to slavery." A full spectrum bigot, "anti-Semitism" also "crept into Webb's crusade." Webb also concurred with Deep South leaders approving "anything that Congress could do to stop the antislavery agitation."[6]

It was Webb who, on July 4, 1834, "published a list of the activities scheduled for the holiday that included an announcement that 'at eleven, the fanatics meet at Chatham-Street Chapel, to have their zeal inflamed by the doctrines of abolition and amalgamation . . . ' Webb felt he could light a match to an already smoldering hostility toward the abolitionists. He was right. A mob broke into the chapel just as abolitionist Lewis Tappan finished reading the American Anti-Slavery Society's Declaration of Sentiments to a racially mixed audience. . . . one of the worst riots of the decade followed, lasting a total of eleven days. Mobs proceeded to break up other integrated abolitionist meetings with their menacing haunts."[7]

With such a background, it should not be deemed surprising that Webb would promote enthusiastically the notion of deporting U.S. Negroes to Brazil, even as this group was sacrificing tremendously to ensure the survival of the government—Webb's government—that was seeking to dispatch them southward. The contemporary historian, Lerone Bennett, has stirred controversy by ascribing this plan to Webb's superior—the President, Abraham Lincoln. After all, Bennett suggests, "in five major policy declarations, including two State of the Union addresses and the preliminary Emancipation Proclamation, the sixteenth President of the United States publicly and officially called for the deportation of Blacks. On countless other occasions, in conferences with cronies, Democratic and Republican leaders and high government officials, he called for colonization of Blacks or aggressively promoted colonization, by private and official acts." In 1862, says Bennett, "largely at President Lincoln's urging, Congress appropriated $600,000 a sum desperately needed . . . to prosecute the war" in order to "begin the colonization process." According to Navy Secretary, Gideon Welles, " 'almost from the commencement of this administration . . . the subject of deporting the colored race has been discussed.' " Lincoln asserted that " 'room in South America for colonization can be obtained cheaply, and in abundance; and when numbers shall be large enough to be company and encouragement for one another, the freed people will not be

so reluctant to go.'" The President created a "Black emigration department without giving it that name," to deport Negroes. "The President and all members of the cabinet, with the exception of Secretary
[Gideon] Welles and Secretary [Salmon] Chase, were in favor of deportation, according to firsthand reports." In 1862 on the front page of the
New York Tribune, the President discussed sending Negroes south of
the border.[8]

But Bennett, the historian, has paid insufficient attention to how the
international situation influenced Lincoln's decision to assert the Emancipation Proclamation and compel his retreat from mass deportation of
Negroes. For in mid-September 1862, the President told a "delegation
of Chicago clergy in mid-September that 'to proclaim emancipation
would secure the sympathy of Europe . . . which now saw no other
reason for the strife than national pride and ambition [and] an unwill-
ingness to abridge our domain and ambition. No other step would be
as potent to prevent foreign intervention,'" he declared cogently. A
Lincoln successor—Woodrow Wilson—acknowledged years later that
the 16th President hoped the Proclamation would "'imperatively prevent that foreign recognition of the Southern Confederacy which he
dreaded.'"

Lincoln, though opposing the war against Mexico, was something of
a novice in foreign policy. Rudolph Schleiden, Minister from Bremen,
recorded that the President had told him that "'I don't know anything
about diplomacy. I will be very apt to make blunders.'"[9] Yet he did
know enough about this hugely important subject to tread carefully
when it came to the question of enslavement of Africans. He had to be
careful for even the Brazilian Foreign Ministry had reason to believe
that "Louis Napoleon" had a "secret treaty," in 1863, "either concluded or in progress, with Jefferson Davis, by which the cession of
Texas is to be received as an equivalent for recognition and for substantial aid to the rebel Confederacy"; the "intrigues of two French consuls
in Texas" determined to "detach her from the Confederacy and reestablish nominally her independence" was likewise not exactly hidden from
view.[10] Both the U.S. and CSA realized that theirs was a conflict that
extended well beyond their own immediate interests and implicated
other powers with dedicated interests of their own—ignoring this simple yet profound reality could prove to be fatal. Thus, Washington "had
proposed an international conference to deal with the subject of emancipated slaves who wished to emigrate from the United States, but the

plans were abandoned after unfavorable responses from the leading European powers."[11] Carl Schurz, U.S. Minister in Madrid, was among those who realized early on that " 'as soon as the war becomes distinctly one for and against slavery, public opinion will be . . . overwhelmingly in our favor.' "[12]

Nevertheless, "on December 1, 1862 in his second annual message, President Lincoln presented a plan for gradual, compensated emancipation coupled with voluntary expatriation after freedom." This was in the face of claims by the Democratic Party that "used three phrases to sum up the alleged consequences of emancipation: 'racial amalgamation,' 'Africanization of America' and 'Free Negroism.' " In response "242 black residents" of California "petitioned Congress in 1862 to settle them in a country where their color would not be a badge of degradation. It seemed to be the policy of the state and the nation, they commented, to discourage the increase of persons of color in their midst and to use every legal means to induce those among them to emigrate." Nodding their heads in agreement at the idea of ousting U.S. Negroes, "such dignitaries as Representatives Francis Blair, Jr. from Missouri, Edward Bates from Missouri and Montgomery Blair from Maryland and Senator James Doolittle from Wisconsin" were "among the framers of these colonization plans."[13] Francis Blair had long been in favor of shipping U.S. Negroes southward, feeling that the "immense distance" had weakened Liberia's attraction as a dumping ground. But "the door is now open in Central America to receive the enfranchised colored race born amongst us," he said as early as 1858, as these "freed blacks hold a place in this country which cannot be maintained."[14]

These plans were so notorious that the Spanish Foreign Ministry got wind of them, noting the words of one member of the "Select Committee on Emancipation and Colonization" in 1862 who declared that "the home for the African must not be within the limits of the present territory of the Union. . . . Hayti and others of the West India islands, Central America and the upper portions of South America and Liberia are all interesting fields on inquiry in relation to the future of the . . . Negroes of the United States."[15]

To be fair, nations shipping huge numbers of their nationals to distant climes was not new, as the example of the poor and the Irish in the U.K. showed. They were dispatched to Australia en masse in the late 18th century and in 1824 London had devised yet another plan, this time "providing a settlement in South America for a portion of the unemployed poor of Great Britain & Ireland who are desirous of an asylum abroad"; the authorities made this scheme seem like a treat in that they were to be sent to a region where "the climate" was "similar to that of the South of France."[16] As indicated by the apparent ease that Portuguese and other European nationals were gaining U.S. citizenship then plunging into the African Slave Trade, there was a kind of ease of nationality then that seems more compatible with today's "globalized," "global village" approach. "As Thomas Jefferson explained in 1793, 'our citizens are entirely free to divest themselves of that character by emigration . . . and may then become the subjects of another power.' " Attorney General Jeremiah Black "forcefully articulated the idea in an official ruling in 1859. He argued that the 'natural right of every free person . . . to leave the country of his birth in good faith and for an honest purpose, the privileging of throwing off his natural allegiance and substituting another allegiance in its place—the general right, in one word, of expatriation, is incontestable.' "[17] More to the point, the inflammatory North Carolinian, Hinton Helper, had long called for "the removal of all African-Americans from America."[18]

And even before the idea had struck Webb, the former U.S. Consul to Buenos Ayres, William H. Edwards, had concluded in 1847 that African labor was the key to developing the Amazon. "The whole territory is as much superior in every respect to the Valley of the Mississippi, as the Valley of the Mississippi is to that of the Hudson," said Edwards. It contained "an area of 950,000 square miles, nearly half the area of the United States in all its territories." But why Negroes for the Amazon? Reflecting a widespread belief, Edwards thought that "it is only in the early morning and late in the afternoon that white men can labour in the open air; but, where a white would inevitably receive a sun-stroke, a Negro labours with uncovered head without injury or exhaustion. The one has capacity to direct and the other the ability to perform and it is difficult to conceive how the resources of Brazil can ever be successfully developed without a co-operation of the two races."[19]

So it was not totally extraordinary that Lincoln and his Brazilian Minister would be discussing deporting U.S. Negroes as the Civil War raged. The "establishment of a colony of liberated Negroes on the Amazon was called to the Minister's attention by newspaper accounts of President Lincoln's suggestion in a message to Congress of the probable necessity of acquiring territory for manumission purposes. Immediately the thought struck Webb that suitable land lay along the Amazon; a little reflection convinced him that every factor pointed toward this as the best spot in the world for such a purpose." U.S. Negroes, thought Webb, "in their African home . . . had lived in a similar latitude" as Brazil's and "were exactly fitted by nature to conditions along the Amazon." Webb's plan "provided for the creation of a joint-stock colonization company" with Lincoln "to appoint the President of the company," who would be none other than Webb himself. "Before transportation to Brazil the manumitted Negroes were to be transferred to the corporation." Webb thought that "'the United States will be blessed by his [the Negro's] absence, and the riddance of a curse which has well-nigh destroyed her.'"[20]

Many of those who worked closely with Webb thought they would be better off in his absence, deeming him the curse. A "heavy-set, foppish man" and a "staunch Whig," Webb had an "abrasive manner and [a] sensitive honor," which "made him a difficult man with whom to work." His "gout and arthritis were aggravated by the humid tropical heat"; already he was "suspicious, stingy, hot-tempered and aggressive" and his multiple maladies did not improve his demeanor. Later Webb "worried himself into the symptoms of a duodenal ulcer." He was "reduced to eating nothing but moistened bread" as a result of his various illnesses; for months he "leaned heavily on crutches and was always liberally medicated with opiates." It was not easy for those of the most sunny of dispositions to stay upbeat in Rio de Janeiro where during summer months, "it seemed to rain constantly; black mud and grey skies framed the usually picturesque mountains." He considered his appointment as "little more than an opportunity to make money through his diplomatic connections." Not only did his eyes glint at the opportunity to make money off the misfortunes of U.S. Negroes, but he "also had great aspirations for monopolizing Brazilian coastal trade." Perhaps it was the "combination of drugs and pain" that "made it impossible for Webb to reason clearly and fulfill his duties expediently," for his grandiose schemes—which had U.S. Negroes at the center—went unrealized.[21]

But it was not for lack of trying. Webb was enthusiastic about the potential logistical nightmare of removing millions of U.S. Negroes thousands of miles southward. He sought to convince Secretary of State Seward that adding U.S. Negroes to the mix in Brazil would benefit both nations. "The Negroes on the opposite coast of Africa, whence Brazil was supplied," he explained, "are a very superior race to the tribes further north, which furnished the slaves for the West Indies and the United States"; the former were "fierce, warlike and intellectual" and seemed prone to "insurrection," unlike their North American counterparts. He was not seeking to defame wholly his erstwhile darker compatriots, declaring, "I insist that 50,000 freed Negroes from the United States would be worth to Brazil more than 100,000 slaves from Africa. . . . the United States will be blessed by his absence," he repeated, speaking of U.S. Negroes. Thus, he concluded, "the northern provinces of Brazil" should become the "future home of the manumitted Negro of the United States. . . . all the freed Negroes of the United States shall be transplanted to the region of the Amazon at the expense of the United States, and there be endowed with land gratuitously by Brazil" and "become citizens of Brazil."[22]

In a lengthy 17-page lawyer-like brief in favor of his proposal, Minister Webb asserted that he was only seeking to follow the lead of the "President" who was "suggesting the means . . . of obtaining a place for colonization"; the "purchase of territory for this wise and philanthropic purpose may be attended with difficulties so embarrassing" as to block the entire scheme, hence the value of a voluntary agreement with Brazil. There he found a "rapidly increasing value of the Negro in the province of Rio de Janeiro and all the southern provinces of the Empire," while the "slave population" was "on the decrease instead of the increase, as with us."[23]

In a "confidential" message, the U.S. legation in Rio de Janeiro stressed further that "the great want of Brazil at this day is labour. From the character of her climate and soil, black labour is preferable to white" [emphasis-original]. Deporting U.S. Negroes would be a boon to both nations, it was insisted. "Time and circumstances, not necessary to be considered in this Paper," it was stressed, "have produced prejudices between the white and black races in the United States, which to [the] honour of Brazil, do not exist here and which render it absolutely impossible, that the two races should live together on terms of social and political equality"; there was an "absolute necessity that the freed Negro should be transported beyond the jurisdiction of the United States where he can never enjoy political or social equality" [emphasis-original].[24]

For a while it seemed that U.S. Negroes were Brazil bound. In a "private and unofficial" message that was, again, "confidential," the government of Brazil initially "conceded" to Webb "for a period of twenty five years and thereafter, until revoked by the government of Brazil, the exclusive right of introducing as apprentices or colonists into the Empire of Brazil, Negros in part or whole the descendants of Africans emancipated or about to be emancipated" by the U.S. There was to be a "joint stock company with a capital not exceeding five millions of dollars," controlled by both nations; each colonist was to receive "one hundred acres of land," a "hut," and "certain agricultural implements."[25]

For a while it also seemed that London would go along with such plans, as long as they could get their slice of the action. In mid-1862, British emissaries were contemplating "the conveyance to St. Croix of free Negroes now in the United States or Negroes who may hereafter be captured by United States cruisers"; at this juncture a major concern seemed to be to "obtain for our West Indian colonies some share in the emigration."[26] There ensued serious debate in London about the "possibility of transferring to the British West [Indies] a large number of free Negroes who have been or may be emancipated by force of events in the United States." The Foreign Office had "received communications from a gentleman named Henderson, a native of the United States, who is now in this country with the object of making large purchases of different kinds on behalf of the Federal Government. . . . he further states as a result of the conversation with Mr. Seward that the United States government would be glad to receive a proposal for carrying these Negroes off to the British West Indies." High on the list were about 100,000 recently freed slaves now in Pennsylvania. London made it clear it did not want U.S. burdens offloaded upon them—"no person should be sent who from old age or sickness were unfitted for field labour."[27] No, said London, those to be deported should be "exclusively of the agricultural class and . . . pure African," not "any persons of colour of the various shades" who Washington "would be the most anxious to be relieved from"; these deportees would be "under indentures for three years."[28] From Government House in Demerara, in the nation that was to become Guyana, there was enthusiasm for this proposal, in light of the vast territory there and the sparse population. "Contraband" Negroes, i.e., escapees from the South, "border state" Negro slaves, "liberated Africans"—i.e., those caught on slavers—all would be welcome.[29] Similar enthusiasm emerged from similarly sparsely settled British Honduras: "some of the landed proprietors are very anxious to introduce coloured labourers," London was informed.[30] The desperate planters there were "making every exertion to obtain labour from China, India, Yucatan, indeed from almost anywhere."[31]

But as time passed, it seemed that London was arriving at the conclusion that U.S. Negroes should stay put. When Lincoln suggested publicly that U.S. Negroes should be dispatched to Central America, London raised the salient point that such a move was probably in violation of the "Clayton-Bulwer" treaty[32] and seemed relieved when states in this region "declined" the U.S. Negroes they were offered.[33] London also interposed the objection that sending these deportees to "New Grenada" or present-day Colombia would also violate this treaty, leading to a temporary pessimism on Seward's part, alleging that there had been "so many difficulties . . . interposed that he scarcely expected [the deportation] be carried out."[34]

In September 1862, when London's representative in Washington reported in "confidential" words that he "had another conversation with Mr. Seward. . . . he told me that the President was still anxious to carry out his scheme" but Guatemala and "San Salvador" were "against the importation of any Negroes. . . . Mr. Seward expressed his conviction that the British colonies would be far better adapted than any other destination for Negro Emigrants," and the "French Government" too did not want to be excluded, as they "were anxious to obtain a share of any Negro emigration" and the "Danish" in St. Croix remained interested too.[35] Seward remained engaged, telling London in a highly detailed proposal that "the number of this class of persons," i.e., deportees, was "augmenting and will continue to increase." Indeed, the "President" had "authorized" Seward to "enter into negotiations upon the subject."[36] "Seward informed me," said London's representative in mid-October 1862, "that the Government would shortly have an embarrassing influx of Negroes upon their hands." London was then suggesting as a way to foil CSA skepticism of this plan "embarkation" of these Negroes from the Northeast—New York, Philadelphia, Boston—not least to "preclude the appearance of taking an unfriendly part against the Southern States near their own borders."[37] But London continued to press difficult questions. As late as 17 January 1863, President Lincoln was asking London if they would accept deportees if they could "avoid all risk of the complications which might be caused if we received Africans claimed as slaves"—this could only complicate relations with the Slave South.[38]

Days before the Emancipation Proclamation was to take effect, Lord

Lyons in Washington was reporting in a "confidential" message that "Mr. Seward proceeded to speak at some length on the general question of the Emigration of the Coloured Population. Men, he said, of very great weight, and indeed the President himself, inclined to the opinion that the most desirable thing for both races was to separate them and to reserve North America exclusively for the Whites. On the other hand, the more ardent members of the Emancipation Party strongly objected to the removal of the Negroes. . . . it was asked whether it was wise to deprive the country of so much muscle and sinew, whether it was prudent to add to the strength of nations which might not be always friends of the United States." Reflecting the sensitivity of the discussions, Lord Lyons added tersely, "I do not think" Seward "would like them [his opinions] to be made public."[39]

In late April 1863, London was still enmeshed in protracted negotiations with Washington about the fate of U.S. Negroes. It was then that "Mr. Hodge, the agent of the British Honduras Company . . . arrived" in Washington and "had interviews with the Secretary of the Interior, with Mr. Pomeroy, Senator for Kansas. . . . he has also had an audience with the President. He tells me," said Lord Lyons, "that he has met with so much encouragement and made so much progress that he hopes to be soon in a position to request me to inform the Lieutenant Governor of Honduras that the time [has] come for proclaiming the Ports in the United States for the shipment of Negroes, under the Act of the Colonial Legislature."[40]

But London seemed to be souring on this grand scheme, as concern grew that they were being manipulated against the interests of the CSA, which "might lead to embarrassing complications."[41] From Jamaica came the suspicion that the entire "scheme" had "originated with speculators."[42] Others thought that U.S. Negroes might wind up being a Trojan horse for Washington, while Radical Republicans in the U.S. fretted that ousting Negroes would be akin to scoring an own goal. Thus, by the summer of 1863, Lord Lyons was cooling to Washington's ideas, particularly accepting "contraband" or escaped slaves from below the Mason-Dixon line—"serious political embarrassment might be caused at the end of the Civil War by our having taken away Negroes of their class," he insisted. London would accept free Negroes, but many of them had little desire to emigrate or were viewed suspiciously by British planters.[43] Hence, the scheme passed into stillbirth—and Lincoln was then poised to "evolve" to the point of accepting the continued presence of U.S. Negroes, not least since his desire to send them away was being extinguished for lack of finding a place to deposit them.

For the other great power of the hemisphere—Spain—was not enthused about an influx of Negroes to their neighborhood, not least to Haiti, whose existence had been causing shudders in Madrid and Havana for decades—though their fallback position was that matters of language and culture would complicate the integration of these potential emigrants and possibly foment handcuffing problems for Port au Prince. The Spanish representatives in Haiti monitored carefully President Lincoln's meeting with Negroes during the height of the war when he sought to convince them allegedly that they should leave the U.S.[44] Madrid took note of Lincoln's generous concession after "several of the Spanish republics . . . protested against the sending of such [Negro] colonists to their respective territories. Under these circumstances," he added magnanimously, "I have declined to move any such colony to any state without first obtaining the consent of its government."[45]

Likewise, Seward was sobering. Brazil and the U.S., he told Minister Webb, "although very widely separated" were the "principal states on this continent [*sic*] and the only two which tolerate that form of human bondage," i.e., slavery. "You think that you discern the finger of God pointing to the Northern provinces of Brazil as the land of promise, rest and restoration of the slaves now in the Southern States of the Republic," he said rehearsing Webb's own arguments. "You ask for the President to negotiate a treaty to effect the removal of such freedmen from their present homes and their colonization . . . in Brazil." Well, said Seward dismissively, "the President cannot, without further consideration, accede to this request." In the first place, like London and Madrid, there was grave doubt if Rio de Janeiro would accept this potential Trojan horse. "We have no right to assume," he said, "that the Empire of Brazil would prefer an expelled caste from this country to other possible supplies of population." Then there was the resistance in Congress, not least from Radical Republicans. It was unclear if "assent of two thirds of the Senate to any treaty based upon an Executive decision upon these questions could now be obtained," not to mention a "majority of Congress" for "appropriations of money to enable the President to execute the treaty." Speaking elliptically—though profoundly—Seward added, it "must not be inferred that the uncertainty of the public mind which I have described is a permanent and unchangeable one," thus, the "Presi-

dent while declining at the present to give you the authority you request, invites a continuance of your discussions."[46]

Actually, Seward's words were reflecting the dissent arising in the
Cabinet and Congress to Webb's bold initiatives. "Your Brazil scheme
does not meet the approval of Chase, Sumner, et al.," Webb was informed, "because they oppose colonization altogether. They say that the
labor must be kept in the country & the South must use it—& must
have it as <u>free labor</u>" [emphasis-original]. On the other hand, he was
told, "The President is ardently for a Central American colonization, as
near at hand & more likely to take with the blacks."[47] "All these subjects remain a subject of earnest but as yet very confused discussion,"
was Seward's frustratingly accurate response.[48]

Even after Brazil nixed the idea of mass migration of U.S. Negroes,
Webb "believed that this hurdle could be surmounted either by the repeal of the law," limiting immigration of those of African descent, "or
by having the company bring in the freedmen before they were techni-
cally free. Seward unofficially approved the plan and he promised that it
would be submitted to the next session of Congress." Yet even this idea
of bringing U.S. Negroes to Brazil as something akin to "indentured servants" in itself was suggestive of how far out of favor the African Slave
Trade had fallen.[49]

But even this scheme proved to be overly optimistic and, as in Brazil,
Washington found that securing a locale for millions of U.S. Negroes
was more than a notion. How would racists react to the arrival of so
many? Would Brazilian nationalists view this group as a Trojan horse?
And what about the Radical Republicans? Would forcing this departure
alienate a significant portion of the party that propelled Lincoln into the
White House in the first place?

Meanwhile, as Webb was plotting to send African-Americans to Brazil,
others were still scheming to transport more Africans from Southern
Africa and its environs across the Atlantic. 1863 seemed to be the
watershed year in this regard with a continued stream of Africans crossing the Atlantic in this year of Emancipation in the U.S., with a fluctua-
tion—up and down—in 1864, before tapering off in 1865, when the
traitorous rebellion in the Slave South was squashed finally. Thus, just
before Christmas 1863, it was reported from Luanda that "during the
greater portion of this year, the Slave Trade has been in a state of great

activity on the coast to the southward of this port,"[50] while six months later it was repeated from the same port that the "coast still swarms with vessels . . . in the service of the Slave Traders" with many having "no papers."[51]

It had long been the goal of London to force the African Slave Trade further south, backing it into a smaller and smaller region—like a boxer pushing an opponent into the corner of the ring—so better as to curb its range and mobility and smash it and this seemed to be working. By the era of the Civil War, the region north of Angola near Sierra Leone was as quiet in terms of trading as Luanda was busy. There had been a favorable "change of public sentiment which [was] produced by the secession of the Southern States and the attempt at disruption of the Union," while the execution of Nathaniel Gordon "struck terror into the parties" so disposed to slaving.[52] "The Slave Trade" it was said as 1864 was about to dawn, "during the last twelve months has been considerably on the decline." Reporting from Sierra Leone, a Royal Navy commander asserted that "the war now existing between the Northern and Southern states of America has, doubtless, very materially assisted the efforts of our cruisers and intimidated the old and long-established agents of the slave dealers on this coast from risking their money and their ships in such uncertain speculation," though there were "no American ships of war of any kind out there."[53]

Soon even Angola seemed to be changing for the better. In early 1865, the Luanda-based Portuguese-British commission, designed to frustrate the African Slave Trade, reported that "the only case brought before them for adjudication during the course of the year 1864 was that of the schooner 'Congo' . . . navigating without papers . . . laden with a cargo that might be easily disposed of to provide the means of purchasing slaves or be bartered for them; that she had an American ensign on board" and "twelve blacks on board unprovided [*sic*] with passports."[54]

As Washington began to enforce more carefully its existing laws against the African Slave Trade and as the fortunes of the CSA began to deteriorate in the face of a Union army replenished with an ebony arm and this treasonous rebellion found itself frustrated in gaining desperately needed diplomatic support in Madrid and Lisbon and London, the number of Africans crossing the Atlantic began to slow down for the first time in years. A turning point had been reached, it seems, in the decades long—nay, centuries long—campaign to hinder successfully the

African Slave Trade. This was reflected in the bold words of Andrew Foote, who once had sailed with the African Squadron. In mid-1862, he forcefully instructed Navy Secretary Gideon Welles, "when this rebellion is crushed, and a squadron is fitted out to enforce the new treaty for the suppression of the African slave trade, as I have had long and successful experience in African cruising. . . . I should be pleased to have command of the African Squadron; but so long as the rebellion continues, it will be my highest ambition," he emphasized, "to be actively employed in aiding in its suppression."[55] Crushing the African Slave Trade and crushing the CSA were increasingly seen as synonymous. Washington signaled its new earnestness when in the spring of 1862 it signed a treaty with London "for the suppression of the African Slave Trade." Finally retreating from the claim of sovereignty, the U.S. acceded to the mutual searching of trips and if the ship examined had "shackles, bolts or handcuffs" or "hatches with open gratings" or an "extraordinary quantity of rice," this would be deemed "prima facie evidence that the vessel was employed in the African Slave Trade."[56]

Indicative of Washington's evolving position on the African Slave Trade was the appointment of Ohioan James Monroe as Consul to Rio de Janeiro in 1863. Theretofore, Brazil had been viewed as a sinecure for anti-abolitionists like Webb or outright pro-slavery elements like Henry Wise and Meade but Monroe was made of different stuff. He "became deeply involved in the antislavery politics of Ohio, with the famous Oberlin-Wellington rescue of 1858 and the ramifications of the Harpers Ferry raid a year later"; unlike many of his predecessors, Monroe was "dedicated to the eradication of slavery" and had a "relationship with [Frederick] Douglass" that "was especially close."[57]

But Brazilian slavery was sufficiently insidious to ensnare the most fervent abolitionist. His household in Rio "relied upon the labors of hired-out servants, who were slaves"; when "the Monroes left to return to Oberlin permanently, Bento begged to go with them to the United States. . . . the use of slave labor with the wages going to the slaves' owners, leaves Monroe open to criticism as a hypocrite."[58] The tortured diplomat "struggled with his conscience over the position he should take regarding Brazilian slavery."[59]

Webb did have a point nonetheless. There continued to be a perceived need in Brazil for African labor. As in the U.S., Africans had been moving from north to south, following the trajectory of economic trends. But with U.S. Negroes not arriving any time soon and the

hampering of the forced recruitment of Angolans and Mozambicans—
"it is now more than eight years since one single debarcation [*sic*] of
Africans has been realized," said Brazil's Minister of Justice in 1864[60]—
more severe means arose. Hence, in the fall of 1864, there were complaints from Montevideo about the "seizure in the Brazilian territory
and the sale there as slaves of Uruguayan citizens and complaints as to
the invasion of the Uruguayan territory by Brazilians and their forcibly
carrying off Uruguayan citizens, in order to sell them as slaves in the
territory of the Empire."[61] Seeking to reassure Brazil that the Emancipation Proclamation was not as sweeping as it appeared, Webb informed
the Marquis d'Abrantes that the "Executive of the United States never
claimed, and has never attempted to exercise the power of manumitting
slaves, except where their masters were in open insurrection," the implication being that there was still a green-light for slavery itself.[62]

Such blatant kidnappings were driven by the effective squeeze placed
on the African Slave Trade to Brazil and a gathering abolitionist sentiment[63] in this South American nation itself. "The slave population is
decreasing," said W. D. Christie, Britain's representative in Rio de Janeiro in early 1863; "there is no possibility of a revival of the Brazilian
Slave Trade," he said with confidence—though there was "no sign of
effort or preparation for the abolition of slavery."[64] From Maranham
came the message on 30 September 1863 that there was "no renewal of
the African slave trade within the limits of this vice-consulate during the
whole of the quarter ending this day."[65]

CSA slave trading operatives were busy, but their attention had been
diverted away from Brazil. In early 1863, London's emissary in Havana
spoke of F. P. Drain, "who had a considerable sum of money with him
and who stated that he was a citizen of the Confederate States," which
was linked with a "suspicious screw-steamer [that] was fitting out for
the Slave Trade at Isla Mugeres on the coast of Yucatan. . . . the steamer
was [none] other than the famous slaver 'Noc Daqui.' "[66] In September
1863, from Sierra Leone there came a report about a "Netherlands barque 'Jane' "; but it was added tellingly, "there can be little doubt" that
"her Dutch nationality was merely nominal and assumed for the purposes of fraud; she was originally an American vessel and had already
been known as a successful slaver under the name of the 'Fleet Eagle,' it
is most probable that her supercargo, an American, who described himself as a native of the Southern or Confederate States of America, was
the real owner of the ship as well as of the cargo."[67] A few months

earlier "the American brig 'Souther' 197 tons" and registered in New Orleans, "sailed the day before yesterday" from Cadiz, "nominally for St. Thomas but in reality for the coast of Africa for slaves." This "old vessel" appropriately was "painted black."[68]

And East Africa continued to present a problem of untold dimensions. "The Slave Trade from this side of the continent," it was said in late 1863 in reference to this vast region, "is carried on to a far greater extent that is generally supposed in Europe." Pointed reference was made to the conspicuous presence of "American merchants" in Zanzibar where this "horrible business" was conducted.[69] In mid-1864, the Royal Navy captured a "schooner without name, papers or colours, fully equipped for the Slave Trade," near the River Congo, that was "until recently . . . employed in running cargoes of cotton between the Confederate States and Havana. The mate, who is apparently an American, states that . . . [this] is the Captain's first voyage in the Slave Trade," though the "crew of five men are European."[70]

These forays from the Slave South reflected this region's desperate circumstance for with enslaved Africans fleeing north and west and with their economy spiraling into desuetude, at this point the CSA not only needed "Cheap Africans," but they also needed Africans plain and simple. They and their "Copperhead" allies[71] sprung into action accordingly but they were finding the going a bit tougher. In early 1862, "the American barque 'White Cloud' a suspected slaver arrived in the River Congo" primed for a dirty venture, but they "met a just and well-merited end" as "she grounded off a point called Scotchman's Head; and the natives, who have lately given a good deal of trouble to the Europeans residing there, made a dash at her in force with a number of canoes and were soon in possession of her. The captain and crew immediately abandoned the vessel; and, destitute of everything but the clothes they stood in, arrived at the French factory at the mouth of the river. . . . the natives proceeded to destroy the rigging and plunder the whole of the cargo."[72]

There was a perceived need for more labor in Brazil during the U.S. Civil War, as this conflict seemed to give a fillip to the Brazilian economy. Writing from Pernambuco in December 1863, a **New York Times** correspondent called this city a "great center of the cotton trade. It has doubled within the past year." But the tectonic shift in attitudes was reflected in rejection of the assumption that only African labor could fill the gap, for this industry was "carried on by white men and free half-breeds"; the "old shallow argument that the 'nigger' alone could stand the hot climate, ergo 'the nigger' must be enslaved, is all exploded. . . . slavery will go, is going, by the board in Brazil."[73] Increasingly it seemed that the U.S. authorities were reconciling themselves—like this **Times** correspondent—to a post-slavery world. "Nine-tenths of the cotton produced in this and adjacent provinces is the result of free labor," agreed the U.S. Consul in Pernambuco in November 1864. There was a recognition that it was slavery itself that had hampered the forces of production, as it was added tellingly, "the production might be enormously increased if any care was given to the cultivation but I doubt if a single plough can be found in the hands of any cotton grower in this province."[74]

This boon for Brazil seemed to be a positive for the U.S. as well, particularly in the Amazon where the idea of expatriating U.S. Negroes had yet to perish. As an economic boom rocked this region, it is easy to imagine how the idea of sending African-American laborers there gained a footing. "The American commerce with this province (the second province in the Empire) is greater than that of any other commercial nation and nearly as great as that of England and France combined!" Seward was informed enthusiastically in August 1862.[75]

Yet despite this rose-tinted economic outlook, diplomatic relations between the U.S. and Brazil were more complicated. After all, Washington had tolerated a host of ministers, such as Meade, who had appealed to Brazil on the basis of slavery, just as they warned that if the Confederates were expropriated of their slave property without compensation, something similar would befall the Empire. Thus, the pro-Confederate **Savannah Daily Morning News** was not alone when in early 1862, it dismissed the idea that the Empire was somehow pro-U.S.[76] "We want no misunderstanding with Brazil," Seward advised Webb. "But we can't consent that she shall harbour pirates and justify it. . . . why does not the Brazilian government adopt the French rule—or even the British. Why stand out alone," he wondered.[77] As late as November 1864, as the CSA was about to writhe in its death throes, the **New York Times** found that "Confederate privateers have been constantly hovering around [Brazil's] ports and while burning United States vessels trading to Brazil off the Brazilian coast, have run into her ports at the first sign of danger," indicating that "Brazil was giving undue protection to the Confederate cruisers."[78]

The perceptive journalist probably had Raphael Semmes of the CSA Navy foremost in mind. Of French descent and born in Maryland in 1809, Semmes—like many leading Confederates—had fought in the war in Mexico.[79] This wartime experience served him well when the Civil War broke out. Sensing correctly that Brazil could be a powerful ally of the CSA, just as disrupting its trade with the U.S. would be similarly potent, Semmes repaired southward where "his veiled threat of calling down on Brazil the vengeance of the Southern Confederacy after it had disposed of its Northern adversary, was most persuasive." Brazilian elites "caved in at once." In a celebratory mood, a "British resident merchant, Mr. Ogilvie, topped off the merry-making by a splendid ball honoring the Confederate visitors . . . the Confederacy was toasted to the starlit skies."[80] As Semmes himself recalled it, while in Brazil in September 1861, he "called upon the President" and "was admitted to an interview. . . . I then stated to him that this war was in fact a war as much in behalf of Brazil as of ourselves, and that if we were beaten in the contest, Brazil would be the next one to be assailed by Yankee propagandists. These remarks were favorably received," he added modestly.[81]

Actually, Semmes may have been the most notorious Confederate on the global scene, sailing from port to port wreaking havoc on the U.S. and its vessels and accepting the hosannas of the adoring. When Semmes arrived in Cape Town—a town whose attitude toward Africans may have been more primitive than that of the CSA—he was welcomed like a conquering hero.[82] "His arrival was more spectacular than had been foreseen. Colonists and natives swarmed." The appreciative Semmes observed, " 'during my entire stay, my table was loaded with flowers and the most luscious grapes and other fruits, sent off to me every morning by the ladies of the Cape, sometimes with and sometimes without a name." This occurred though "commercially the Civil War was a disaster for South Africa, as it deprived the Cape of the transatlantic market for her wool and gave other nations a chance to establish themselves." Even today a song is still sung there about Semmes's ship, the "Alabama." Lord De Villiers, later the Chief Justice of the Cape and then of the Union of South Africa, was in 1863 during Semmes's visit, "still a student" in London but heard enough about Semmes's incursion to echo the sentiments of many of his compatriots when he said, " 'I wish the Southerners well with all my heart . . . slaveholders though they may be.' " What had made Semmes so inspirational was that he held out the prospect that those who wished to keep Africans in bondage, could yet prevail. After all, "during his previous raids around the Cape of Good Hope Semmes captured no fewer than fourteen Northern Vessels, thereby providing busy times for the shipbrokers."[83] The CSA had reason to believe it could rely upon a "Racist International" that included Brazil and South Africa to help them triumph in the war.

This was unsettling to Washington but it was partially to blame for the U.S. had persisted in dispatching "reliable" slaveholders as ministers to Brazil in the antebellum era. Thus, Henry Wise was not only "for some years upon the Committee of Naval Affairs," but he also had an "acquaintance with naval officers resulting from that fact and from his long residence at Rio de Janeiro"; he was well positioned to provide useful intelligence to the CSA.[84] It was not only the loss of the ships but the possibility they could then be deployed in obtaining valuable capital —in the form of enslaved Africans—for the CSA. It was as if Semmes was bouncing between Rio de Janeiro and Cape Town, turning the South Atlantic into a Confederate lake as he raided U.S. shipping, e.g., when "the 'Tuscaloosa' . . . a barque of 500 tons captured by the 'Alabama' off the coast of Brazil" and was brought to "Simon's Bay" in South Africa.[85] The bold Semmes not only requested "supplies and repairs" in South Africa, but he also sought "permission to land 33 prisoners." Then his reception was so rhapsodic that he stayed on longer than expected, with "heavy seas" given as the reason for the delay.[86] Following Semmes, more rebel ships were arriving regularly in South African waters. "No American war-ships have yet appeared here," said a U.S. diplomat glumly, "but they are anxiously looked for." Semmes, on the other hand, was celebrating, "offered" a hefty "4000 [pounds]" for a ship he had captured, which could go a long way in fueling the CSA's rebellion.[87] The "damage done by Raphael Semmes to the commerce of the United States" amounted to "ten millions of dollars." Yet despite this mayhem he inflicted on the U.S. during the course of his treasonous revolt, after the war his "statue" was placed prominently on "Mobile's busiest thoroughfare, standing near the sea he so long loved and dominated."

It was as if the racist world recognized that the arrival of Semmes was akin to a last hurrah for the African Slave Trade, now in its twilight, which had brought so much wealth to so few and so much misery to so many.[88]

In Mexico the sardonic Semmes left a tombstone that said, "in memoriam of Abraham Lincoln, President of the late United States, who died of nigger on the brain, 1st January 1863."[89] With such a putrid attitude toward the Emancipation Proclamation, it should not be deemed overly surprising that his approach to a Brazil with more than a modicum of the darker-skinned, was hardly benevolent—despite the cooperation he received at the highest levels. Yes, he "found the country attractive but Brazilian society displeased him so violently that after the war, when an emigration scheme to Brazil was mooted in the Confederacy, it met with Semmes' forceful disapproval. 'The effete Portuguese race,' " he sputtered, " 'had been ingrafted [*sic*] upon a stupid, stolid Indian stock in that country. . . . this might be a suitable field enough for the New England schoolma'am and carpet-bagger, but no Southern gentleman should think of mixing his blood or casting his lot with such a race of people.' "[90]

In his memoir Semmes also speaks of meeting a Brazilian governor, "his complexion, like that of most Brazilians, was about that of a side of tanned sole-leather." Even as this politician was treating him to a feast—it was "quite substantial," he thought—the color-obsessed Semmes could not take his eyes off "her ladyship, the governess . . . a very sprightly and not uncomely mulatto" and "her two little children" with "rather kinky, or, perhaps, I should say curly hair." But the high-minded Semmes was "a man of the world and was not at all dismayed by this discovery." His counterparts were more concerned about their mutual taste for bondage than the matter of color, so Semmes was garnished during his stay with "fat turkeys and bouquets, instead of remonstrances." But the ungrateful Semmes could only think of the countenances of his hosts, who were "only a better class of Portuguese," a "swarthy population, the chief features of which are *sombreros* and garlic." He was disgusted with "amalgamation" in Brazil, thinking it provided a poor example for North America, as it was leading to a "mongrel set of curs" that would "cover the whole land." He was more pleased with South Africa where "the African had met the usual fate of the savage, when he comes in contact with civilized man. He had been thrust aside and was only to be seen as a straggler and stranger in his native land." As he saw it, "the inhabitants of the Cape Colony seemed to resemble our own people" in their penchant for white supremacy.[91] Interestingly, on Semmes's ship "the vast majority were British nationals but there were also . . . Frenchmen, Lascars and other Continentals and Asians," there was even a "man of color on

board," slave " 'contraband' " who served as "mess orderly"—but to
Semmes those who served him and his cause were no more than "water-
front riffraff."[92]

Thus it was that this racist marauder, Semmes, found himself off the
coast of Brazil during the Civil War; alongside him was John McIntosh
Kell, who fondly recalled later "we were a week or more in Bahia,
enjoying all the hospitalities of its citizens and the salubriousness of
its climate";[93] these well-treated buccaneers were "permitted"—in the
words of U.S. Consul James Monroe—"to burn three American vessels
within three miles of the shore." This was "barbarous, cowardly and
ruinous to our commerce," he said, "and was made all the more irritat-
ing by the fact that it received substantial aid from England."[94] James
Watson Webb was outraged by Brazilian complicity and demanded satisfaction.[95] In a brutally detailed 37-page reproach, he denounced this
"unfriendly act" toward the U.S.[96]

Semmes's ship was a behemoth, "220 feet long and 32 feet wide,
with a draft when fully loaded of 15 feet" and "rated at 1040 tons.
Each of the two horizontal steam engines was rated at 300 horsepower,
but her trial run indicated that her maximum total power was close to
1000 horsepower. Her bunkers could carry 350 tons of coal. She was
equipped with a double set of sails, a condenser to produce fresh water
from seawater and spare equipment and supplies sufficient for a long
voyage." Washington could not be pleased by the fact that it was the
British who were central to the "construction, arming, escape and supply" of this vessel, along with "other Confederate raiders"; besides
South Africa and the U.K. itself, Semmes was greeted rapturously in
Jamaica, Trinidad, and other outposts of the British Empire. Thus, these
"raiders," e.g., the one that destroyed U.S. shipping off the coast of
Brazil, were "the most serious source of continuing tension between
the United States and British governments during and following the
Civil War."[97]

That it was a serious source of continuing tension between the U.S.
and Brazil is an understatement. The U.S. Consul in Bahia, Thomas
Wilson, was livid when the "Alabama" arrived there in the spring of
1863. Semmes and Co. stayed for a week and were allowed to take on
coals and supplies, as if Bahia were part of the CSA. Wilson vainly
urged the "President of the province" to bar this "but without effect.
. . . on the morning of the 13th," he told Seward, "I found that another
piratical steamer called the 'Georgia,' bearing the rebel flag, had entered

this port. She called for coals and supplies and other supplies which she was allowed to take on board." Wilson "renewed the protest," again to no avail. Wilson was doubly upset when an "English barque . . . attempted to furnish supplies to [these] pirates."[98] Bahia seemed to be adopting a form of what they termed "strict neutrality" that favored the CSA, as when it referred in official documents, to "the states of the South of the American Confederacy" and "the Northern states of the same Confederation" — such circumlocution could be viewed as a whopping verbal blunder or a smooth pro-CSA evasion.[99]

Wilson was beyond anger about this. When "Semmes arrived" in Brazil "on the 6th day of September 1861," he was "granted permission to obtain . . . supplies and treated . . . in all respects as" if he were captaining a "<u>regular man of war</u>" [emphasis-original], this "against the protest" of the U.S. about this "unfriendly conduct" of the Brazilians. Brazil was terming the CSA a "<u>de facto</u> government, having in the field large armies, making war upon the United States and that the Imperial government had conceded to those states the right of belligerents, in conformity with the laws of nations and the dictates of humanity." The U.S., which for the longest time had resisted collaborating with Britain against Brazil in an attempt to extirpate the African Slave Trade, was now facing the dire prospect of the two teaming up against Washington: Semmes's ship not only was built in England but also "sailed from the port of Liverpool with an English crew and flying the British flag," it "never having been in a port under the control of the <u>insurgents</u>" [emphasis-original].[100]

Semmes's deeds instilled fear on those being transported on U.S. vessels. Writing in mid-1862, U.S. Consul in Para, William Richard Williams, expressed grave "apprehensions . . . regarding Southern privateering in the vicinity of this port. . . . three vessels within the last four months have disappeared very strangely."[101] A worried Minister Webb instructed the Bahia Consulate "to grant no circumstances from this port to American vessels, unless the masters of said vessels first *take and subscribe* before you, an oath to support the Constitution" [emphasis-original].[102]

James Monroe of Ohio spent 49 days at sea on his way to Rio during the Civil War. It was "mostly uneventful," "somewhat wearisome" with "homesickness" being a major emotion. With time on his hands, he "discovered that my old friend the North Star had disappeared from the sky—had gone behind the great polar," then he saw the "Southern

Cross which came into view about the same time with its four rather dim points of light," which let him know that he was nearing the "Deepest South." Then his reverie was interrupted; his vessel just "evaded another ship" which "would have sent us to the bottom. The mysterious stranger, though it was very dark, had carried no lights. One captain thought her officer must have been drunk." Monroe had other suspicions. He was worried about bumping into Semmes, especially in light of the "proclamation of Emancipation,"[103] which he was known to despise—and for which he was thought to be seeking substantial retribution.

Semmes was not a master of public relations, finding it difficult to downplay his Negro-phobic attitudes, e.g., in a well-circulated letter to the **London Times** where he denounced a competing newspaper and "kindred Negrophilist associates" who he found "particularly virulent and abusive" after they correctly termed him a " 'pirate.' "[104]

A sensible London was not willing to back a loser and as the war grinded on, Semmes's escapades were replaced in the public mind with contrasting images. In the late spring of 1863, the "Palace of the Government" in Pernambuco reported that "the commanding officer of the steamer 'Florida' of the Confederate States of the American Union [*sic*] which lies at the anchorage of the port of this capital" requested "coal," adding that "like favors have been conceded to ships of the Confederated States in their need by many unions." The vessel would not be allowed to stay for more than 24 hours; it was "reckoned from the reception of the dispatch and that during the interval" the ship obtained "coal, fresh provisions and" was able to "make repairs to the machinery."[105] The commander of the CSA vessel objected, arguing that he needed at least four days—a request that was quickly granted by João Silveira e de Souza on behalf of the "Palace."[106] Just after that, the U.S. Consul in Pernambuco, Thomas Adamson, had the "painful necessity of reporting the destruction of another American ship by the pirate 'Florida.' "[107] It was as if Brazil was just one more state in the Confederate States of America.

When this CSA ship arrived at Bahia in the late fall of 1864, the U.S. Consul there "went at once" to "consult with Capt. Collins in regard to what might be done to destroy her. I found Capt. Collins extremely anxious to do everything that he could do in conformity with international law to secure the pirate," said Thomas Wilson; "[he] did not wish to violate the sovereignty of Brazil by attacking her in the harbor"

—but what was the alternative? Wilson was "urging Capt. Collins to sink her in port and not trust to the uncertainties of a chase at sea. He still declined."[108]

But it was not long before the appropriately named Commander Napoleon Collins of the U.S. Navy abruptly changed his mind and rammed his ship squarely into the CSA "cruiser 'Florida,'" accepted her surrender, and "with the Brazilian fort guns ablaze and warships giving chase, towed his quarry out to sea and eventually to the United States."[109] U.S. Consul Wilson was now elated about the "capture of the piratical cruiser 'Florida.' . . . these pirates have made the ports of Brazil a basis for obtaining supplies and repairing their machinery and also a rendezvous where they have met their consorts and <u>tenders</u>, every facility for so doing having been accorded to them by the authorities of the ports which they entered, sanctioned by the Imperial Government. Thus the pirates were enabled not only to prey upon the commerce of the [U.S.] in the waters adjacent to the coast of Brazil but also <u>within those subject to the jurisdiction of the Brazilian government</u>" [emphasis-original].[110] U.S. Navy Secretary Gideon Welles was unapologetic about the ensuing uproar. Yes, there was a "great outcry" among the "English press and people," but it was "Brazil herself" which had "in the first instance done wrong. She has given refuge and aid to the robbers whom she does not recognize as a government. . . . Brazil and other governments who have given shelter, comfort and aid to the piratical vessels that have plundered our commerce under a pretended flag which neither Brazil nor any other nation recognizes committed the first great wrong."[111]

Secretary of State Seward told the Brazilian Foreign Ministry bluntly that "in the year[s] 1862 and 1863 remonstrances were addressed by us to the Government of Brazil against the policy, different as it was from that of all other American states, in regard to the furnishing of shelter and a haven [for] pirates"—with "no satisfactory result."[112] As if he were instructing a mannish schoolboy, Seward rebuked Brazil, adding "this Government disallows your assumption that the insurgents of this country are a lawful belligerent." He accused the Empire of committing an "act of intervention in derogation of the law of nations, and unfriendly and wrongful as it is manifestly injurious to the United States." Semmes and his sort were "enemies of the human race," Seward charged angrily, while the "wrongs and injuries" inflicted by the CSA on the U.S. with Brazil's connivance meant that the latter "justly owes reparations to the United States."[113] Seward had a point: "during the first two years of the war even the ports of far-off Brazil were used as occasional depots [by rebels] for arms to be shipped through the blockade to the coast of Texas."[114]

The fire-eater, Edmund Ruffin, robustly begged to differ. "The Brazilian government acted with vigor in regard to the capture of the 'Florida.' The exequatur of the U.S. Consul at Bahia was revoked," while "the principal courts of Europe, also, have sent such strong protests against this violation of the law of nations, that Lincoln's government is alarmed & has manifested clear indications that it will back down as it did in the case of the Trent."[115]

C. M. Morris of the CSA Navy was predictably irate. "I came to this port for the purpose of procuring provisions for my crew and getting certain necessary repairs to enable me safely to continue my voyage," he told the Brazilian president, and instead he was hijacked by "cowardly and treacherous" Yankees, engaged in the "most base and cowardly outrage."[116] The "Governor's Secretary" treading delicately was "authorized to tell" Morris that "His Excellency was very sorry to say that your Government not being recognized by any nation, he could not keep up an official correspondence with you so as to answer your protest which he considered quite right."[117] The CSA spun this as a "flagrant outrage upon the territorial sovereignty of Brazil,"[118] but they could not obscure the point that even the slaveholding Empire was reluctant to truck with an outlaw regime bent not only on slavery but reviving the African Slave Trade as well.

But the pro-slaveholding forces of the Empire were of a different view. There was "ineffective fire [from] Brazilian ships and forts" as the CSA vessel was "towed. . . . Two Brazilian ships pursued" to no avail but then "an angry mob which a few hours later attacked" the U.S. "consulate and defaced the American coat of arms." The next day a "small company of soldiers" were dispatched by the Empire to protect the consulate. Seward promised to repatriate the CSA ship but instead it was sunk in Hampton Harbor, Virginia and Commander Collins was promoted.[119]

With it was sunk the Confederate dream of an alliance with Brazil that would guarantee the eternity of slavery and the African Slave Trade sunk with it. Washington came to realize that it had jeopardized its own existence by seeking to conciliate the Slave South with their despicable traders in human flesh, while Brazil came to recognize that it was risking war with its more powerful northern neighbor by doing the same. But the rebellious traitors—at least not all of them—did not surrender. Some instead thought the better part of wisdom would be to expatriate to Brazil, with their enslaved Africans in tow, thereby making concrete James Watson Webb's ever-shrinking vision of U.S. Negroes building the Empire.

U.S. slavery had proven over the years that it was influenced by global —particularly hemispheric—currents. Thus, one reason U.S. Negroes remained in North America was because of the reluctance of certain nations—especially Brazil—to receive them as the Civil War was unfolding, just as this South American nation's friendliness to the CSA was exceedingly helpful to this regime. But what would be Brazil's reaction to the arrival of former U.S. slaveholders on their shores?

10

Confederates to Brazil

The post–Civil War South was not a congenial place for those who held the African Slave Trade dear. Inevitably this also had an impact on Brazil, now sporting the once coveted but currently uncomfortable crown of being the heavyweight champion of slavery. Two simple cases of how Washington dealt with slavery in Brazil illustrate how the demise of this institution in North America undermined its continuation in South America. On 1 July 1862, William Harris, a U.S. national, died without a will in Bahia. The U.S. Consul there complained ineffectually that Brazil "interfered" in the administering of his estate so that all his property including "even a poor slave girl" was "sold"; the "authorities sent their armed police after her and she too was put up and sold at auction." But what seemed to upset him most was that "not a cent has ever reached the heirs of Mr. Harris who live in the city of New York" [emphasis-original].[1] Certainly no meaningful protest ensued.

But by 1868, times had changed. As William Seward—who acquiesced in the Harris case—explained, "a Portuguese subject Bernadino de Souza Pinto residing in the city of Recife, in Brazil, had a slave named José who was induced to run away to New York on board of the United States brig schooner. . . . [The] American Consul . . . refused to take the necessary steps" to retrieve him, to which his owner objected. Figuratively thrusting out his chest as he bestrode his high horse, Seward explained to the representative of this embittered loser of valuable property that "slavery is not only unknown here but is forbidden and disallowed. . . . no law of the United States forbids slaves in foreign ports from the use of merchant vessels in foreign ports . . . from enjoying rights of asylum in the United States."[2]

The annihilation of the CSA and the undermining of their "Copperhead" allies did not magically end the role of U.S. nationals in the African Slave Trade. In August 1865, months after guns had been stilled in

North America, familiar news was coming from Luanda: "two American whaling ships . . . on the coast with . . . 800 slaves."[3] In July 1865, the "Bark Dahomey" purchased in Lisbon, then transferred to New York, was in and out of Havana and suspected of slaving—though "the owners have never been in the slave business."[4] Then there was "the arrest" in Philadelphia after Lincoln's murder "of a Portuguese slaver and blockade runner named John Celestina who was suspected of being connected with the conspiracy to murder the leading officers of the Government."[5] Just as the existence of slavery in Brazil had given an enormous boost to the ambitions of the CSA, the demise of the CSA was correspondingly a detriment for this slave nation; yet the continued existence of African slavery in Latin America, even after it had been extinguished in North America, would continue to provide a base for remnants of the Slave South and their allies.

There were thousands of Confederates now in an analogous position —deprived of valuable property but unlike the gentleman from Recife, they had to endure the added indignity of living as close to their former property—who were now perceived as incredibly cheeky—as lips and teeth. To many, this transcended being intolerable, it soared beyond unendurable. Hence, many packed their bags and moved to an ally of the now vanquished CSA where slavery continued—and did continue —until 1888: Brazil. Thus, it was not surprising when as early as mid-May 1865, the verbose Mary Chesnut noted in her diary, "Isabelle writes that Rosser & Young have escaped—one to Maximilian, the other to Brazil."[6]

Even before the war's conclusion, the **New York Times** had detected signs of emigration. In fact, this trickle southward was an early indication of the failing fortunes of the CSA. "New from Europe," the **Times** announced in October 1864, "is the curious item that 'several wealthy Southern planters from South Carolina propose settling Brazil.' One gentleman is expected to arrive there with an odd quarter of a million in some sort of money."[7] A few weeks later it was observed that "a good many wealthy Southern planters are removing to Brazil and settling here. They go there in order to hold their slaves in peace."[8] During this same period, the U.S. Consul in Para, the Amazon, reported the arrival of "Dr. A. A. Blandy, a dentist recently resident in Baltimore"; he "fled from the U.S. to avoid a criminal prosecution for having swindled a Jew" and, suspiciously, "arrived at this port in the British brig . . . with a false passport." He was a "blatant secessionist" and complained incessantly about " 'outrages by Butler's black soldiers on [white] women in the South.' "[9]

And even before this, there "was a significant interest in Brazil on the part of Southerners prior to the Civil War. This interest, in fact, went all the way back to . . . James Edward Calhoun, a brother of the well-known Southern firebrand," who "made a number of friends in Brazil while serving on the crew of the USS Boston" in the 1830s. In 1852, "several planters approached the Brazilian Minister in Washington, proposing to settle with a thousand slaves along the Amazon. And talk of annexation spread."[10]

Thus, an alert listener at Appomattox may have heard a fellow officer of Robert E. Lee discussing the fact that he had already been in touch with the Emperor of Brazil about migrating. Captain Frederick N. Colston and "General Alexander" were chatting about this. The latter "said that he was going to try to go to Brazil and I wanted to go with him," said the eager Captain. "I have an interesting letter from him from the 'Brandreth House, N.Y., April 22nd 1865' telling of the inability of getting there and asking that it be communicated to Latrobe, General Longstreet's A.A.G. who also thought of going."[11] Weeks later, Jedediah Hotchkiss, Stonewall Jackson's famed topographer, was following up aggressively on these plans.[12]

How many Confederate expatriates were there after the Civil War? Estimates vary. Eugene C. Harter claims a figure of "twenty thousand or so," but this may be too high;[13] my own highly speculative guess is that the figure may be half that many.

In December 1865, Henry Shipley Stevens of Ohio was on his way to Brazil "to look up old customers and find new ones" and on board his vessel were a "group to which I wish to call your especial attention. Here are ten patriarchal looking gentlemen, who, with five or six younger ones, go out to Brazil to gain their freedom in a land of slavery; to escape from their old homes in Mississippi and northern Alabama, to go to nearly the last place on the globe where they can hold slaves." However, even then, he thought the number of Dixie refugees entering Brazil was miscalculated. "From what I learn," he said, "the number of Southerners who have gone to Brazil and who are preparing to go, has been under-estimated at the North. These people on board seem to belong to that middle class of farmers, so common to the South—the men who did most of the fighting at the behest of their superiors—who are still belligerent, though confessing to a lost cause. They are all zealous defenders of slavery." These also included a "General and one or two officers who have earned their titles by hard fighting," but the "unpardonable economy of truth" on their part and on the part of their fellow Confederates hampered Stevens' ability to guess how many of their kind were migrating.[14] Opinions about the numbers and class origins of the exiles vary, but what is broadly true is that racial animus and/or anger with the U.S. were factors in every case.

To where in Brazil did they decamp? in what was once characterized as "the largest planned migration ever to take place from the United States." There were six settlements and all failed except one at today's "Americana,"[15] appropriately in the south of that huge nation. Since Brazil was a "slave holding nation," said U.S. diplomat James Monroe, the Confederates were "received with much friendly attention and even with distinction by Brazilian officials at the Capital and in the interior"; they "bought or leased lands, bought or hired slaves" but "in less than a year," they began drifting back to the U.S., often disillusioned with Brazil, at times poorer since "many of the slaves whom they had bought, or for whose services they had contracted, ran away and it was not easy to recover them."[16]

The Empire, which was seeking to attract immigrants from Europe, at the same time they were turning away those of African descent, was open to accepting Euro-Americans, who were hostile to the U.S.[17] The passage from New York to Rio de Janeiro was a hefty $122, though "this money was to be refunded by the government of Brazil upon arrival in the country," suggestive of how eager the Empire was for these émigrés.[18]

Though many in succeeding generations have denied it, there is little question that there were two intertwined matters that drove so many from the U.S. to move so far: hatred of the federal government and a desire to continue African slavery.[19] "The tide of emigration setting towards Brazil is becoming every day more and more deep and general," reported the **New York Herald** in September 1865; "they abhor the idea of political equality with their former slaves; and rather than submit . . . they would expatriate themselves altogether."[20] The son of Matthew Fontaine Maury, the early champion of seizing the Amazon, remarked in mid-1866 in words that captured a widespread feeling, "I am so thoroughly anti-Yankee and pro-Confederate that I will always allow my feelings to run away with me when on this subject."[21] Why the anger? One unnamed rebel summed it up when he emphasized the "unconstitutional confiscation of my Negroes" and the related "belief" that the "Radicals will prevail" in Washington [emphasis-original].[22] During the war Green Ferguson's job was "capturing runaway slaves and escaped Yankee prisoners of war. The tools of his trade were a horse and 4 fox hounds. After the war federal troops arrested him and took him to New York City. . . . Green escaped and returned [home] to South Carolina. Later he was among the first to travel to Brazil," where he stayed—and "died a lonely and disappointed man in 1905."[23] But when queried in 1868 from his new home in São Paulo, Ferguson was acidly bitter when asked rhetorically why he should return to the U.S. "You tell me that your country is bankrupt and that the Negroes rule. Again, I ask, what do you wish me to return to the United States for?" especially since, said Ferguson, "I left the United States to avoid this state of affairs." He was content in Brazil though having been there "about sixteen months" where he was "free from tyranny and misrule."[24]

Like Ferguson, George Barnsley decided, "I have no other hope but emigration." Why? "I cannot conscientiously take an oath to the U.S. Government."[25] Like other Confederates, he could not rationalize swearing an oath of affirmation to a government that he had just sought to overthrow and which now, in turn, had overthrown slavery ruining thousands in the process. "In the advertisements sent out for the purpose of soliciting colonists, the promoters," Frank McMullen and William Bowen of Texas "sounded the warning that no persons would be considered unless they could qualify morally and politically—that is, be Southerners and hold proslavery sentiments."[26]

In the early postbellum era in Virginia, a Confederate was asked if he thought a " 'friendly feeling' " between the former warring combatants could ensue. " 'No sir, never,' " he replied firmly. " 'The people of the South feel they have been . . . most tyrannically oppressed by the North. All our rights have been trampled upon. We knew that we had a perfect right to go and leave you,' "[27] he declared, restating the rationale for secession—in his view, it would be akin to Britain not being able to depart the European Union. In 1867, the Confederate J. D. Porter observed the growing "feeling that the Negroes will take this country," meaning the U.S., "and that the whites will have to abandon it"—this was "taking holds of the minds of our people."[28]

James Gaston arrived in Brazil in September 1865. He wrote at length apprising his fellow Confederates of the opportunities available there. "Negroes are not admitted into Brazil from other countries unless free-born," he said sadly, "and even should they be citizens of the latter after being born in slavery, it does not authorize them to be received here. Regarding this, a matter of much moment to those whose Negroes would be willing to come with them to this country, I urged the importance of some modification." However, the "Minister" told him, "this element would not be a very desirable addition to the population of this country." There was a "questionable propriety to admit this particular class of free Negroes in a country where slavery exists," in any case, "and the influence of these freedmen upon other free Negroes and upon slaves in Brazil might tend to bring about similar scenes to those which have been enacted in the process of emancipation in the United States."[29]

As early as December 1865, the **Times** reported on "these 'Caucasians'" in Florida opposed to the new order: "we have heard these embittered men talk of the attraction of life in Brazil, of its freedom from 'niggers' and 'nigger worshippers,' the latter term now being applied to the majority of Northern men who come South to engage in business."[30]

Thus, "there was not a single state south of the Potomac and Ohio rivers that did not have its society for the promotion of emigration." "Several" of these émigré planters went straight to the "slave marts of Rio de Janeiro and elsewhere and made purchases" upon arrival. Near "Petropolis . . . Captain [James] Johnson of Florida purchased a large plantation (fazenda) with its supply of Negro laborers," i.e., "many Brazilian slaves." "Names prominent in the antebellum South were not infrequently heard" in Brazil. "Russell, a Louisiana planter, leased a plantation and its Negroes for ten years"; "ten miles from the City of Rio de Janeiro Major [Duncan] McIntyre bought fazenda Ipahiba, with its one hundred and thirty Negroes."[31] It was like old times for McIntyre as he "began to grow sugar cane, oranges and coffee"—"business was good."

"One of the original settlers recalled years later that her people came to Brazil because they wanted to continue a system"—slavery—"that was no longer legal in the United States." Unfortunately—for these émigrés—they did not consult the vast amount of memoirs penned by those who had traversed Brazil on their way to California during the Gold Rush, for if they had they would have recognized that for those who harbored an ideology of "race" like themselves, Brazil was something less than hospitable. "The social mobility enjoyed by Negro freedmen and the relaxed attitude taken toward miscegenation shocked most Southerners."[32]

Furthermore, though some were able to circumvent this provision, Brazil was firm in asserting that " 'no slaves can be imported into Brazil from any country whatsoever.' "[33] "General [Wallace] Wood of the late so-called [CSA] has lately arrived here," said Edward Thornton of the British legation in Rio de Janeiro in November 1865. He wanted to bring "60,000 souls" to Brazil but the relevant Ministry told him straightforwardly that "no Negroes, either slaves or free, can be admitted into the country." He and those like him "must previously dispose of them" before arriving; "the greatest desire on the part of the Brazilian Government and authorities in general here," added Thornton, was "that no importation of Negroes should take place."[34]

Moreover, many of these Confederates—like their counterparts in 1849—were disconcerted to see those they deemed to be Negro wielding weapons as soldiers and police officers.[35] "Many Confederados of the first generation never quite got used to [this] practice," e.g., those defined as Negro in the U.S. exerting power in Brazil, for "to them, a man with any black blood was black and should stay in his own society."[36] The U.S. Consul in Para had noticed this disillusion on the part of his erstwhile compatriots. "The immigrant from the South if he would be successful in Brazil must leave his prejudices behind him," he insisted. "If he abandons his home only because he is indignant at the assertion of equal rights on the part of those who until recently were judged to have no rights at all, he will find here that the free black, or at least the black man born free, has all the privileges of a white citizen, and greater privileges than the white man if a foreigner" [emphasis-original].[37] But it was not easy to leave these prejudices behind at the port of embarkation, like so much unnecessary baggage. Herbert H. Smith of Brooklyn was typical in the disgust that he felt in Brazil; "people who talk of 'amalgamation' as a blessing to be hoped for," he declared, "should study it here [in Brazil] where it is almost an accomplished fact. The mixed races are invariably bad."[38] Smith's presence was not anomalous for in 1867, the Reverend A. A. Porter averred, " 'there are more immigrants in Brazil from New York than from the South. They come here to get employment in the government works and are disappointed. . . . [Southerners] buy large farms and several slaves on a credit.' "[39] The presence of these Northerners was not inconsistent with the antebellum ethos of the African Slave Trade and, perhaps, accounts for the varying figures as to how many from the U.S. actually migrated to Brazil. Yet clashes between Northerners and Southerners did become a flashpoint in Brazil, suggesting more ideological variation in the migration of the former, as their regional conflict seemed to be exported; in early 1867 in Rio de Janeiro, a "party of Northerners attacked and attempted to burn a sawmill belonging to the Southerners."[40]

John Codman, who left the U.S. for Brazil during the heat of Reconstruction, wound up on a ranch 20 miles from Rio de Janeiro "where the cattle ran wild and Negroes became very much like them." "No people has attempted the experiment [with miscegenation] more recklessly than the Brazilians," he declared.[41] J. D. Porter would have agreed with him. Writing from Brazil in 1867 to his cousin, John D. Templeton, in Waxahatchie, Texas, he thought this was the "country to which Southerners should emigrate"; competition was not stiff, given the "extreme stupidity of this people in the useful arts," reflected in their "refusing to use the plow"; the "moral leprosy [is] far more to be feared here than the physical," he concluded. "The social and religious ideas of this country are a disgrace to the age" and "the priesthood are as immoral as the laity."

But setting aside moral rot and rank incompetence, there was an overriding factor that made Brazil attractive. "The rumors you have heard to the contrary notwithstanding," he told his cousin, "slavery will not be abolished soon in this country and when done, as most probably it will be, this government is not going to make paupers of Africans. In proof—Negroes are advancing in price and Southerners are all wanting to buy." In other words, the participation of U.S. nationals in the African Slave Trade had not ended with the conclusion of the Civil War but had taken on a new form and migrated, as U.S. nationals kept dealing in dark human flesh, be they in Brazil, Venezuela, Egypt, or the South Pacific. Porter was candid in confronting the "objections to Brazil being urged," toward "Negro Equality." Keep in mind, he declared, that "the poor African [here] unless mixed with better blood rarely attains a social or civil eminence. And with a few exceptions, his blood taints whatever it mixes, so that few of this class ever reach the upper strata in Brazilian life." Compare the U.S. he added derisively, where "the best part of the white race" were little more than equal with Africans while the "policy of the dominant party of the U.S. is to efface all social distinctions—a policy clearly indicated in . . . forcing Negroes into omnibuses, street and railroad cars, hotels (and so forth) and a policy that, like all their other ideas will ultimately prevail, and does now to a greater extent in the U.S. than in Brazil."[42]

For with all its differences with the U.S. over the question of the configuration of "race" and the role of the African, Confederates were flocking to Brazil because of one major reason: As the intrepid British traveler, Richard Burton, put it, upon his arrival in Brazil right after the U.S. Civil War, "those of 'pure white blood' even being poor, would receive a treatment that in their countries of origin were reserved only to the most fortuned: 'as a field for the white man no country equals . . . Brazil.' "[43]

The search for a "white paradise" coupled with profound pessimism about the prospects for the U.S. drove many away from the reconstructed Union. Writing from São Paulo in 1874, one emigrant opined that "the Southern States" were "on the eve of a war of races and within the last few days a dispatch has arrived in this country by telegraph that it has already commenced and that several thousand had been killed." Typically, this dire foreboding was yoked to a deep skepticism about the U.S. government which had just escaped being toppled. When the Civil War began, it was expected that "the Northern people and the Federal government will side with the Negro, that it will come I have no doubt and the sooner the Southern people may prepare for it the better." As for Brazil, bright optimism prevailed: though it would "not pay a man of my age," said the writer only identified as Whitaker, "to go to planting coffee beans as it takes four years under the most favorable circumstances to realize and crop from them," the good news was that "Negroes have advanced in price quite materially."[44]

Indeed, there were some Confederates who saw their defeat in the Civil War as a mere setback, a pricking skirmish in an ongoing conflict. Their goal was to use Brazil as a springboard for constructing a newer slave empire that, ultimately, could reverse the outcome of the Civil War. In the spring of 1866, a correspondent in Venezuela, Dr. Henry Price, told Lafayette McLaws of plans to establish a colony in Venezuela; "so soon as we have 1000 inhabitants," he was told, "we should organize a Territorial Government—when 50,000 (allowing us to count Indians) a State Government. It is perfectly understood, if we so desire, [we] may establish slavery—Brazil furnishing market. Fortunately for our scheme the most intimate friendship & confidence exists between myself" and high level officials. "I was a States Rights Democrat & Secessionist from principle after John Brown's raid. My belief in the orthodoxy of slavery is as firmly fixed as my belief in [the] Bible." These plans were capacious, calling for "trade" in the "entire Valley of the Amazon, even to [the] foot of the Andes in Peru & Bolivia." "Open the Slave Trade" was also a goal. "We can at once establish a state or in one with any form of government we please" with more "Confederate soldiers to be recruited." This was no last minute scramble either as this idea had been bruited "as early as 1857. At the fall of Richmond I devised the plan & opened with the Government" in Caracas, said the ever-prepared Dr. Price.[45]

Actually, the arrival of so many Confederates was, in a sense, contrary to the impact that the Civil War—and, especially, its accoutrement, Emancipation—had on Brazil. For as the British emissary, Edward Thornton, reported in December 1865, "events that have lately taken place in the United States have inspired Brazil with a feeling of isolation and shame that she should be the last on this continent to wipe off such a stain from her institutions and are producing a moral pressure which it will be difficult for her Government to withstand."[46] "One of the first shock waves" that hit Brazil "resulted from the outcome of the American Civil War," according to historian Robert Toplin. "News of the sudden demise of the Western Hemisphere's largest slave society [*sic*] frightened Brazilian leaders."[47] It was the "abolition of slavery in the United States, which helped inspire a national policy of gradual emancipation through 'free birth.'"[48] Months after Appomattox, one Brazilian journal asserted that a "hydra headed monster is rearing up and looming in the future, in a short time and Brazil will be the only country in the civilized world where slavery is tolerated."[49]

The Empire had to be concerned that Washington might want to retaliate given its own newly found abolitionism and Brazil's own favorable attitude toward the CSA. As the Civil War was winding down, high-ranking U.S. Senator, Charles Sumner, told the scientist, Louis Agassiz, who was about to visit Brazil, "of course, you will see the Emperor of Brazil" and "if he gives you an opportunity I hope you will not fail to let him know that there are good friends of Brazil here who think that a grave mistake was made when this Power, naturally friendly to the United States, consented to follow the lead of Lord Russell in elevating our rebels to the condition of lawful belligerents on the ocean. It is difficult to see all the consequences of this act," though he added, "I wish that the Brazilian government could see the mistake that has been made & cancel it."[50] But as Brazil opened its doors to obdurate, recalcitrant Confederates, Senator Sumner was poised to challenge the Empire. "How would it do to suspend diplomatic relations with Powers maintaining Slavery? This would bear on two countries only —Spain & Brazil. Such an act on our part could not fail to have important consequences. I do not think these two countries could stand against the pressure."[51]

Sumner's potential demarche was understandable. As Henry Shipley Stevens floated south to Brazil in early 1866 he met aboard his vessel, a "rebel Colonel" who "was formerly on Stonewall Jackson's staff, but afterwards went into the blockade running trade and has made successful trips. The object of his visit to Brazil was to dispose of several of the blockade runners. There are now fifteen in the harbor of Rio. Several of them have been sold to the government"[52]—and it was unclear what had happened to the others. In a confidential memorandum in 1865, the Brazilian Foreign Ministry was informed that "the undersigned Brigadier General of the Confederate States and Chief of staff to Gen'l Beauregard at the request of the latter, has sought this interview with His Excellency the Minister of the Brazils, to tender to the Emperor the services of General Beauregard as a Military Engineer without commission"; he wanted to "devote all the skill and aptitude he has to the defence of Brazil."[53] After the murder of President Lincoln, CSA General Edward Porter Alexander feared that he would be suspected and "instantly mobbed & lynched," so he "wore a U.S. Army private's overcoat, only dyed black instead of its original blue" and immediately "went to see the Brazilian Minister. He read my letters & told me that if I should go to Brazil he had no doubt I could secure a commission in the Brazilian army." Knowing that such activity might be viewed widely as subversive and incompatible with his diplomatic status, the Minister "seemed to be actually afraid lest my being in his house might bring a mob on him."[54] Maximilian's Mexico "was still desperate for experienced military assistance. Some top Confederate generals and militarists were already serving in Mexico. More could be drawn there" to assist his continuing plots for reclaiming land seized by the U.S. in 1848.[55] George Barnsley, scion of a prominent Georgian family, groaned in August 1865, "I have not the shadow of an excuse. I am utterly ruined —in hopes, in fortune and all save honor gone. . . . No I must go," he insisted, "if there is no hope in Brazil, could I not do well in Mexico—I could get a position there in the Army" [emphasis-original].[56] Brazil, a veritable cobelligerent of the CSA, during the Civil War, was now accepting the most retrograde, unforgiving rebels, along with some of their military materiel: Washington would have been negligent if it had failed to view this as a further act of belligerence.[57]

And even before the war ended, there was another concern. As the Dixie migration accelerated "in some quarters of the United States apprehension was felt less the cotton industry in Brazil, stimulated by exiles from the South, might offer keen competition to the same industry."[58] "The production of the Indies, Egypt and Brazil, will be larger than ever the coming season," said one reporter in early 1868, "and that it will be furnished cheaper than in previous years. Under all these circumstances, it may be hard to see where grounds of hope are to be found for the revival of American cotton."[59]

The rebel émigré James Gaston certainly thought so too: "the yield here is better than in the United States," he declared, "and the fibre of the cotton is superior to the average quality grown in the South, which, taken with the fact that it grows two years in succession from the same stalk, give that grown here an advantage over the plants in the United States. Our views as to the probability of failure in the labor [of] our Negroes in the South, lead us to think that cotton may be produced in this . . . country cheaper than in the South and that the market will be supplied principally by Brazil at no distant day."[60]

Brazil in these minds would not only become an Empire of slavery, challenging the U.S. in the vital economic sphere, but as well—and, perhaps, more dangerous in the long run—a "contra" base of opposition tailor-made for CSA diehards.

Yet, as time passed, there was less incentive for Brazil to welcome these migrants warmly despite the apparent advantages they offered; instead, these sojourners came to resemble a rotting mackerel in the moonlight that was shining brightly as it invaded the olfactory. Consequently, Northern U.S. propaganda was unleashed against these Confederates, who were beginning to be seen not as quirky malcontents but as potential counter-revolutionaries. The **New York Times** in December 1865 warned that Confederates "having thereby strengthened" the "Empire, these Coriolanuses shall return, 'leading a power 'gainst Rome; vowing revenge as spacious as between the oldest and the youngest thing.'"[61] This journal looked askance at the unsupported claim that "50,000 families" would be moving south; they highlighted the Brazilian point that "no slaves and not even free colored people will be permitted to enter. Was this hint necessary? Did our Southern friends expect to bring any part of this, their former wealth?" "I wonder," it was said, "how they will like to find that such man a gentleman of color, as is most likely to be the case," as "government officer, judge, or something like it. . . . I wonder how the Protestant part of them will like to be excluded from voting for Electors and other officers?" it was said in reference to the blatant pro-Catholic bias of Brazil. "The Southern slaveholder, the chivalrous aristocrat will have now to begin to do what his despised Yankee neighbor never thought it a shame to do—he will have to work for himself." Confederates carried a "secret longing to found another slaveholding Power on this soil," speaking of Brazil, but seemed unaware that "the Brazilians are beginning to talk very seriously of abolishing slavery legally and forever."[62]

Undeterred, early on J. H. Blue of Missouri alerted the Brazilians—and irked Washington—when he announced in September 1865 that those potential emigrants, like himself, wished to align with "the Emperor Louis Napoleon of France, the Emperor Don Pedro of Brazil and the Emperor Maximilian of Mexico"; they were "forming a triumvirate more mighty than ancient Rome and more hopeful than the Anglo-Saxon"—and the U.S.[63]

Unsurprisingly, there was palpable enthusiasm—initially in Brazil—about the arrival of these rebel migrants. It was the "leading topic of the journals throughout this Empire for several months," said the U.S. emissary in Rio de Janeiro in 1867; "representatives from the Southern States . . . professing to be agents to locate lands for hundreds and thousands of people, have stated, that not only thousands of families, but that even an hundred thousand families, would come to Brazil." These representatives were "received with the utmost distinction possible to high dignitaries." Suggestive of the revenge they might seek against Washington was the "boast" of "many of them . . . that they are secessionists and of their hatred to the Yankeess. . . . they are, with few exceptions, '*de facto*' just as much rebels today as when in arms against it" [emphasis-original]. However, the emissary, William Van Vleck Lidgerwood, envisioned difficulties ahead for these revenge-seekers: "many Brazilian officials, and specially of the lower order," he said, "are men of African descent; and the American immigrant from the Southern States, especially if congregated in any number, being accustomed to order men of color, would soon make himself obnoxious to this class, and difficulties would ensue; and under such circumstances, though he had left the United States without a passport, intending never to return to it, cursing our country and its institutions, he would remember in his time of need that he was born an American citizen."[64]

Nevertheless, when CSA General Wallace Wood arrived in October 1865 in Brazil with "several other gentlemen of the Southern states to fix upon a locality for a settlement of Southerners," he was greeted enthusiastically. A "spontaneous demonstration was set up" by the "most influential Merchants and Brokers" of São Paulo. When he appeared "at the window of the Exchange Hotel," he was "loudly cheered." Though Wood in his remarks to the assembled could " 'speak to you in English only,' " that did not quell the cheering throngs. "We shall bring to your country, as speedily as facilities will admit of it," cried Wood, "50,000—aye one hundred thousand families of the best and most energetic and most enterprising citizens of North America."[65] General Wood was being greeted like a conquering savior. "An hour before sunset" on the "Rua de Dereta, the main street in the city, on which the Exchange Hotel, where he had taken rooms was located," began "filling for the distance of three blocks or squares in front of the hotel with a dense mass of humanity and a band of music, while the windows, balconies and housetops of the buildings in the city were thronged with women and children, waving handkerchiefs and miniature flags of Brazil and the States. In response to loud and repeated 'vivas for General Wood,' that gentleman appeared in one of the balconies of the hotel, where, in his representative character, he was welcomed with deafening shouts, the band playing 'Dixie.' "[66]

This "encouraging immigration and more especially that of those citizens of the United States who are dissatisfied with the state of matters there," crowed one insider in Brazil, was "meeting with great favor from all classes, both in Rio and the provinces"; moreover, "the initiation of the new mail line of steamers between Brazil and New York" was "hailed" similarly with "much satisfaction" as a harbinger of a day when talented migrants and goods alike would flow effortlessly from north to south.[67]

The **New York Times** was not pleased with General Wood, who hailed from the rebel stronghold that was Mississippi and was a "longtime resident of New Orleans." This "middle-aged man, a lawyer and editor, a fluent writer" and "forcible speaker" was "appointed the chief agent of associations of immigrants of four counties in Mississippi."

Their reporter seemed dumbfounded about his "enthusiastic" reception and the fact that "no passport was asked of him—he had none—and his baggage was permitted to be taken to his hotel without the surveillance of the customs."[68]

A segment of public opinion in Brazil, on the other hand, was decidedly excited about the prospect of this mass departure. The Confederates, it was said, were "an educated, intelligent, industrious and wealthy class of persons"; indeed, "no such community has ever decided upon expatriation" and this could only be a boon for Brazil. For just as the "Lombards introduced by their expatriation to England the sciences, arts, capital and commercial usages—and in like manner as the Portuguese and Spanish Jews conveyed with them to Holland sufficient wealth to make that country one of the richest in means—so will the Confederates elevate Brazil to a high standard of literacy, scientific and commercial prosperity, which she is so much entitled to." The "average amount of capital which the Confederates may bring with them, will be [considerable] . . . [and] this alone is worthy of attention" particularly compared with the amounts brought by "Europeans who go to the United States."[69] Like a star professor attracting other stellar faculty to an academic department, it was said that a "gentleman from the Cape of Good Hope" asserted that a "thousand persons were either started or preparing to leave Southern Africa for Brazil, seeing in this country a future for their efforts which they vainly looked for there." Thus, "great anxiety was manifested by the Northerners to discourage the emigration which is taking place in the Southern States."[70]

What was the natural source of immigrants to Brazil—akin to the British and Western Europeans to the U.S.? According to Dr. Antonio Francisco de Paula Souza, Minister of Agriculture in 1866, it was the Confederates; in fact, he thought, this migration would be "counterbalancing the tendency of European emigration to the United States." Reaching for an analogy, he posited provocatively that the "revocation of the Edict of Nantes wearied by religious fanaticism from the weakness of an old king, threw out of France more than 400,000 of the most energetic, industrious and wealthy individuals"—and, he thought, history was repeating itself with this time Brazil being the beneficiary.[71]

Ironically, these Negrophobic, slave hungry Confederates were seen by some as a means by which Brazil could avoid a servile revolt. "Many persons and in an especial degree foreigners, pretend to foresee another St. Domingo in Brazil," said one Brazilian periodical nervously in 1867;

"others at the least a second Jamaica on a grander scale." The "Brazilian," it was said incongruously, "naturally turns his eyes to the United States for the initiation of the solution, for a clue to guide the country from the labyrinth of difficulties which surround this matter" since "Brazilians lack that ruthlessness, that inhuman energy of the North American which prefers to destroy the savage to conciliating and civilizing him, and will as readily root out the black if he proves contumacious."[72] Evidently, it was not realized that whatever dearth in "ruthlessness" possessed by Euro-Brazilians in dealing with Africans was due more to their lesser numbers compared with the "North American" than anything else.

On the other hand, some of the migrants from the north held views about Brazil that were similarly uncomplimentary to residents of this giant land. John Codman, for example, argued bluntly in 1867, "let the Monroe Doctrine in its modified sense be extended to Brazil. Let us make an American state of it, without the process of annexation. . . . and as the Indians have died away from among us, and the Africans are now perishing, so will this composite, mongrel, effete race disappear from the world. It is destiny." As Codman saw it, "it does not seem that this people can compete with the Anglo-Saxons." "If God did make 'of one blood all the nations on the earth,' it was a long time ago," he added sarcastically; "and now the blood is so certainly not the same, that He can alone restore it to its original purity. All the endeavors of miscegenationists have proved failures" for "no people has attempted the experiment more recklessly than the Brazilians." The arrival of northern migrants would mark a turning point for Brazil: "years hence, it may appear that one of the results of our civil war will have been the repeopling of this land from the starting-point of the few dozens of Americans who have landed here." Codman had first arrived in Brazil in 1847 and then sought to "take off every restriction upon the slave trade between Africa and Brazil" and continued to think that "Brazil cannot be supplied with labor unless there shall be a species of coolie trade between that country and Africa . . . black labor from the nearest market is therefore a necessity for Brazil, even if the result of its importation should eventually be a black empire." Of course, there were ways to circumvent this, he informed his English-speaking audience, pointing to "an enterprising Portuguese," who was "very poor" but "undertook to make money systematically . . . by the increase of his [Negro] 'stock,'" recognizing that "mulattoes are as valuable as Negroes. Think, then, by what double prostitution he succeeded in obtaining two in each season—one being the half of his own flesh and blood, the other belonging in the same proportion to his wife! So it went on, year after year, the children being sold when of suitable age; and by this commerce the worthy couple lived and prospered!" But ultimately, he thought, Maury's plan of a de facto annexation of Brazil by the U.S. would be attained by other means.[73]

Matthew Fontaine Maury, the celebrated Virginian who had done so much to draw antebellum attention to Brazil, became a staunch Confederate. Though he had touted the Amazon endlessly, ironically his odyssey did not lead to a Brazilian residency—though it still speaks volumes about why this South American nation did not become the mass site of exile that it promised to be and why those who had been so pro-Brazilian slavery were equally anti-U.S. after the Civil War.

No blurry-eyed idealist he, Maury in the fall of 1860 as war loomed, engaged in hard-boiled speculation about how "land and Negroes" would be "affected by disunion."[74] Deciding that "land and Negroes" would not be adversely affected by war, Maury sought to devise a plan in Virginia "of organizing all the remaining white population in the border & tide water counties into a home guard to act in case of inroads & marauders as guerrillas. . . . Gen'l Lee who highly approved of the plan is going to carry it into effect," since Maury "being a cripple"[75] was unable to effectuate his martial rhetoric.[76]

Instead, Maury became a roving ambassador for the CSA, stirring up trouble for the U.S. in Europe particularly.[77] He became a highly personal antagonist of Lincoln.[78] He prayed and worked for a war between London and Washington, so as to bail out the CSA.[79] Still, while in London he was aggressively "pursuing . . . researches" concerning increasing the "destructiveness of the torpedo" so as to better destroy U.S. vessels.[80]

France was his next stop, where its takeover of Mexico had raised hopes for further assistance to the CSA. But he came up empty there too[81] though he seriously sought "alliance with France." In a breathtaking 27-page document, virtually unrivaled in the annals of those who have sought to destroy the U.S.—and even more ironic given Maury's continuing iconic status in the nation he sought to exterminate—Maury was pointing to a future building of a Panama Canal which would increase immeasurably the value of a California that he was offering to

Paris and would, simultaneously, reduce the value of Brazil as a way-station to the Golden State.[82] Yet, despite Ferdinand Maximilian, the Archduke of Austria and new ruler of Mexico, cooing to Maury about his "flattering" of him and his "friendship," California was not returned to the nation that once controlled this territory.[83]

But this was not due to Maury's lack of trying. More than most, Maury had an acute sense of the power of geography—geopolitics, to use the current term—and, as he saw it, the advent of the Panama Canal would be the new link between east and west in North America, thereby reducing somewhat the importance of Cape Horn—and Brazil. California, said Maury to those who intended the U.S. harm, intended to get as much capital from Washington for internal improvements as it could—e.g., a transcontinental railway, which would too reduce the value of Brazil and Cape Horn as a link between the east and west of North America—then bolt.[84]

Yet it was hard to place any trust in an inveterate schemer. For just as Maury first plotted against Brazil on behalf of the U.S., then against the U.S. on behalf of the CSA, then against the interests of Brazil, he wound up scheming against his vaunted CSA on behalf of Mexico, offering to join the Archduke in Mexico, when it seemed that his treacherous revolt against Washington was failing ignominiously. Again, this was of a piece with the times, when so many Portuguese nationals, for example, gained U.S. citizenship for—it seemed—little reason beyond facilitating their participation in the African Slave Trade. Citizenship, patriotism, and allegiance to Washington had a different import back then to those who held slavery dear.

The Archduke remained appreciative of Maury's "valuable and friendly" approach, and his "flattering concern"; he was "particularly attracted" to Maury's "observations on the present state of affairs in California" and was "much indebted" for his interlocutor's "frankness and detail."[85]

These glowing words were not enough for Maury so he went a step further. Again, he held out the prospect of Mexico regaining California, which—if it had happened—would have helped to solidify French domination; and, the altruistic Maury would have been graciously willing to volunteer to administer this immense region on the Archduke's behalf. A master of oceanography with vast knowledge of South America, he reminded that iron-clads quietly sent around Cape Horn at an early opportunity would find themselves complete masters of the coast; "for the Federals have nothing in the Pacific that could cope with them." Maury was ready to tender his resignation in the "Confederate Navy . . . whenever you may require my services."[86] Weeks later he repeated to the Archduke, "I am heartily at your command whenever you may need my services."[87]

Chickens had come home to roost: The U.S., which countenanced Maury's plotting against Brazil, set the stage for his going over to the CSA, which laid a foundation for his then waltzing into the arms of Mexico. But that last scheme also proved unavailing. By 1865, Maury was searching desperately for a new homeland, aghast as he was at the prospect of returning to the hated U.S. By April of that fateful year, his ward since 1838, J. M. Maury, who had risen to the post of lieutenant in the CSA military, was languishing in a Union prison. "I am so restless and miserable that I don't know what to do with myself," he told his "father." "I cannot read or eat or sleep . . . this news from the South is so overwhelming! Gen'l Lee surrendered!" he wailed. "Who would have ever have thought the noble Army of Northern Virginia would have come to such an end. . . . oh it is sad and humiliating to think of this terrible disaster. To be beaten in a quarrel of our own seeking was bad enough, but to think that all this blood has been shed, all this misery inflicted for nothing, is a sad, sad retrospect indeed. . . . it has almost made me sick. . . . there is a weight at my heart which it seems to me I shall always carry, for how can we ever hold our heads up again, anywhere in the whole world. . . . can't you say something to comfort me," he asked Matthew Maury, who so boldly had led the South into war but now was equally bereft of answers.[88]

A few weeks later, Maury was "off San Domingo," on his way to Havana, groaning that "this Confederacy has come to a miserable wreck"; Maury was "utterly astounded at the brick-row tumble of our armies; and at the ignoble end of the Confederacy"; he was "grieved and mortified beyond expression." He was humiliated by the "great calamities that have been brought upon us"; "the soil of Virginia has now for me no charms," he concluded, since "its future is black with misery and utterly horrid. I have no wish to see it." What to do then? "In my judgment," said Maury, "the only course that becomes them and that is left to those noble sons and daughters who have graced the fall of the noble old state is expatriation," i.e., "finding . . . a new country." Since the "future of every true hearted Virginian is a life dragged out under the yoke amidst secret spies and truculent informers," the "best service that I can make the state is to propose an asylum" [emphasis-original].[89]

But where was the question. Just before the war, "His Majesty the Emperor" of Russia generously gave Maury a "diamond broach."[90] After the war began, a Russian Grand Duke invited him to live in that nation given "the present political whirlpool in your country" and since "your name is well known in Russia."[91] Ironically, Maury who had done so much to trumpet the charms of Brazil chose exile not there but in Mexico, a choice that may have been motivated by his corrosive grudge against Washington and his surmise that Paris—despite his coming up empty there—could inflict more damage on his now despised former homeland. By September 1865, he was in Mexico City encouraging Confederate emigration though his prospectus did not sound enticing, warning as it did about "guerrillas" [emphasis-original]—"to avoid any molestation from these," he advised, "immigrants, especially the first comers, should travel in company and establish themselves, for mutual protection and convenience, in settlements of not less than a dozen or two."[92]

Still, Maury may not have ruled out Brazil altogether—or anywhere else on the planet—excepting the U.S., of course. Writing from Mexico's "Office of Colonization" in October 1865, he grimaced as he recounted how "the Yankee papers now have it that 'Professor Maury, the vilest of traitors has asked for pardon.'" Maury was horrified: "In the name of Jesus," he exclaimed, "what do I want with a 'pardon.' I have no idea of going to the U. States in the future. . . . I may want to go to the U.S., I may want to go to Siberia" since "if colonization fails, Mexico is no place for me" [emphasis-original].[93]

Maury was floundering; he was "afraid to leave" his "dear wife" in Virginia, "afraid," as he was, "of troubles there": "I thought England the best place for you to wait," he told her. "I may not come back" to the U.S., now wavering as he sensed that though slavery may have been banned, Negrophobia had not. "This thought is way down deep among the remote contingencies of the future. It is not to be mentioned, except with injunctions, even to the most reticent." He considered going to "Halifax to bide my time," then was "consulting" about "buying some Cordova land—in the olden times Cordova was the garden spot of New Spain" but, he said sadly, "when slavery was abolished suddenly fifty years ago—as with us—down it went—and its splendid haciendas and baronial old mansions are now in ruins." He continued to hold out hope for Mexico, though it seemed to be fading fast: "colonization is not a chimera," he insisted: "We have letters. Thousands are dying to come."[94] By December 1865, he was negotiating for a hacienda in Mexico.[95] His son, Richard, was likewise championing emigration since Virginia was deemed "not a fit place to live in now. All must come to Mexico. If they stay" a catastrophe of the first order would occur: "they will [have] to free their nigs" and, worse, "will very likely have a nig tax collector coming around." The solution: "set all the nigs free and then bring them along as persons owing passage money to be paid in labour. Then they can be held as peons til the debt is discharged. That is you pay them but can compel them to work for you as long as they owe you money or labour."[96] Something similar was proposed for Brazil, but the Empire's reluctance to admit Africans of any kind—free or slave—turned the devious toward Mexico.

The Maurys were convinced: migration to the region south of formerly Confederate Texas was the refuge of choice, a keen site for the establishment of a "contra" base. Hence, in March 1866, Maury was still touting Mexico and denouncing the U.S., "that Yankee despotism called the Union."[97] But soon his fortunes had taken another dip, as in May 1866, "the banker with whom I had deposited my 'little money' went down in the London panic week before last," he groused, "and I lost all the money & more too that I brought away from Mexico." Back at his new Central American home "intriguers set to work and colonization was going so badly and the opposition [of] the Minister was so vexatious" that "immigrants were returning in disgust." Now he was contemplating the "hard blow" of having "to give Mexico up."[98]

A year later he was back in London, as he continued to find the "future of the South" to be "very dark." As he saw it, only slavery—along the lines of Brazil—could save the South, otherwise the dreaded social equality would ensue. "Go among the Pa. [farmers]" and "you will [find] the colored labor & the white upon the most perfect terms of equality, and the wife and daughters of the farmer serving meals to them both and standing behind their chairs." Maury did not think that "Va. Gentlemen" were "quite prepared for wife and daughter to do that," but that seemed to be where the nation he hated was going. "Barriers have already broken down between the blacks & the whites which two years ago, your wisest statesmen did not have the sagacity to think were in the round of possibilities."[99] It was all too depressing. But Maury continued to plot revenge against Washington. In the summer of

1866, for example, Maury's son did "hear from" his "father frequently. He, with my mother and sister are now in Paris," he remarked, "where he was called by the Emperor" and where he had received funding "ever since he went over there in '63."[100]

Maury was miserable. In 1868, he was still in London complaining about what had befallen his once beloved Virginia. "The Jamaican planters were paid for their Negroes and had 7 years notice to prepare for emancipation. None of them are there now who could get away. One of them told me last night," he said, "that his plantations yielded him $30,000 a year—that he sold it on emancipation about 30 years ago for $5000 & that the purchaser—his former manager—still owes some $25,000." The "Dutch since that war began emancipated their slaves—in Surinam and Jansen tells me that that colony is already Africanized. The South is no place," he concluded, "for any gentleman with wife and daughters to live . . . nor will it be until the contest is now brewing and going on there between blacks & whites, is finally settled."[101] With emancipation Negroes had to depart, as he had proposed in the 1850s or as Webb had proposed in the 1860s, for if they did not, North American would become "Africanized" in any case. But where was a man of this opinion to live if the Western Hemisphere was his goal?

By 1870, Maury was continuing to carp. "Napoleon has brought his dynasty to an end," he said mournfully, "as ingloriously as Jeff Davis did the Confederacy." But by then, he had made his peace and was back home, teaching at the Virginia Military Institute in Lexington, though he was continuing his dream of moving, "I suppose to Florida, perhaps to Cuba."[102] But if his oldest son's views reflected his father's, Maury would not be happy in the remaining slave citadels of Havana or Rio de Janeiro. "Did you ever fall in with an educated Frenchman who was not an infidel" [emphasis-original], Richard Maury asked his father. "If you have, you are more fortunate than I have been. It may be all prejudice but I have a very poor opinion of every country save those where the [majority] of believers are Protestants" [emphasis-original]; it was a "very special Providence," he added consolingly, "that carried you away from Mexico & that prevented your linking your fortunes with those of L. Napoleon."[103]

Maury's peregrinations in Western Europe were far from innocent. After Appomattox, "he felt himself at liberty to impart to the sovereign[s] there the secret of his discoveries concerning his new made science" of perfecting torpedo destructiveness. "Most of the European powers sent representatives to his school of instruction—all of them have built upon his beginnings, the most powerful branch of their naval armaments. To France he [also] imparted his secret," his son, Richard, confessed, thereby jeopardizing the security of the nation, the U.S., he had come to loathe.[104]

F. H. Farrar of Point Coupee, Louisiana, also wound up in Mexico where he observed presciently of the U.S. in 1866 that the "time is not far distant when the West and South, politically united will control this government for many a year to come."[105] Certainly the reactionary politics of Maury, who sought to deport U.S. Negroes to Brazil, then sought to split California from the Union, was not inimical to a subsequent conservative upsurge.

Maury's odyssey was emblematic of those of his persuasion and generation. He first saw Brazil as a "safety valve," sensing that the system of slavery could not survive unless it could expand. Then he signed on to the quixotic CSA, which sought to build slavery in one nation in a nation based on slavery. Then he tried to return California to Mexico with himself as ruler. He found no solace in London and, finally, returned home to a changed Virginia. Why not move to Brazil where slavery survived? The prevalence of a reviled popery was one deterrent, no figment for a man who descended from Protestants and who had endured unpleasant times in France. Like so many others, Maury found it hard to accept the eradication of the socioeconomic system that was slavery—and its complement: the African Slave Trade. Yet the dilemma of Maury and other rebels was more intractable: for they had to make the severe adjustment to accepting as human what had theretofore been treated as a commodity. The more profound adjustment sheds light on why Maury would seek to ally with France and Mexico against the U.S., while still others would seek to bolster Brazil as the ultimate redeemer of slavery and the African Slave Trade. Moreover, by the time Maury discovered that he was virtually a man without a country, the death of Reconstruction was returning Virginia to a time that he found much more agreeable, a situation that was impelling more migrants to Brazil to return to their erstwhile homeland.

Though the statue to Maury in Virginia has yet to be toppled, he was emblematic of the treasonous anti-Washington sentiments that animated the Civil War. Like those thousands of rebels who fled the U.S., he was also symptomatic of the fluidity of citizenship that was not unusual during this time, a fluidity that facilitated anti-government revolts or, in an earlier day, facilitated switching flags in midocean in order to more effectively participate in the African Slave Trade. Yet these rebels came to find that the despised U.S. had certain attractions—the English language, an advanced infrastructure, a significant number of Protestants—that Brazil's tolerance of slavery could not overcome, and even that "advantage" was eroding rapidly.

11

The End of Slavery and the Slave Trade?

"Steve" was a freed Negro from the U.S. said to have "come with his former master Judge Dyer" to Brazil after the Civil War. But like many migrants, Dyer chose to return to the U.S., so "Steve continued to work the lumber mill given to him when Dyer elected to return to Texas, and he found it to be very profitable. . . . Steve adopted the surname of Columbus Wasson, Judge Dyer's son-in-law and settled down on the Rio Una north of Iguape to operate his business. Hard work, patience and good sense paid off handsomely" and "he accumulated a considerable fortune"; he became as "well off" as a "Turkish Pasha and died highly respected"—he "always held that he was a true American," though his surname was now Vassão.[1] "Steve" was not alone. "The John Cole family of Georgia took one of their former slaves, 'Aunt Sylvy' to Brazil because"—supposedly—"'she refused to be left behind.'" Certainly, "some of the American settlers who could afford to do so bought or hired Brazilian slaves to assist them in their labors. But the blacks were said to be slow workers and many of them ran away to São Paulo or to other cities."[2] Such reactions were an incentive for rebel migrants to arrange for the importation of their "former" slaves, even though this was of questionable legality. Just as certainly, some of the rebels "proposed that the Brazilian Empire encourage immigration of American former slaves because of their superior technical knowledge of cotton production," this was a continuation of Maury's old dreams about dispatching U.S. Negroes to the Amazon.[3]

This chapter concerns the travails of émigrés from the former Slave South in Brazil. Their adjustment was difficult. Some could not accept that those deemed to be Negro in the U.S. seemed to be viewed as being on their level in Brazil. Some could not overcome the formidable barriers of language and religion, while others could not adapt to a level of underdevelopment that was daunting. As a result, a considerable number swallowed their anger and pride and returned to the U.S.

It is unclear how many U.S. Negroes migrated with their "former" masters to Brazil after the Civil War. It is clear, however, that after the Civil War, Washington did make good faith efforts to squash slavery and the African Slave Trade: in June 1870, a pact was forged between the U.S. and U.K. that indicated this trend.[4] Yet, it was striking that as the African Slave Trade was winding down, revving up was the "coolie" trade, involving the transport of Chinese laborers globally in conditions that mimicked its predecessor.[5] Even before the end of the Civil War, there were reports of "two ships" that "were supposed to be American vessels sailing under Portuguese colors to avoid . . . capture by the Confederate steamer 'Alabama' " that stopped in Cape Town on its way from Macao to Havana, filled to the brim with Chinese laborers.[6] Portuguese involvement in the African Slave Trade continued in the 20th century,[7] in any case, and, strikingly, despite Washington's official anti-bondage stance, the U.S. continued to supply Portugal with arms that, presumably, could have been useful in suppressing revolts in Lisbon's huge African colonies by incipient slaves.[8] Indeed, even in the 21st century, there are continuing allegations indicating that not only does the slave trade continue but that there are also more slaves today than there were during the height of the African Slave Trade.[9]

Godfrey Barnsley was born in Derbyshire in Britain in 1805 where he was part of the commercial aristocracy, then moved on to Savannah in 1824. A father of seven, he fought with the CSA at Manassas, an indicator of what he thought was at stake—he controlled 10,000 acres and 24 enslaved Africans.[10]

But by early 1867, there was a "cloud of apprehension" and "anxious doubt about our political future"; it "rests heavily on Georgia and on me alike," Barnsley was told, "and which I strive in vain to shake off, a kind of vague expectation of some painful change." The question nagging Barnsley's comrade and other rebels was if "the radicals [will] be able to effect what they propose? If they do," he assured, "I am sure Brazil or any other land would be the refuge of all who could meet the costs of transportation."[11]

By the spring of 1867, Barnsley's son, George, had accepted this advice and decamped to Brazil. "There are now nearly 500 emigrants

224 | *The End of Slavery and the Slave Trade?*

from the South at this hotel," he told his father; "we receive food gratis and lodging also" and suggestive of how warmly they were embraced, "this evening the Emperor and Minister paid us a visit" and both were "[greeted] by cheers. He is a fine looking gentleman," he said of this ruler, "and is much interested in, especially, our colony. . . . I am sure of success," he said manfully, "and do not regret leaving the States."[12]

Why were so many from the former Slave South in southern Brazil?[13] As J. D. Porter put it, "the political situation of the South is as bad as its worst enemies could wish, or as our most gloomy fears had foreboded [*sic*]," thus the migration flow continued, "contrary to all reasonable expectations these Southern merchants who say that the emigration feeling is somewhat abated and especially as to Brazil."[14] He added that "our leading Southern papers have recently lost all Federal printing by order of the military governors. They are very needy and might accept some from patronage from the Brazilian government," not least since Brazil had "natural advantages . . . over almost any other part of the globe." He urged the "Brazilian government" to install "agents in the interior of this country," meaning the U.S. "to encourage and facilitate emigration."[15]

James McFadden Gaston was "chief surgeon of the South Carolina [CSA] forces." Then "the Reconstruction period was upon them and he knew only too well how it would try men's souls. . . . [his] personal property had vanished and his money was useless, being in Confederate notes"—what options did he have? Yet, despite the ill-repute in which he was held, still "it was necessary for Dr. Gaston to make this journey" to Brazil "very quietly, because of the suspicion with which all Southern men were watched at this time," especially those heading south who were often viewed as so many Coriolanuses, seeking revenge and a base for it. "His Confederate uniform still worn for lack of other apparel, was a passport among his own people, but might have detained him if he met Federal officers." Like others, Gaston was "able to secure free passage" in October 1865 from New Orleans south. He was only one among many, indicative of the "general inclination among Southern people at this time to leave the scene of desolation around them." "There are many reflections crowding upon my mind this morning," he informed his spouse in December 1865; high on the list was the "blending of fear with hope as to your situation in the midst of comparative strangers, and surrounded by a race that has so recently changed its relations to the white inhabitants of the country."[16]

J. Marshall McCue concurred with the views of Gaston, Barnsley, and other migrants. He trumpeted the virtues of Brazil, stressing the "liberality of the government of Don Pedro . . . the delightful climate and most luxuriant soil, with all the products of our north temperate zone, added to the delightful fruits and vegetables of the tropics, fine water . . . and extreme healthfulness all combined, cause thousands of our down-trodden people, sad as it may be to expatriate themselves and to leave the graves of their fathers and Virginia, proud, glorious noble old Virginia, and to find a home down there. You would be surprised, my dear sir, to learn of the number who not only think of this, but have determined to do so. Your unworthy correspondent is of this number," he emphasized. But why? Why travel thousands of miles to a land where the language was foreign and the situation less than steady? "We are now under a military satrap whose ipse dixit overrides our code," said this Virginian. "I have given my last vote. My bo[y] Sander (ex-slave) yet in my employ, in the estimation of our masters in Washington, is a better man than your unworthy correspondent. My spirit is too unbending to brook this, to submit to it. I will not do it," he stressed [emphasis-original]. "Painful as I admit it to be, I will not remain in Virginia, but will cast my fortunes with many who have fixed on the sunny lands of Brazil," which was "destined to be one of the greatest wheat growing regions we know of," since the "soil and labor"—slave labor —"and climate are there superior to any in the States for producing wheat."[17]

His interlocutor, Cyrus McCormick was dubious, despite McCue's impassioned persuasiveness. Why leave, he mused, since the former slaveholders still held the whip hand and the former slaves were mostly illiterate and poverty-stricken.[18] But McCue was not convinced. "Your idea of whites of [the] South controlling the voting of the Negroes is quite erroneous," he said in June 1867. "Some of us [thought] so too, but we abandoned the idea some time ago" for now "Negroes and low whites are in ascendancy. So our prospects are gloomy in extreme," and, he added balefully, "if I could sell my property for its value, I would go tomorrow" to Brazil. "As one of the biggest planters in Alabama wrote me," he said, " 'I go to Brazil because I feel satisfied that I will never more be permitted here to enjoy the fruits of my own industry in peace and tranquility.' " That was not all, as McCue went on to cite words he agreed with zealously: " 'we can't forget the past and I never expect to be reconstructed. It causes my blood to boil and tingle to look upon the Star Spangled Banner, I once loved but will love it no more forever.' "[19]

Lucita Hardie Wait agreed heartily with such sentiments. Hailing from an old Southern family, she was actually born in Brazil after the war. Her great-grandfather, James W. Miller of Gainesville, Georgia, "had prospered before the war and lost all during the war," as "idle and mischievous savages" were set "loose everywhere." But like others, she and her family had maintained a "southern interest in the tropics [that] reaches back into the era of 'Manifest Destiny.' " And when "land was offered" at the "unbelievable price of 22 [cents] an acre," her ancestors hopped on a boat and wound up in "Santa Barbara, about seventy-five miles southwest of São Paulo, the Chicago of Brazil."[20] By early 1867, one of her treasured ancestors observed happily " 'in less than two years we will have paid for the place" in Brazil "with the addition of a gin, ginhouse and screw, and eight valuable Negroes.' "[21]

This flow of rebels southward was also due in part to a "Brazilian emigration scheme," which was "carrying crowds of newly-arrived Irish and Southern ex-slaveholders to the slave-working Empire of Brazil. There is a Brazilian emigration society that desires to obtain for that country a new infusion of foreign blood and it has provided $150 gold for each immigrant."[22] Many of these emigrants had traveled via New Orleans, "the majority of them had donned the Confederate gray," and the "majority of them" were "from Texas," and, thus, had probably experienced life under Mexican rule, under Texas sovereignty, under U.S. suzerainty, then that of the CSA—so what was one more sovereign, what did citizenship mean anyway?[23]

George Barnsley was in São Paulo, site of an ongoing boom. "Rents are very cheap"; he had a "very good house, with four good rooms, kitchen and other rooms for servants . . . all for $3.00 per month. Food is quite cheap. . . . people are extremely kind, in fact, I never knew such hospitality and genuine kindness." There were also problems: he was "invited to a ball given by the musical society at Iguape," but he didn't speak Portuguese, which limited his ability to bond. Still, the "young ladies were very pretty," even better, "some" were "quite fair— blondes"—in fact. Brazil was a "paradise for idlers" and, thus, the migrants who were "displeased" were "men who are afraid to work."[24]

By the spring of 1868, George Barnsley had been "naturalized" and "taken the oath of allegiance." He was not unwilling to fight for his new nation, noting that "my two years in the war department in Richmond gave me a very good idea of what men to use in my plans." He was "shocked" by a murder back in the U.S. and "was afraid he had been murdered by the Negroes and under the impulse of horror of the thought," he "determined to return to the States at all hazards." But he quickly got over this thought and expressed "no desire to return to the States to live permanently"; "if after making money I desire another clime, I will go to Europe," he resolved.[25]

But it did not seem that would be necessary for by early 1872, the younger Barnsley—a medic—was now in Rio de Janeiro and had "already gained quite as good a reputation here as I had in São Paulo" and had "furnished" his "house very comfortably and handsomely."[26] Julia Louisa Hentz Keyes also traveled from the U.S. to Brazil during this period and she too was initially pleased with what she encountered; she declared, "we were surrounded by friends, some from the home we had left in Alabama, some from different parts of the Southern States." They were from Montgomery, cradle of the Confederacy, Louisiana, Texas, etc.—a "common interest made us feel near to each other," she said. One "common interest" was slavery. "Today Captain Johnson moves to his new home," she said in the early postwar period; "he has bought a large plantation and Negroes." His was "the finest I have seen in Brazil or anywhere else" with "6000 orange trees . . . and numberless fruits. Orange trees are so abundant that he has been digging up many from his fields. I have visited several planters in this neighborhood. With one I spent a night and found him more like an American than I have met with in their homes. They speak three, four and five languages and have many things just like Southerners." "Maj. McIntyre has at last, bought a place with one hundred and thirty Negroes," she added. "Capt. Johnson has bought one with fifty seven Negroes—he already had six or eight," presumably brought from the U.S. "Russell has bought a [plantation] and Negroes also." Though there was "an Episcopal Church and English schools in Rio," she thought the "province of Sau (Sao) Paulo will be the great center of American enterprise in Brazil. There are many now located there, planting and prospering and others are going. The Southerners," she announced accurately, "are scattered from the Amazon to Buenos Ayres," a distance of thousands of miles. Matthew Maury's oceanographic enterprise had not been unavailing for "Brazil [was] not near so far from the U.S. as it once was. You can run down in a month from Baltimore very pleasantly for $100."[27]

J. D. Porter of the Slave South joined her in enthusiasm. "When I reach home," one correspondent was informed, "I shall exert myself in favor of emigration to Brazil and in furtherance of the cause, I trust you will neglect no opportunity to promote the establishment of a line of steam transports directly from the South to Rio de Janeiro."[28] Joseph Weed also thought there was good reason for migrating. In 1874, writing from Rio de Janeiro, he found that "the roads were built by Americans and are owned by them" and it was "so profitable an investment that they have become suddenly men of large wealth."[29] In 1872, Robert S. Merriwether was elated to announce that the "profits made in manufacturing cigars must be enormous. . . . Mr. Lane told me that a few of the Confederates about [Santa] Barbara raised some nice Cuban or Paraguayan tobacco and made it up at home; and their cigars became quite the [talk of] Rio; finding their way to the Emperor himself." Merriwether, who was on the scene in Brazil, found that "after the second year the lands are more easily cultivated than those in South Carolina and Georgia." He had arrived in 1865 "and spent some months exploring the country, and selected this province, Sao Paulo &," he added triumphantly, "have no reason to regret my choice."[30] Charles Hall was also exuding mirth. This Georgian migrant "lived on the farm" of "about 660 acres" at "Bom Retiro" for "sixteen years"; he had roots in Georgia also.[31]

But soon deep and profound doubts began to intrude on the consciousness of these wayward rebels. One reason among many that Brazil would be so willing to accept these fleeing rebels was because it was then involved in a bloody war with Paraguay and suspected that those with military skills freshly displayed could be of use in this conflict. The rebels, on the other hand, were not as convinced as to why they should flee from the frying pan of one recently concluded war to the fire of a blazing one. Still, CSA General Edward Porter Alexander early on during this war "had made up my mind that if ever a white flag was raised I would take to the bushes. And, somehow, I would manage to set out of the country & would go to Brazil. Brazil was just going to war with Paraguay, & I could doubtless get a place in their artillery," earn credits in turn with the regime, and, perhaps, be in a position to maneuver his new homeland into becoming a powerful antagonist against his antagonist—the U.S.[32]

Alexander was among those who participated directly in two of the transforming events of the hemisphere since the "Paraguayan war bears the same relation to the history of South America that the American

Civil War does to that of North America."³³ But, ironically, Africans trumped the rebels in both cases, serving as the decisive force in breaking the back of the CSA, while in Brazil "serving in the army became identified with the worst forms of slavery," guaranteeing opportunists like Alexander would find themselves sharing a trench with those they routinely despised, not least since "by the second half of 1865 desertion had become a national phenomenon." As this was occurring, "the victory of the Union in the American Civil War had forced powerful Brazilian groups to realize that conditions had so decisively turned against slavery that any explicit defense of the institution should be fruitless. . . . the Brazilian Emperor declared that the direction of events in America compelled the Brazilian government to consider the future of slavery 'because the same thing that happened during the abolition of the traffic should not happen again.' "³⁴ So potent was the Paraguayan Question in Brazilian politics then, that the **New York Times** hooted at what they deemed to be the lack of sophistication among rebel migrants, who did not sense this issue. "How could the promise of a homestead," be believed, "especially when it is known that all lands in Brazil worth anything are monopolized by the slaveholders"—"or does there lurk in them, an intention to make recruits of the men thus bound by a bond, and to send them on the scene of the bloody war in Paraguay."³⁵

Hence, the rebels were fleeing to Brazil, often on the premise that they could continue to enjoy the tasty fruits of the labor of enslaved Africans, when Brazil itself was in the process of reconsidering this noxious practice. "In consequence of the abolition of slavery," announced a report filed by Brazil's Foreign Ministry, "considerable numbers of recent slaveholders in our Southern States contemplate a removal to Brazil where the African race are still kept under the restraints of the 'peculiar institution.' "³⁶ "Many believe," said the Reverend Ballard S. Dunn in 1866, "that foreigners cannot hold property in Brazil; particularly in slaves. This is utterly without foundation," he huffed, "I know many Southern gentlemen, who have bought large numbers of slaves, and much real estate, during the last year."³⁷ He may have had in mind the maternal grandfather of the subsequent advisor to Martin Luther King, Jr., Clifford Durr. James Henry Judkins came from a "large landowning and slaveholding family" that was "unwilling to adjust to the changed South at the war's end and, in particular, refusing to accept the reality of emancipation"—so they moved to Brazil "hoping there to reestablish their lost plantation world. He and his colleagues, he later wrote, had 'no faith in their ability to manage freed slaves.'" This grandfather, said Durr, was the "'greatest influence on his life'"— though it was unclear if this were in a wholly negative or positive sense.[38]

But the rebels could hardly be comforted when Ignacio Barboza da Silva, Brazil's emissary in Washington, remarked contemptuously in May 1865 about the capture of Jefferson Davis, late of the CSA, allegedly dressed in the clothes of a woman; this diplomat did not seem particularly enthusiastic about the fact that "inveterate prejudice exists" and "continues" in the U.S. "against" this reviled "African race."[39] After all, it was not long before the conclusion of the "war in the United States" had "convinced" enslaved Africans in Brazil "that they will all be freed," according to a Brazilian official in Para, thereby spurring mass discord amongst them and helping to alter attitudes in South America about slavery itself.[40] Not long after that, the Brazilian Andre Reboucas was visiting New York City but due to his modicum of melanin was barred from public accommodations. "I realized that the reason I was being refused rooms was a problem of color," he lamented. He speedily protested to Brazil's Consul who got a room in a "third class hotel" for him "under the condition that I eat in my room and never in the restaurant"—"I was obliged to take a bath in a barber shop," he added sadly.[41]

Thus, the faces of the escaping Confederates were suspended somewhere between a smile at the prospect of abandoning the hated abolitionist U.S. and a frown when they came to recognize that what they thought was an Empire for Slavery was morphing into something else altogether. If they had listened more carefully, these émigrés could have saved themselves a long journey. John F. Pickett, a former Confederate emissary in Mexico, "believed that no Confederate veteran would find emigration to Brazil acceptable. Brazilians, Pickett contended, lacked the same social prejudices against blacks that were felt by most Southerners."[42] In 1866, the Reverend Ballard S. Dunn warned potential Southern sojourners in Brazil. "The sidewalks of the principal streets being narrow," he advised, "and our hero large and portly, lo! He is jostled, by a Brazilian citizen of African descent: who presumes to apologize, by raising his hat and moving politely on. He has scarcely recovered from this rude shock of free-Negroism, when he espies, at the very next corner, a man, apparently white, conversing upon terms of perfect equality, with another citizen of the same extraction, as black as can be.

Here is proof, positive, of the existence of that hateful thing, 'Negro equality.' "[43]

"Even the importation of free Africans is prohibited by law," declared Brazil's Minister of Agriculture,[44] referring to a long-standing bar. "On arriving," one Northern U.S. journalist wrote jubilantly, the migrant "finds himself unable to go from place to place without a passport; he can buy slaves for one-fifth part, or less, than the former price [in the] South, but the slave cannot do one-hundredth part as much work as an Alabama cotton slave," and—worse—"he finds officers of Government, at the Custom-house, judges and officers in the army, are colored men. It is endurable to see a white man, or nearly white" in such posts "but to see black men among chief officers of Government and owners of slaves, this reverses all former theories" and was profoundly unsettling. "And Brazil, that seemed at a distance to be a Paradise, seems on a nearer view to be a Paradise lost"—yet "steamer loads of these deceived men [were] coming to Brazil every month only to repeat the disappointments of their predecessors."[45] In November 1865, James McFadden Gaston seemed almost stunned when he discovered that "Negroes are not admitted into Brazil from the U.S. unless born free, even should they be citizens of the latter"—which meant that seeking to smuggle Negroes into this nation was even more questionable than it might be otherwise. Then a few weeks later, he seemed even more surprised when "we were called upon in the evening by the Vicar of this municipality, who is a mulatto of more than ordinary intelligence. . . . he is a native of Bahia and I understand," he said admitting his ignorance of where he was now residing, "there are many people there of this mixed blood. The prevalent idea [was] that the dark complexion of many of the people in this warm climate is attributed to climate," said this willfully naïve surgeon.[46]

Gaston was distraught when he discovered there was a "very serious difficulty" that was "likely to meet our people in the matter of securing a regular and reliable system of labor the cultivation" of cotton and other crops. "There are many who may be hired at moderate price, but they are inexperienced in the use of the plow and do not understand the proper use of the hoe, so as to cultivate the cotton to the best advantage. Neither do they have the skill in picking cotton which is found among the Negroes of the South," he added in a note of misplaced nostalgia for those they had only recently abused—a note ironically and frequently found among these émigrés.[47] "In this respect," Dr. Gaston added, "a few of these [U.S.] Negroes would prove very advantageous" in Brazil.[48]

Julia Keyes concurred with him. The "Negroes . . . all look cheerful and happy" she said upon arrival in Brazil. "We find very little difference between the Negroes here and those in the States except in the amount of work they seem able to do. Our American house servant," she sniffed, "will accomplish more than twice as much without trying."[49]

Dr. Gaston, who was "profoundly pro-slavery," and whose "fondest dream was to be a plantation owner in the style of Low Country antebellum slave plantations of South Carolina," transplanted to Brazil, met a Priest, "a mulatto of more than ordinary intelligence; but my prejudice to being associated with those having the Negro blood could not be so entirely put aside as to make me feel at ease with this colored gentleman," he sputtered; in fact, such bias was "one of the basic reasons for the overall collapse of any extensive migration of Southerners to Brazil."[50] The oft surprised Gaston was taken aback once more "with the freedom which was allowed some Negro children" in Brazil "in coming into the room occupied by the family and with the attention given them," whereas such temerity would hardly be tolerated in the Slave South.[51]

Captain James A. Thomas of the CSA visited Brazil in 1866 with a "view to migrating to that country, but owing to the mixed race of inhabitants, he thought it an undesirable location to bear his children."[52] Julia Keyes was of like mind. While in Rio de Janeiro in 1867, she noticed that "females could not walk even to visit a near neighbor without a servant in attendance and it was often difficult to tell which was the mistress, their complexions being the same. Among them, however, were some Negroes as black as Ethiopians."[53] Ballard Dunn, formerly of the Slave South, then at Iguape, Brazil, "mocked the Southern emigrant who returned to the U.S. He 'poor mouthed' him because he could not put up with 'Negro Equality' and gave up his efforts to remain in Brazil when confronted by the 'rude shock of free Negroism'"; indeed, "if one were to select a single factor that truly kept the emigrant Southerner separated, with exception, from the Brazilian world in the arriving and the first generation born in Brazil, it was this cultural question."[54] The migrating ancestors of Lucie Hardie Wait "thought they would buy slaves—and get rich easily" so "they bought slaves but could talk to them, only [communicating] by signs," which complicated things tremendously.[55]

The U.S. diplomat James Monroe observed that many of the rebel migrants "'bought . . . slaves'" upon arrival but these promptly "'ran away, and it was not easy to recover them. . . . the fugitives secured places of refuge among their fellow slaves [on other plantations] and the Brazilian planters themselves were thought to be unsympathetic and unhelpful in the work of rendition.'" The rebels, who may have counted on some sort of "racial" solidarity with their Brazilian counterparts, instead discovered ruefully that the "snobbery evinced by Confederates towards their Brazilian neighbors was reciprocated in full by Brazilian planters who wished to discourage American competition."[56]

Dr. Gaston detected a "little feeling of jealousy on the part of those engaged in the cotton culture here, lest an emigration of Southern cotton planters to this country may lead to a cheapening of the article"[57]— and a worsening of the already tenuous relations between Brazilian and former Slave South planters.

Though some Brazilian elites may have welcomed these migrants, others viewed them as unneeded competition. Thus, Joseph W. Weed found that "many of the professions cannot be practiced without becoming a citizen of Brazil."[58] "Professional men, doctors and lawyers are required to undergo an examination in Brazil in coming from the U.S.," which an aghast Dr. Gaston considered to be unfair—and which also served to foil many potential competitors.[59]

The recent arrivals were learning quickly that there was real meaning to Brazil being a former Portuguese colony—meaning that included language barriers and more. "I have been so surprised to find so few Negro laborers outside of the coffee houses, as compared with what I expected," said the visiting Southerner, Joseph W. Weed, in 1874, sounding disappointed. "The Portuguese, about 10,000 of whom come over annually, have almost driven the darkies out of the city & [supplanted] his place as a laborer," he said, sounding disappointed, "while the value of the Negro has risen & has been taken to the interior plantations, to grow coffee."[60]

The visiting scholar from the U.S., Louis Agassiz, accompanied by his spouse, Elizabeth, sensed these changing tides during his post–Civil War sojourn in Brazil. "Captain Bradbury asked the proprietor of the island whether he hired or owned his slaves. 'Own them—a hundred and more; but it will finish soon,' he answered in his broken English. 'Finish soon! How do you mean?'" he was asked. "'It finish with you, it finish here, it finish everywhere.' He said it not in any tone of regret or complaint, but as an inevitable fact. The death-note of slavery in the United States was its death-note everywhere. We thought this significant and cheering," the couple opined. The message they were bringing back home was contrary to what had propelled the Confederates southward. "We may have something to learn here in our own perplexities respecting the position of the black race among us," they said; "the absence of all restraint upon the free blacks, the fact that they are eligible to office, and that all professional careers are open to them, without prejudice on the ground of color, enables one to form some opinion as to their ability. . . . the result is on the whole in their favor" since Africans did "compare well in intelligence and activity with the Brazilians and Portuguese," though since the latter were a "less energetic and powerful race than the Anglo-Saxon" and since slavery was "more odious" than in the U.S., it was unclear how universal were their maunderings, it was thought.[61] Racial biases against Africans were colliding with ethnic biases against Brazilians and Portuguese.

The perceived antipathy of Brazilian planters complicated further the tangled stay of the migrants. Besides having to adjust to being thrown into intimate gatherings with those who back home would have been deemed to be mere Negroes, the Southern sojourners had a more basic and formidable obstacle—language. "The greatest trouble to an American is the language," concluded Julia Keyes, for "until he learns it he cannot succeed well at anything without assistance or at any rate, he labors under a serious disadvantage."[62] Dr. Gaston studied French while en route to Brazil which "served as a means of communication in polite society or at court," then "quickly picked up Portuguese phrases"; but "his wife, coming later, never obtained good use of the language" though he was "able to take the oral and written examination" for his profession and "to write his thesis credibly in the Portuguese language."[63] "The Southerners are the Jews of the American Republic," announced the **New York Times**, "and yet they will never find a home in foreign countries where a different language, other customs and the want of means prevent a barrier to their welfare."[64] Diehards, who no longer could stomach the hegemonic Northern states, were "more inclined to go to California, Texas and the northwestern states," said J. D. Porter of Alabama, than "Brazil and some even incline towards Honduras," for "until recently Brazil was a terra incognita to most of us," not least due to the language barrier.[65]

Some might have wished they had gone to Honduras instead of Brazil. One recent migrant complained that he had "failed in [the] cotton crop the past season owing to a drought of seven weeks" and would not "make more than 1/2 bale per acre of cotton." He began to wax nostalgic in this pivotal year of 1876, offering "hope" that the "South may obtain all she may desire or expect to obtain in this election," while adding morosely, "I feel quite lonesome, so far from all relatives or old acquaintances and now never expect to meet any of them again."[66] Even Dr. Gaston, who adjusted better than most, having picked up Portuguese, admitted that he was "often sorely tempted to despondency. Again and again he hoped for mail, only to be disappointed."[67]

Soon the inevitable occurred. Disgusted with the underdevelopment of Brazil compared to the U.S., upset with the state of race relations, unable to communicate in an alien tongue, bothered by the often less than friendly attitudes of the locals, and often bordering on misery, a growing number of rebel migrants swallowed their corrosive doubts about the U.S. and returned to their homeland. Such returns were often blared in the **New York Times,** that was far from friendly to the CSA, in any case. "There arrived at the Central Hotel [in Montgomery] last night a party of ladies and gentlemen who left Brazil last month," it was reported in August 1867; "they give affecting and pitiful accounts of the sufferings of many hundreds of deluded Southerners," recounting that "there is no regularly organized Government in Brazil—there is no society." One among them, "Capt. Jack Phelan, who is so well-known and admired in Montgomery, has, we learn, left with a large number of other young men, to make California their home."[68] Rebel colonies had been established throughout the hemisphere, including Mexico, Honduras, and "the village of San Javier in the Argentine Republic" but it was "Brazil that promised the most, and perhaps led to the bitterest disappointment. It is from Brazil that have now returned, disheartened and disgusted, six score of those colonists who left comfortable homes here in 1867," it was said in early 1870.[69]

This souring was mutual. General Wood, who had been greeted so effusively in Brazil, turned up in Natchez where he was "elected County Attorney"—"sic transit Gloria Braziliensis" was the response in Brazil.[70] More specifically, the Vice Consul in New Orleans of Brazil, informed his Foreign Ministry that "W. W. Wood, soi dissant General is, [we] learn now in the city of Natchez. . . . he has delivered some public lectures upon Brazil, since his return but I cannot learn of his having made any movement relating to immigration to that country. He does not appear to enjoy the esteem of the better class of the population of Mississippi." Even then, in May 1866, migrants were still leaving for Brazil from this busy port, including a "highly respected sugar planter. . . . several families in all some 30 persons, mostly planters from the western part of Louisiana"[71]—but already opinions of such an exodus were being transformed.

One source in Rio de Janeiro in the year following these migrants leaving said that "we regret to say that many mere speculative Americans have been attracted hither by this liberality and kindness of the Government towards their countrymen and look upon it as a mine from which they can dig out favors and subsidies, on specious pretexts and without the slightest wish or intention to serve their emigrating countrymen or Brazil." Worry was now arising that "the immigration which was calculated at first hundreds will be thousands, perhaps tens of thousands," thus reaffirming that old saw about being careful about what is desired.[72] There was, for example, Charles Edward Lewis Stuart, "calling himself General of the late Confederate army," who had "forged" and was also "swindling by false representations."[73]

The grumbling soon became louder. "What can it be which makes United States diplomacy unappreciated and unsuccessful in every country?" it was asked querulously. "Is it that the 'Manifest Destiny' is inscribed too strongly in the demeanor and language of their diplomats," i.e., "the intention of its rulers to imitate the policy and the example of its Roman predecessor." And what about the "Monroe Doctrine," now "openly avowed to mean nothing short of the absorbing of all the independent American states into the northern republic." Worry was expressed about Washington's view of the all-important war in Paraguay.[74] Thanks but no thanks was Brazil's terse and telling reply to the U.S. offer to mediate this conflict.[75]

Why should Brazil trust the U.S., a nation with a sworn policy of anti-slavery? Consider that in 1873, President U.S. Grant—who had led the victorious Union army against the de facto Brazilian ally, the CSA—entertained the revival of the age-old Radical Republican dream of placing a "discriminating duty on slave-grown products"—a measure that had Brazil in the crosshairs. It would be beneficial, the cigar-smoking, whiskey-swilling President was told, "not only for its political effect at home" but, as well, "it would promote, greatly stimulate in fact, the culture of sugar in Louisiana, Texas and Florida." As for the negative effect on Brazil, well, it was said, this nation was "profiting from us immensely from its sale [of coffee], the proceeds of which go mainly to purchase British goods," and, thus, merited no special favors. "The world would look with favor" upon this special duty and, besides, it would "protect our freedmen from the unpaid labor of foreign slaves." In other words, the U.S. was placing pressure on Brazil to alter its economy fundamentally and profoundly.[76] Typically, this line was bolstered in the **New York Times** as a prominently placed interview asserted that a duty on slave-grown products "would promote—greatly stimulate in fact—the culture of sugar in Louisiana, Texas and Florida."[77]

This proposal was not unusual. After abolishing slavery, the U.S. advocated for Brazil to do the same, not least so it would not gain a competitive advantage in certain markets, just as after London barred slavery it sought to squelch the African Slave Trade. Thus, as early as 1867, James Watson Webb declared that Brazil, being "next to ourselves, the great power on the American continent," was "in imitation of us" "considering the means of immediately commencing the gradual manumission of her slaves." The blunt Webb suggested, "let her begin the work by at once manumitting 50,000 of her able-bodied Negroes. Let her, if need be, follow our example [*sic*] and *buy* them from their masters at our bounty rate of $1000 per head, give them freedom, and make them earn that freedom as soldiers and as freedmen" [emphasis-original], for—he said definitively—"there can be no doubt that Brazil will get rid of slavery altogether within the next 30 years." As he saw it, the "Emperor" was "the head and front, the very soul of the movement for the emancipation of all slaves within thirty years—the work to commence now, by immediate legislation. Of course, if he should abdicate, the movement ceases, and therefore the advocates of the slave interest would be well pleased to get rid of him on any terms. They'll not succeed," said Webb confidently though if the rebel migrants had anything to do with it—many of whom had come to Brazil precisely because it perpetuated slavery—the Emperor would not succeed.[78]

Thus, émigrés from the former Slave South, were increasingly being seen as a threat to the security of the U.S. Perhaps, not coincidentally, the Northern U.S. press at this moment began to unleash an inundation of inflamed accounts about their plight and the presumed questionable occurrences in Brazil itself, e.g., their "national currency" being "more extensively counterfeited than that of any other country in the world."[79]

The **New York Times** informed its readers in May 1871, of "established colonization agencies in New York, Richmond, Savannah,

Mobile and New Orleans"; the **Anglo-Brazilian Times,** published in Brazil, was designed with these potential migrants in mind. Soon a "number of very estimable gentlemen, among whom were tobacco growers from Virginia, Alabama and Mississippi and extensive sugar planters from the famous Red River district of Louisiana and Middle Texas . . . emigrated with their families to the provinces of Sao Paulo and Espiritu Santo, in lower Brazil. Whole districts of the finest land in the South, from Maryland to Texas, were sacrificed for a mere song. Entire counties were almost completely depopulated by the great exodus of reputable emigrants and disreputable adventurers." But soon, said the **Times,** Brazil began to sour on these sojourners as they "refused to comply with their contract by colonizing the interior, and remained in the vicinity of the capital, eking out a miserable existence, as best they could. After making the City of Rio a perfect pandemonium for nearly two years, they were sent home at Government expense. . . . these misled people have since learned a terrible lesson of sad experience," as "every day in the gay thoroughfares of the Brazilian Capital, are to be seen hundreds who have, years gone by, reveled in luxury and affluence, and who are now actually begging from door to door and making a poor, pitiful effort to drown their miseries by spending the pittance thus obtained in the nearest drinking booth, where potent libations of villainous *aguadiente*—the vilest decoction in Christendom—is peddled for the smallest fraction of a cent." In sentence after sentence, this journalist heaped mounds of scorn on this exile:

> The writer of this sketch was walking down the Rua Dereita, the great boulevard of Rio de Janeiro, one evening last January, when he was [intercepted] by a miserable, ragged and squalid-looking object, who implored him, "for God's sake, give me only a *vinte* (less than a quarter of a cent) to get something to eat." The wretched man said that he had been in Brazil four years. He had left a young wife and child in Baltimore, and had emigrated with many others, whom he said were then as destitute as he, hoping to repair his fortunes, but instead, he had been going rapidly down hill ever since he had first landed on Brazilian soil. The gentleman . . . said that he was a graduate of the Jefferson College Medical School in Philadelphia, and had at one time a large and lucrative practice in Richmond, Va. When reaching Brazil he had at first endeavored to practice medicine among the American colonists of the Sao Paulo province but the colonists were as poor as he, and he was

finally compelled to return to Rio de Janeiro sick at heart and much more sick in body. Wandering about the dingy streets . . . he at last applied to the city authorities for employment [and] accepted work on the public highways.

Shortly thereafter, he was "found dead in a filthy hovel in an obscure section of the city. Being a Protestant he was denied a Christian burial by the ecclesiastical authorities." Worse was to come. "In a remote quarter of one of the lowest precincts of the capital is a rickety little building"; "over the door of the dilapidated hovel is a sign in glaring capitals" reading " 'the Dixie Free and Easy Concert Saloon.' " There "as vile a set of scoundrels as ever cut a throat, is all that remains of a man, who was once a might among his people—a man who has been the Mayor of one of the principal cities of the United States, and also a prominent officer in the Southern army." Nearby in "the penal colony of Ferdinand de Naronba are two or three gentlemen criminals who were once respected citizens of the South, but who, having lost all their worldly possessions in the United States, were tempted to emigrate to Brazil by visions of speedy affluence and freedom from toil" by dint of slavery. They "recklessly plunged into an abyss of fraud and forgery, and as a consequence are now enduring a miserable existence on the lonely island of Naronba as Brazilian convicts. A very intelligent gentleman who was formerly an extensive sugar planter on the Bayou Sara in Louisiana, recently stated, while on a visit to Rio from his new home in the province of Sao Paulo, that he was not alone among the Southern colonists when he said that he was intensely disgusted with the country and would willingly return to his good old home in Louisiana if he had but the means." In painful detail was recounted the story of the "seizure . . . of two daughters of a prominent citizen of Memphis" and "the subsequent enslavement of the fair Southerners, to satisfy the cruel claims of a hard-hearted Brazilian, to whom the father had become peculiarly indebted for a large amount."[80]

Godfrey Barnsley, the Georgian migrant from a family once rich in enslaved Africans, took umbrage to this widely circulated article, as did many of his fellow émigrés. Contrary to the reporter's observations, Barnsley was outraged about the explosive allegation that "white men's daughters and Americans were sold." The émigrés were wounded by the idea that they had descended downward on the level of civilization by moving to Brazil; "it is a great mistake," he said, "to consider this country in a semi-barbarous condition" for "to say that white people are sold is beyond measure stupid; it is not even calumniative [*sic*], for that word carries an idea of some basis to the assertion." He disputed the notion that the Emperor himself was pro-abolitionist; he spoke of how "well" these colonists were doing, though he acknowledged that "more than a hundred Southerners went to Espiritu Santo" and now "that colony is totally abandoned"; and, yes, in the "Rebeira Province" of São Paulo, "three distinct colonies" were now "totally deserted." But what about "Santa Barbara, São Paulo," where "250 to 300, babies included," were doing fine, with some, he stressed, "<u>accumulating riches</u>." The idea of "seeing hundreds of Americans in Rio destitute" was "simply false" and those seen in such a state were "<u>not Americans</u>" [emphasis-original] but "mostly Irish, and it is possible the greater part of them were particular pets of the New York police." It was "true that the Brazilian Government sent them back to the States, as rubbish" but they were not "Americans." However, reality was hard to ignore, even for the ideologically committed, so Barnsley's defense was as damning as the original indictment. "I will state candidly," he said, "that a greater portion are <u>discontented</u> and propose <u>eventually</u> to return to the States and for that end are saving" [emphasis-original] because of "dissimilarity of language and customs; difficulties of transportation, low price for skilled labor; difference in religion; inability to vote and be 'sovereigns'; disgust—for the Brazilian idea that a man who sweats from work is not a gentleman; and finally—the most potent of all—that this country offers and gives nothing for the American, which he cannot get in his own country." Thus, "more than two thirds of them that have come have already returned," and the "rest may be expected to follow, sooner or later." Barnsley himself gave up valuable ground to Brazil's detractors by acknowledging "I am no lover of these people and though naturalized, intend to return to the States at an early date."

But what seemed to irk Barnsley was not the alleged inaccuracies in accounts of what was happening to rebel migrants in Brazil, but the general inattention in the U.S. itself to events in its neighbor. "There are <u>eight</u> or more superb packet lines to England, France, Italy and Germany, and only <u>one</u> to the States" [emphasis-original]—and this one "receives a subsidy from the Brazilian Government to enable it to continue. Europe furnishes iron, coal, dry goods, wines, fancy articles, all kinds of machinery, carriages, etc. America sends flour and patent medicines!"[81]

That Barnsley would be compelled to give resonance to some of the most damaging allegations made about the migration to Brazil served to underscore how ill-fated this adventure was. For in his private moments he acknowledged that he and many others were enduring a painful adjustment to this new land. "The whole country is infested with ants," there were "scarcely any vegetables for sale," "the only fruits are oranges and bananas," there were "scarcely any flowers," the "only fare is beef, rice and beans, with once in a while potatoes and yams." Barnsley was a doctor and he was disgusted that among those claiming this lofty title in Brazil was a "pure charlatan without the least knowledge of the profession of medicine, yet to these men are entrusted the lives of the miserable slaves, simply because they think it economical." "Almost everything comes from abroad which is used for clothing, for house use, for agricultural use," which was a "great drawback." The culture was oppressive. "Another great restraint to my happiness," he complained, "is that a stranger cannot become intimately acquainted with the Brazilians unless he becomes identified with them in customs, bragging and lying"; "among the women," there was "no education, and having nothing to do except scandalize, if one tries to become intimate his life is rendered a constant torment." Thus, he had kept his family "apart, as much as possible." Education among men was little better, as they were "very superficial and rarely one encounters a person who can hold a conversation on any subject beyond the more commonplace of affairs of daily life." "I am wasting away precious years," he cried, "I must get away from this country as soon as possible. This desire is the grand absorbing aim, to which everything else becomes subsidiary" [emphasis-original].[82] But as time passed, he found himself "doomed to remain in this country for years yet. . . . my heart yearns once more to be among my own people. . . . I grow sad and sickened with my lot." How could he be so "foolish as to enter into voluntary exile," which had contributed to "pecuniary embarrassment" since his "whole career in Brazil has been one continued misfortune dragging to the ground every time I attempt to rise."[83]

But being blunt, Barnsley could not ignore that a bunch of slaveholders were not humanity's best advertisement. "The conduct of Americans in Brazil has not been creditable to themselves or to the nation which they represent," he admitted; they "swindle when they get a chance" and the Brazilians not being "a stupid people" were "fast learning" this.[84]

This dispirited adventure of Confederates in Brazil was reassuring to the national ego of the U.S. but in a contradictory manner. It served to discredit slaveholders and slavery which both the CSA and Brazil represented, while it buttressed rudimentary notions of white supremacy, which their South American neighbor was thought to have violated by not penalizing sufficiently "inter-racial" sexuality. Writing from the U.S. legation in Rio de Janeiro in the summer of 1871, James R. Partridge seemed almost heartened to find of the "between three and four hundred" rebel migrants "self-exiled" in São Paulo, "very many" were now "exceedingly anxious to avail themselves of the generosity of our Government, which they are now glad to call their Government also, to return to the home they left."[85] They had "lost everything," he said, were "without employment or the means of returning." He was "aware" that to "relieve persons . . . from the consequences of their deliberate folly in leaving their own country" was a discomfiting signal to transmit in a nation grounded in the idea of personal responsibility for one's actions; and "if men alone were concerned," he would be "silent," but there were too many "women and children" involved to do so.[86] While in Para, the U.S. emissary found exiles in "destitute circumstances," both "dissatisfied" and "living frugally," all of which underscored the value of remaining true to the U.S. itself.[87] Back in the U.S. newspaper columns were filling with tales of exiles returning disgusted with their Brazilian experience—though their reluctance to repudiate slavery itself meant the U.S. Negro would have been served better by their absence.[88]

Treating the bedraggled return of these former exiles as the final victory of the Civil War, in late 1875, the **New York Times,** exaggerating for dramatic effect, found "something significant in the return to the United States of the last detachment of the American emigrants to Brazil. . . . no such exodus had ever taken place from" this country, thus distinguishing the loyalist exile after the Revolution since these were actually British nationals who chose to remain so. "Some timid people," it was announced victoriously, "affected to see in this migration the beginning of a depopulation of the lately rebellious States. The total strength of the movement was finally put at fifteen hundred. It now appears likely that not one-half that number were left" in Brazil, a nation whose "primitive business habits . . . seem excessively wasteful and dilatory." But now a benevolent Washington "sent men-of-war after the Southern fugitives. But they were sent in answer to a call for help, not in anger," i.e., as reconciliation between the former Slave South and the North at the expense of the U.S. Negro.[89]

Thus, as the **New York Times** put it, 750 out of an estimated 1500 U.S. nationals remained in Brazil as the pivotal year of 1876 approached. This may have been an underestimation, a reflection of the Northern press's antipathy to these émigrés and their concomitant desire to downplay their significance. The émigrés provided lethal ammunition to their detractors with their incessant complaining and their festering anti-Washington sentiments. Still, the devolutionary spiral of slavery in Brazil meant that any dream of restoring the equivalence of African and chattel was rapidly coming to a close.

Epilogue

Despite the return to the U.S. of so many disgruntled exiles, others remained in Brazil where they continued to shape their new homeland, just as they had molded their old. Thus, "when a Senator opposed to slavery was assassinated on the eve of Brazil's emancipation" in 1888, "the Confederados"—as they came to be called—"were at first suspected."[1] Those with U.S. ties may have been innocent in this instance but others were a more troublesome presence in Brazilian internal affairs. In early 1888, a "police delegate of the municipality who sympathized with the antislavery movement was sheltering refugees in his home." This was at a time when many plantations were "being abandoned" in anticipation of slavery's 1888 demise and, thus, "angry slave proprietors decided to take action. They were led by two naturalized Brazilians, James Ox Warne and John Jackson Clink, immigrants from the United States, who had fought for the Confederacy during the Civil War. The two incited the planters by telling them that they had 'cockroach blood' and that under such circumstances a revolution would have occurred in any other country." They "bludgeoned" the "young man to death," along with others deemed to be abolitionist sympathizers.[2]

As early as 1867, the exile, John Codman, had signaled that many of his fellow émigrés would not be enthusiastic about the demise of slavery —and the concomitant final strangulation of the African Slave Trade— in their new homeland. "Soon the pressure of the abolition party in Brazil, aided by the influence of Brazil and the United States, will terminate slavery altogether," he said with rancor, referring to "the anti-slavery party" as "already a disturbing political element." "The shock upon society will not be so great there as it has been here," he added generously, "and the absence of distinctions of color [sic] will aid in incorporating the black into the body politic," though he warned that "coming as we did from a country where we knew too well how much of the pretended love for the Negro has emanated from that political ambition which has made him the mere tool for the purposes of party and of power," he advised Brazilians to adopt an alternative course.[3]

The Confederates had seemed to be a people without a nation—or a hemisphere—as their attempt to revive the "peculiar institution" ran aground on the shoals of Brazilian abolitionism. Unwilling to reconcile with abolitionism, they had even more difficulty adapting to a substantive role for the formerly enslaved in politics. The latter did not make it easy for them, for as in the U.S. they came to take quite seriously their newly forged citizenship rights. Thus, in April 1869, a group of African-Americans petitioned President Grant; they wanted some of their number to be appointed not only for diplomatic posts in Liberia, Haiti, and other Latin American nations but, as well, wanted their leader—Frederick Douglass—appointed Minister to Brazil, indicative of their viewing this South American nation as part of the Pan-African world.[4]

As was to happen so often in coming decades, these petitioners were to be sorely disappointed. For continuing the antebellum tradition of appointing "reliable" white Southerners as chief diplomats in Brazil, the revival of this practice after the war was a troubling signal that though slavery and the African Slave Trade might have virtually disappeared, the ideology that underpinned both was very much alive. Thus, with Reconstruction's demise, dispatched to Brazil was Henry W. Hilliard, a "strong, unrepentant rebel"; in fact, "there was not in the city of Augusta in the Summer of 1865, after the termination of the rebellion, a more decided rebel than this man Hilliard"—he was a "'last ditch rebel.'"[5] Hilliard, born in Cumberland County, North Carolina in 1808, was admitted to the bar in Athens, Georgia in 1829, and in 1831 was "elected to a Professorship in the University of Alabama" before Jefferson Davis "commissioned him as a Brigadier-General in the Provisional Army of the Confederate States."[6] A self-described "Union man" wrote in anguish about the "active part taken by" Hilliard in "causing the separation of the state of Tennessee from the Union in 1861"—the "union men of 1861 are indignant and ashamed," it was said, "that such a person should represent in a foreign country the Government they loved more than life."[7]

Hilliard sought to reassure the doubting, issuing a "long statement as to the industrial results of emancipation" in the U.S.; his "able and temperate letter, coming from a Southern man who was engaged in the rebellion," said one news report in 1880, "has greatly encouraged the friends of immediate emancipation in Brazil, while it has somewhat offended the Brazilian Bourbons. It is also pleasant to remark that the Emperor thanked Mr. Hilliard for his letter."[8]

Even the approach of abolition in 1888 did little to alter the reinstated policy of sending white Southerners to represent U.S. interests in Brazil, reversing the wishes of African-American petitioners. Thomas J. Jarvis of North Carolina represented a tightly woven strand of U.S. representation—"reliable" white Southerners providing undistinguished leadership. "I would gladly [trade] the magnificence of Rio for the simplicity of home," he said at one point, "and when I say home I mean North Carolina."[9] He had expected a "seat in the President's Cabinet" but he was "under obligation to the Party" and was "bound" to accept the post in Brazil. "I did not desire this place," he wailed, and wanted the "Party" to "withdraw" his "name" but he was refused,[10] and though he found "Petropolis" to be "the prettiest mountain city I ever saw,"[11] Jarvis's stay marked the beginning of a new trend in U.S.-Brazilian relations, whereby the inflamed issues of enslavement and the African Slave Trade were no longer the defining characteristic and third-rate politicians had to be cajoled to move southward.

Even before the advent of abolition in Brazil, U.S. emissaries were getting increasingly grumpy about Brazil. Reporting from Rio de Janeiro in 1879, John C. White, was not sympathetic to his host country, remarking that "with the exception of the blacks, Brazilians do not perform manual labor, and very few of them are engaged in trade"; a "professional existence or a political office is the wish and work of the Brazilian." Yes, it was "popular to say that this country is an Eldorado for Americans with energy and money and many American newspapers have pictured Brazil as the land of plenty," but he disagreed. "Eventually the trade of this country will be controlled by our country," he predicted, "but it will take time." In the meantime, a replay of previous decades was still in play as Britain and Brazil seemed to be in a virtual marriage: "English capital, English goods, English subsidized steamship lines, and English influence" remained to "be met, checked and overcome."[12]

Another perennial was Maury's dream of having U.S. Negroes develop Brazil. Hilliard reported that "de Lesseps has applied to the Emperor of Brazil to supply him with laborers" for construction of the Panama Canal and was informed that "15,000 Negroes will be furnished . . . under this arrangement." Hilliard was dismissive, however, observing that "the application may have been made but it will lead to nothing."[13] Though not enthusiastic about Brazilian Negroes moving closer to the U.S. by coming to Panama, Maury's idea of sending U.S. Negroes to Brazil was another matter altogether. For at that moment a U.S. contractor had "determined to send colored men to Brazil to work upon the Madiera and Mamore Railroad. It is more than probable that 500 will go out [to] Rio de Janeiro" and it was added a bit optimistically, "the Brazilian government will make no objection to their landing."[14] "Over 300" of these were "residents of Washington," which may have been pleasing to those in the nation's capital concerned with the growing "colored" population there.[15] Yet this latest attempt to rid the nation of this problematic population was encountering a familiar roadblock, as the "contractors for the Brazil railroad" were informed by "the Brazilian Secretary of State that colored men would not be permitted to enter the Empire as part of the working force of the contractors."[16] Then after that was negotiated, the "Senate" had to pass a bill "authorizing the issue of passports free to colored citizens going to Brazil," as the previous $5 charge "practically prevented many colored men," from traveling southward.[17]

As some in Brazil saw it, these men were "best fitted for the work, to which the Brazilian Minister in Washington would not consent, he doubting the legality of an introduction of free blacks into Brazil"; then the "Government telegraphed last week to declare to him that American citizens, whatever their color, can be brought. This is an important boon," it was reported, "and will greatly facilitate the construction."[18] It seemed that Brazil and the U.S. were evolving toward a more "modern" conception of the role of the formerly enslaved; i.e., they would not be barred solely because of their color but, instead, could be slated to labor in certain posts precisely because of that still disabling factor.

Then other factors intruded. As excited Negro men began to meet in Washington, this "gave rise to a report that secret meetings" were "being held by the working men of the District in furtherance of a labor strike to be started throughout the country in August next and that these meetings were arranged by representatives of Western labor organizations." On the other hand, as "an impression prevailed that colored men who would go to Brazil would be consigned to slavery, the requisition could not be filled." Rather vainly "the agent explained that Brazil was averse to permitting the settlement of colored men in that country and [that] laws forbid such settlement. These laws, however, have been suspended with reference to such colored men as would go to Brazil to assist in constructing the railroad and those who would go would be furnished passports free by the United States, Congress having passed an act recently for this purpose." Pay would be "$1.50 per day and their expenses to Brazil and return, provided they will remain two years." Finally, it was determined that "about 60 laborers were obtained," who would depart soon, which lent optimism that such employment would mean "labor strikes will be reduced in proportion to the number of idle men that will be given employment and taken from a community largely overstocked with laborers."[19] Maury's dream of Brazil as a "safety valve" for the U.S. was being realized, albeit not in the manner he originally intended.

But the difference now was that U.S. Negroes themselves were beginning to look southward longingly, their interest stirred by both the atrocities they were forced to endure regularly and the spotlight being shown on Brazil as a result of the export of black workers to build a railroad. In 1886, the all-black AME Church in the U.S. passed "resolutions reviewing the history of Negro emancipation in the United States and expressing sympathy with the movement for the gradual emancipation of slaves in Brazil," which were "unanimously adopted. The resolutions were translated into French and an engrossed copy forwarded to the Emperor of Brazil."[20] In the year of abolition, 1888, A. A. Jones, a "prominent colored leader" in Indianapolis—"formerly of Virginia"—declared, " 'we are going to weed some of the Southern States of the colored population.' " Why? Well, for starters, " 'the Democracy will not let them vote; they do not appreciate the value of colored labor and we propose to get the voters and their families out of the country. . . . we propose to send them to South America. Brazil is the objective point. Everybody down there is dark, and there is no trouble on the score of color. We will get many of them away this summer,' " he said sanguinely. " 'Missouri' " Negroes would be an initial target. " 'We have enlisted men with money in the enterprise,' " he added, " 'and we are systematically preparing for the exodus. We will have plenty of funds when the time comes for action.' "[21]

Reverend Jones was not singular in his desire for mass Negro emigration to Brazil. That same year of abolition, 1888, a "rumor" reached Washington and Rio about a "scheme" said to "have originated in Topeka, Kansas for starting a great emigration of colored people from the

Southern States to South America." Apparently, there was a distinct fear of the "probability" of these potential émigrés "being sold into slavery," though it was felt that "President Cleveland's administration would not tolerate such a scheme for a moment."[22]

This was part of a larger "scheme of colonizing African laborers in South and Central America . . . affecting many states and hundreds of thousands of people." "Several well-known colored men . . . of means met three years ago to consult as to the best method of relieving their people from the condition that prevailed in the extreme Southern States." They quickly "arrived at the conclusion that South America was the land that would give them shelter and a home." These men "all with some wealth and some of them counting with six figures, sent out educated agents," as "the Guianas, Brazil and the Argentine Confederation were examined"; this was "quietly effected by a secret organization whose head is in Topeka" as the idea was to "carry off more than a million of laborers from the cotton, sugar and rice fields." "Important concessions would be made by the Brazilian and Argentine governments in the way of land and immunity from taxation," it was expected, while "owing [to] the mixed blood already existing in some of those countries their color will not debar them from political and social preferment."

The **Rio Daily News,** which reported this story, was skeptical. "If these agents visited Brazil," it was said, "they succeeded wonderfully well in keeping themselves and their purposes well out of sight and if any inducements have been offered they have been verbal and through secret channels." "No colony of American Negroes will ever [be] prosperous and contented in South America, especially in Brazil," it was predicted confidently. "The language, laws, customs and institutions of all these countries, except British Guiana, are foreign to them"; indeed, huffed this journal, "it is our candid opinion that there is not one single country in South America where they will be treated as well as in the United States." Like their Confederate opposite numbers, these U.S. Negroes evidently did not realize that "without railways, steamship lines, and markets, and without government protection against Indians and lawless characters, the chances of their making even a bare living are very slight"; "they cannot expect help from Brazil, for the country is already poor and already overburdened with beggars and parasites. . . . chances are that they will starve or be degraded to the level of the savages about them." "If the American colony at Santarem on the

Amazon could not maintain itself, what can the less energetic Negro expect? Every one of the American colonies in this country has failed and disappeared, except that of Santa Barbara and it is certain that no Negro colony can do better." Hitting a sensitive nerve, the paper proclaimed, that these Negroes "may find less prejudice against his color here in Brazil, more opportunities for association and amalgamation, but to gain those he must make infinite sacrifice and suffer infinite loss."[23]

Before this ambitious scheme petered out, it was reported that it was "making rapid progress" in "eight states," though skepticism about its prospects reigned. These Negroes were focusing on Brazil and Argentina, "where they are told that there is no prejudice against their color." Settling "on the highlands of the Southern tributaries of the Amazon, [was] an absurd chimera," it was suggested. "In the end," it was said, "the consulates of the United States in this country, will soon be overrun with destitute Negroes, and the United States government will have to send for them, just as it did for some of the white emigrants after the rebellion."[24]

Thus, there was no takeoff for this ambitious scheme of colonization though about twenty years later a number of U.S. nationals sought to revive the filibustering of the previous century.[25] For it was in 1907 that "nine men went to Brazil in November to conquer a state of 2,000,000 inhabitants," a plot that also failed miserably.[26] All were "dressed in khaki uniform of the American army" and were "well armed with revolvers and Remington rifles,"[27] though they were portrayed as mentally unbalanced, others were not so sure.[28]

Though perhaps not lineal descendants, they were, at least, ideological descendants of the "Confederados" who had descended upon Brazil in the years following the Civil War. Some among this latter group remained in Brazil as the 20th century wound down and they were carrying on the traditions of their ancestors; thus, "such words as 'nigger' " were used "with the same abandon" as by their "slave-owning ancestors" and they were "very conservative politically."[29] When then Governor Jimmy Carter of Georgia visited Brazil just before his capture of the White House in 1976, he was so "overcome with the joy of finding an old-time Southern town" he "wept." His spouse, Rosalynn Carter, "found the gravestone of an ancestor named Wise."[30] Confederate flags continued to flutter in these neighborhoods that time forgot.[31] Some of these descendants had honored their ancestors' pledge to construct a nation to challenge the U.S. that so many of them abhorred. Jose Luiz Whitaker Ribeiro, for example, was President of Engesa, "Brazil's largest arms exporter" and a challenger to the U.S. in this lucrative market; he was descended from Joseph Whitaker who had fled Georgia in 1866.[32] This was consistent with the martial and adversarial spirit that had animated the initial wave of Confederate migrants. Interviewed in 1978 in Brazil, Elizabeth McAlpine MacKnight did not seek to prettify the reason her Alabama-born father—who had served as Jefferson Davis's bodyguard—had migrated to Brazil. "Till the day my father died," she exclaimed, "I reckon he always had a kind of hatred for the Yankees."[33]

Thus, abolition descended upon Brazil without any mass effort of U.S. Negroes to find a more welcoming home south of the border. If this had occurred, they would have encountered a land that may have perplexed these migrants. For as one analyst has put it, "the situation in Brazil is better characterized by the saying 'the poor white person is black and the rich [black] person is white.' This comparison might suggest a possible amendment to the African-American perspective 'or I can be black, become rich, go to Brazil and become white!'" In the U.S. "no white person can acknowledge any African ancestry, because by definition anyone with African ancestry is black," while "even [former] President Fernando Henrique Cardoso acknowledged having 'um pen a cozinha,'" i.e., "'one foot in the kitchen,' an expression referring to his having had a black ancestress."[34]

On 14 May 1888, writing from Petropolis, Thomas J. Jarvis, the U.S. Minister there, still distraught about being away from his beloved North Carolina, noted, almost in passing, "yesterday the General Assembly of Brazil finally passed and the Princess Imperial Regent approved a law abolishing slavery in Brazil. . . . I therefore do not share in the fears expressed by some as to its immediate effect on the various industries."[35]

Meanwhile in Albany, New York, the "sixty-eighth Annual Conference of the African Methodist Episcopal Church," meeting on their nation's national holiday in 1888, designated a committee to "prepare resolutions to be sent to the Brazilian Minister at Washington, by him to be conveyed to" the Emperor, "thanking [him] for freeing the slaves in Brazil."[36] And with that a curtain was rung down on one of the more inglorious chapters in their nation's history: the promiscuous participation of U.S. nationals in the African Slave Trade to Brazil.

Reportedly, in a 2002 meeting between U.S. President George W. Bush and then Brazilian President Fernando Henrique Cardoso, the former asked, " 'Do you have blacks too?' " Bush's aide, Condoleezza Rice—who happened to be of African descent—"noticing how astonished the Brazilian was, saved the day by telling Bush 'Mr. President, Brazil probably has more blacks than the USA. Some say it's a country with the most blacks outside Africa.' "[37]

The widespread circulation of this story in Brazil may suggest lingering feelings there about how U.S. nationals transformed the demographic makeup of this South American colossus by dint of the illicit African Slave Trade.[38]

Similarly, though there is little concern in the U.S. about a real or imagined security threat emerging from Brazil, the reverse is not necessarily the case. Matthew Fontaine Maury and his dream of seizing the Valley of the Amazon may not be forgotten either; a sensitive nerve in Brazil was exposed in June 2005, when it was reported that "suspicions run wild that 'hegemonic' powers like the U.S. have desires on the vast region," meaning the Amazon; "many are convinced that foreign powers, in particular the [U.S.] are making plans for a takeover of the world's biggest tropical forest to secure the rights to its seemingly limitless natural resources, from wood to gems to medicinal herbs. In a national survey released last month, 75% of Brazilians polled feared a foreign invasion provoked by their country's natural riches."[39]

U.S. nationals have continued to stream into Brazil, this time attracted by tourist attractions, particularly the lovely beaches of Rio de Janeiro, once the site of black bodies floating in nearby waters. Reversing the journey taken by Pedro Parris, who was kidnapped in East Africa, then dragged to Brazil before decamping to the U.S. where he became a citizen, the popular U.S. singer, Dionne Warwick, has become something of an émigré in Brazil, where she maintains a residence. "Brazil is my real home now," she says. "I love everything about Brazil: the land, the people and the culture."[40] She was preceded by the popular jazz clarinetist, Booker Pittman—a lineal descendant of Booker T. Washington—who migrated permanently to Brazil in 1937, where he died in 1969.[41]

For just as Frederick Douglass and his contemporaries jousted about whether Brazil was a racial "horror" or "paradise," this discourse continued in the era following slavery's abolition in 1888.[42]

The latest African-American to confront this question at length is the prominent **Washington Post** columnist, Eugene Robinson. Posted to South America as a correspondent by this newspaper, he traveled throughout the nation and felt compelled in 1999 to wax at length about what he saw, most notably the parallels. "Some hear Salvador's music," he rhapsodized, "and think of New Orleans, others meet the city's black intellectuals and think of New York." "There was no shortage of people I'd have classified as white," he remarked, "but they seemed a distinct minority. The acid test, for me, was that most of the people I saw would have looked seriously out of place at an American country club. To the extent that the identity of a nation is equivalent to the identity of its people, then Brazil was by my lights a great black nation—unadvertised as such, but a black nation nonetheless." Like many before him, Robinson was comparing the so-called one drop rule of the U.S.—where any hint of African ancestry consigns one to the category of "black"—and the more flexible Brazilian system, which has been interpreted in North America as a denial of "blackness" but actually is a reflection of a huge nation colonized by relatively small Portugal, then being inundated by Africans in the 19th century (not least because of the actions of U.S. nationals), that, in turn, generated a desire to create intermediate buffers between black and white.

Coming from a mostly black Washington, D.C., Robinson was struck by the parallels after he stumbled—literally—over black corpses, victims of a tightly linked web of poverty, crime, and violence, in Rio de Janeiro, one of this sprawling city's many scandals. "The inference I drew," he asserted wearily, "was that young black men were seen as expendable in Brazil. . . . I was ready to get on my high horse about all this, until on reflection I realized that that could be a pretty good description of the way young black men were seen in the United States as well."[43]

If Robinson had been in Rio de Janeiro in 2005, no doubt he would have been struck by yet another macabre display of black corpses. For it was then that one of the world's largest slave burial grounds was unearthed, a mass grave where thousands of corpses were abandoned by slave traders well before abolition in 1888. Experts say that as many as 20,000 bodies may have been dumped ignominiously in the Cemiterio dos Prietos Novos or the Cemetery of the New Blacks.[44] Yet a mystery remained as to whether the burying of these corpses was the result of the depredations of U.S. nationals during the heyday of the illicit slave trade approximately 160 years ago.

Notes

NOTES TO THE INTRODUCTION

1. In this sense this book is akin to previous books of mine. See e.g. Gerald Horne, **From the Barrel of a Gun: The United States and the War Against Zimbabwe, 1965–1980,** Chapel Hill: University of North Carolina Press, 2001: This book is an account of U.S. policy toward this land in South-Central Africa, along with a narrative focused on the actions of U.S. nationals—especially mercenaries—there. Here Zimbabweans are incidental to the telling of this central story. See also **Black and Brown: African-Americans and the Mexican Revolution, 1910–1920,** New York: New York University Press, 2005: This book looks at Mexico through the eyes of African-Americans in the context of the Revolution. Here Mexicans are incidental to the telling of this central story. Hence, the book at hand is not actually comparable to those works that examine the African Diaspora, either generally or as it relates to Brazil. See e.g. James H. Sweet, **Recreating Africa: Culture, Kinship and Religion in the African-Portuguese World, 1441–1770,** Chapel Hill: University of North Carolina Press, 2003. James Lorand Matory, **Black Atlantic Religion: Tradition, Transnationalism and Matriarchy in the Afro-Brazilian Candomble,** Princeton: Princeton University Press, 2005; Linda M. Heywood, ed., **Central Africans and Cultural Transformation in the African Diaspora,** New York: Cambridge University Press, 2002; Julius Scott, "The Common Wind: Currents of Afro-American Communication in the Era of the Haitian

Revolution," Ph.D. dissertation, Duke University, 1986; Pierre Verger, **Bahia and the West African Trade, 1549–1851,** Ibadan: Ibadan University Press, 1964; Least of all is this book written as a history of Brazilian slavery. See e.g. Flavio dos Santos Gomes, **Expêriencias Atlânticas: Ensaios e Pesquisas Sobre a Escravidao e o Pós-Emancipação no Brasil,** Passo Fundo, Brasil: Universidade de Passo Fundo, UPF Editora, 2003; Maria Helena Machado, **Crime e Escravidão: Trabalho, Luta e Resistência nas Lavouras Paulistas, 1830–1888,** São Paulo: Editora Brasiliense, 1987; Joseli Mendonca, **Cenas da Abolição: Escravos e Senhores no Parlamento e na Justiça,** São Paulo: Editora Fundação Perseu Abramo, 2001; Leonardo Dantas Silva, **Abolição em Pernambuco,** Recife: FUNDAJ, Editora Massangana, 1988; Hebe Castro, **Das Cores do Silêncio: Os Significados no Sudeste Escravista, Brasil Século XIX,** Rio de Janeiro: Nova Fronteira, 1998; Nor is this book—as such—a comparative history: see e.g. Richard Graham, "Slavery and Economic Development: Brazil and the U.S. in the 19th Century," **Comparative Studies in Society and History,** 23 (Number 4, October 1981): 620–655; Celia Azevedo, **Abolitionism in the United States and Brazil: A Comparative Perspective,** New York: Garland, 1995.

2. Joseph E. Inikori and Stanley L. Engerman, eds., The Atlantic Slave Trade: Effects on Economics, Societies, and Peoples in Africa, the Americas and Europe, Durham: Duke University Press, 1992, 9.

3. Joseph E. Inikori, "The Struggle against the Trans-Atlantic Slave Trade," in Sylviane A. Diouf, ed., **Fighting the Slave Trade: West African Strategies**, Athens: Ohio University Press, 2003, 170–198, 170–171. But see David Eltis, et al., "A Participação dos Paises da Europa e das Américas no Tráfico Tranatlântico de Escravos: Novas Evidências," **Afro-Asia**, 24 (2000): 9–50: This authoritative article suggests that 12 million enslaved Africans crossed the Atlantic and that it is unlikely that there were more than 13 million, with about 10.4 million landing alive. See also Philip D. Curtin, **The Atlantic Slave Trade: A Census**, Madison: University of Wisconsin Press, 1969: estimates here are lower than those of Inikori. See also James Rawley, **The Transatlantic Slave Trade: A History**, New York: Norton, 1981: this author's estimates are also lower than those of Inikori.

4. Gwen Midlo Hall, **Slavery and African Ethnicities in the Americas**, Chapel Hill: University of North Carolina Press, 2005, xiv, 95; David Eltis, et al., eds., **The Trans-Atlantic Slave Trade**, Cambridge: Cambridge University Press, 1999. Hall argues that the renowned Eltis database "undercounts the massive Portuguese and Brazilian slave trade voyages."

5. Jose C. Curto and Paul E. Lovejoy, eds., **Enslaving Connections: Changing Cultures of Africa and Brazil During the Era of Slavery**, Amherst, New York: Humanity Books, 2004, 11. See also W. D. Christie to Earl Russell, 5 August 1860, in **British Parliamentary Papers: Correspondence Relative to the Slave Trade, Volume 64, No. 47, 1861–1862**, Shannon: Irish University Press, 1969.

6. A. J. R. Russell-Wood, **Slavery and Freedom in Colonial Brazil**, Oxford, U.K.: Oxford University Press, 2002, 27, 113, 117.

7. David Eltis, **Economic Growth and the Ending of the Trans-Atlantic Slave Trade**, New York: Oxford University Press, 1987, 14.

8. Leslie Bethell, **The Abolition of the Brazilian Slave Trade: Britain, Brazil and the Slave Trade Question, 1807–1869**, London: Cambridge University Press, 1970, x.

9. Hugh Thomas, **The Slave Trade: The Story of the Atlantic Slave Trade: 1440–1870**, New York: Simon and Schuster, 1997, 743, 746, 862. Thomas argues that Philip Curtin, whose estimates of the Atlantic Slave Trade, are lower than those of Inikori's, was "understandably baffled" —"like most of his successors"—"as how to face the vast Portuguese-Brazilian slave traffic. . . . Curtin underestimated both the illegal Cuban and Brazilian trades in the nineteenth century." See Ibid., Philip Curtin, **The Atlantic Slave Trade**. See also Jean-Michel Deveau, "Pedagogy of the History of the Slave Trade," in Doudou Diene, ed., **From Chains to Bonds: The Slave Trade Revisited**, Paris: UNESCO, 2001, 397–415, 408: "the period of the clandestine slave trade between 1815 and 1860 appears to have been significantly underestimated." Still, an estimate based on Curtin's figures shows that Brazil imported more enslaved Africans during the 1841–1850 decade—338,000—than any other. See E. Phillip LeVeen, **British Slave Trade Suppression Policies, 1821–1865**, New York: Arno Press, 1977, 7.

10. Stanley S. Stein and Barbara H. Stein, **The Colonial Heritage of Latin America: Essays on Economic Dependence in Perspective**, New York: Oxford University Press, 1970, 148.

11. Robert Fogel and Stanley Engerman, **Time on the Cross: The Economics of American Negro Slavery**, New York: Norton, 1989, 14, 28, 52.

12. W. E. B. Du Bois, **The Suppression of the African Slave Trade to the United States of America, 1638–1870**, Baton Rouge: Louisiana State University Press, 1969, 162.

13. Captain Brunwick Popham, U.K. to Admiral George Elliot, 24 December 1838: "it has been mentioned by Spaniards and Portuguese slaving on this coast" of Africa "that, were it not for the active coopera-

tion of the Americans, the slave trade would very materially decline—in fact be but feebly carried on. I do not doubt, from all I hear, that the citizens of the United States (generally of Baltimore) are more deeply interested in the slave-trade to Havana and Brazil than is generally supposed," in **Reports in Congress: Slavery Agitation and John Brown**, 1860, 370835-49 [unclear provenance], *Huntington Library–San Marino, California.* See also e.g. Joao Baptista Moreira, Portuguese Legation in Rio De Janeiro, to Lisbon, 10 August 1851, "Diplomatas Portugueses no Rio," *Archivo Histórico-Diplomático, Ministério dos Negocios Estrangeiros–Lisbon,* re: A Portuguese national buying a U.S. ship, renaming and reflagging it before it sails to Angola. Similar content is reflected in J. B. Moreira to Lisbon, 29 November 1850 and other letters in this file reflecting transfer of U.S. registered ships to Lusophone nationals planning trips to slave-hunting grounds. In the same archive in Lisbon, see John C. Calhoun to William Figaniere, Consul General of Portugal in New York City, 24 June 1850, [translation] Legation of Portugal in Washington, Correspondence with the U.S. Government, 1835–1869, A 28, M17, Torre 4 Piso, Estante 1, 15: "The usual course of the slave trade in Brazil has been for the slaver to take out an original crew of Americans to Cabinda, or some other place on the African coast, there discharge the crew, upon which the vessel is sent back to Brazil with a cargo of slaves, navigated by 'passengers.' " For a typical case of direct U.S. involvement, see "U.S. vs. Cyrus Libby, May Term 1846, General Case Files, U.S. Circuit Court for District of Maine, Records of Circuit Courts of United States," Record Group 21, *National Archives and Records Administration–Waltham, Massachusetts.* See also U.S. Consul in Bahia to U.S. State Department, 6 May 1850, Record Group 59, Roll 1, T331, **Records of the U.S. Department of State, Dispatches from U.S. Consuls in Bahia, Brazil, 1850–1906,** *National*

Archives and Records Administration–College Park, Maryland: "I have been threatened with protests, abandonments, damages . . . for refusing to grant papers to American vessels condemned at this port (sold at public sale) to enable them to proceed to the coast of Africa" to get "cargoes of slaves." Sadly, reconstructing some of this history is problematic since there was a "distressed state of affairs . . . in this consulate" with an " 'Aegean Stable' " of strewn files. In same file see also Chief of Police, Bahia, to U.S. Consulate, circa November 1850 [translated from Portuguese]: "foreign vessels" of U.S. origin "having brought to this port on board of their vessel, liberated slaves" in violation of the "law of 7th of November 1831 . . . subject themselves to a penalty of one hundred mil reis for every person so brought and also the expenses." See also Report, 23 June 1852, FO 115/124, *Public Records Office–Kew Gardens, London:* ". . . the Brazilian slave merchants intend to employ vessels belonging to the United States in that [slave] traffic." This made sense in that U.S. reluctance—and its power to enforce its wishes—to allow vessels with the Stars and Stripes to be searched for potential slaving, was an immense boost to this illegal trade. See also in same file the letter from Henry Southern in Rio de Janeiro, 16 August 1852; see also Alexander Majoribanks, **Travels in South and North America,** New York: Appleton, 1853, 62, "Jose Cliffe, M.D., a native of the United States, settled in the Brazils and for some time engaged in the slave trade [and] it seems had made large profits. . . . he pronounces the slave trade the most lucrative one under the sun, yielding from one to three hundred per cent, slaves being generally bought in Africa for 5 [pounds] and sold in Brazil for 75 [pounds]."

14. Ibid., Leslie Bethell, **The Abolition of the Brazilian Slave Trade,** 189, 184. See also Craig M. Simpson, **A Good Southerner: The Life of Henry A. Wise of Virginia,** Chapel Hill: University of North Carolina Press, 1985, 63.

15. See Richard Carl Froelich, "The United States Navy and Diplomatic Relations with Brazil, 1822–1871," Ph.D. dissertation, Kent State University, 1971, 393: "In the decade 1840–1850, fifty-two slaving ships flying the United States flag cleared Rio de Janeiro only a few of which were ever captured. During the five year period ending in 1845, sixty-four American vessels were sold in the capital alone, most of which because of their design were undoubtedly employed as slavers. . . . commerce between Brazil and Africa during the nineteenth century was negligible, so it must be assumed that these ships were utilized as slavers. While there is no way of estimating the total number of slaves brought into Brazil on American-flag vessels, the figure must surely run into the hundreds of thousands."

16. Manolo G. Florentino, "Slave Trading and Slave Traders in Rio de Janeiro, 1790–1830," in Ibid., Curto and Lovejoy, eds., Enslaving Connections, 57–79, 67.

17. Ibid., David Eltis, 199.

18. Mame-Kouna Tondut-Sene, "The Travel and Transport of Slaves," in Ibid., Doudou Diene, 15–21, 15. See also Ibid., James H. Sweet, Recreating Africa, 60.

19. Patrick Manning, "The Slave Trade and Demographic Evolution of Africa," in Ibid., Doudou Diene, 103–118, 114.

20. Ibid., Gwen Midlo Hall, Slavery and African Ethnicities in the Americas, xiii; Eric Anderson, "Yankee Blackbirds: Northern Entrepreneurs and the Illegal International Slave Trade, 1815–1865," M.A. thesis, University of Idaho, 1999, 349: "capital earned in the slave trade also contributed to industrialization during the first decades of the nineteenth century."

21. Manisha Sinha, The Counterrevolution of Slavery: Politics and Ideology in Antebellum South Carolina, Chapel Hill: University of North Carolina Press, 2000, 136, 151–152, 153.

22. See e.g. Eric Walther, The Fire-Eaters, Baton Rouge: Louisiana State University Press, 1992, 32, 150:

23. See e.g. Jesse T. Carpenter, The South as a Conscious Minority, 1789–1861, Gloucester, Massachusetts: Peter Smith, 1963, 179–180.

24. Statement by W. L. Garrison, in Stephen B. Oates, ed., The Approaching Fury: Voices of the Storm, 1820–1861, New York: HarperCollins, 1998, 153.

25. Joseph A. Stout, Jr., Schemers and Dreamers: Filibustering in Mexico, 1848–1921, Fort Worth: Texas Christian University Press, 2002, 53.

26. Matthew Fontaine Maury, "Direct Foreign Trade of the South," De Bow's Review, 12 (Number 2, February 1852): 126–148. Like many other Virginians, Maury opposed the illegal African Slave Trade; critics of these Virginians argued that this view was motivated by the profits garnered in the Upper South by selling enslaved Africans "down the river" to e.g. Alabama—where enthusiasm for reopening the trade was more intense. See e.g. John M. Wayland, The Pathfinder of the Seas: The Life of Matthew Fontaine Maury, Richmond: Garrett & Massie, 1930, 78–79. See also Lawrence F. Hill, Diplomatic Relations Between the United States and Brazil, Durham: Duke University Press, 1932, 140: "the section of the United States which gave greatest support to abolition also gave greatest encouragement to the foreign slave trade. Furthermore, the support accorded these apparently antagonistic movements was at floodtide at about the same time. . . . the owner of the 'Bangor [Maine] Gazette' preached abolition in the columns of his paper at the same time he was engaged in building ships which he knew were to be used in the illicit trade."

27. See Matthew F. Maury to William Graham, U.S. Secretary of the Navy, 14 August 1850, Washington Oficios, 1848–1851, Arquivo Histórico do Itamaraty, Rio de Janeiro.

28. Letter from William Marcy, 20 April 1853, Oficios, 1852–1853, Arquivo Histórico do Itamaraty, Rio de Janeiro.

29. See e.g. W. S. W. Ruschenberger, Notes and Commentaries During a Voyage

to Brazil and China in the Year 1848,
Richmond: McFarlane & Ferguson, 1845,
60, 62, 120, 121. The author, who made
his first visit to Brazil in 1834 observes
that "the entrance to the harbor of Rio de
Janeiro is admirably defended" though a
"brave mind directing a sufficient number
of skillful gunners in these forts might render this passage very perilous" though a
"force afloat would find it difficult to conquer the forts of Rio. . . . the standing
army of Brazil is so small as scarcely to
merit the name" while "the navy is not
effective . . . and there is no prospect of
improvement."
 30. Robert E. May, **Manifest Destiny's
Underworld: Filibustering in Antebellum
America,** Chapel Hill: University of North
Carolina Press, 2002, 116.
 31. See Memo, no date, Box 1, **Edwin
James Papers,** *University of South
Carolina–Columbia.*
 32. James W. C. Pennington, **A Narrative of Events from the Life of J. H. Banks,
An Escaped Slave, From the Cotton State,
Alabama, in America,** Liverpool: M.
Rourke, 1861, 5.
 33. U.S. Congress. House of Representatives. 37th Congress, 2nd Session. Report
Number 148, "Report of the Select Committee on Emancipation and Colonization
with an Appendix." ES US 587, R42, *Bowdoin College.*
 34. Najia Aarim-Heriot, **Chinese Immigrants, African Americans and Racial
Anxiety in the United States, 1848–1882,**
Urbana: University of Illinois Press, 2003,
64: it was "better for free blacks to be colonized in a country where they could have
political rights and dignity. . . . some of the
men who would become radicals in the
1860s (for example, Salmon P. Chase,
Benjamin F. Wade, Thaddeus Stevens and
Samuel C. Pomeroy) favored the scheme at
one time or another."
 35. "Marquis d'Abrantes" to James
Watson Webb, 24 June 1962, Box 7,
Folder 100, **James Watson Webb Papers,**
Yale University. See also Nicia Vilela Luz,
Amazônia Para Os Negros Americanos (As

Origens de Uma Controvérsia Interna-
cional), Rio de Janeiro: Editora Sage,
1968.
 36. See Memo of Mariano Alvarez,
Legation of Spain in Haiti, 8 July 1862,
File: "Haiti," H2523/003, *Ministerio de
Asuntos Exteriores–Madrid.*
 37. Letter from Legation of U.S. in
Ecuador, 1 January 1863, Record Group
48, Microfilm No. 160, Roll 3, **Department of the Interior,** *National Archives and
Records Administration–College Park,
Maryland.*
 38. See Lord Lyons to "My Lord," 27
January 1863, FO5/934, *Public Records
Office–Kew Gardens, London.*
 39. Ibid., James W. C. Pennington, A
Narrative of Events of the Life of J. H.
Banks . . . , 69, 89.
 40. Ibid., Craig M. Simpson, A Good
Southerner, 61.
 41. **Report of the Committee on Slaves
and Slavery in Relation to the Importation
of African Slaves,** Austin: John Marshall &
Co., 1857, *American Antiquarian Society–
Worcester, Massachusetts.* See also Arn-
abella G. Odell, "Reopening the African
Slave Trade in Texas," M.A. thesis, Univer-
sity of Texas-Austin, 1946. See also Earl
W. Fornell, "The African Slave Trade to
the Texas Gulf Coast," no date, *Barker
Center for American History, University of
Texas–Austin:* "in the 1850s a prime slave
could be sold for as much as $1500 in
Texas"; hence, "according to one estimate"
many hundreds of "Africans were
imported into Texas" in 1838 alone. See
also Michael Rugeley Moore, "Settlers,
Slaves, Sharecroppers and Stockhands: A
Texas-Plantation Ranch, 1824–1896,"
M.A. thesis, University of Houston, 2001,
85: "British Consul William Kennedy at
Galveston estimated that between 1833
and 1843 over 500 African slaves were
smuggled into Texas from all places other
than the United States, while a later historian believes the estimate would be closer
to 2–3,000 during this period."
 42. Washington Irving to John C. Calhoun, 16 October 1844, in Clyde Wilson

and W. Edwin Hemphill, eds., **The Papers of John C. Calhoun, Volume 20, 1844,** Columbia: University of South Carolina Press, 1991, p. 91.

43. Serge Daget, "France, Suppression of the Illegal Trade and England, 1817–1850," in David Eltis and James Walvin, eds., **The Abolition of the Atlantic Slave Trade: Origins and Effects in Europe, Africa and the Americas,** Madison: University of Wisconsin Press, 1981, 193–217, 202.

44. Gardner W. Allen, ed., **The Papers of Francis Gregory Dallas,** New York: Naval History Society, 1917, xlvii.

45. See Lord Lyons to Mr. Cass, 23 May 1859, in U.S. Congress. House of Representatives, 2nd Session, Ex. Doc. 7, "African Slave Trade." Message from the President of the United States. 6 December 1860. Volume 2, 337. *New York Historical Society.*

46. William Law Mathieson, **Great Britain and the Slave Trade, 1839–1865,** New York: Octagon, 1967, 165.

47. Duke of Newcastle to Sir Philip E. Wodehouse, December 1861, GH 1.286.173, *State Archives–Cape Town.* A similar message was sent to Queensland, Australia. See Letter to Queensland Governor, 26 December 1861, RSI A46196, **Original Despatches from the Secretary of State, Volume II,** 1861, *Queensland State Archives–Brisbane.*

48. Laird W. Bergad, **Slavery and the Demographic and Economic History of Minas Gerais, Brazil, 1720–1888,** New York: Cambridge University Press, 1999, 42.

49. W. Lorman to Samuel L. Southard, Secretary of the Navy, 2 March 1826, Rare Pam. 2351, U.S. Congress. House of Representatives. Doc. No. 119, 19th Congress, 1st Session, Washington, D.C., 1826, *Maryland Historical Society–Baltimore.*

50. See Inventory, **Wright-May-Thom Family Papers,** MS 2416, *Maryland Historical Society–Baltimore.*

51. Ibid., Eric Anderson, "Yankee Blackbirds," 244, 310. See also "Testamento de Manuel Pinto da Fonseca," 22 May 1854, Tabeliao: Antonio Simão de Miranda, Livro 20, 20 bairro de Lisboa, XV-R-72 (32) 1854. Arquivo Historico do Ministério das Finanças, *Arquivo Historico da Torre do Tombo–Lisbon.* See also Phyllis Martin, "Family Strategies in Nineteenth Century Cabinda," **Journal of African History,** 28 (1987): 65–87.

52. Maxwell, Wright & Co., **Commercial Formalities of Rio de Janeiro,** Rio de Janeiro: T. B. Hunt, 1834, *Barker Center for American History, University of Texas–Austin*: There were 62 U.S. vessels in the port of Rio in 1819; 104 in 1823—and 619 by 1833. See also Silke Strickrodt, " 'Afro-Brazilians' of the Western Slave Coast in the Nineteenth Century," in Ibid., Jose Curto and Paul Lovejoy, eds., **Enslaving Connections,** 212–244, 250, 224, "Samuel da Costa Soares . . . who was Portuguese by origin and [a] naturalized citizen of the United States was apparently one of the old traders on the coast, based at Ouidah." See also John David Smith, **Black Judas: William Hannibal Thomas and 'The American Negro,'** Athens: University of Georgia Press, 2000, 134: "In 1867 Brazilian native Augustus Archer da Silva, a naturalized American citizen, entered the Luanda [Angola] market as U.S. commercial agent. . . . he began trading operations in palm oil, kernels, coffee and groundnuts two hundred miles up the Cuanza River." See also Roquinaldo Ferreira, **Slaving, Trade, and Creolization in the Black Atlantic,** forthcoming (I thank Professor Ferreira for sharing his findings with me): da Silva was also a major slave dealer in partnership with another U.S. national, John Willis, John Sparhawk, and Robert Brookhouse. They were part of a relatively large U.S. business community in Luanda. Between 1840 and 1860, the U.S. lagged behind only Portugal and Brazil in the number of ships entering this port. Brookhouse, based in Salem, Massachusetts, was a major economic force in Angola. Major slave dealers in Angola were part of a slaving circuit that also

included frequent stops in Rio de Janeiro, Charleston, New Orleans, and New York. U.S. nationals with dual—especially Luso-phone citizenship and/or connections—were essential to the illegal trade.

53. See Report, circa 1802, Legado No. 22, 9-31-1-8, *Archivo General de la Nación–Buenos Aires, Argentina*: The ship once called the "Lenox," owned by a U.S. national, went to Africa to buy Negroes for Montevideo. It sank off the coast of Africa.

54. See Volume 0541, Sessions Laws, 1834, Page 0137, passed 25 February 1835, *Maryland State Archives–Annapolis*: "An act to authorize William . . . Wright to bring into this State, certain Slaves. . . . now resides in Rio de Janeiro, whither he went as U.S. Consul of the United States, carrying with him two Negro slaves, Frederick and Maria, who have since had two children, Edward and Lewis, and the said Wright intending to return to this State, is desirous to bring said slaves into this State." He was authorized to do so.

55. Ibid., Roquinaldo Ferreira: Antonio Severino de Avellar was an active dealer in Congo and Angola, whose cousin was the Consul of Hamburg in New York. Mary Catherine Karasch, "The Brazilian Slavers and the Illegal Slave Trade, 1836–1851," M.A. thesis, University of Wisconsin-Madison, 1967, 22: "as late as 1853–1854 a Governor-General of Angola shipped a cargo of slaves to Brazil." See also David R. Murray, **Odious Commerce: Britain, Spain and the Abolition of the Cuban Slave Trade,** Cambridge: Cambridge University Press, 1980, 104: London charged that the U.S. Consul in Havana, Nicholas Trist—who "later negotiated the Treaty of Guadalupe-Hidalgo"—was "aiding United States vessels engaged in the Cuban slave trade." Ibid., Eric Anderson, 296, 306: "the Secretary of the U.S. Navy was a supporter of the slave trade as late as 1842. . . . the Brazilian, Domingo Rodrigues Souto, an employee in the U.S. consulate in Santos, Brazil, also acted in concert with slavers disembarking slaves near that

port." Isaac Mayo of the U.S. Navy and Commodore in the African Squadron that was tasked to halt the illicit trade was a slaveholder; there were "scores of slaves toiling on his Maryland plantation" and he remained in this business "until his dying day." See C. Herbert Gilliland, ed., **Voyage to a Thousand Cares: Master's Mate Lawrence with the African Squadron, 1844–1846,** Annapolis: Naval Institute Press, 2004, 35.

56. Ibid. Roquinaldo Ferreira.

57. See e.g. John McKeon, U.S. Attorney, to William Marcy, Secretary of State, 10 November 1854, [translation]: Legation of Portugal in Washington, Correspondence with the U.S. Government, 1835–1869, A 28, Torre 4 Piso Estante 1, 15, *Archivo Histórico-Diplomático, Ministério dos Negocios Estrangeiros–Lisbon*: "William Figaniere, Consul General of Portugal . . . was called as a witness for the defence of the trial of James Smith indicted for having carried slaves on board the American brig 'Julia Moulton' "; it was suspected that this diplomat too was involved in the trade; on the stand, he refused to answer certain questions. In the same file, see also William Marcy to William Figaniere, 2 August 1856. In the same file, note also the curious increase of Portuguese Consuls appointed in Savannah, New Orleans, Norfolk, etc., as the Civil War approached. A Portuguese Vice-Consul in Baltimore, Augusto Lopes Baptista was "arrested for trial under a charge of being concerned with the slave trade." The accused also had extensive dealings with the "Consulado Brasiliero" and shipping to Rio de Janeiro. See Augusto Baptista to New York Consul, 31 December 1849, [translation]: Legation of Portugal in Washington, Correspondence of Vice-Consuls of Portugal in the U.S., 1839–1887, Torre 4, Piso, Estante 1, 7. A28, M9, *Archivo Histórico-Diplomático, Ministério dos Negocios Estrangeiros–Lisbon*. See also Clipping, 26 October 1858: Baptista "for several years resided in Baltimore and for some time acted as Portuguese Vice

262 | *Notes to the Introduction*

Consul in that city . . . ceased to hold that office and was dismissed the service of Portugal on the 5th of June 1857; that is so soon as it was ascertained that Baptista had assumed that name, his real one being Domingos Jose da Costa Florim a Brazilian subject, who had been indicted at Rio de Janeiro for the deviation of the public funds." See also Augusto Baptista to William Figaniere e Marao, 31 October 1856, [translation]: Legation of Portugal in Washington, Correspondence Received from Various Individual Portuguese and Americans, 1835–1888. A28, M15. Torre 4, Piso, Estante 1, 13, *Archivo Histórico-Diplomático, Ministério dos Negocios Estrangeiros–Lisbon*: Re: "purchase of the schooner Charles F.A. Cole . . . which is turned out of having been engaged in the slave trade and for which offense I am charged of fitting her out. On the 20th . . . my trial commenced." Jury "after deliberating on the case the whole night and part of the next day . . . [was] unable to agree on a verdict." In this era there was a fluidity of citizenship and diplomatic representation that facilitated the slave trade. In the same file as the previous see D. Ponce of Savannah to Figaniere, then Chargés d'Affaires in Baltimore, 22 March 1837: "I have a letter of recent date from the Spanish Consul General, in which he states that it is perfectly consistent with propriety that one and the same person may hold both offices of Spanish and Portuguese Vice-Consul." See also H. V. Huntley, U.K. emissary in Angola to Earl Russell, 24 January 1861: "Senhor Pamplona, whose proceedings with reference to the Slave Trade are so well known . . . is now in the United States for [the] purpose, it is said, of residing there a sufficient period to enable him to claim naturalization papers and then return here. . . . his object in becoming a citizen of the [U.S.] is to enable him to work his lanchas on the north of the Portuguese territory under the American flag." In **British Parliamentary Papers: Correspondence Relative to the Slave Trade, Volume 64, Number 47, 1861–1862,**

Shannon: Irish University Press, 1968. See also **Report of Mr. Kennedy of Maryland. The Committee on Commerce of the House of Representatives of the United States on the Memorial of the Friends of African Colonization Assembled in Convention in the City of Washington, May 1842 . . . Together with all the Diplomatic Correspondence Between the United States and Great Britain on the Subject of the African Slave Trade,** 27th Congress, 3rd Session. Report No. 283, Washington, D.C.: Gales and Seaton, 1843: Campbell J. Dalrymple, Havana to Lord Palmerston, 19 January 1839. The U.S. Consul in Havana was "also acting as Portuguese Consul," which facilitated disguising U.S. ships as Portuguese for illicit purposes.

58. Philip E. Nothway, "Salem and the Zanzibar-East African Slave Trade, 1825–1845," **Essex Institute Historical Collections,** 90 (Number 2, 1954): 123–154, 124.

59. Major F. B. Pearce, **Zanzibar: The Island Metropolis of Eastern Africa,** London: Fisher Unwin, 1920, 134, 192: "In 1859 no less than 19,000 slaves were openly imported into Zanzibar, about half of whom were subsequently shipped" to the Western Hemisphere, "to Arabia and the Persian Gulf."

60. Manuscript by Cyrus Brady, 1948, Box 1, **Cyrus Brady Papers,** *Peabody Essex Museum–Salem, Massachusetts.*

61. See Russel Lawrence Barsh, " 'Colored' Seamen in the New England Whaling Industry: An Afro-Indian Consortium," in James F. Brooks, ed., **Confounding the Color Line: The Indian-Black Experience in North America,** Lincoln: University of Nebraska Press, 2002, 76–107, 77, 78, 91.

62. Ibid., Manuscript by Cyrus Brady.

63. Kathryn Grover, **The Fugitive's Gibraltar: Escaping Slaves and Abolitionism in New Bedford, Massachusetts,** Amherst: University of Massachusetts Press, 2001, 268: "the percentage of mariners in the city's workforce of color dropped steadily between 1836 and 1856, from 35.6 percent in the earlier year to

14.9 percent in the later one." See also
Nigel Randell, **The White Headhunter:
The Story of a 19th Century Sailor who
Survived a South Seas Heart of Darkness,**
New York: Carroll and Graf, 2003, 221:
"the result of low pay and miserable work-
ing conditions was that by the 1840s of the
18,000 men in the Pacific whaling fleet,
one half were greenhorns and more than
two-thirds of them deserted every voyage."
This provided fertile ground for slavers,
which were more lucrative than declining
whalers. See also, Gerald Horne, **The
White Pacific: U.S. Imperialism and Black
Slavery in the South Seas after the Civil
War,** Honolulu: University of Hawaii Press,
forthcoming.
    64. Lt. Pegram Harrison, "A Blind Eye
Toward the Slave Trade," **Naval History,**
10 September 1996, Vertical File-Slave
Trade, *U.S. Naval Academy–Annapolis*:
"between 1837 and 1862, U.S. officers
arrested only 106 vessels for violation of
the slave trade act—an average of four a
year. . . . its orders . . . made it clear that
the Navy's first mission was not to suppress the slave trade but to protect the
growing American-West African commercial trade and the sovereignty of U.S. vessels from search by the British. The
commodores were instructed almost inci-
dentally to go through the motions of suppressing the slave trade and to even that
much with great restraint."
    65. Hugh G. Soulsby, **The Right of
Search and the Slave Trade in Anglo-American Relations, 1814–1862,** Baltimore:
Johns Hopkins University Press, 1933,
137.
    66. **New York Herald Tribune,** 15
August 1859, H1470/0046/04, *Ministerio
de Asuntos Exteriores–Madrid.*
    67. Robert Pierce Patrick, Jr., "In the
Interest of the South: The Life and Career
of Duff Green," Ph.D. dissertation, University of South Carolina, 2000, 334.
    68. Lawrence Jennings, **French Reaction
to British Slave Emancipation,** Baton
Rouge: Louisiana State University Press,
1988, 77.

    69. See e.g. Harvey Wish, "The Revival
of the African Slave Trade in the United
States, 1856–1860," **Mississippi Valley
Historical Review,** 27 (Number 4, March
1941): 569–588, 572.
    70. Ibid., Lawrence Jennings, 84.
    71. **The Standard and River Plate News,**
[Buenos Aires], 5 January 1865, *Biblioteca
Nacional de Argentina–Buenos Aires.*
    72. See Thomas Adamson to William
Seward, 21 November 1863, Roll 7,
**Despatches from U.S. Consuls in Pernam-
buco, Brazil, 1817–1906.**
    73. Jose Araugo Pereira to Francisco
Carneiro de Campos, 14 September 1831,
Oficios da Missão Diplomática Brasiliera
em Washington, Oficios, 233/3/1, *Arquivo
Histórico do Itamary, Rio de Janeiro.*
    74. See e.g. **The Cosmopolitan,** [Buenos
Ayres], 23 November 1831, *Biblioteca
Nacional de Argentina, Buenos Aires*:
Readers were informed that according to
one on-the-scene report, " 'we are all in a
state of confusion here. . . . number of
brigands is supposed to be from 100 to
150, chiefly on horseback and armed with
fowling pieces.' " As if there were a contagion at play, nearby in this same edition
was a report noting, "accounts received at
Montevideo from Rio Janeiro [*sic*] state
that . . . the Negroes had murdered from
60 to 70 of the whites. Troops had been
sent from Pernambuco."
    75. U.S. Consul to Secretary of State,
John Forsyth, 11 February 1835, T344,
**Despatches from U.S. Consuls in Pernam-
buco, Brazil, 1817–1906,** Roll 1, *National
Archives and Records Administration–College Park, Maryland.* (Note: attached to
this letter are contemporaneous accounts
of this revolt from e.g. **Periódico Politico,
Moral Literario,** and **Noticioso.**)
    76. See Report, 23 March 1843,
H2523/003, *Ministerio de Asuntos Exteriores–Madrid.* Similarly, Spanish diplomats
monitored Haiti relentlessly for abolitionist
sentiment, which would be of relevance to
Cuba and Puerto Rico.
    77. See e.g. Report, 12 March 1853,
Monrovia, 1850–1853, "Correspondencia

Recebida, Correspondencia Expedida,"
Archivo Histórico do Itamaraty, Rio de Janeiro: Brazil's representative, who spent over a year in Liberia studying the prospects for emigration, found his mission hampered by internal strife. Liberia's President in discussing this issue with him assailed the U.S. because of that nation's rampant racism and favorably contrasted Brazil—or so said this Brazilian diplomat. Concern was expressed that Brazilian emigrants were not fluent in English. See e.g. João José Reis, **Slave Rebellion in Brazil: The Muslim Uprising of 1835 in Bahia,** Baltimore: Johns Hopkins University Press, 1993, 221.

78. See the voluminous reports about the Brown-led revolt in H1470/0046/04, *Ministerio de Asuntos Exteriores–Madrid.*

79. Report from Rio, 16 December 1837, Record Group 84, **Records of Foreign Service Posts, Brazil,** *National Archives and Records Administration–College Park, Maryland.*

80. Ibid., Thomas Adamson to William Seward, 21 November 1863, Record Group 84.

81. Robert Edgar Conrad, **The Destruction of Brazilian Slavery, 1850–1888,** Malabar, Florida: Krieger, 1993, 48: "It was the outcome of the military conflict in North America that most greatly undermined Brazilian slavery and awakened opposition to it, for the survival of slavery in the United States had given defenders of Brazilian slavery one of their best arguments."

82. Malcolm Rohrbaugh, "No Boy's Play: Migration and Settlement in Early Gold Rush California," **California History,** 79 (Number 2, Summer 2000): 25–43, 25.

83. Oscar Lewis, "South American Ports of Call," in John Walton Caughey, ed., **Rushing for Gold,** Berkeley: University of California Press, 1949, 57–66, 60.

84. Rhoda Blumberg, **The Great American Gold Rush,** New York: Bradbury, 1989, 37.

85. Reverend Robert Walsh, **Notices of Brazil in 1828 and 1829, Volume 2,**

Boston: Richardson, Lord & Holbrook, 1831, 190.

86. See address by Douglass from **New York Daily News,** 14 January 1865, **New York Herald,** 14 January 1865, in John Blassingame and John R. McKivigan, eds., **The Frederick Douglass Papers; Series One: Speeches, Debates and Interviews, Volume 4: 1864–1880,** New Haven: Yale University Press, 1991, 59.

87. Robert S. Levine, ed., **Martin R. Delany: A Documentary Reader,** Chapel Hill: University of North Carolina Press, 2003, 264–265.

88. Robert L. Hall, " 'Illegal Aliens' from Africa: The Clandestine Overseas Slave Trade from Africa to the United States, 1808–1865," Paper Presented at Colloquium of the African American Studies Center, Boston University, 2003. See also **Tallahassee Floridian and Journal,** 6 August 1859 and 10 November 1860. See also James Paisley Hendrix, Jr., "The Efforts to Reopen the Slave Trade in Louisiana," M.A. thesis, Louisiana State University, 1968, 20: the "number of illegal importations into the entire South between 1808 and 1860 [was] as high as 270,000. In the decade of the 1850s, [Du Bois] finds the illicit traffic to have been almost 'a reopening of the slave trade.' "

89. Report from Ben Slocumb, 21 November 1859, Record Group 48, Roll 4, **Records of the Department of Interior,** Microfilm No. 160, *National Archives and Records Administration–College Park, Maryland.*

90. See Report from U.K. Consul in Galveston, 30 May 1843, FO 701/27, *Public Records Office–Kew Gardens, London.* See e.g. Consul Arthur Lyons in Galveston to Lord John Russell, 31 August 1860, FO 701/27.

91. **New York Times,** 15 August 1867.

92. See e.g. Letter from William Seward to Madrid, 8 May 1866, H1472, *Ministerio de Asuntos Exteriores–Madrid:* "official information has just been received at this department that a steamer is now fitting out at New Orleans for the purpose of

taking a cargo of Negroes from some point near Pensacola, Florida to Cuba . . . another vessel, bound on the same errand, will follow in a day or two"; Report by Acting U.K. Consul in Puerto Rico, Francis H. Cowper, 23 August 1865, FO 115/447, *Public Records Office–Kew Gardens, London*. See Douglas Audenreid Grier, "Confederate Emigration to Brazil, 1865–1870," Ph.D. dissertation, University of Michigan-Ann Arbor, 1968, 164. See also, Ibid., Hugh Thomas, **The Slave Trade**, 739–740. See also Lord Palmerston to Consul Arthur Lyons in Galveston, 5 December 1851, FO 701/27, *Public Records Office–Kew Gardens*. Letter from "Granville," 13 February 1852, FO 115/124, *Public Records Office–Kew Gardens*. H. S. Fox to U.S. Government, 4 November 1837, FO 285/1, *Public Records Office–Kew Gardens*. R. Hesketh, U.K. Consul in Rio de Janeiro, to James Hudson, 29 September 1850, FO 420/11, *Public Records Office–Kew Gardens*. Consul William Kennedy to the Earl of Aberdeen, 10 July 1843, FO 701/27, *Public Records Office–Kew Gardens*.

93. See Register, 17 November 1888, M468, Roll 1, **Despatches from U.S. Consuls in Zanzibar, British Africa,** *National Archives and Records Administration– College Park, Maryland*: There was a "suspicion" that in this year that slavery was banned in Brazil, the "Solitaire," a vessel from Boston, which had just arrived from Mozambique was "engaged in" the "Slave Trade." See also Report, 17 November 1888, Roll 4.

NOTES TO CHAPTER 1

1. Robert M. Levine and John J. Crocitti, eds., **The Brazil Reader: History, Culture and Politics,** Durham: Duke University Press, 1999, 2.

2. Elizabeth Donnan, ed., **Documents Illustrative of the History of the Slave Trade to America, Volume 3: New England and the Middle Colonies,** Washington,

D.C.: Carnegie Institution of Washington, 1932, 405, 406, 412–413.

3. Ibid., Elizabeth Donnan, **Volume 4: The Border Colonies and the Southern Colonies,** Washington, D.C.: Carnegie Institution of Washington, 1935, 255.

4. See Rhode Island Historical Society, "Rhode Island and the African Slave Trade: John Brown and the Colonial Economy of Slavery," Providence: RIHS, 2003; see also Christy Millard Nadalin, "The Last Years of the Rhode Island Slave Trade," **Rhode Island History,** 54 (Number 2, May 1996): 35–50, 35, 37. J. Stanley Lemons, "Rhode Island and the Slave Trade," **Rhode Island History,** 60 (Number 4, Fall 2002): 95–104. See also John Atkins, **A Voyage to Guinea, Brasil and the West Indies,** London: Caesar Ward and Richard Chandler, 1735.

5. See e.g. Letter, 26 January 1762, Box 15, Folder 1, **Hunter Family Papers,** *Newport Historical Society–Rhode Island*: "some merchants have made vast [sums] of money by the Guinea Trade lately; they have ordered their slaves directly from the Coast to Monto Christo where they received a higher price for their Negros than in any of [the other] islands." See also Robert Champlin, **A Rhode Island Slaver; Trade Book of the Sloop Adventure, 1773–1774,** Providence: Shepley Library, 1922. See also Bill of Sale for a Negro Slave brought to U.S. by Daniel Olney after being bought in the Rio de la Plata, South America circa 1805, Box 593, **Brown Family Papers,** *Brown University–Providence*. See also "The Journal of an African Slaver, 1789–1792," **Proceedings of the American Antiquarian Society,** 39 (October 16, 1929): 379–465.

6. Edwin S. James, "The Last Confederates Live in Brazil," 1991, Box 1, **Edwin James Papers,** *University of South Carolina–Columbia*.

7. Letter from Jean Luzac in Leyden, 14 September 1780, in Gregg L. Lint, ed., **Papers of John Adams, Volume 10,** Cambridge: Harvard University Press, 1996, 150.

8. Tommy Todd Hamm, "The American Slave Trade with Africa, 1620–1807," Ph.D. dissertation, Indiana University, 1975, 83, 96, 121, 179, 233, 247: "in 1805 Montevideo attracted more American slavers than Havana."

9. Marie-Jeanne Rossignol, The Nationalist Ferment: The Origins of U.S. Foreign Policy, 1792–1812, Columbus: Ohio State University Press, 2004, 130.

10. Thomas Jefferson to John Jay, 4 May 1787, in Julian Boyd., ed., The Papers of Thomas Jefferson, Volume 11, 1 January to 6 August 1787, Princeton: Princeton University Press, 1955, 339.

11. Ibid., Marie-Jeanne Rossignol, 148.

12. A. Leon Higginbotham, In the Matter of Color: Race & the American Legal Process: The Colonial Period, New York: Oxford University Press, 1978, 380, 382.

13. Bernard Bailyn, To Begin the World Anew: The Genius and Ambiguities of the American Founders, New York: Knopf, 2003, 133.

14. Saul L. Pandover, Jefferson, Old Saybrook, Connecticut: Konecky, 1980, 390.

15. See e.g. Garry Wills, 'Negro President': Jefferson and the Slave Power, Boston: Houghton Mifflin, 2003, 5.

16. Ibid., Christy Millard Nadalin, 39. See also Susan Herlin Broadhead, "Trade and Politics on the Congo Coast: 1770–1870," Ph.D. dissertation, Boston University, 1971.

17. See Letter from Mozambique, 7 February 1806, Box 7, Elisha Potter Papers, Rhode Island Historical Society–Providence: Potter, born in Rhode Island, was a lawyer and a graduate of Harvard. He was the Democratic candidate for Governor of this state in 1858 and 1859. See also Kenneth Scott, "George Scott, Slave Trader of Newport," American Neptune, 12 (Number 3, July 1952): 222–228, 222.

18. See "Records of Rhode Island vessels copied by Dr. Charles Chandler in 1944 from the National Archives at Rio de Janeiro, Brazil." Box 6, Charles Chandler Papers, Rhode Island Historical Society.

See also Letter from Gustavus K., circa 1810, Causten Family Papers, Georgetown University; Documents, 1791, Box 1, Folder 25, Slavery in the U.S. Collection, American Antiquarian Society–Worcester, Massachusetts.

19. See "Trader's Book," MSS9001, Rhode Island Historical Society: Covering the early years of the 19th century, this fascinating document concerns Rio de Janeiro, Bahia and the R.I. trade.

20. Letter from Downing Street, 17 April 1813, GH1/8/63, State Archives–Cape Town.

21. Elizabeth Donnan, "The New England Slave Trade after the Revolution," New England Quarterly, 3 (Number 2, April 1930): 251–278, 257: "James DeWolfe [sic] elected to the Senate for the United States in 1820, had by that time accumulated a fortune in the slave trade." On this Senator, see also Joseph Curtis to Timothy Pickering, 10 January 1817, HR 14AC17.4, S.29, Record Group 233, Records of House of Representatives, Select Committee on African Slave Trade, National Archives and Records Administration–College Park, Maryland.

22. See e.g. Walter Minchinton, et al., eds., Virginia Slave Trade Statistics, 1698–1775, Richmond: Virginia State Library, 1984, 77, 79, 83, 165, 173.

23. Ibid., Eric Anderson, "Yankee Blackbirds: Northern Entrepreneurs and the Illegal International Slave Trade," 8.

24. Ibid., William Law Mathieson, Great Britain and the Slave Trade, 1839–1865, 138.

25. See, "Synopsis of U.S. District Court of Louisiana Case Papers" re: "importation of slaves into any port or place within the jurisdiction of the United States," Tulane University–New Orleans: numerous cases are listed including e.g. #216, "U.S. vs. Schooner L'Esperence, 1809, bringing slaves from Cuba to New Orleans." There are numerous such cases listed, suggesting that Africans were routinely trans-shipped from this island to the U.S. See also #326, "U.S. vs. James Metcalf," 1810; #376, U.S.

vs. William Carter and U.S. vs. Louis Aury, 1810, concerns "Santo Domingo," i.e., "Portuguese brigantine that arrived some time ago in this port," New Orleans "with one hundred and six or eight Negroes on board"; U.S. vs. Schooner Cometa, 1816, bringing Negroes from Colombia to Jamaica to New Orleans; #1095, "Don Juan Constante," concerning bringing 186 Africans to New Orleans in 1817 via Africa and Havana; #1183, U.S. vs. Brig Joseph and cargo, 1818, involving Venezuela; #1685, U.S. vs. J. B. Zangronis, 1821; Like 1809, another year when slave trading cases increased dramatically, something similar occurred in 1821. See also #2904, 1830. Some of these cases concern individuals seeking to sell their Negroes upon arriving in New Orleans, e.g. #1432, U.S. vs. Schooner Mary, 1819, involving a resident of Puerto Rico. The controversy surrounding the jump in the enslaved population of the U.S. from, say, 1790–1820, i.e., whether it was due substantially to natural increase should also take into account the trans-shipments from the hemisphere, which were a routine part of slave commerce. See James McMillin, **The Final Victims: Foreign Slave Trade into North America, 1783–1810**, Columbia: University of South Carolina Press, 2004.

26. See Letter from Evan Lewis, Wilmington, Delaware, 23 December 1816, Record Group 233, HR 14AC17.4; S29, **Records of House of Representatives, Select Committee on African Slave Trade:** In the same file, see the following: Letter from Isaac Briggs, 5 February 1817; Letter of Elisha Tyson, 3 January 1817. Isaac Briggs to Timothy Pickering, 24 December 1816. See also Deposition of Francis Scott Key, 22 April 1816. In same Record Group, see also the records of the **Select Committee to Inquire into Humane and Illegal Traffic of Slaves in Washington, D.C.:** Report by Baltimore Grand Jury, circa 1816. See also Letter to John Randolph, "Chairman of the Committee for Investigating the Conduct of Traffickers in

Slaves and Kidnappers in the United States," 29 April 1816.

27. Ibid., Leslie Bethell, **The Abolition of the Brazilian Slave Trade**, 299.

28. **Report of the Committee to Which Was Referred So Much of the President's Message as Relates to the African Slave Trade.** February 9, 1821, E446/U45, *Virginia Historical Society–Richmond.*

29. U.S. Department of State. **Message from the President of the United States, Transmitting (In Pursuance of a Resolution of the House of the Representatives of the 4th Ultimo) Information on the Subject of the African Slave Trade,** Washington, D.C.: Gales & Seaton, 1821, *Virginia Historical Society–Richmond.*

30. **Report of Mr. Kennedy of Maryland. The Committee on Commerce of the House of Representatives of the United States on the Memorial of the Friends of African Colonization Assembled in Convention in the City of Washington, May 1842 . . . Together with all the Diplomatic Correspondence Between the United States and Great Britain on the Subject of the African Slave Trade,** 27th Congress, 3rd Session. Report No. 283, Washington, D.C.: Gales & Seaton, 1843, 290, *Huntington Library–San Marino, California.*

31. Ibid., Leslie Bethell, **The Abolition of the Brazilian Slave Trade**, 23. See also "Private Papers Relating to the Negotiation in London Between the British Plenipotentiaries and the Plenipotentiary on the Part of the United States of America, January to August 1824," FO 414/2 and "Convenção Addicional ao Tratado de 22 de Janeiro de 1815 entre os muito altos e muito Ponderosos Senhores de Portugal, do Brazil, e Algarves e el-Rei do Reino Unido da Grande Bretanha e Irlanda: Feita em Londres Pelos Plenipotenciarios de huma e Outra Corte em 28 de Julho de 1817 e ratificada por Ambas. . . . Rio de Janeiro na Impressão Regia 1817." FO 129/15, *Public Records Office–Kew Gardens.* See also Robert Thorpe, **A Commentary on the Treaties Entered into Between His Britannic Majesty and his Most Faithful**

Majesty . . . , London: Longman, Hurst, Rees and Brown, 1819. See also Anti-Piracy Treaty re: "Negros en la Costa de Africa," 6 October 1824, S10-C2-A1-3, *Archivo General de la Nación–Buenos Aires.* See also Hugh G. Soulsby, **The Right of Search and the Slave Trade in Anglo-American Relations, 1814–1862,** Baltimore: Johns Hopkins University Press, 1933, 35. See also Dieudonne Gnammankou, "The Slave Trade to Russia," in Ibid., Doudou Diene, **From Chains to Bonds,** 65–73.

32. Ananias Dortano Brasahemeco, **Rights of Portugal in Reference to Great Britain and the Question of the Slave Trade,** no city, no publisher, 1840, 154, *New York Historical Society.*

33. **Message from the President of the United States. Transmitting the Information Required by a Resolution of the House of Representatives, of 27th February last, in Relation to the Suppression of the African Slave Trade.** 18th Congress, 1st Session. Washington, D.C.: Gales & Seaton, 1824. *Virginia Historical Society–Richmond.*

34. U.S. Congress. House of Representatives. 19th Congress, 1st Session. Report 281: **Suppression of the Slave Trade,** 22 May 1826. *Virginia Historical Society–Richmond.* See also "Information Concerning the Present State of the Slave Trade," 1824, 23–24, Tw*99v2, *Historical Society of Pennsylvania–Philadelphia:* "During the year 1822 it has been estimated from the best information that can be obtained, that an aggregate of *one hundred thousand* slaves have been torn from Africa and carried into the American colonies—and some of them into the United States. . . . this country indeed is the *only neighboring market to which they can be taken.* . . . a trade in slaves has been carried on upon the southern coast of the United States. That the vigilance of the United States' vessels cruising there, has *only checked,* not abolished that trade" [emphasis-original].

35. See e.g. George Graham, Esq., to U.S. Secretary of State, 9 September 1818, in Ibid., **Report of Mr. Kennedy of Maryland,** E448/U57.

36. See e.g. William C. Davis, **The Pirates Laffite: The Treacherous World of the Corsairs of the Gulf,** Orlando: Harcourt, 2005, 155, 326; Steven Deyle, **Carry Me Back: The Domestic Slave Trade in American Life,** New York: Oxford University Press, 2005.

37. See Document, 16 October 1817, in Mary Jo-Kline, ed., **Political Correspondence and Public Papers of Aaron Burr,** Princeton: Princeton University Press, 1983, 1171–1172.

38. Ibid., Richard Carl Froehlich, "The United States Navy and Diplomatic Relations with Brazil, 1822–1871."

39. Joseph Ray to John Quincy Adams, 18 February 1818, T344, Roll 1, **Despatches from U.S. Consuls in Pernambuco, Brazil, 1817–1906,** *National Archives and Records Administration–College Park, Maryland.*

40. John Quincy Adams, U.S. State Department, to Don Manuel H. de Aguirre, 27 August 1818, S10-C1-A5-1, *Archivo General de la Nación–Buenos Aires.* Of course, this nation—though not as blatantly as neighboring Brazil—was also implicated in the African Slave Trade: See Document, unclear date, S10C-43A-8-2, **Tribunal de Cuentas Esclavos-Juzgados,** 1810–1813; see also Legado No. 22, 9-31-1-8, 1802: re: African Slave Trade. In this same file see the 28 September 1801 document concerning buying of 25 slaves ["veinte y cinco esclavos"] at 30 pesos per slave ["treinta pesos por cada esclavo"]; see also Report of a 14 November 1804 voyage to Africa, arriving in Montevideo with 301 enslaved Africans: *Archivo General de la Nación–Buenos Aires:* "ha vendido . . . negra Angola llamada Ana," i.e., the sale of an Angola woman in the area north of B.A. Though the U.S. did not open diplomatic relations with Haiti—not least because of the slavery issue—until decades later, at this early date, the nation that was to become Argentina was moving

in that direction. See exchange of letters between Alejandro Petion of Haiti and the "Director Supremo de las Provincias Unidas del Rio de la Plata," 18 November 1816, S10-C1-A10-3, *Archivo General de la Nación.*

41. John Graham to John Quincy Adams, 1 August 1819, Record Group 84, Volume 007, **Records of Foreign Service Posts, Brazil,** *National Archives and Records Administration–College Park, Maryland.*

42. John Graham to Minister of Foreign Affairs, 18 October 1819, Record Group 84, Volume 007, **Records of Foreign Service Posts, Brazil.** See also **Message from the President of the United States, Transmitting Copies of a Correspondence with the Governor of Brazil in Relation to an Alleged Blockade by the Naval Force of Brazil, the Imprisonment of American Citizens and the Demand Made by the Charge d'Affaires of the U.S. of His Passports and the Cause Thereof,** 20th Congress, 1st Session, Ex. Doc. No. 281, House of Representatives, Washington, D.C.: Gales & Seaton, 1828.

43. **Freedom's Journal,** 14 September 1827. See also **Correspondence Between Senhor Jose Silvestre Rebello, Charges des Affaires of HM the Emperor of Brazil, Resident at Washington . . . and Citizens Antonio Gonsalves da Cruz, Consul General of the Same Empire, Resident in Philadelphia,** Philadelphia: Stavely & Bringhurst, 1824. *American Antiquarian Society–Worcester, Massachusetts.*

44. Ibid., Robert M. Levine and John J. Crocitti, eds., **The Brazil Reader,** 351.

45. Mary C. Karasch, **Slave Life in Rio de Janeiro, 1808–1850,** Princeton: Princeton University Press, 1987, 3. See also U.S. Consul to Abel P. Upshur, Secretary of State, 20 December 1843, Roll 2, **Despatches from U.S. Consuls in Pernambuco:** "the death of one of our fellow countrymen at this place, he was a mulatto and was named Samuel Smith, his occupation that of innkeeper and his house was known as the Union Hotel. . . . originally

from Maryland but has been many years in this place as also in Bogota." He left a sizeable estate. See also G. T. Snow, U.S. Consul to John C. Calhoun, U.S. Secretary of State, 17 August 1844, Roll 3: "my painful duty to advise [of] the death of a fellow countryman. . . . William H. Nicholson, a black . . . native of Philadelphia . . . discharged from the Barque Globe of that port and being subsequently seized with fits was placed by men in the British Hospital." U.S. Consul to Lewis Cass, Secretary of State, 20 May 1858, Roll 5: "the death of George Eldridge, a black seaman. . . . he died. . . . his death is supposed to have been caused by injuries received in a fight with another man." Strikingly, the U.S. State Department was directly involved in selling enslaved Africans belonging to U.S. nationals in Brazil who died without wills. See Charles Smith to Daniel Webster, 15 June 1841, Record Group 59, Roll 1, T478, **Records of the Department of State, Despatches from U.S. Consuls in Para, Brazil,** *National Archives and Records Administration–College Park, Maryland*: "The slave Antonio Maria belonging to said estate [of Hayward Pierce] and at that time disposed of, in consequence of some difference of opinion among the heirs whether he should be sold or not has since by my orders been sold at public auction, in conformity with the General Consular instructions, and vouchers of which I have on this occasion, transmitted to the Treasury Department together with the balance amounting to Two hundred ninety nine dollars four and a half cents." See also John Gillmer, U.S. Consul to "His Excellency Francisco Gonsalves Martins, President of the Province of Bahia," 5 April 1852, Record Group 59, Roll 1, T331, **Despatches from U.S. Consuls in Bahia:** William Harris of New York had just died and in his estate was a "black girl named Joanna . . . now in the house of the undersigned for safekeeping. . . . and the undersigned presumes that his heirs in the United States would hardly consent that she should be again sold into slavery," though he would deliver her to the "competent authority."

46. Ibid., Leslie Bethell, **The Abolition of the Brazilian Slave Trade**, 42.

47. Condy Raguet to John Quincy Adams, 5 October 1824, **Condy Raguet Papers,** *Historical Society of Pennsylvania.*

48. Manolo G. Florentino, "Slave Trading and Slave Traders in Rio de Janeiro, 1790–1830," in Ibid., Curto and Lovejoy, eds., **Enslaving Connections**, 57–79, 57.

49. James Bennett to John Quincy Adams, 1 August 1821, Roll 1, **Despatches from U.S. Consuls in Pernambuco.** See also Statement by R. S. Long, 15 July 1821, Roll 1: "I left the island of [?] . . . in the Portuguese sloop . . . with 35 slaves as cargo. . . . voyage was illegal. . . . I have suffered. . . . I have been in prison 22 months."

50. Ibid., David Eltis, **Economic Growth and the Ending of the Transatlantic Slave Trade**, 195.

51. Francisco Vidal Luna and Herbert S. Klein, **Slavery and the Economy of São Paulo, 1750–1850**, Stanford: Stanford University Press, 55.

52. See Translated Document, circa 1854, FO 128/48, *Public Records Office–Kew Gardens.*

53. F. Torres Texugo, **A Letter on the Slave Trade Still Carried On along the Eastern Coast of Africa Called the Province of Mozambique**, London: J. Hatchard & Son, 1839, 20, 41, 57. The author also speaks of an illness called "Itacas" which supposedly only afflicted European males after sexual intercourse; they received chills, cold, intense pain in the back of the neck and loins and could be fatal. The cure was to burn the patient with sea sand put aflame, which was placed in a linen napkin and rubbed slowly over the body but particularly on the parts affected; "the blacks are exempt from this disorder which is more fatal in Quilimane, on the mainland, than in the island of Mozambique."

54. Rudolph Said-Ruete, **Said Bin Sultan, Ruler of Oman and Zanzibar, His Place in the History of Arabia and East Africa**, London: Alexander-Ouseley, 1929, 125. See "Brig Ann," 1827–1829, Box 29-30-31, #91-20, 1827A4: registered in Salem, this ship visited Zanzibar, Mombasa, Comoros Islands, etc.; Log of "Ship Louisa," 1826–1829, Box 29-30-31, #91-65, 1826L: **The Essex Institute Collections, Manuscript Logs and Journals,** *Peabody Essex Museum–Salem, Massachusetts.*

55. See e.g. Norman Robert Bennett, "Americans in Zanzibar: 1825–1845," **Essex Institute Historical Collections**, 95 (Number 3, 1959): 239–262.

56. Ibid., Manuscript by Cyrus Brady, 1948.

57. John H. Galey, "Salem's Trade with Brazil, 1801–1870," **Essex Institute Historical Collections**, 107 (1971): 198–222, 206. See also Ibid., Leslie Bethell, **The Abolition of the Brazilian Slave Trade**, 189.

58. Cyrus Townsend Brady, Jr., **Commerce and Conquest in East Africa**, Salem: The Essex Institute, 1950, 98.

59. See letter, 26 September 1836, Box 3, Folder 8, **Gardner Family Papers,** *Peabody Essex Museum.* See also **Putnam Family Papers**, Box 1, at same site, for further detail on U.S. trade with Brazil in the 1830s.

60. Kabengele Munanga, "The African Presence in Brazil," in Ibid., Doudou Diene, 302–315, 302.

61. H. M. Brackenridge, **To Buenos Ayres, Performed in the Years 1817 and 1818, By Order of the American Government**, London: Sir Richard Phillips, 1820, 20, 19, 30, 33: "the prejudice with respect to complexion, did not appear to me as strong as in the United States. This may be owing to the great number of persons of colour, who own large fortunes and possess wealth and consequence. I remarked several mulatto priests, and in one instance a Negro. . . . the Inquisition was never established here, very fortunately for the Jews, who are numerous and whose outward conformity has never been strictly scrutinized."

62. Henry Bradley, **Voyage from the United States to South America Performed During the Years 1821, 1822 & 1823**, Newburyport: Herald Press, 1823, 36.

63. Manoel Cardozo, "Slavery in Brazil as Described by Americans, 1822–1888," **The Americas**, 17 (Number 3, January 1961): 241–260, 241, 244, 255.

64. Thomas H. Bennett, **A Voyage from the United States to South America**, Newburyport: Herald Press, 1823, 12.

65. Ibid., Thomas H. Bennett.

66. Ibid., Rev. Robert Walsh, **Notices of Brazil in 1828 and 1829, Volume 1**, 83, 257; **Volume 2**, 179.

67. **The Standard and River Plate News** [Buenos Ayres], 15 April 1866.

68. **The Cosmopolitan** [Buenos Ayres], 7 December 1831.

69. **The Cosmopolitan**, 4 January 1832: "while taking his supper . . . he overheard three African Negroes, one of whom appeared to be a servant of our own, conversing in Arabic, a language he himself spoke fluently, respecting the intended robbery."

70. **The Cosmopolitan**, 4 January 1832; **The Cosmopolitan**, 20 June 1832.

71. Condy Raguet to Henry Clay, 26 October 1825, **Condy Raguet Official Letters, 1824–1827**, *Historical Society of Pennsylvania–Philadelphia.*

72. Condy Raguet to John Quincy Adams, 12 May 1825, **Condy Raguet Official Letters.**

73. Report, 17 December 1833, Record Group 84, Volume 012, **Records of Foreign Service Posts, Brazil**, *National Archives and Records Administration–College Park, Maryland.* The U.S. authorities kept a close eye on the Brazilian military, especially its composition. See e.g. Condy Raguet to John Quincy Adams, 5 October 1824, **Condy Raguet Official Letters.** Condy Raguet to John Quincy Adams, 31 January 1825, **Condy Raguet Official Letters.** See also Raguet to Henry Clay, 20 March 1826. See also Condy Raguet to John Quincy Adams, 11 March 1825, **Condy Raguet Official Letters.**

Condy Raguet to John Quincy Adams, 12 May 1825.

74. Report to U.S. Secretary of State from Rio de Janeiro, 3 September 1831, Record Group 84, Volume 013, **Records of Foreign Service Posts, Brazil.**

75. Berlarmin C. Condo, "Returning Afro-Brazilians," in Ibid., Doudou Diene, **From Chains to Bonds**, 55–64, 56.

76. Joseph Ray to Secretary of State John Forsyth, 29 March 1838, Roll 2, **Despatches from U.S. Consuls in Pernambuco:** "the place was fired in many directions and commenced burning furiously; spirits of turpentine & other combustible materials having been prepared many days previous."

77. Condy Raguet to Henry Clay, 12 April 1826, Record Group 84, Volume 009, **Records of Foreign Service Posts, Brazil;** see also Condy Raguet to John Quincy Adams, 1 February 1823, Record Group 84, Volume 008, **Records of Foreign Service Posts, Brazil.** See e.g. U.S. Congress. House of Representatives. Committee on Foreign Affairs, 20th Congress, 1st Session. Report No. 212, 25 March 1828: "attack upon" the "character" of Raguet, who "had been bribed by the Government of Buenos Ayres to pursue measures designed to interrupt the harmony between the Governments of the United States and Brazil."

78. Condy Raguet to Henry Clay, 14 February 1826, **Condy Raguet Official Letters.**

79. Condy Raguet to Henry Clay, 23 November 1825, **Condy Raguet Official Letters.**

80. Report, 16 December 1837, Record Group 84, Volume 017, **Records of Foreign Service Posts, Brazil.** See also Condy Raguet to Henry Clay, 31 October 1826, **Condy Raguet Official Letters:** "Monarchy has been thrice attempted in America, but without success. Dessalines, Christophe and Iturbide afford sad examples of the instability of illegitimate moves in this hemisphere of liberty"—and Brazil's Emperor was thought to be no different.

81. See Report, 18 July 1834, "Oficio do Consul Brasiliero na Filadelfia," Oficios, 233/3/1, *Arquivo Historico do Itamary*: "graves desordens em Nova Iorque" [grave disorder in New York] including destruction of certain churches ["destruicao de certas igrejas"] with an issue being whether Jesus Christ was a mulatto ["Jesus Christo era um mulatto"].

82. Martin Van Buren to Don Miguel Calmon, 25 May 1830, MS 1467, **William Wright Papers,** *Maryland Historical Society–Baltimore.*

83. "Dear Sirs," from Baltimore, 13 January 1836, Box 2, **Wright-May-Thom Family Papers,** *Maryland Historical Society–Baltimore.*

84. William Wright to Maxwell Wright in Rio de Janeiro, 14 January 1836, Box 2, **Wright-May-Thom Family Papers.**

85. Letter from William Wright, 9 January 1835, Box 2, **Wright-May-Thom Family Papers.**

86. See "Letter Book of William Wright, Consul of the U.S. of America Rio de Janeiro 1826," Box 4, **Wright-May-Thom Family Papers.**

87. See Letter, 1831, Box 2, **Wright-May-Thom Family Papers.**

88. Letter, 29 April 1837, Box 2, **Wright-May-Thom Family Papers.**

89. George W. Slocum, U.S. Consul in Rio de Janeiro to John Forsyth, Secretary of State, 16 October 1839, in Ibid., **Report of Mr. Kennedy . . .**

90. Report from George Elliot, Royal Navy, 22 July 1839, in Ibid., **Report of Mr. Kennedy . . .** In same document see also H. S. Fox to John Forsyth, 19 August 1840: In 1838 "nineteen vessels and in the year 1839 twenty-three vessels bearing the flag of the Union [U.S.] left Havana for the coast of Africa, under the strongest suspicion of being engaged in the slave trade."

91. Congressman Charles Miner, "An Extract from a Speech . . . in the House of Representatives of the United States in 1829 on the Subject of Slavery and the Slave Trade in the District of Columbia

with Notes," A67, 973.7112, *Peabody Essex Museum.*

92. U.S. Congress. House of Representatives. 19th Congress, 1st Session, Letter from the Secretary of the Navy, Samuel L. Southard, Doc. No. 119, 7 March 1826, Rare Pam. 2351, *Maryland Historical Society–Baltimore.*

NOTES TO CHAPTER 2

1. Ibid., Joseph E. Inikori, "The Struggle against the Transatlantic Slave Trade," 170–171.

2. John Oriji, "Igboland, Slavery and the Drums of War and Heroism," in Ibid., Sylviane A. Diouf, ed., **Fighting the Slave Trade,** 121–131, 129.

3. Ibid., C. Herbert Gilliland, ed., **Voyage to a Thousand Cares: Master's Mate Lawrence with the African Squadron,** 1844–1846, 73.

4. George Coggeshall, **Thirty Six Voyages to Various Parts of the World, Made Between the Years 1799 and 1841,** New York: Library Editions, 1970 [orig. published 1858], 551.

5. Joseph Story, "Piracy and the Slave Trade," in William W. Story, ed., **The Miscellaneous Writings of Joseph Story,** Boston: Charles C. Little and James Brown, 1852, 122–147, 141.

6. E. I. Barra, **A Tale of Two Oceans,** San Francisco: E. I. Barra, 1893, 92. See also **Reports in Congress: Slavery Agitation and John Brown,** 1860, 370835-49 [unclear provenance], *Huntington Library*: N. P. Trist, U.S. Consul in Havana to U.S. Secretary of State, 28 September 1840: "to break up the slave trade from Africa to Cuba, would be to injuriously affect, at least in a commercial point of view, the prosperity of that island; whilst, to leave the same slave-trade free to flow from Africa to Brazil, would be to confer a benefit upon that portion of our continent. . . . the trade to Cuba is to that of Brazil as six to ten. For every six vessels captured on their way to Cuba, there ought, therefore to be ten captured on their way to Brazil,"

yet since 1838, "of the slavers captured in the five preceding years, not quite *one-tenth* [emphasis-original] were destined to Brazil or fitted out from thence!" He suggested that London concentrated on the trade to Cuba since it was more closely tied to the U.S. than Brazil; "and it is but recently that the idea of stimulating Brazil as a cotton growing country, by means of British capital, into rivalry with the United States, has been relinquished for the plan of accomplishing the same end with the *free* labor of Hindoostan."

7. See e.g. Campbell J. Dalrymple to Lord Palmerston, 19 January 1839, in Ibid., **Report of Mr. Kennedy of Maryland,** *Huntington Library*: On one slave voyage a single ship makes "nearly $300,000, of which, therefore, two-thirds was net profit. So long as such returns can be effected, we fear that no efforts whatever will be effectual in suppressing this traffic."

8. Ibid., Richard Carl Froelich, "The United States Navy and Diplomatic Relations with Brazil, 1822–1871," 371, 375. For an intriguing account of the African Squadron, see Harry Gringo, **Tales for the Marines,** Boston: Phillips, Sampson, 1855. See also Horatio Bridge, **Journal of an African Cruiser: Comprising Sketches of the Canaries, the Cape de Verds, Liberia, Madeira, Sierra Leone and other Places of Interest on the West Coast of Africa,** New York: Putnam, 1853, 177.

9. See Charles Bell, Lieutenant Commander, U.S. Brig Dolphin to Hon. James K. Paulding, Secretary of the Navy, 28 July 1840, 534–6, in Ibid., **Report of Mr. Kennedy of Maryland.**

10. Robert Edgar Conrad, ed., **In the Hands of Strangers: Readings on Foreign and Domestic Slave Trading and the Crisis of the Union,** University Park: Pennsylvania State University Press, 2001, 93.

11. See Lord Palmerston to Mr. Stevenson, 27 August 1841, in Ibid., **Report of Mr. Kennedy of Maryland,** *Huntington Library.* See also H. S. Fox, U.K. to John Forsyth, 30 October 1839, in Ibid., **Report of Mr. Kennedy of Maryland.**

12. William Peter to Lord Palmerston, 17 February 1851, FO 115/117, *Public Records Office–Kew Gardens.* See also Peyton Skipwith to John H. Cocke, 20 May 1839, in Bell Wiley, ed., **Slaves No More: Letters from Liberia, 1833–1869,** Lexington: University Press of Kentucky, 1980, 48–49: "I see daily the Star Spangled Banner unfurled on the coast of Africa as a protection for the slaver to keep the British man of wars from takeing [*sic*] them. . . . a disgrace to her banner."

13. **American Sentinel,** [Bath], 14 May 1857, Box 3, Folder, "Slavery/Slave Trade," **African-Americans in Maine Collection,** *Maine Historical Society–Portland.*

14. Ibid., Lt. Pegram Harrison, "A Blind Eye Toward the Slave Trade."

15. **Freedom's Journal,** 28 December 1828.

16. **Frederick Douglass' Paper,** 8 April 1853.

17. **North Star,** 5 October 1849. See also **Colored American,** 3 August 1839.

18. Ibid., Eric Anderson, "Yankee Blackbirds," 309.

19. See U.S. Department of State. **Message from the President of the United States. Transmitting Copies of Dispatches from the American Minister at the Court of Brazil, Relative to the Slave Trade.** 20 February 1845. House Documents, Serial No. 148, Doc. 148, 28th Congress, 2nd Session: George William Gordon, U.S. Consul, Rio de Janeiro, to Henry Wise, 23 September 1844: "The Brig 'Sooy' . . . owned at Bahia and was recently sold there by American owners" was "captured" with "580 slaves . . . landed from her near Bahia." See also U.S. Department of State. **Message from the President of the United States. Information in Relation to the Abuse of the Flag of the United States in Subservience of the African Slave Trade, and the Taking Away of Slaves the Property of Portuguese Subjects.** 14 March 1844. Senate Documents, Serial No. 434, Doc. No. 217, 28th Congress, 1st Session.

20. Ibid., Senate Documents, Serial No. 434, Doc. No. 217: Brazilian Legation in

Philadelphia to U.S. Secretary of State, Abel P. Upshur, 10 July 1843: An "American whaling barque . . . the 'Romulus' . . . kidnapped or carried away . . . on the 18th of July 1842, from Maio, one of the Cape Verde islands, a valuable Negro man, named Pedro Timas, represented as a good sailor, an excellent swimmer and a superior diver . . . belonging to Antonio Soares Timas"—and he wanted his Negro back. See also Brazilian Legation to Abel Upshur, 23 November 1843: Captain Daniel Borden of the "American whaling barque, the 'Pantheon' of Fall River," Massachusetts, while in Cape Verde kidnapped a "young, intelligent and valuable Negro, named Marcelino, a journeyman carpenter and sailor."

21. Lord Howden to Lord Palmerston, 12 November 1847, in **British Parliamentary Papers: Correspondence Relative to the Slave Trade, Volume 64, Number 34, 1847-1848.** Shannon: Irish University Press, 1969, 251. British Library–London.

22. **Message of the President of the United States,** 31st Congress, 2nd Session, Ex. Doc. 6, 17 December 1850, Report from R. M. Hamilton, U.S. Consul in Montevideo. See also Carl Norman Haywood, "American Whalers and Africa," Ph.D. dissertation, Boston University, 1967, 26, 29, 33, 36, 41, 45, 54, 133, 134.

23. Consul Archibald in New York to Lord Lyons, 1 February 1861, in Ibid., **British Parliamentary Papers: Correspondence Relative to the Slave Trade, Volume 64, Number 47.**

24. Commander Andrew H. Foote, **Africa and the American Flag,** New York: Appleton, 1854, 347.

25. Abel P. Upshur to Matthew Perry, 30 March 1843, in Kenneth E. Shewmaker, et al., eds., **The Papers of Daniel Webster: Diplomatic Papers, Volume 1, 1841-1843,** Hanover: University Press of New England, 1983, 817-823.

26. Joseph C. Dorsey, **Slave Traffic in the Age of Abolition: Puerto Rico, West Africa and the Non-Hispanic Caribbean,**

1815-1859, Gainesville: University Press of Florida, 2003, 202-203.

27. C. Wise to Secretary of Admiralty, 28 October 1858, FO 541/1, *Public Records Office–Kew Gardens.* See also Ibid., C. Herbert Gilliland, ed., **Voyage to a Thousand Cares,** 5: An "American crew might sail an American-flag ship to Africa, taking along as passengers a second crew composed of Portuguese, Spaniards or other non-U.S. citizens. These, as slaves were about to be loaded, a prearranged 'sale' would be transacted, turning the ship over to the second crew under a new flag. The second (non-American) crew would take the ship and slaves back across the Atlantic."

28. Rev. J. Leighton Wilson, **The British Squadron of the Coast of Africa,** London: James Ridgway, 1851, 26. See also Mary W. Tyler Gray, **Stories of the Early American Missionaries in South Africa,** no date, no publisher, *National Library of South Africa–Cape Town.*

29. Lieutenant Forbes, **Six Months Service in the African Blockade from April to October 1848 in Command of HMS Bonetta,** London: Bentley, 1849, vi, 101, 105. See also James Riley, **Loss of the American Brig Commerce Wrecked on the Western Coast of Africa in the Month of August 1815 with an Account of Tombuctoo, and the Hitherto Undiscovered Great City of Wassanah,** London: John Murray, 1817.

30. Ibid., C. Herbert Gilliland, ed., **Voyage to a Thousand Cares,** 80-81.

31. Deposition of George Slocum at Rio de Janeiro, 11 September 1841, vfm 190, *G. W. Blunt White Library–Mystic, Connecticut.*

32. Abdul Sheriff, **Slaves, Spices and Ivory in Zanzibar,** London: James Currey, 1987, 47. See also Rudy Bauss, "The Portuguese Slave Trade from Mozambique to Portuguese India and Macau, and Comments on Timor, 1759-1850: New Evidence from the Archives," **Cameos Center Quarterly,** 6/7 (Number 1 & 2, Summer/Fall 1997): 21-26. See also "The Journal

of an African Slaver, 1789–1792," Proceedings of the American Antiquarian Society, 39 (October 16, 1929): 379–465.

33. Charles H. Bell and John S. Paine to
Daniel Webster, 10 May 1842, in Ibid.,
Kenneth E. Shewmaker, et al., eds., **The
Papers of Daniel Webster: Diplomatic
Papers, Volume 1, 1841–1843**, 550–556.

34. Cornwallis Rickets to Rear-Admiral
Dacres, 29 April 1847, in Ibid., **British
Parliamentary Papers: Correspondence Relative to the Slave Trade, Volume 64, Number 34.**

35. James Hudson to Lord Palmerston,
16 December 1848, in **British Parliamentary Papers: Correspondence Relative to
the Slave Trade, Volume 55, Number 36,
1849.** See also R. W. Beachey, **The Slave
Trade of Eastern Africa**, London: Rex
Collings, 1976, 20: "British naval forces
were pitifully inadequate for the task facing them. . . . the demands made on its
dozen ships were excessive. Five vessels
alone were on patrol at St. Helena during
the exile of Napoleon there, until his death
in 1821. Not more than one or two ships
ever got as far north as Quelimane [East
Africa]. Two vessels could not effectively
keep watch over the whole East African
coast and western shores of Madagascar.
. . . in 1854, Commodore Talbot had only
three vessels to deploy between Delagoa
Bay and Zanzibar, over 1300 miles of
coastline"; besides, "slavers were well
informed as to the movements of these
few British cruisers"; see also Lieutenant
Barnard, R.N., **Three Years Cruize in the
Mozambique Channel for the Suppression
of the Slave Trade**, London: Bentley, 1848,
50, 51.

36. Vice-Admiral Dacres to the Secretary of the Admiralty, 1 December 1848, in
Ibid., **British Parliamentary Papers: Correspondence Relative to the Slave Trade, Volume 55, Number 36.**

37. Lord Russell, London to Sir A.
Magenis, Mozambique, 16 April 1861, in
Ibid., **British Parliamentary Papers: Correspondence Relative to the Slave Trade, Volume 64, Number 47.**

38. Percival J. Parris, "Pedro Tovookan
Parris," **Old-Time New England**, 63
(Number 3, January-March 1973): 61–68,
62, 67. See also Inventory, **George Frost
Richardson Papers**, *Maine Historical Soci-
ety–Portland*: Richardson of Brunswick,
Maine, owned the ship that brought Parris
across the Atlantic, the "Porpoise." Said
ship was commanded by Cyrus Libby of
Scarborough, Maine when it was seized in
Brazil by the USS Raritan. Libby wound up
as a school-teacher in Australia. Gordon,
born in Exeter, New Hampshire, attended
Phillips Exeter where he was "valedicto-
rian"; by 1830 he was heading an importing firm, then served on the Boston City
Council from 1831 to 1836. He became a
Whig and was appointed as a Consul in
Rio, where he served from 1843–1846.

39. See Clipping, 28 February 1988,
Maine Historical Society. The adopted
father of Pedro Parris, Virgil Parris, was a
"square-jawed Jacksonian, former Congressman, one-time acting Governor of
Maine and an amateur astronomer." He
had "taken a liking to Pedro during the
long trial" of his captors. After the trial he
took him to his house "high above the
wilds of Oxford County, Paris Hill was the
19th century's American Acropolis. Topped
by great elms and white mansions, it was a
hotbed of Maine's antislavery movement
and the hometown of more Congressmen,
Cabinet members and Senators—including
future Vice President Hannibal Hamlin—
than any other square mile of America."
Though a "sense of loneliness colors
accounts of Pedro's life in Maine"—"his
closest friends were children"—when he
died, "his funeral" was "one of the most
fully attended that had been held in the
village." Ibid., Percival J. Parris.

40. For various affidavits, contracts,
and letters cited herein see "U.S. vs. Cyrus
Libby, May Term 1846, General Case Files,
U.S. Circuit Court for District of Maine,
Records of Circuit Courts of United
States," Record Group 21, *National
Archives and Records Administration–
Waltham, Massachusetts.*

41. Deposition of Mark Tanner, 7 January 1845, Roll 18, **Letters Received by the Secretary of the Navy from Commanding Officers of Squadrons, 1841–1886, Brazil Squadron,** *National Archives and Records Administration–Washington, D.C.* Hereafter designated as **Brazil Squadron Letters.**

42. U.D. Congress. House of Representatives. 2nd Session. 12 March 1849. Ex. Doc. No. 61, **Correspondence Between the Consuls of the United States at Rio de Janeiro, & with the Secretary of State on Subject of the African Slave Trade.**

43. Deposition of Charles Hendricks, 7 February 1845 in Ibid., Roll 18, **Brazil Squadron Letters.**

44. Deposition of John Williams, circa 1845, in Ibid., Roll 18, **Brazil Squadron Letters.**

45. "Examination of Guilheme, an African boy," 28 April 1845 and "Statement of George Williams," 13 March 1845, in Ibid., Roll 18, **Brazil Squadron Letters.**

46. "Examination" of Pedro Parris, 1 February 1845, in Ibid., Roll 18, **Brazil Squadron Letters.** Of course, there were other examples of the U.S. seeking to enforce the law against the slave trade. See e.g. Small's Deposition, Case 15, Box 23, Copy Misc. Mss., **Gratz Mss.,** *Historical Society of Pennsylvania–Philadelphia*: In February 1845 the "Sea Eagle" from Boston was "lying in the harbor of Rio." Z. H. Small of Massachusetts had gone to Cabinda months earlier; he saw on board the U.S. ship " 'Agnes' . . . several hundred Negroes, most of them in the hold but a few on deck. . . . the American flag had been previously taken from the 'Agnes' " and "either 485 or 585 Negroes taken on board." Another ship flying a U.S. flag, the " 'Monte Video' took on board something over eight hundred Negroes on this occasion." See also Ibid., C. Herbert Gilliland, 276: the African Squadron in December 1845 captured a U.S. slaver with "eight hundred fifty human beings . . . crammed naked below deck into a space of less than

2000 square feet." The ship had been built in New Jersey.

47. **Portland Pleasure Boat,** 7 August 1846, *Maine Historical Society–Portland.*

48. Testimony of William Page, 12 February 1845, **Correspondence with the British Commissioners at Sierra Leone, Havana, Rio de Janeiro, Surinam, Cape of Good Hope, Jamaica, Loanda, and Boa Vista, Relating to the Slave Trade from January 1 to December 31, 1845, Inclusive . . . ,** London: Parliament, 1846, *Western Reserve Historical Society–Cleveland.*

49. Edward Porter to Lord Palmerston, 31 March 1848, in Ibid., **British Parliamentary Papers: Correspondence Relative to the Slave Trade, Volume 55, Number 36.**

50. J. Kennedy to Lord Palmerston, 20 December 1849, in Ibid., **British Parliamentary Papers: Correspondence Relative to the Slave Trade, Volume 55, Number 36.**

51. A. Oaksmith, Master of U.S. Brig to John Gillmer, 26 July 1852, Record Group 59, Roll 1, T331, **Despatches from U.S. Consuls in Bahia, Brazil.**

52. Report from Lieutenant Commander Wood, 24 June 1852, Record Group 59, Roll 1, T331, **Despatches from U.S. Consuls in Bahia, Brazil.**

53. Leslie M. Harris, **In the Shadow of Slavery: African Americans in New York City, 1626–1863,** Chicago: University of Chicago Press, 2003, 213.

54. Robin Law and Paul E. Lovejoy, eds., **The Biography of Mahommah Gardo Baquaqua: His Passage from Freedom in Africa and America,** Princeton: Markus Weiner, 2001, 45, 61. See also **Diario do Rio de Janeiro,** 4 October 1847; **National Anti-Slavery Standard,** 15 July 1847, 29 July 1847, 12 August 1847.

55. Samuel Moore, **Biography of Mahommah Gardo Baquaqua,** Detroit: George E. Pomeroy, 1854, 6, 9, 34, 35, 44, 45, 48, 51, 56, 58. This narrative can be found at http://docsouth.unc.edu.

56. Captain Joseph Tucker to Richard

Hawley Tucker, 22 August 1848, **Tucker Family Papers,** *Bowdoin College.*

57. James Hudson to Lord Palmerston, 5 August 1848, in Ibid., **British Parliamentary Papers: Correspondence Relative to the Slave Trade, Volume 55., Number 36.**

58. C. Syvill, Captain, and Senior Officer on the East Coast of Africa to His Excellency, Rodrigo Luciano d'Abreu de Lima, Governor General of Mozambique, 26 May 1847, [translation]: Correspondence of the Mixed Commission at the Cape of Good Hope, 1846–1852, *Archivo Histórico-Diplomático Ministério dos Negocios Estrangeiros–Lisbon.*

59. Lt. Paul Gibson to C. Syvill, 20 May 1846, Ibid., Correspondence of the Mixed Commission at the Cape of Good Hope, 1846–1852.

60. Letter from Conde Tojal, Department of State for Foreign Affairs, 18 March 1850, [translation]: Legation of Portugal in Washington, Correspondence of the Portuguese Government, 1850–1859, Torre 4, Piso Estante 1, A28, M3, *Archivo Histórico-Diplomático, Ministério dos Negocios Estrangeiros–Lisbon.*

61. Letter from J. B. Clay, 30 April 1850 in Ibid., Correspondence of the Portuguese Government, 1850–1859.

62. John C. Calhoun to William Figaniere, 19 February 1845, [translation]: Legation of Portugal in Washington, Correspondence of the U.S. Government, 1835–1869, Torre 4, Piso Estante 1, 15, A 28, M17, *Archivo Histórico-Diplomático, Ministério dos Negocios Estrangeiros–Lisbon.*

63. John C. Calhoun to William Figaniere, 24 June 1850, in Ibid., [translation]: Legation of Portugal in Washington, Correspondence of the U.S. Government.

64. Edward Everett to William Figaniere, 28 February 1853, in Ibid., [translation]: Legation of Portugal in Washington, Correspondence of the U.S. Government. Lisbon was also concerned about how its nationals were treated in the U.S., particularly those deemed to be "colored." See W. Wallace Davis to William

Figaniere, 3 March 1853, [translation]: Legation of Portugal in Washington, Correspondence of the Vice-Consulates of Portugal in the U.S., 1839–1887, Torre 4 Piso, Estante 1, 7. A28, M9, *Archivo Histórico-Diplomático, Ministério dos Negocios Estrangeiros–Lisbon.* See also John Hampton, Washington, D.C., to William Figaniere, 29 May 1852, [translation]: Legation of Portugal in Washington, Correspondence of the Foreign Legations and Consulates in the U.S., Torre 4 Piso Estante1, I, A28, M10, *Archivo Histórico-Diplomático, Ministério dos Negocios Estrangeiros–Lisbon.*

65. See e.g. Report from Lt. Matson of Royal Navy, 9 October 1839, in Ibid., **Report of Mr. Kennedy of Maryland,** *Huntington Library*: "I captured the Portuguese schooner 'Constitucão' . . . having on board 344 slaves. This vessel was sailing under American colors, and by the name of 'Dolphin.' " Later, "I captured . . . the Portuguese schooner 'Zete de Abril' having on board 427 slaves and dispatched her to Sierra Leone. . . . I had several times boarded this vessel during the last three months; at which times she was sailing under American colors and by the name of 'Mary Cushing.' . . . it is quite evident that this, as well as all slavers hoisting the American flag are sailing with false colors and papers."

66. Lord Palmerston to Sir Hamilton Seymour, 29 March 1847, in Ibid., **British Parliamentary Papers: Correspondence Relative to the Slave Trade, Volume 64, Number 34.**

67. Report of Mixed Commission, 2 January 1849, in Ibid., [translation]: Correspondence of the Mixed Commission at the Cape of Good Hope, 1846–1852.

68. Report, 2 June 1851, in Ibid., [translation]: Correspondence of the Mixed Commission at the Cape of Good Hope.

69. See e.g. **Cape Argus,** 22 July 1857; **Natal Mercury,** 2 July 1857.

70. George Stoner to Secretary of Navy, 26 October 1850, in Ibid., Roll 23, **Brazil Squadron Letters.**

71. William Graham to George Stoner, 5 November 1850, in Ibid., Roll 23, **Brazil Squadron Letters.**

72. See also Report from Rio de La Plata, circa 1850, in Ibid., Roll 23, **Brazil Squadron Letters.**

73. Letter from U.S. Department of State, 26 May 1853, in Ibid., Roll 25, **Brazil Squadron Letters.** See also Report from Rio de Janeiro, 22 May 1842, in Ibid., Roll 14, **Brazil Squadron Letters.** See also Nathaniel Hawthorne, ed., **Journal of an African Cruiser . . . by an Officer of the U.S. Navy,** [Horatio Bridge], New York: Wiley and Putnam, 1845, 51.

74. Letter from Andrew Boyd Cummings, 27 December 1853, **Andrew Boyd Cummings Papers,** *U.S. Naval Academy–Annapolis:* "Their musical instruments consisted of a barrel with a piece of parchment drawn tight over the head. One darky as black as any of Pluto's disciple sits straddle of one end & beats this sort of drum with his hand while another sits at the other end beating on the barrel with sticks. . . . tis the best place to practice languages I have ever been in that even Macao or Canton. . . . mosquitoes about the size of hummingbirds are buzzing about my ears & making anything else than a pleasant noise."

75. Andrew Boyd Cummings to "Dear Mother," 1 February 1858, **Andrew Boyd Cummings Papers:** "This is the third time we have been here" in Benguela; "two Americans in jail here, awaiting their trial on charge of stabbing a man in Fish Bay, they have been here in prison several months." He was irked when the "authorities" were "trying to humbug with us when the Captain gave them at a certain time in which to bring them to trial, at the exception of that time he gave them notice he would land a force & take them."

76. George Jackson to "My Lord," 20 September 1851, FO 115/124, *Public Records Office–Kew Gardens.*

77. James Hudson to Rear Admiral Reynolds, 3 February 1850, FO 420/11, *Public Records Office–Kew Gardens.* For the clash over the African Slave Trade in the Brazilian press, see e.g. **Philathropo,** 1 February 1850; **Correio Mercantil,** 20 January 1850; **Correio da Tarde,** 17 January 1850, 21 January 1850.

78. James Hudson to Lord Palmerston, 11 February 1851, FO 420/11, *Public Records Office–Kew Gardens.*

79. Ibid., R. W. Beachey, **The Slave Trade of Eastern Africa,** 20.

80. Letter from Andrew Boyd Cummings, circa 1850, **Andrew Boyd Cummings Papers:** "the affair between the English & Brazilians has all blown over or rather ended by John Bull carrying the point. The Legislative Assembly was in session at the time of the disturbance & passed or rather revived an old law, prohibiting the importation of slaves under the severest penalties, if some of our disinterested abolitionists could see the condition of the slaves in this place, abolitionism would cease for a while in the United States, in many instances they do not receive the attention given to horses or cattle in other countries." He described the Emperor as "repulsive."

NOTES TO CHAPTER 3

1. Ibid., Francisco Vidal Luna and Herbert S. Klein, **Slavery and the Economy of São Paulo, 1750–1850,** 64, 133.

2. Ibid., Robert M. Levine and John J. Crocitti, eds., **The Brazil Reader,** 79, 135: "the decade of the 1850s was the golden age of coffee and the society based on it in Vassouras. . . . between 1800 and 1852 during the period when some European nations began to turn against the institution of slavery and pressure slave traders to cease, more than 1,600,000 slaves arrived in Brazil."

3. Ibid., Joseph C. Dorsey, **Slave Traffic in the Age of Abolition,** 5.

4. See e.g. Ibid., Mary Catherine Karasch, "The Brazilian Slavers and the Illegal Slave Trade, 1836–1851," 17, 19, 30: Jose Bernardino de Sa used "American-built steamers capable of transporting

1000 to 15,000 slaves each trip. He had the 'Cacique' especially built in New York." Jenkins and Company, "founded about 1845 or 1846" was a leading financier of the trade and "its leading men consisted of an American from New York named Jenkins." "American calico cloth and other items specifically designed for the African coast were consigned to [Manuel Pinto da Fonseca] in Rio. . . . he then made a pretense of chartering American ships to carry these American as well as British goods to Africa, but actually he bought them. Since American ships were not searched by British cruisers for slave equipment, such as shackles, . . . Fonseca's ship, manned by an American crew, flying an American flag and carrying Portuguese passengers (the crew to bring her back from Angola), then loaded trade goods for the coast." See also Ibid., Hugh Thomas, **The Slave Trade**, 739–740.

5. See "Canning" to "Gentlemen," 17 May 1843, FO 131/1, *Public Records Office–Kew Gardens*. On the influx of Africans see **Diario do Rio de Janeiro**, 11 August 1841.

6. See Ship Arrivals from Rio de Janeiro, 1843, Box 3, Folder 9, **Gardner Family Papers**, *Peabody Essex Museum*.

7. Ibid., Joseph C. Dorsey, 85.

8. Ibid., Leslie Bethell, **The Abolition of the Brazilian Slave Trade**, 287.

9. Ibid., Eric Anderson, "Yankee Blackbirds: Northern Entrepreneurs and the Illegal International Slave Trade," 281–282.

10. Massachusetts Senate, "Report and Resolves on the Subject of the Foreign Slave Trade," No. 35, February 1839, 973.7111, F26.1, *Peabody Essex Museum*.

11. Bruno Gujer, "Free Trade and Slavery: Calhoun's Defense of Southern Interests against British Interference, 1811–1848," Ph.D. dissertation, University of Zurich, 1971, ii, 115.

12. John C. Calhoun to Lt. James E. Calhoun, 24 December 1826, in Ibid., Clyde Wilson and W. Edwin Hemphill, eds., **The Papers of John C. Calhoun, Volume 10, 1825–1829**, 238–239.

13. John C. Calhoun to Henry A. Wise, 25 May 1844, in Ibid., Clyde Wilson and W. Edwin Hemphill, eds., **Volume 18**, 621.

14. Memo from John C. Calhoun, 12 August 1844, Record Group 84, Volume 017, **Records of Foreign Service Posts, Brazil**.

15. John C. Calhoun to William King, 12 August 1844, in Ibid., Clyde Wilson and W. Edwin Hemphill, eds., **Volume 19**, 1990.

16. John C. Calhoun to Duff Green, 8 September 1843, in Ibid., Clyde Wilson and W. Edwin Hemphill, eds., **Volume 17**, 445.

17. Duff Green to John C. Calhoun, 18 October 1843, in Ibid., Clyde Wilson and W. Edwin Hemphill, eds., **Volume 17**, 511.

18. Duff Green to Abel Upshur, 17 October 1843, in Ibid., Clyde Wilson and W. Edwin Hemphill, eds., **Volume 17**, 579–580.

19. Ibid., Bruno Gujer, 117.

20. See St. George L. Sioussat, "Duff Green's 'England and the United States': With an Introductory Study of American Opposition to the Quintuple Treaty of 1841," **Proceedings of the American Antiquarian Society**, 40 (15 October 1930): 175–275, 231, 235, 238, 241, 261, 269.

21. Ibid., Robert Pierce Patrick, Jr., "In the Interest of the South: The Life and Career of Duff Green," 204, 209.

22. Report to Abel P. Upshur from Rio de Janeiro, 7 January 1844, Record Group 84, Volume 017, **Records of Foreign Service Posts, Brazil**.

23. See Lewis Cass to Daniel Webster, 3 October 1842, **Correspondence Between Lewis Cass and Daniel Webster in Relation to the Quintuple Treaty**, Cincinnati: Enquirer, circa 1844, HT 993, C343, **Western Reserve Historical Society**, *Cleveland*: "my protest against the ratification of the Quintuple Treaty for the suppression of the African Slave Trade." See also Harral C. Landry, "Slavery and the Slave Trade in Atlantic Diplomacy, 1850–1861," **Journal of Southern History**, 27 (Number 2, May 1961): 184–207, 192; see also Andrew C.

McLaughlin, **Lewis Cass,** New York: Chelsea House, 1980.

24. John M. Baker, **A View of the Commerce Between the United States and Rio de Janeiro,** Washington, D.C.: Office of the Democratic Review, 1838, 5, 53, G. W. *Blunt White Library–Mystic, Connecticut.*

25. Margaret Lockhart (Allen) Davis to "My Dear Father," 1843, Box 1, Folder 3, **Allen Family Papers,** *Peabody Essex Museum.*

26. Margaret Lockhart (Allen) Davis to "My Dear Grandfather," December 1845, Box 1, Folder 3, **Allen Family Papers.** See also James Birkhead, **Pro-Form Sales and Invoices of Imports and Exports at Rio de Janeiro with Tables, Remarks,** Salem: William Ives & Co., 1838.

27. Chaplin Conway to spouse, 24 April 1849, Box 1, Folder 3, **Chaplin Conway Papers,** *Peabody Essex Museum.* There was also a Salemite community in Para. See e.g. Letter to "Dear Friend," 8 December 1836, Box 1, Folder 4, **Putnam Family Papers.**

28. Rev. Pasco Grenfell Hill, **Fifty Days on Board a Slave Vessel in the Mozambique Channel in April and May 1843,** New York: J. Winchester, New World Press, 1843, 6.

29. Letter from Rio to Abel P. Upshur, 5 January 1844, Record Group 84, Volume 017, **Records of Foreign Service Posts, Brazil.**

30. "List of American Vessels Sold at the Port of Rio de Janeiro," Box 1, **George William Gordon Papers,** *New York Public Library.*

31. John Crampton, Washington, D.C., to Lord Palmerston, 2 April 1849, FO 84/773, *Public Records Office–Kew Gardens.* See also "List of Vessels Under the United States Flag Reported by Her Majesty's Consul at Bahia and Rio de Janeiro—to have cleared out from these Ports for the Coast of Africa from the 1st of January 1848 to the 31st of March 1849," FO 84/773, and "List of Vessels Under the United States Flag Reported by Her Majesty's Consuls at Bahia and Rio de Janeiro to have entered those ports from the Coast of Africa from the 1st of January to the 31st of March 1849," FO 84/773, *Public Records Office–Kew Gardens:* Of the latter, vessels were sailing mostly from Ambriz, Congo, and Angola.

32. "Departure of American Vessels from the Port of Rio de Janeiro for the Coast of Africa." Box 1, **George William Gordon Papers.**

33. "Arrivals of American Vessels at the Port of Rio de Janeiro from the Coast of Africa." Box 1, **George William Gordon Papers.** See also Brig Cherokee, Box 82–85, 91–45, 1849: this ship, reputedly implicated in the slave trade, sailed from Salem to Zanzibar, Muscat, Aden, etc.; see also 91–73, 1845, Bark Emily Wilder sailed from Salem to East Africa also in pursuit of the slave trade; 91–53, 1857, Bark Goldfinch, from Salem to "Ambriz & Loanda (only)" for similar purposes.

34. George Gordon to Secretary of State, 27 August 1845, Box 1, **George William Gordon Papers.** On 25 September 1845, Gordon asserted, "'since the beginning of the year 1840, sixty four American vessels had been sold at the port of Rio" and "subsequently employed in the Slave trade, and during the same period there had departed from the port of Rio de Janeiro for the coast of Africa, fifty six American vessels; and forty American vessels had arrived at that port from the Coast, in all ninety six American vessels ... between Rio and the African continent.'" See American Party, Massachusetts, State Executive Committee, **The Record of George Gordon . . . ,** Boston: The American Headquarters, 1856, *New York Public Library.*

35. See **British Packet and Argentine News,** 20 April 1844 and 6 July 1844, *Biblioteca Nacional de Argentina.*

36. Ibid., Eric Anderson, "Yankee Blackbirds: Northern Entrepreneurs and the Illegal International Slave Trade," 108, 110, 122, 126, 152, 153, 154, 190, 192. See also Ibid., David R. Murray, **Odious**

Commerce: Britain, Spain and the Abolition of the Cuban Slave Trade, 104.

37. Ibid., William Law Mathieson, **Great Britain and the Slave Trade, 1839–1865,** 164.

38. Robert Hesketh to Lord Palmerston, 19 February 1847, in Ibid., **British Parliamentary Papers: Correspondence Relative to the Slave Trade, Volume 64, Number 34.** See also James Hudson in Rio de Janeiro to Lord Palmerston, 16 December 1848, in Ibid., **British Parliamentary Papers, Volume 55, Number 36, 1849.** See also U.S. Congress. Senate. **Message from the President of the United States,** 28th Congress, 1st Session, *Virginia Historical Society–Richmond*: Letter from Earl of Aberdeen, 14 March 1844; in same document see George Slocum, U.S. Consul in Rio de Janeiro to Daniel Webster, 5 October 1841: Victor Alexander of the ship "Sophia" says "he is the only survivor" after his vessel was "fitted as a slaver immediately on her arrival at Benguela," Angola, took on slaves; the U.S. flag was hoisted, then on arriving in Brazil "the Portuguese assumed the command and hoisted the flag of Montevideo."

39. J. J. C. Westwood, Rio de Janeiro, to Lord Palmerston, 17 February 1848, in Ibid., **British Parliamentary Papers, Volume 55, Number 36.**

40. U.S. Congress. Senate. 31st Congress, 2nd Session. Ex. Doc. No. 6, **In Compliance with a Resolution of the Senate, a Report of the Secretary of State, with Documents Relating to the African Slave Trade.** 17 December 1850. David Tod to Mr. Clayton, 8 January 1850, citing "Mr. Profitt" in 9 February 1844.

41. Ibid., Leslie Bethell, **The Abolition of the Brazilian Slave Trade,** 287.

42. Michael Craton, **Sinews of Empire: A Short History of British Slavery,** Garden City: Doubleday, 1974, 290.

43. Report, 19 July 1844, Record Group 45, in Ibid., Roll 17, **Brazil Squadron Letters.**

44. Edward Hopkins to Commander of U.S. Naval Forces, Brazil, 26 June 1844, in Ibid., Roll 17, **Brazil Squadron Letters.**

45. Letters, 21 June 1844 and 17 June 1844, in Ibid., Roll 17, **Brazil Squadron Letters.**

46. Letter to George Bancroft, Secretary of the Navy, 7 November 1845, in Ibid., **Brazil Squadron Letters.**

47. Henry A. Wise to James Buchanan, 6 March 1946, Record Group 84, Volume 018, **Records of Foreign Service Posts, Brazil.** This kind of thing was not unusual. See Deposition of William Larrenson, 21 January 1847, FO 128/48, *Public Records Office–Kew Gardens*: This "native of the Kingdom of Norway . . . shipped on board the Brig 'Senator' of Boston" in "the month of December . . . for a voyage to the coast of Africa," to the "River Congo," where it "took in nine hundred and forty three Negroes, of this number a great many died on the passage to Brazil, three hundred and seventy three blacks and three white men, as I was told; the remainder were landed at a little place to the north of Cape Frio. . . . the cause of the great number of deaths was the want of water; the blacks were not allowed a pint of water per day. The first night we went to sea I was told that seventy four died, this was because the ship was too full; they were men, women and children. The deck and the hold were both as full as they could be. We were twenty two days on the passage; we had no colours up on the voyage. I was turned ashore where the slaves landed, without being paid any wages . . . excepting the month's advance which I received at Rio."

48. Fleet Surgeon to Lawrence Rousseau, 6 January 1846, in Ibid., Roll 19, **Brazil Squadron Letters.** See Letter, 5 August 1844, in Ibid., Roll 17, **Brazil Squadron Letters:** "R. D. Taylor . . . suffers from Epilepsy . . . a severe return of the convulsions. . . . recommend his return to the United States."

49. Letter, 24 August 1843, in Ibid., Roll 16, **Brazil Squadron Letters.**

50. See e.g. Deposition from George C.

Kholler, circa 1845, FO 128/48, *Public Records Office–Kew Gardens*: This "native of Norway . . . shipped on board the American brig 'Senator' " at Rio de Janeiro to Africa; "at Cabinda," he said, "I was so sick with fever that I was insane. . . . we took on board nine hundred and thirty three slaves—seventy four died in the hold the first night from suffocation, the slaves lying on top of each other, the hold was so crowded . . . only six hundred and fifty men were alive when we landed the slaves."

51. Letter from U.S. brig in "harbour of Montevideo," 5 November 1848, in Ibid., Roll 20, **Brazil Squadron Letters**: "A deserter from my vessel was shot dead by a person near the lines of defense of the city of Montevideo and another deserter was wounded and taken prisoner."

52. Report, 5 February 1842, in Ibid., Roll 14, **Brazil Squadron Letters.** See also "Official Document" from "Department of Foreign Relations" of the "Argentine Confederation" in "Buenos Ayres," 27 November 1845, in Ibid., Roll 19, **Brazil Squadron Letters.** See also Letter from U.S.S. Brandywine, off the coast of Montevideo, 22 March 1848, in Ibid., Roll 20, **Brazil Squadron Letters**: "The present state of affairs between the Provinces of the Republic of the Argentine Republic and of Uruguay renders it important that a part of our Naval Force should be ready at this place to watch over, and if necessary, give protection to the persons and interests of the citizens of the United States." See also Report, 22 February 1843, in Ibid., Roll 15, **Brazil Squadron Letters.** See Report, G. Pendergrass, U.S. Navy, Montevideo, 30 September 1845, in Ibid., Roll 18, **Brazil Squadron Letters.**

53. Report from W. H. Smiley, U.S.S. Enterprise, 1 March 1844, in Ibid., Roll 16, **Brazil Squadron Letters**: "George Ogelby was shot . . . a short distance from this place," i.e.. Patagonia; "the Negro who shot this man . . . by order of Senor Pedro Crespo." See related adjacent letter from Nicholas Garcia, March 1844: "they

were warned off the place by those who were in charge but the sailors considering themselves superior in number, resisted with knives in hand." Thus, "measures to put in rigorous confinement the Negro man." See also Report, 28 December 1847, Roll 19, in Ibid., **Brazil Squadron Letters**: "assassination of two sailors belonging to the U.S. Brig Bainbridge."

54. See Letter, 22 February 1843, in Ibid., Roll 14, **Brazil Squadron Letters.**

55. G. F. Snow, U.S. Consul, Pernambuco, to Commanding Officer of the "Bainbridge," 9 June 1845, in Ibid., Roll 18, **Brazil Squadron Letters.**

56. See also Report, circa 1843, in Ibid., Roll 14, **Brazil Squadron Letters**: There were vessels entering the port near Pernambuco from England, Brazil, Portugal, Sardinia, Hamburg, Spain, France, Holland, Russia, Austria, Denmark, Denmark, Montevideo, etc.; see also Report, circa 1845, in Ibid. Roll 17, **Brazil Squadron Letters.**

57. Lawrence Pennigton to Dan Turner, 10 July 1845, in Ibid., Roll 18, **Brazil Squadron Letters.**

58. Letter from John Gillman, George Carey, et al. 24 May 1845, in Ibid., Roll 18, **Brazil Squadron Letters.**

59. Gorham Parks to Brazil Squadron, Rio de Janeiro, 12 July 1848, in Ibid., Roll 20, **Brazil Squadron Letters.**

60. William Brent, U.S. Legation, Buenos Ayres, to Commodore F. H. Gregory, Brazil Squadron, 11 December 1845, in Ibid., Roll 19, **Brazil Squadron Letters.** See also J. Graham, Consul, B.A., to F. H. Gregory, circa 1845, in Ibid., Roll 19, **Brazil Squadron Letters**: "the citizens of the United States, merchants and others in Buenos Ayres suffer much inconvenience and detriment in their business from the difficulty of communicating with other places during the blockade."

61. Letter from C. Morris, Brazil Squadron, Rio de Janeiro, 13 February 1843, in Ibid., Roll 15, **Brazil Squadron Letters**: "informed by the British legation that four or five vessels filled with slaves and wearing the flag of the United States,

might be expected daily on the coast, coming direct from Africa." See also Report, 28 January 1848, in Ibid., Roll 19, **Brazil Squadron Letters:** In Rio de Janeiro a U.S. ship was "suspected of fitting out for a voyage for the coast of Africa for the purpose of returning with a cargo of slaves. . . . follow said vessel to sea and ascertain her true character" and, if need be, "send her either to New York or Boston; Report from Gorham Parks, U.S. Consulate, Rio de Janeiro to Brazil Squadron, 11 July 1848, in Ibid., Roll 20, **Brazil Squadron Letters:** A U.S. "brig" just landed in Rio "with a large number of blacks. . . . this information is communicated to you with the hope that you will at once send a sufficient force to secure said vessel with her Master and crew"; see also George Stoner, Brazil Squadron to H. H. Locke, U.S. Consul in Montevideo, 22 December 1848, in Ibid., Roll 22, **Brazil Squadron Letters:** "American vessels having slave cargoes on board & bound to the coast of Africa, to clear from this port," i.e., Rio, "for Montevideo or Buenos Ayres for the purpose it is said of avoiding the heavy duties upon goods destined direct for Africa."

62. See **Journal of Sandwith Drinker**, 1840, *Peabody Essex Museum.*

63. Charles Ward to "His Highness, the Sultan of Muscat," 21 November 1848, Box 1, Folder 1, **Charles Ward Papers**, *Peabody Essex Museum.*

64. Charles Ward to U.S. Government, 21 February 1846, Box 1, Folder 1, **Charles Ward Papers.**

65. Thomas Nalle to "Dear Mother," 1 April 1840, MSS1, N1495a51, **Thomas Nalle Papers**, *Virginia Historical Society*: Nalle "had been several times in Sierra Leone, Monrovia & Bassa Cove" where he had "seen some of the Negroes that were formerly owned by Doctor Hawes" back home. "They are dissatisfied, said they had rather be in Virginia in Slavery than here. . . . just as you might imagine a Negro would be if left entirely to himself, lean hungry sterility & squalid wretchedness seems to pervade the whole coast."

66. U.S. Congress. Senate. 28th Congress, 2nd Session. **Message from the President of the United States, Information Relative to the Operations of the United States Squadron on the West Coast, The Condition of the American Colonies There, and the Commerce of the United States Therewith**, *Virginia Historical Society*: Letter from Joel Abbot, 6 November 1844 and Letter from US Ship Saratoga, Port Grande, Island of St. Vincent, 5 September 1843.

67. U.S. Congress. House of Representatives. 2 March 1849. Ex. Doc. 61, **Correspondence Between the Consuls of the United States at Rio de Janeiro, & with the Secretary of State on the Subject of the African Slave Trade:** Gordon Parks, U.S. Consul to "Mr. Buchanan," 20 August 1847: "One house in particular is deeply involved in this traffic. That house, lately established, consists of an American named Jenkins from New York. . . . nearly the whole of the slave trade [is] in American bottoms, is transacted by this house of Jenkins and company." Mariners on the whaler, "Fame," were told that this was to be a typical whaling expedition before traveling to East Africa to pick up slaves— and apparently circumvented possible capture by sailing through the open back door that was the Indian Ocean, then the Pacific; in same document see also Parks to Buchanan, 4 December 1848 on Krafft.

68. Ibid., Joseph Dorsey, **Slave Traffic in the Age of Abolition**, 85.

69. Commander Bossanquet to Commander Jones, 12 June 1844, in **Correspondence with the British Commissioners at Sierra Leone, Havana, Rio de Janeiro, Surinam, Cape of Good Hope, Jamaica, Loanda, and Boa Vista, Relating to the Slave Trade, from January 1 to December 31, 1845 Inclusive**, London: Parliament, 1846, *Western Reserve Historical Society–Cleveland.* See also Report from Foreign Office, 12 July 1849, FO 84/773, *Public Records Office–Kew Gardens*: "Slave traders of Brazil had determined to abandon the system of employing Brazilian

vessels without flag or papers and that they intended to trust their speculation on future to foreign bottoms and to employ vessels under the United States flag," particularly near Angola: "there is nothing to obstruct slave traders in this course, as no American vessel of war had been to Loanda or has been heard of to the South of the line since 1847."

70. See "Papers Relating to the Convention Between Great Britain and Brazil on [the] Slave Trade," 1845, FO 115/89, *Public Records Office–Kew Gardens*.

71. Letter to Foreign Office, 20 October 1845, FO 115/89, *Public Records Office*.

72. Earl of Aberdeen to Foreign Office, 30 July 1845, FO 115/89, *Public Records Office*: Referring to a Spanish slave ship: "New Orleans had been her principal port of rendezvous on her return from the coast of Africa and that she had cleared from that port on her last voyage and . . . the American collector who last cleared her knew well the nature of the market she was proceeding to when she left New Orleans."

73. Letter to Foreign Office, 29 December 1845, FO 115/89, *Public Records Office–Kew Gardens*: "supposed introduction of coloured persons from those islands [Bahamas] into Florida, there to be sold as slaves."

74. Consul William Kennedy to the Earl of Aberdeen, 18 May 1844, FO 701/27, *Public Records Office*. See also Report from UK Consul in Galveston, 30 May 1843, FO 701/27, *Public Records Office*: There was an estimate of "five hundred and four slaves" brought to this Texas town over the previous decade, including those who had been kidnapped: "there seems to be no recognized party in Texas favourable to the abolition of slavery"; see also William Kennedy to Earl of Aberdeen, 31 December 1845, FO 701/27: "two hundred and forty seven Negro slaves have been landed at this port from New Orleans during this and the immediate preceding month. It is probable that this amount

does not include the whole number brought to Galveston in the course of the last two months. A considerable number have, it is said, been introduced by way of [the] Red River. Annexation, it is evident, will add greatly to the slave population of Texas."

75. Commander Bossanquet to Commander Jones, 2 July 1845, in Ibid., **Correspondence with the British Commissioners.** . . .

76. Ibid., **Correspondence with the British Commissioners.** . . . In this volume see e.g. Commodore W. Jones report, 5 January 1845; Captain P. C. Dumas to Secretary of the Navy, 15 August 1845; Deposition of Jeremiah McCarthy, 26 December 1842.

77. P. C. Dumas, Rio de Janeiro, to U.S. Consul, 29 July 1844, Box 1, **George William Gordon Papers:** "I just arrived from Africa in the French Bark . . . as a passenger after having made abandon of my Brig Cyrus of New Orleans. . . . British Commander of the 'Alert' who took my papers away and trampled my flag."

78. Ibid., **Correspondence with the British Commissioners.** . . . See e.g. H. R. Foote to Commodore Jones, 24 February 1845: "The 'Atilla' was formerly an American vessel called the 'Glencliff.' She arrived at Cabinda . . . under American colours. . . . when it was discharged she was sold to the Brazilian slavedealers and conveyed 800 slaves to the Brazils"; see also J. Oake to Commander Jones, 22 April 1845: "captured . . . for being engaged in the Slave Trade, as there were actually on board 685 Negroes, shipped at Cabinda . . . and bound for the Brazils . . . under American colours . . . of New Orleans . . . manned by 27 persons, prisoners landed from prizes detained by Her Majesty's cruisers, which system I have reason to believe is pursued to a great extent on this part of the coast"; see also Earl of Aberdeen to Foreign Office, 2 July 1845, FO 115/89, *Public Records Office–Kew Gardens*: "the American schooner brig 'Washington Barge' . . . sailed from Bahia

with a general cargo for the coast of Africa on the 1st of December 1844 and that she has returned to that Port on the 20th April last under the Brazilian flag and with the name of 'Fantasima' " with "upwards of 600 slaves." See also Letter to Foreign Office, 20 October 1845, FO 115/89, *Public Records Office–Kew Gardens*: "The United States vessel 'Hazard' . . . had been sold . . . to a slave trader at Whydah and had immediately afterwards sailed from that Port with 370 slaves on board." See Reginald Levinge, Commander, to "Sir," 25 May 1847, FO 268/4, *Public Records Office–Kew Gardens*: Writing from "Whydah," about "six miles S.E. of Lagos . . . [a] suspicious schooner" was detected and the officer went to "board her"; this was an "American schooner" and "the Master of her was highly indignant at having been brought to"; the "British Consul's report from Bahia" rates her, i.e., the "Eleanor," as a "notorious slaver. . . . I was obliged to tell him I would fire into him if he did heave to which he then did" though "the Master refused to show" papers initially. In same file see also Peter Godfrey to "Sir," 3 May 1847: "this vessel's name is mentioned in . . . list of vessels sailing out of Bahia for the purpose of slave traffic on the west coast of Africa"; the vessel was registered in New York City. See also Report from Foreign Office, 26 June 1849, FO 84/773, *Public Records Office–Kew Gardens*: "United States barque . . . shipped a cargo of 800 slaves at Ambriz," while another U.S. vessel "carried off 800 slaves from the same place."

NOTES TO CHAPTER 4

1. Henry A. Wise to George N. Jones, 29 June 1855, Box 1, **Henry Wise Papers**, *Virginia Historical Society–Richmond*.
2. Ibid., Garry Wills, **'Negro President,'** 204.
3. Ibid., Craig M. Simpson, **A Good Southerner**, 36.
4. Henry A. Wise to William C. Whitecomb, 17 November 1859, **Henry Wise Papers, *American Antiquarian Society–Worcester, Massachusetts*.**
5. John Blassingame and John R. McKivigan, eds., **The Frederick Douglass Papers; Series One: Speeches, Debates and Interviews, Volume 3: 1855–1863**, New Haven: Yale University Press, 1985, 405.
6. William Lee Miller, **Arguing about Slavery: The Great Battle in the United States Congress**, New York: Knopf, 1996, 478.
7. Ibid., Mary Catherine Karasch, "The Brazilian Slavers and the Illegal Slave Trade, 1836–1851," 27.
8. Don E. Fehrenbacher, **The Slaveholding Republic: An Account of the United States Government's Relations to Slavery**, New York: Oxford University Press, 2001, 177.
9. Letter to Henry Wise, 17 July 1839, Box 1, Folder 1, **Henry Wise Papers**, *Peabody Essex Museum*.
10. See **James Buchanan, His Doctrines and Policy as Exhibited by Himself and Friends**, circa 1856, including a "Virginia View of Mr. Buchanan" by Governor Henry Wise, 13 June 1856, *American Antiquarian Society–Worcester, Massachusetts*.
11. James P. Hambleton, M.D., **A Biographical Sketch of Henry A. Wise, with a History of the Political Campaign in Virginia in 1855**, Richmond: J.W. Randolph, 1856, xii.
12. Steven Deyle, **Carry Me Back: The Domestic Slave Trade in American Life**, New York: Oxford University Press, 2005, passim.
13. Ibid., Craig Simpson, 61. See also Barton H. Wise, **The Life of Henry A. Wise of Virginia, 1806–1876**, London: Macmillan, 1899, 109: According to Wise's grandson, Henry Wise was an "accomplished linguist" who apparently spoke Portuguese. See also Adele Toussaint-Samson, **A Parisian in Brazil: The Travel Account of a Frenchwoman in Nineteenth-Century Rio de Janeiro**, Wilmington: Scholarly Resources, 2001, 85: "The Emperor of Brazil speaks seven languages,

Portuguese, Latin, Spanish, Italian, French, English, German and . . . Hebrew."

14. Letter to Henry Wise, 20 January 1838, Box 1, Folder 1, **Henry Wise Papers,** *Peabody Essex Museum.*

15. Ibid., James P. Hambleton, M.D., xxxiv.

16. Ibid., Bruno Gujer, "Free Trade and Slavery," 208, 212. See also Ibid., Craig Simpson, 61.

17. Report from Henry Wise, 11 October 1844, in Ibid., Clyde Wilson and W. Edwin Hemphill, eds., **Volume 20,** 71.

18. Report from Henry Wise, 11 October 1844, in Ibid., Clyde Wilson and W. Edwin Hemphill, eds., **Volume 20,** 77. See also Henry Wise to "Dear Bob," 15 March 1846, **Confederate Military Leaders Collection,** *Museum of the Confederacy–Richmond, Virginia*: "when I first arrived here I found the U. States seal in the hands of one of Fonseca's agents, a man named [Souto] at Victoria as Consular agent of the U. States. He actually caused the slave deck to be fitted to the Monte Video at that place, for which Capt. Pendleton was lately convicted at [Baltimore]. I caused his exchequer to be immediately revoked."

19. Report from George Gordon, 3 December 1844, in Ibid., Clyde Wilson and W. Edwin Hemphill, eds., **Volume 20,** 453.

20. Henry Wise to John C. Calhoun, 12 January 1845, Record Group 84, Volume 017, **Records of Foreign Service Posts, Brazil.**

21. Henry Wise to "Mr. Calhoun," 12 January 1845, in Ibid., Ex. Doc. No. 61, **Correspondence Between the Consuls of the United States at Rio de Janeiro.**

22. Henry Wise to John C. Calhoun, 11 October 1844, **Henry Wise Papers,** *Virginia Historical Society–Richmond.*

23. Report, 25 May 1842, Record Group 84, Volume 017, **Records of Foreign Service Posts, Brazil.**

24. Henry Wise to John C. Calhoun, 18 February 1845, in Ibid., Ex. Doc. 61.

25. Memo from Henry Wise, 30 January 1845, in Ibid., Ex. Doc. 61.

26. Memo, 24 January 1845, in Ibid., Ex. Doc. 61.

27. Henry Wise to James Buchanan, 27 July 1847, **Henry Wise Papers,** *Virginia Historical Society-Richmond.*

28. Henry Wise to James Buchanan, 12 April 1847, **Henry Wise Papers.**

29. **New York Times,** 28 April 1884.

30. Henry Wise to "Dear Bob," 15 March 1846, **Confederate Military Leaders Collection.**

31. See U.S. Congress. Senate. 30th Congress, 1st Session. Ex. Doc. No. 28, **Message from the President of the United States.** Letter to Editor of the 'Evening Mail,' 3 March 1848: This "'British Merchant'" asked, "and who are they whose calumnies against our merchants and manufacturers are thus re-echoed in the House of Commons? Who is Mr. Wise. . . . Mr. Wise is, I believe, one of the most reckless and unscrupulous advocates of slavery even in the United States, and, like Mr. Tyler, himself a large slaveholder. He is known to have publicly declared that he would uphold slavery with the last drop of his blood."

32. See American Party, State Executive Committee, **The Record of George Wm. Gordon. The Slave Trade at Rio de Janeiro, Seizure of Slave Vessels, Conviction of Slave Dealers, Personal Liberation of Slaves & Practice Against Theory. Lovers of Freedom, Read! Read! And Vote for the Best Man,** Boston: The American Headquarters, 1856, *New York Public Library*: Gordon, born in Exeter, New Hampshire, was of Scottish origins. He was the "Know-Nothing" candidate for Governor of Massachusetts in 1856. See also F. R. Anspach, **The Sons of the Sires; A History of the Rise, Progress and Destiny of the American Party and its Probable Influence on the Next Presidential Election to which is Added a Review of the Letter of the Hon. Henry A. Wise Against the Know-Nothings. By An American,** Philadelphia: Lippincott, 1855: Wise railed against those who sought to limit the immigration of Irish Catholics to the U.S.

33. Report from Henry Wise in Rio de Janeiro, 14 December 1844, in U.S. Department of State. **Message from the President of the United States, Transmitting Copies of Despatches from the American Minister at the Court of Brazil, Relative to the Slave Trade.** 28th Congress, 2nd Session. House Documents, Serial No. 148, Doc. 148, 20 February 1845.

34. Henry Wise to James Buchanan, 1 May 1845, in Ibid., Ex. Doc. No. 61, **Correspondence Between the Consuls of the United States at Rio de Janeiro. . . .**

35. Ibid., House Documents, Serial No. 148, Doc. 148, Henry Wise to "Maxwell, Wright," 9 December 1844.

36. *Daily Union* [Washington, D.C.], 18 September 1845, Washington, Oficios, 1845–1847, *Archivo Histórico do Itamaraty–Rio de Janeiro*: "I observe the United States papers are filled with statements and remarks upon the proceedings of Mr. Wise at this place," i.e., Rio, "in relations to vessels and persons engaged in the trade to the coast of Africa."

37. See Letter from U.S. Department of State, 13 March 1846, Washington Oficios, 1845–1847: "acknowledging . . . protest of the Brazilian government against the Act of the British Parliament . . . which declares Brazilian vessels engaged in the slave trade liable to be tried before the High Court of Vice Admiralty in the dominions of Her Brittanic Majesty." In same file see bill from November 1846 seeking to limit the slave trade by requiring that vessels e.g. should carry "at least sixty gallons of water" and no more than "two [passengers] to every five tons of such vessel."

38. Frederick Jones to Gaspar Jose Lisboa, 6 November 1846, Washington Oficios, 1845–1847.

39. Letter from Mary E. (Jones) Carr, 1844, **James T. Jones Collection,** *Huntington Library–San Marino, California.*

40. Report, 13 July 1847, Washington Oficios, 1845–1847.

41. **Salem Register,** 16 August 1847, Washington Oficios, 1845–1847.

42. Clipping, circa 1848, Washington Oficios, 1848–1851.

43. Henry Wise to William Wright, 9 March 1845, MS 1467, **William Wright Papers,** *Maryland Historical Society–Baltimore.*

44. Henry Wise to William Wright, 22 May 1845, **William Wright Papers.**

45. Ibid., Henry Wise to William Wright, 9 March 1845.

46. Solomon B. Davies to William Wright, 28 May 1845, **William Wright Papers.**

47. Henry Wise to "Gentlemen," 3 July 1845, **Wright-May-Thom Family Papers.**

48. John Mason, U.S. State of Department, to William Wright, 4 April 1845, **William Wright Papers:** "your letter . . . requesting the opinion of this Department as to the legality of sales of vessels of the United States at Rio de Janeiro deliverable on the coast of Africa, as to chartering of such vessels for the purpose of taking cargoes to that coast and requesting to be informed of this government in regard to these subjects . . . the policy of this government, as shown by the laws of the United States, is both to encourage the construction, equipment and navigation of vessels by our citizens and to deter them from participating in the African slave trade."

49. Edward Livingston in Washington, D.C. to William Wright in Rio de Janeiro, 1 December 1831, **William Wright Papers.**

50. Circular from Maxwell, Wright in Rio, 17 January 1845, Box 2, **Wright-May-Thom Family Papers,** *Maryland Historical Society–Baltimore.*

51. Letter from William Wright, circa 1835, Box 2, **Wright-May-Thom Family Papers.**

52. Letter from Rio by William Wright, 18 January 1832, Box 2, **Wright-May-Thom Family Papers.**

53. Edward Livingston to William Wright, 3 November 1831, Box 2, **Wright-May-Thom Family Papers.**

54. Robert Wright in Rio de Janeiro to William Wright, 23 November 1841, **Wright-May-Thom Family Papers.** See also

Ibid., Eric Anderson, "Yankee Blackbirds," 311–312.

55. J. S. Rebello to Joshua Cohen, 5 February 1841, 2432, Maryland Manuscripts, *University of Maryland–College Park.*

56. Evelyn M. Cherpak, ed., A Diplomat's Lady in Brazil: Selections from the Diary of Mary Robinson Hunter, 1834–1848, Newport: Newport Historical Society, 2001, 16.

57. See Ibid., Evelyn M. Cherpak, ed., 17, 207, 260–261, 276, 41, 42, 229, 269, 277, 400, 355. See also John Morgan, U.K. Consul in Rio Grande do Sul to Lord Palmerston, 15 February 1848, in Ibid., British Parliamentary Papers: Correspondence Relative to the Slave Trade, Volume 55, Number 36. See also Lord Howden to Lord Palmerston, 20 March 1848, in Ibid., British Parliamentary Papers: Correspondence Relative to the Slave Trade, Volume 55, Number 36. See also Extracts from the Evidence Taken Before Committees of the Two Houses of Parliament Relative to the Slave Trade, London: Ridgway, 1851, 75, *National Library of South Africa–Cape Town.*

58. Lord Howden to Lord Palmerston, 31 December 1847, Ibid., British Parliamentary Papers: Correspondence Relative to the Slave Trade, Volume 64.

59. Ivor Debenham Spencer, The Victor and the Spoils: A Life of William L. Marcy, Providence: Brown University Press, 1959, 258.

60. Freedom's Journal, 10 October 1828.

61. John C. Calhoun to James Buchanan, 24 March 1845, in Ibid., Clyde Wilson and W. Edwin Hemphill, eds., Volume 21, 441.

62. John C. Calhoun to Thomas G. Clemson. 23 June 1845, in Ibid., Clyde Wilson and W. Edwin Hemphill, eds., Volume 21, 597.

63. David S. Heidler, Pulling the Temple Down: The Fire-Eaters and the Destruction of the Union, Mechanicsburg: Stackpole, 1994, 122, 123.

64. See Jefferson Davis, "Remarks on the Slave Trade," 22 January 1851, in Lynda Lasswell Crist, et al., eds., The Papers of Jefferson Davis, Volume 4, 1849–1852, Baton Rouge: Louisiana State University Press, 1983, 154–155.

65. North Star, 21 August 1848.

66. National Era, 4 November 1847.

67. Milo Milton Quaife, ed., The Diary of James K. Polk During his Presidency, 1845 to 1849, Volume 2, New York: Kraus, 1970, 351.

68. Frederick Moore Binder, James Buchanan and the American Empire, Selinsgrove: Susquehanna University Press, 1994, 146–147. See also G. B. Wright, "Hon. David Tod: Biographical and Personal Recollections," Ohio Archaeological and Historical Publications, 8 (1900): 107–131, 111. Tod was appointed to succeed Wise in Brazil after the latter was "recalled at the request of Brazil in consequence of his arbitrary course which threatened to involve our country in war with that Empire."

NOTES TO CHAPTER 5

1. Journal of Charlotte Gardner, circa 1852, Box 1, William Bunker Gardner Papers, *Huntington Library–San Marino, California.*

2. Captain William Harwar Parker, Recollections of a Naval Officer, 1841–1865, New York: Charles Scribner's, 1885, 25.

3. George Shepard, "Addresses of Rev. Professor Shepard, and Rev. S. L. Caldwell to the California Pilgrims from Bangor, Maine," Bangor: Smith & Sayward, 1849, *Huntington Library.*

4. Raymond A. Rydell, "The Cape Horn Route to California, 1849," Pacific Historical Review, 17 (Number 1, February 1948): 149–163, 162, 150, 149. See also "Cape Horn and Cooperative Mining in '49," Century Magazine, 42 (Number 1, May 1891): 579–594, 593: Statistics kept by Mr. Edward King, "harbor master of San Francisco during that period, the Custom House records having been destroyed

by the great fire of May 4, 1851" indicate
that " 'passenger arrivals by sea in San
Francisco in 1849' " via Cape Horn was
15,597 and via Panama 6489. Interestingly,
from Pacific ports the figure was 9217. See
also Oscar Lewis, "South American Ports
of Call," **Pacific Historical Review**, 18
(Number 1, February 1949): 57–66, 60:
"in the first three months of 1849, eighty-
six California bound ships put into the
harbor" at Rio; "sometimes a dozen
arrived in a single day bearing as many as
a thousand passengers." See also William
McCollum, **California as I Saw It**, Los
Gatos, California: Talisman, 1960: There
were also Brazilian 49ers arriving in California; 23 are listed here.

5. Letter from A. H. Cazzam, circa
1849, Box 1, **Peter Remsen Papers**, *State
Historical Society of Wisconsin–Madison.*

6. John B. Goodman III, **The Gold
Rush: Voyage of the Ship Loo Choo
Around the Horn in 1849,** Mount Pleasant, Michigan: The Cumming Press, 1977,
xix.

7. George G. Webster, **The Journal of a
Trip Around the Horn**, Ashland: Lewis
Osborne, 1970, 32.

8. See George Gardner, **Travels in the
Interior of Brazil, Principally Through the
Northern Provinces and the Gold and Diamond Districts during the Years 1836–
1841**, London: Reeve, Benham and Reeve,
1849.

9. Diary of Joshua Vincent, Acc. 2656,
20 November 1846, *San Diego Historical
Society.*

10. John Charles Duchow, **The Duchow
Journal: A Voyage from Boston to California 1852,** no city: Mallette Dean, 1959, no
page no.

11. Letter to spouse, 4 March 1852,
Box 1, Folder 6, **Chaplin Conway Papers**,
Peabody Essex Museum.

12. "From Boston to San Francisco
Around Cape Horn," 1864, MSSHM
60313, *Huntington Library.*

13. Hinton Helper, **The Land of God:
Reality versus Fiction**, Baltimore: Helper,
1855, 278–279. See also Judson A. Gre-

nier, "Colonel Jack Watson: Copperhead
Assemblyman in Civil War California,"
The Californians, 12 (Number 5, year
unclear): 14–35, 18, *California State
Library–Sacramento*: There was talk of a
" 'coup d'etat' " in the state to take Southern California out of the state and union
on pro-slavery grounds.

14. **Savannah Daily Morning News**, 26
August 1850.

15. Gerald Stanley, "The Politics of the
Antebellum West: The Impact of the Slavery and Race Issues in California," **Journal
of the West**, 16 (Number 4, October
1977): 19–26.

16. Donald Jackson, **Gold Dust**, New
York: Knopf, 1980, 101.

17. Oscar Lewis, **Sea Routes to the Gold
Fields: The Migration by Water to California in 1849-1852**, New York: Knopf,
1949, 135.

18. John H. Beeckman to "My Dearest
Wife,"27 February 1849, **John H. Beeck-
man Collection**, *California State Library–
Sacramento.*

19. Ruth S. Nash, **High Seas to High
Stakes or Around Cape Horn to the Gold
Rush**, Bloomington, Indiana: First Books,
2000, 49.

20. C. S. Stewart, **Brazil and La Plata:
The Personal Record of a Cruise**, New
York: G. P. Putnam, 1856, 150.

21. Journal of Julius Howard Pratt, no
date, Folder qq, *Connecticut Historical
Society–Hartford.*

22. Ibid., John B. Goodman III, **The
Gold Rush**, xvi.

23. Journal of C. H. Keefe, 1849, *University of California–Berkeley*. See also
Ibid., Mary C. Karasch, **Slave Life in Rio
de Janeiro, 1808–1850**, 332. See also Benjamin Brewster to "My Dear Mother,"4
March 1849, *G. W. Blunt White Library–
Mystic, Connecticut.*

24. Salvador A. Ramirez, **From New
York to San Francisco via Cape Horn in
1849: The Gold Rush Voyage of the Ship
'Pacific,' an Eyewitness Account**, Carlsbad,
California: The Tentacled Press, 1985, 57,
68. See also John Chauncey Mason,

"Memories of Long Ago," no date, Folder V, *Connecticut Historical Society*: "there were nineteen ships in the harbor" when he arrived in 1849, "all going to California; we had to wait about ten days before our turn came to have our water casks filled." See also Christian Miller to "Dear Father . . . ," 27 April 1849, 74/194C, **Christian Miller Letters**, *University of California–Berkeley*: "there are not less than 1500 Americans bound to California in the city of Rio Janeiro. Before our arrival there were about 60 vessels put in this port for water. . . . it will take about four months before we arrive in California."

25. Ibid., Journal of Julius Howard Pratt.

26. Charles Mansfield, **Paraguay, Brazil and the Plate: Letters Written in 1852–1853**, Cambridge: Macmillan, 1856, 30.

27. Journal of William Carshaw, 1846–1847, *Huntington Library.*

28. Letter to George Stoner, 8 October 1849, in Ibid., Roll 23, **Brazil Squadron Letters**: "the population . . . including blacks—the town contains from six to eight thousand inhabitants. . . . the climate is mild and . . . salubrious." See also Letter from Andrew Boyd Cummings, 8 November 1847, **Andrew Boyd Cummings Papers**, *U.S. Naval Academy–Annapolis.*

29. Brian Roberts, " 'The Greatest and Most Perverted Paradise,' " in Kenneth N. Owens, ed., **Riches for All: The California Gold Rush and the World**, Lincoln: University of Nebraska Press, 2002, 71–89, 74.

30. Letter from Mary Smith, 11 October 1853, **Letters of Mary Smith**, *Yale University.*

31. John H. Beeckman to "My Dearest Wife," 27 February 1849, **John H. Beeckman Collection.**

32. John H. Beeckman to Spouse, 8 March 1849, **John H. Beeckman Collection.**

33. A. H. Cazzam to "Dear Sir," 11 November 1849, Box 1, **Peter Remsen Papers**, *State Historical Society of Wisconsin–Madison.*

34. See Diary of Horatio Chapman,

circa 1849, Box 1, Folder 11 (ell/ell), **California Gold Rush Collection**, *Connecticut Historical Society–Hartford.*

35. "Narrative of Henry Beckett, taken from the 'Tacoma Sunday Ledger,' " 26 February 1893, *Washington State Historical Society–Tacoma.* See also "Journal of a Voyage Taken by George Stevens Aboard the Sailing Vessel 'North American' . . . Sailing Around Cape Horn from New York to San Francisco, April 1 to August 31, 1852," *California Historical Society–San Francisco*: "the city [Rio] is strictly guarded by coloured soldiers. . . . a guard also extends for some miles out of the city, probably to prevent the escape of slaves."

36. Captain Joseph Hamilton to Captain Richard H. Tucker, Jr., 8 March 1849, **Tucker Family Shipping Papers**, *Bowdoin College–Maine.*

37. Edward M. Brown, **An Ocean Voyage: Around Cape Horn, 1849–1850**, No city, 1900, *Huntington Library.*

38. Roger Conant, **Mercer's Belles: The Journal of a Reporter**, edited by Lenna A. Deutsch, Seattle: University of Washington Press, 1960, 69.

39. Anonymous Diary, 1849, c-F216, **Honeyman Collection**, *University of California–Berkeley.*

40. W. S. W. Ruschenberger, **Notes and Commentaries During a Voyage to Brazil and China in the Year 1848**, Richmond: McFarlane & Ferguson, 1854, 79.

41. Ibid., George Coggeshall, **Thirty Six Voyages to Various Parts of the World, Made Between the Years 1799 and 1841**, 550. See also, Ibid., Salvador A. Ramirez, 59. See also Letter of Condy Raguet, 8 November 1824, **Condy Raguet Official Letters**, *Historical Society of Pennsylvania.*

42. Journal of Thomas Williams, 1849, *University of California–Berkeley.*

43. "Diary of Ship 'Robert Bourne,' " 1849, *Huntington Library.*

44. Ibid., W. S. W. Ruschenberger, 120.

45. Anonymous Journal, 1849, 77/160c, *University of California–Berkeley.*

46. Diary of Ebenezer Sheppard, 1849,

California Historical Society–San Francisco.

47. Thomas Ewbank, **Life in Brazil; or a Journal of a Visit to The Land of the Cocoa and Palm**, New York: Harper & Brothers, 1856, 188.

48. Milton Stevens to "My Dear Mother,"4 May 1849, Box 1, **Milton Stevens Papers**, *Huntington Library, San Marino, California.*

49. Ibid., "Diary of Ship 'Robert Bourne.' "

50. C. S. Stewart, **Brazil and La Plata: The Personal Record of a Cruise**, New York: G. P. Putnam, 1856, 72.

51. Ibid., Brian Roberts, 74.

52. James Orton, **The Andes and the Amazon or Across the Continent of South America**, New York: Harper & Bros., 1870, 323.

53. Journal of James Lamoureaux Pangburn, 1849, *J. Porter Shaw Maritime Library–San Francisco.*

54. Letters of Mary Smith, 25 September 1853, *Yale University.*

55. John Pomfret, **California Gold Rush Voyages, 1848–1849: Three Original Narratives**, San Marino: Huntington Library, 1954, 108, 109.

56. Samuel C. Upham, **Notes of a Voyage to California via Cape Horn Together with Scenes in El Dorado in the Years 1849–1850**, Philadelphia: Upham, 1878, 68.

57. L. M. Schaeffer, **Sketches of Travels in South America, Mexico and California**, New York: James Egbert, 1860, 14.

58. Clipping, circa 1846, **Henry Wise Papers**, *American Antiquarian Society.* See also Gaspar Jose de Lisboa to President James Buchanan, 21 August 1847, **Mason Family Papers**, *Virginia Historical Society.*

59. Errol Wayne Stevens, **Incidents of a Voyage to California, 1849: A Diary of Travel Aboard the Bark 'Hersilia' and in Sacramento**, Los Angeles: Western History Association, 1987, 22. See also Journal of C. H. Keefe, May 1849, *University of California–Berkeley.*

60. Ibid., Edward M. Brown, **An Ocean Voyage**, 58.

61. Journal of John R. McFalan, 1850, *Huntington Library.*

62. Ibid., W. S. W. Ruschenberger, 62.

63. Joseph Lamson, **Round Cape Horne: Voyages of the Passenger Ship James W. Paige from Maine to California in the Year 1852**, Bangor: O. F. and W. H. Knowles, 1878, 26.

64. John Esaias Warren, **Para; Or Scenes and Adventures on the Banks of the Amazon**, New York: G. P. Putnam, 1851, 62.

65. Diary of Richard Morton, 1857–1858, *Virginia Historical Society.*

66. Journal of J. L. Ackerman, 23 September 1849–1 February 1854, *University of California–Berkeley.*

67. Journal of Samuel Adams, 1849, **Samuel Adams Papers**, *California Historical Society–Sacramento.*

68. Ibid., Milton Stevens to "My Dear Mother."

69. Ibid., Samuel C. Upham, 88.

70. Diary of James Woods, 1849, *Huntington Library.*

71. James Delgado, ed., **The Log of Apollo: Joseph Perkins Beach's Journal of the Voyage of the Ship 'Apollo' from New York to San Francisco, 1849**, San Francisco: Book Club of California, 1986, 47.

72. Ibid., Diary of James Woods.

73. Ibid., Salvador Ramirez, 61.

74. Anonymous Journal, 1849, 77/160c, *University of California–Berkeley.*

75. James T. Jones to Mary E. (Jones) Carr, 1844, **James T. Jones Collection**, *Huntington Library.* Others disagreed.

76. See "Travel Sketches of C. B. Richard," 1846–1849, *New York Historical Society*: "the slave population is five-fold that of the whites" and continually replenished as "slave ships fitted out in Brazilian ports bound for the African coast" were ever present. See also Lonnie J. White and William R. Gillespie, **By Sea to San Francisco, 1849–1850: The Journal of Dr. James Morison**, Memphis: Memphis State University Press, 1977, 12: "the conditions of this unfortunate class [slaves] is

very little above that of the beast of burden. They are not permitted to wear shoes. By this they are distinguished from the free Negro. . . . I saw several children running about entirely naked. The men frequently are naked above the loins and in some instances had no covering except the loins. . . . they are generally cheerful and happy."

77. Ibid., Salvador A. Ramirez, 63.

78. Anonymous Journal, 1849, 77/160c, *University of California–Berkeley.*

79. Ibid., Journal of C. H. Keefe.

80. Albert Lyman, **Journal of a Voyage to California and Life in the Gold Diggings and Also a Voyage from California to the Sandwich Islands,** Hartford: Dexter & Bro., 1852, 42.

81. Anonymous Journal, 1849, c-F 216, **Honeyman Collection,** *University of California–Berkeley.*

82. M. J. Randall, **The Adventures of a Captain's Wife Going through the Straits of Magellan to California in 1850,** New York and San Francisco: A. Roman and Co., 1877, 10.

83. Ibid., Diary of Richard Morton.

84. Journal of Thomas Williams, March-September 1849, *University of California–Berkeley*: "The manner the poor slaves eat their food, which is rice and fish, when I saw them they had . . . no knife, fork or spoon, they scoop it up in their hands and [throw] it in their mouths. . . . their jaws don't open and shut like we white people, they work their jaws, like an ox chewing his cud, or the horse his hay or grain."

85. Anonymous Journal, 1849, 77/160c, *University of California–Berkeley.* See also Journal of Ralph Cross Pendleton, March-July 1852, *Huntington Library.*

86. Ibid., Thomas Ewbank, 440. See also Ibid., Thomas Ewbank, 436: "Common punishments" were a "Negro in a mask, and a Negro wearing the usual pronged collar, with a shackle around one ankle and secured to a chain suspended from his waist."

87. John H. Beeckman to Spouse, 17 March 1849, **John H. Beeckman Collection.**

88. Ibid., J. Lamson, **Round Cape Horn,** 43.

89. Ibid., Errol Wayne Stevens, **Incidents of a Voyage to California, 1849,** 24. See also Griffith Meredith, "Meredith's Journal of a Voyage from New York, 1849, via Cape Horn to San Francisco," *California State Library–Sacramento*: "We went to Capt. Cathcart's house and had quite a chat with him, he is a native of Massachusetts. . . . he is a very wealthy man. Now he has a fine house" and was growing "sugar" and "has 25 or 30 slaves to work for him." See also Oscar Lewis, "South America's Ports of Call," **Pacific Historical Review,** 18 (Number 1, February 1949): 57–66, 58: "At the height of the California Rush, St. Catherine's was overrun with Yankees."

90. See letter to George Stoner, 8 October 1849, in Ibid., Roll 23, **Brazil Squadron Letters:** "On my recent visit . . . I found the American interest prosperous and well represented in the person of Robert S. Cathcart, Acting U.S. Consul. . . . he has resided in the country upwards of twenty years, is conversant with the language. . . . hence our Government would do well in my judgment to confirm the appointment."

91. **Godey's Lady Book,** August 1853.

92. Journal of Daniel S. Hayden, 1849–1852, *Huntington Library.*

93. "Log Book Manuscript Journal of 'California Packet,' Boston to San Francisco, March 4, 1850 to August 24, 1850," *Huntington Library.*

94. Anonymous Journal, 1849, 77/160c, *University of California–Berkeley.*

95. Ibid., Ruth S. Nash, 46, 47. See also Ibid., Charles Mansfield, 29: This visiting British scientist found Pernambuco to be a "dreadfully dirty place; there is not a drain of any sort, and all imaginable filth lies in the streets. . . . two-thirds of the population seems to be naked Negroes, in cotton drawers."

96. Ibid., Brian Roberts, 80–81, 84.

97. Diary of Samuel Whiting, 1849, *Rhode Island Historical Society–Providence.*
98. Ibid., "Narrative of Henry Beckett."
99. Ibid., Journal of Thomas Williams.
100. Ibid., Albert Lyman, 36.
101. Ibid., Thomas Ewbank, 116.
102. Ibid., Diary of Richard Morton.
103. Levi Holden to Charles, 26 December 1848, **Levi Holden Papers,** *Rhode Island Historical Society–Providence.*
104. **Godey's Lady Book,** June 1853.
105. Ibid., Diary of Richard Morton.
106. L. J. Hall, **Around the Horn in '49: Journal of the Hartford Union Mining and Trading Company,** Wethersfield, Connecticut: Hall, 1898, [originally published in 1849], 77, *Huntington Library.*
107. J. D. B. Stillman, **Seeking the Golden Fleece: A Record of Pioneer Life in California,** San Francisco: A Roman & Co., 1877.
108. Anonymous Journal, 1849, 77/160c, *University of California–Berkeley.*
109. A. H. Cazzam to Peter Remsen, 5 October 1848, Box 1, **Peter Remsen Papers.**
110. Journal of Ralph Cross Pendleton, 1852, *Huntington Library.*
111. Ibid., J. Lamson, 43.
112. Ibid., Diary of James Woods.
113. Ibid., C. S. Stewart, 408.
114. Ibid., Diary of Richard Morton.
115. William H. Edwards, **A Voyage up the River Amazon Including a Residence at Para,** London: John Murray, 1847, 52.
116. **North Star,** 5 May 1848. Douglass's forbearance was even more striking since "African Americans" venturing south of the U.S. "traveled under the constant menace of enslavement by slave hunters and bandits. . . . kidnappers made a lucrative business of selling captives to the South American slave market." See Shirley Ann Moore, " 'Do You Think I'll Lug Trunks?' African-Americans in Gold Rush California," in Ibid., Kenneth N. Owens, ed., **Riches for All,** 161–175, 164.

117. **Frederick Douglass' Paper,** 21 May 1858.
118. **Frederick Douglass' Paper,** 5 January 1860.
119. Ibid., Diary of Richard Morton. See also Rev. Walter Colton, U.S. Navy, **Deck and Port or Incidents of a Cruise in the United States Frigate Congress to California,** New York: A. S. Barnes, 1852, 112–113.
120. Ibid., Samuel C. Upham, 88.
121. John H. Beeckman to Wife, 27 March 1849, **John H. Beeckman Collection.**
122. Ibid., Thomas Ewbank, 267, 195, 439. See also Ibid., Charles Mansfield, 29.
123. Ibid., Samuel C. Upham, 89. See Ibid., Jacob D. B. Stillman, 40.
124. See also **Frederick Douglass' Paper,** 19 February 1852. See also Robert Edgar Conrad, ed., **Children of God's Fire: A Documentary History of Black Slavery in Brazil,** Princeton: Princeton University Press, 1983, xvi, xviii: "After years of concentrated study of Brazilian slavery and abolition, and after reading extensively on slavery in the United States, I have become convinced that the *physical conditions* endured by slaves in Brazil made life there considerably more precarious and uncomfortable—again the physical sense—than it was for most slaves in the United States" [emphasis-original], while the higher standard of living in the U.S. trickled down to slaves. On the other hand, "some blacks and mulattoes in Brazil enjoyed social advantages that were normally denied to their counterparts in the American South or even in [the] free states of the North."

NOTES TO CHAPTER 6

1. See Southern Pamphlet #4704, Annual Report of the Matthew Fontaine Maury Association, 1920, *University of North Carolina–Chapel Hill.* See also John A. Coke, Henry Miller, and Branch B. Morgan, "Memorials of Three Great Virginians: Matthew Fontaine Maury, Robert Edward Lee and Thomas Jonathan

('Stonewall') Jackson," Richmond: United Daughters of the Confederacy, 1924, *University of North Carolina–Chapel Hill.*

2. **All Hands, April 1998, N.972**, Vertical File, Defense Mapping Agency, *U.S. Naval Academy, Annapolis.*

3. A. C. W. Bethel, "The Golden Skein: California's Gold-Rush Transportation Network," **California History**, 77 (Number 4, Winter 1998–1999): 250–275, 255.

4. Colonel William Couper, **One Hundred Years at VMI, Volume 3**, Richmond: Garrett & Massie, 1939, 158–172.

5. James P. Reddick, Jr., "Herndon, Maury and the Amazon Basin," **United States Naval Institute Proceedings**, 97 (Number 3/817, March 1971): 56–63, 58, 59, 62, 63.

6. Charles Lee Lewis, "Matthew Fontaine Maury: An International Figure," **The Southern Magazine**, 1 (Number 9, January 1935): 9–11, 43, 10.

7. See e.g. John W. Wayland, **The Pathfinder of the Seas: The Life of Matthew Fontaine Maury**, Richmond: Garrett & Massie, 1930, 77, 78, 79. See also Frances Leigh Williams, **Matthew Fontaine Maury: Scientist of the Sea**, New Brunswick: Rutgers University Press, 1963; Patricia Jahns, **Matthew Fontaine Maury & John Henry: Scientists of the Civil War**, New York: Hastings House, 1963.

8. **London Telegraph**, 25 February 1873.

9. See "Inducements to the Colored People of the United States to Emigrate to British Guiana, Compiled from Statements and Documents Furnished by Edward Carbery, Agent of the Immigration Society of British Guiana and Proprietor in that Colony," Boston: Kidder and Wright, 1840, 7, *Kansas State Historical Society–Topeka*: "Conditions" in the U.S. "which render the position of the colored man in the United States so mortifying and uncomfortable are wholly unknown in British Guiana. In this respect all are equal." See also James O'Toole, **Passing for White: Race, Religion and the Healy Family, 1820–1920**, Amherst: University of

Massachusetts Press, 2002, 33: "Orestes Brownson wrote bluntly in the middle of the Civil War, expressing the fond hope that should slaves win their freedom, they would simply 'drift away' to Central and South America."

10. Percy Alvin Martin, "The Influence of the United States on the Opening of the Amazon to the World's Commerce," **Hispanic American Historical Review**, 1 (Number 2, May 1918): 146–162, 146.

11. Monroe Edwards, **The Life and Adventurer of the Accomplished Forger and Swindler**, New York: H. Long & Brother, 1848, 14, 17, 18, 22, 27, 31, 32, 47–48, 82.

12. See e.g. Ibid., Robert E. May, **Manifest Destiny's Underworld**, 241.

13. Charles Smith, Consul, to John Forsyth, Secretary of State, 20 July 1836, Record Group 59, Roll 1, T478, **Records of the Department of State, Dispatches from U.S. Consuls in Para, Brazil**: "the disturbances which this Province has seen for the last year unhappily afflicted are supposed to be at an end." "Five American merchant vessels" were "in port at this time," along with "two French and English ships of war." But see also The Diary of H. B. Towne, Misc. Vol. 185, *G. W. Blunt Library–Mystic, Connecticut*: Born in Andover, Massachusetts in 1798, this sailor visited Para in the 1830s and noted, "there has been more political troubles at this place than any other. . . . some considerable trade is effected by Americans at Para" though "seldom do we see one of our government's vessels at Para." As for Bahia, he noted that "of late few American vessels trade there. . . . I believe also the blacks (slaves) exceed the whites 3 or 4 to one."

14. Amory Edwards to Capt. I. D. Wilson, 6 January 1847, Box 1, **Peter Remsen Papers**, *State Historical Society of Wisconsin-Madison.*

15. De Facto Passport of Peter Remsen, circa 1847, Box 1, **Peter Remsen Papers.**

16. Letter to "Dear Madam," 3 December 1847, Box 1, **Peter Remsen Papers.**

17. Undated, circa 1848, Box 1, Peter Remsen Papers.

18. G. T. Snow to Commanding Officer, 9 June 1845, Record Group 59, Roll 2, T344, Despatches from U.S. Consuls in Pernambuco, Brazil.

19. Walter Stapp to Lewis Cass, 30 October 1858, Record Group 59, Roll 2, T344, Despatches from U.S. Consuls in Pernambuco, Brazil.

20. Letter to Daniel Webster, 14 May 1851, Record Group 59, Roll 1, Despatches from U.S. Consuls in Bahia.

21. John Julius Pringle to William Pringle, 14 September 1841, 11-325-2, Mitchell-Pringle Collection, *South Carolina Historical Society–Charleston.* See also Steven C. Topik, **Trade and Gunboats: The United States and Brazil in the Age of Empire,** Stanford: Stanford University Press, 1996, 53, 54.

22. Chart, "American Vessels Arriving at & Departing from Bahia, Brazil from the 1st of January to the 30th June 1851 inclusive," Record Group 59, Roll 1, Despatches from U.S. Consuls in Bahia.

23. Consular Report, 31 December 1857, Record Group 59, Roll 2, T478, Records of the Department of State, Despatches from U.S. Consuls in Para, Brazil, *National Archives and Records Administration–College Park, Maryland.*

24. Consular Report, 30 November 1859, Record Group 59, Roll 2, Despatches from U.S. Consuls in Para.

25. Ibid., Consular Report, 30 November 1859.

26. Henry Dewey to William Marcy, 8 November 1855, Record Group 59, Roll 2, Despatches from U.S. Consuls in Para.

27. Mark Williams to Henry Dewey, 8 September 1855, Record Group 59, Roll 2, Despatches from the U.S. Consuls in Para.

28. Henry Dewey to William Marcy, 12 July 1855, Record Group 59, Roll 1, T478, Despatches from U.S. Consuls in Para, Brazil.

29. Ana Maury to "My Dear Cousin," 2 December 1853, Box 1, **Matthew Maury Papers,** *Duke University.*

30. Sam Houston to S. L. Southard, 20 February 1825, **Miscellaneous Southard,** *New York Historical Society.*

31. General Dabney Herndon Maury, **Recollections of a Virginian in the Mexican, Indian and Civil Wars,** New York: Scribner's, 1894, 16.

32. Matthew Maury to "My Dear Sir," 18 June 1829, Box 1, **Matthew Maury Papers,** *Duke University.*

33. See **Smithsonian,** 14 (Number 2, March 1984): 170–186, Vertical File, Defense Mapping Agency, *U.S. Naval Academy–Annapolis.*

34. Ibid., A. C. W. Bethel, "The Golden Skein," 255.

35. Matthew Maury to William Lewis Herndon, 2 April 1850, in J. G. de Roulhac Hamilton, ed., **The Papers of William Alexander Graham, Volume 3, 1845–1850,** Raleigh: State Department of Archives and History, 1960, 433–434.

36. Henry Lee Norris to Daniel Webster, 31 December 1850, Record Group 59, Roll 1, T478, Despatches from U.S. Consuls in Para, Brazil.

37. William Lewis Herndon, "Extracts from My Journal, 1828–1850," **William Lewis Herndon Papers,** *New York Historical Society.*

38. William Lewis Herndon, **Exploration of the Valley of the Amazon, 1851–1852,** New York: Grove Press, 2000, 248, 258, 263, 274–275, 324, 342, 56, xiv.

39. John Schroeder, **Shaping a Maritime Empire: The Commercial and Diplomatic Role of the American Navy, 1829–1861,** Westport: Greenwood Press, 1985, 109, 106–107.

40. John Crampton to London, 8 August 1853, in James J. Barnes and Patience P. Barnes, eds., **Private and Confidential: Letters from British Ministers in Washington to the Foreign Secretaries in London, 1844–1867,** Selinsgrove, Pennsylvania: Susquehanna University Press, 1993, 79.

41. William K. Scarborough, ed., **The Diary of Edmund Ruffin, Volume 1: Toward Independence, October 1856–**

April 1857, Baton Rouge: Louisiana State University Press, 1972, 386.

42. **New York Times,** 24 August 1854.

43. **New York Times,** 16 May 1854.

44. Matthew Maury to William Graham, 14 August 1850, Washington Oficios, 1848–1851, *Archivo Histórico do Itamaraty–Rio de Janeiro.*

45. "Extract from the Rio [de] Janeiro Correspondence of the 'Observator,' " no date, Box 17, Folder 306, **William Graham Papers,** *University of North Carolina–Chapel Hill.*

46. Letter to William Graham, 13 April 1852, Box 8, Folder 125, **William Graham Papers.**

47. John F. Cady, **Foreign Intervention in the Rio de la Plata, 1835–1850,** Philadelphia: University of Pennsylvania Press, 1929, 160.

48. Letter from J. G. Chapman, 22 June 1852, Box 8, Folder 129, **William Graham Papers.**

49. Millard Fillmore to William Graham, 30 June 1852, Box 8, Folder 130, **William Graham Papers.**

50. Millard Fillmore to William Graham, 22 June 1853, Box 8, Folder 143, **William Graham Papers.**

51. Matthew Maury to William Graham, 8 October 1852, Box 8, Folder 137, **William Graham Papers.**

52. Matthew Fontaine Maury, "Direct Foreign Trade of the South," **De Bow's Review,** 12 (Number 2, February 1852): 126–148, 140, 142, 143, 144, 145, 146, 147, 148.

53. Matthew Maury, "Shall the Valleys of the Amazon and the Mississippi Reciprocate Trade," **De Bow's Review,** 14 (Number 2, February 1853): 136–145, 145.

54. Matthew Maury, "The Amazon and the Atlantic Slopes of South America," Washington: Franck Taylor, 1853, F2546, *Virginia Historical Society.*

55. U.S. Congress. House. 33rd Congress, 1st Session. Miscellaneous No. 22, "Free Navigation of the Amazon River. Memorial of Lieutenant Maury, in behalf

of the Memphis Convention in Favor of the Free Navigation of the Amazon River." 3 March 1854, *Virginia Historical Society.*

56. Matthew Maury to William Graham, 7 October 1850, Box 5, Folder 76, **William Graham Papers.**

57. Matthew Maury to Mrs. Blackford, 24 December 1851, in Jacqueline Ambler Caskie, ed., **Life and Letters of Matthew Fontaine Maury,** Richmond: Richmond Press, 1928, 119, 121.

58. Nannie Corbin, **A Life of Matthew Fontaine Maury,** London: Low, Marston, Searle and Rivington, 1888, 132.

59. Letter from Matthew Maury, 8 October 1852, in Ibid., J. G. de Roulhac Hamilton, ed., **Volume 4,** 1961, 418.

60. See Ibid., James P. Reddick, 63.

61. **Provincial Freeman,** 3 June 1854.

62. **National Era,** 31 August 1854.

63. **National Era,** 29 June 1854.

64. **Provincial Freeman,** 27 May 1854.

65. **Provincial Freeman,** 29 April 1854.

66. **Frederick Douglass' Paper,** 31 March 1854.

67. **National Era,** 23 June 1853.

68. Matthew Maury to William Figaniere, 8 September 1856, [translation]: Legation of Portugal in Washington, Correspondence Received from Various U.S. Authorities and Establishments, 1837–1888, Torre, 4 Piso, Estante 1, 17, A38, M 19, *Archivo Histórico-Diplomático, Ministério dos Negocios Estrangeiros–Lisbon.* There are many letters in this file between the two.

69. J. A. Dahlgren to William Figaniere, 24 March 1857, in Ibid., A38, M19, Lisbon.

70. J. A. Dahlgren to William Figaniere, 14 April 1857, in Ibid., A38, M19, Lisbon.

71. Matthew Maury to William Figaniere, in Ibid., A38, M19, Lisbon.

72. U.S. Patent Office to William Figaniere, in Ibid., A38, M19, Lisbon.

73. Letter from Matthew Maury, 14 July 1859, in Ibid., A38, M19, Lisbon: Thanks for your "Royal Letter Patent from His Majesty-Your King conferring upon me the 'Degree of Officer of the Most

Ancient and Most Noble Order of the Power of Swords, of Valor, Loyalty and Merit.'"

74. See e.g. Matthew Maury to the "Grand Duke Constatine, Lord High Admiral of the Russian Navy," 22 October 1855, Box 5, **Matthew Maury Papers,** *Library of Congress–Washington, D.C.*: "I have received by the hands of the Russian Minister, the autograph letter which Your Imperial Highness . . . had the kindness to write me. . . . I am proud of it and hold in high esteem the commendation which the Great Admiral of the Russian Navy bestows upon my humble labors"; in the same file see also the following: "Tomard" to Maury, 18 November 1855: Lavish praise heaped on Maury along with the query re: "keeping perfectly clear for navigation the entrance of the harbor" and the "Suez Canal"; Maury to Tomard, 2 January 1856: Re: Suez Canal, "it is a work worthy of the age"; he also speaks of building a "double track railroad about 420 miles long . . . from Caspian Sea to the Persian Gulf"; "Minister Resident of the Republic of Bremen" to Maury, 28 December 1855: "it affords me great pleasure to hand you in the name of my Government the accompanying Gold Medal"; "Imperial Academy of Science of Russia," to Maury, 29 December 1855: "its high esteem for your scientific labors in the domain of astronomy, has elected you its corresponding member"; In Box 6 of the same collection see also William Marcy, U.S. Department of State, to Maury, no date, "transmitting to you . . . a Gold Medal which His Majesty the King of the Netherlands has been pleased to confer upon you in consideration of your services to science"; Letter from Legation of Denmark in Philadelphia, 11 November 1856 to Maury: another commendation.

75. Maximillian to Matthew Maury, 2 December 1860, Box 10, **Matthew Maury Papers,** *Library of Congress.* See also "Ferdinand Maximilian, Arch Duke of Austria," to Matthew Maury, 10 December

1857, **Matthew Maury Papers,** *Virginia Military Institute.*

76. A. Mathieu, Paris, to Matthew Maury, 24 February 1860, in Ibid., J. G. de Roulhac Hamilton, ed., **Volume 5, 1973,** 151–152: France awards him a "Gold Medal."

77. Matthew Maury to Maximilian, 10 November 1863, Box 19, **Matthew Maury Papers,** *Library of Congress.*

78. Letter to Matthew Maury, 25 August 1865, Box 23, **Matthew Maury Papers,** *Library of Congress.*

79. Matthew Maury to "My Dear Children," 1 March 1866, **Matthew Maury Papers,** *Virginia Military Institute.*

80. Matthew Maury to Corbin, 21 June 1870, **Matthew Maury Papers,** *Virginia Military Institute.*

81. **London Telegraph,** 25 February 1873.

82. Charles Mial Dustin, "The Knights of the Golden Circle: The Story of the Pacific Coast Secessionists," **Pacific Monthly,** 26 (November 1911): 495–504, 495.

83. Ibid., Manisha Sinha, **The Counterrevolution of Slavery,** 137.

NOTES TO CHAPTER 7

1. Ibid., Joseph Dorsey, **Slave Traffic in the Age of Abolition,** 210.

2. Ibid., David R. Murray, **Odious Commerce,** 304. See also Ibid., David Eltis, **Economic Growth and the Ending of the Trans-Atlantic Slave Trade,** 216: "In 1856 a group of old Brazilian slave traders now involved in the Cuban trade made the last recorded attempt to introduce slaves from Africa into Brazil." See Warren Howard, **American Slavers and the Federal Law, 1837–1862,** Berkeley: University of California Press, 1963, 46: "by 1851 the Brazilian slave trade was vanishing, never to revive." But see Report from Rio de Janeiro, 4 March 1853, FO 128/48, *Public Records Office–Kew Gardens:* "worry" expressed that "two slavers from the coast of Africa were daily expected to arrive and

land their slaves to the northward. . . . apprehensive of a resuscitation of slave dealing enterprises"; Letter from Rio, 5 February 1853, FO 128/48: "a person who has given much useful information to [me]" about the slave trade says "a North American brig, whose name has not transpired, was chartered by the agents of Thomas Costa Ramos, now a fugitive from this country for slave trading . . . and that she sailed after taking a crew and water on board . . . for the coast of Africa intending to engage in the forbidden traffic"; Letter from Rio, 14 February 1853, FO128/48: "the fact of a North American brig fitted out for [trade] in port of Montevideo"; B. F. Hallett, Office of U.S. Attorney-Massachusetts, to William Marcy, 5 January 1857, Record Group 59, Roll 1, **Despatches from U.S. Consuls in Bahia**: "the schooner Mary E. Smith . . . was fitted out for the slave trade in Boston and escaped tho warrants figured against her. . . . she went direct to Africa, took her cargo of slaves and was captured by the Brazilian government"; Edmund Gabriel, Luanda, Angola, to Earl of Malmesbury, 10 October 1858, FO541/1, *Public Records Office–Kew Gardens*: "Dr. Saturnino de Souza e Oliveira, the Brazilian Consul General . . . received intelligence that some parties here are forming a design to introduce slaves into the Brazils by landing them in Guayana [sic] and afterwards removing them overland to Para and the other provinces in the north of that country." Edmund Gabriel to Earl of Malmesbury, 15 April 1859, FO541/2, *Public Records Office*: More rumors of a plan for "introduction of slaves into the northern provinces of the Brazils, by way of Guiana." Edmund Gabriel to Lord Russell, 29 September 1859, FO541/2: "The Brazilian subject Francisco Antonio Flores of whose connection with the slave trade in this province" is well known, returned to Luanda. He had been "expelled" in 1854 by the Portuguese. He was "thoroughly skilled in the art of corrupting all the authorities around him. . . . notorious not only as a slave trader but as the chief instigator of that Traffic on this part of the coast"; a "guest of Flores" and accompanying him was "Senhor Joaquim Guedes de Carvalho Menzes" who had served as "Arbitrator" on slave trade cases. See also Rear Admiral Fred Grey to Secretary of Admiralty, 21 March 1859, FO541/2: "I have no means of judging whether it is possible that any [slavers] may have landed in any part of the Brazilian territory."

3. Christopher Lloyd, The Navy and the Slave Trade: The Suppression of the African Slave Trade in the Nineteenth Century, London: Frank Cass, 1968, 179.

4. Philip S. Foner, **Business & Slavery: The New York Merchants and the Irrepressible Conflict**, Chapel Hill: University of North Carolina Press, 1941, 164. See also David A. Ross, "The Career of Domingo Martinez in the Bight of Benin, 1833–1864," **Journal of African History**, 6 (Number 1, 1965): 70–90, 87: "One of the most important of these 'new' [slave] dealers was J.A. Machado, of New York, who in 1856 sent out a relative, Samuel da Costa [Soares], to organize his shipments of slaves. The position of the old traders as middle men in the trade was destroyed." See also Letter from New York to Thomas R. dos Santos, 28 December 1858, [translation], Correspondence of the Consul General in New York, 1839–1888, A28, M8, Torre 4, Piso Ensentell 6, *Archivo Histórico-Diplomático, Ministério dos Negocios Estrangeiros–Lisbon*: "I had no 'trouble' in the proper acceptation of the word when the Martinho de Mello was about to sail on suspicion of her being in the slave trade. . . . the vessel alluded to was about to engage in the slave trade, she was boarded before leaving the wharf by the Deputy Marshall," which was an "annoyance"; the "visit of such an unnecessary and utterly uncalled for character. . . . I am too well known in this city to suffer in reputation."

5. **New York Times**, 9 March 1857; see also **New York Times**, 28 June 1856. **New York Times**, 15 July 1857.

6. New York Herald, 15 August 1859: Mandingoes "as slaves for general work" were "considered superior to the other tribes. The best agricultural laborers are to be found among the Congoes. . . . there is a tribe called the Carobali who appear to have a higher intellectual organization than either of those named . . . they are said to make capital peddlers and traders and for this reason they are employed at such occupations in cities and towns"; they supplied a "large majority of the water sellers of Havana and other cities."

7. See Anne Farrow, et al., Complicity: How the North Promoted, Prolonged, and Profited from Slavery, New York: Ballantine, 2005, 125, 124.

8. See William McBlair, to Isaac Toucey, Secretary of the Navy, 18 December 1857, in U.S. Congress. House. 36th Congress, 2nd Session. Ex. Doc. 7. African Slave Trade. Message from the President of the United States. 6 December 1860. *New York Historical Society.*

9. Ibid., David S. Heidler, Pulling the Temple Down, 81.

10. Dickinson, Hill & Co., Account Book, 1855–1858, Octavo, Volume 3, Slavery in the U.S. Collection, *American Antiquarian Society.* In same collection see also Letter to Mr. Stokes, 12 February 1861, Box 1, Folder 8: "there was one man sold here today for $1350." See also Isabel Howell, "John Armfield of Beersheba Springs," Tennessee Historical Quarterly, 2 (March 1943, March-June 1944): 3–60, 5: this major trader "handled thousands of black Africans" though his "letters and records seem to have been systematically destroyed."

11. Weekly Herald, circa 1858, Box 1, Folder 4, Henry Wise Papers, *Peabody Essex Museum.*

12. Ibid., Manisha Sinha, The Counter-revolution of Slavery, 142, 143, 149.

13. William K. Scarborough, ed., The Diary of Edmund Ruffin, Volume 2, Baton Rouge: Louisiana State University Press, 1972, 67, 285.

14. James K. Greer, Louisiana Politics, 1845–1861, Baton Rouge: Louisiana State University Press, 1930, 191.

15. Betty L. Mitchell, Edmund Ruffin: A Biography, Bloomington: Indiana University Press, 1981, 124.

16. Ibid., Eric H. Walther, The Fire-Eaters, 284.

17. William O. Scroggs, Filibusters and Financiers: The Story of William Walker and His Associates, New York: Macmillan, 1916, 212.

18. James Carson Jamison, With Walker in Nicaragua or Reminiscences of an Officer of the American Phalanx, Columbia, Missouri: E. W. Stephens, 1909, 99; see also General William Walker, The War in Nicaragua, Mobile: S. H. Goetzel & Co., 1860, 262.

19. Robert G. Harper, "An Argument Against the Policy of Re-opening the African Slave Trade," Atlanta: C. R. Hanleiter, 1858, P11003, *Western Reserve Historical Society–Cleveland.*

20. The Campaign Union, 16 October 1860.

21. Reports, circa 1859, H1470, 0046/04, *Ministerio de Asuntos Exteriores–Madrid*: Note was taken of the 31 August 1859 New York Daily News which contained an address of Jefferson Davis with the headline, "Slavery and the Slave Trade defended. . . . Cuba a necessity." There was grave concern in Madrid about this latter point.

22. Report from Spanish Consul in Galveston, 11 January 1856, H1890, *Ministerio de Asuntos Exteriores–Madrid*: "constituye a aquella ciudad en uno de los centros mas activos de conspiracion permanente contra Cuba."

23. De Bow's Review, 1 October 1860.

24. James Oakes, The Ruling Race: A History of American Slaveholders, New York: Norton, 1998, 231.

25. Weekly Herald, circa 1858, Box 1, Folder 4, Henry Wise Papers, *Peabody Essex Museum.*

26. Henry J. Raymond, "Disunion and Slavery: A Series of Letters to W. L. Yancey

of Alabama," New York, 1861, *American Antiquarian Society.*

27. Speech by Henry Wilson, 21 May 1860, 973.7111 A75, *Peabody Essex Museum.* See also Rev. J. Leighton Wilson, D.D., "The Foreign Slave Trade. Can it be Revived without Violating the Most Sacred Principles of Honor, Humanity and Religion," July 1859, 973.7111 W74.3, *Peabody Essex Museum.*

28. South Carolina. General Assembly. Report of the Special Committee on Slavery and the Slave Trade. Columbia: 1857. E438/S721. *Virginia Historical Society–Richmond.*

29. Report of Committee of General Assembly, circa 1856, Item 03233, Series 165005, *South Carolina State Archives–Columbia.* See also Emerson Etheridge, "The Revival of the African Slave Trade," Delivered in the House of Representatives, 21 February 1857, 973.7111, A75, *Peabody Essex Museum.* See also Frederick Law Olmsted, **The Cotton Kingdom,** New York: Modern Library, 1984, 479.

30. Report of Committee of General Assembly, 1856, Item 00096, Series 165005, *South Carolina State Archives.*

31. Report of Committee of General Assembly, circa 1858, Item 03846, Series 165005, *South Carolina State Archives.*

32. **Savannah Daily Morning News,** 11 October 1858.

33. **Savannah Daily Morning News,** 23 November 1858.

34. **Savannah Daily Morning News,** 25 May 1859.

35. **Savannah Daily Morning News,** 9 March 1860.

36. **Savannah Daily Morning News,** 12 May 1860.

37. **Savannah Daily Morning News,** 19 May 1860.

38. Joe Gray Taylor, "The Foreign Slave Trade in Louisiana after 1808," **Louisiana History,** 1 (Number 1, Winter 1960): 36–43, 40.

39. **New York Times,** 16 May 1854.

40. Harvey Wish, "The Revival of the African Slave Trade in the United States, 1856–1860," **Mississippi Valley Historical Review,** 27 (Number 4, March 1941): 569–588, 572, 581, 582.

41. Republican Association of Washington, Under the Direction of the Congressional Republican Executive Committee, Tract No. IV, "The Slave Trade," 1859, P7638, *Western Reserve Historical Society.*

42. R. W. Russell to "My Dear Sir," 30 September 1856, [translation]: Correspondence of Legation & Consulates of Portugal in the U.S., 1852–1867, *Archivo Histórico-Diplomático, Ministério dos Negocios Estrangeiros–Lisbon.*

43. Letter from Clarence Stanton, Maysville, Kentucky, 25 July 1859, [translation]: Correspondence of Legation & Consulates of Portugal in the U.S., 1852–1867: He asked Portugal's Consul General in New York if he could "permit a native of the United States to hold a position either in the Navy or Army of Portugal. I am very desirous of entering into the service of Portugal. . . . I am the son of R. H. Stanton, late a member of the House of Representatives from Kentucky, I am nineteen years of age."

44. J. A. Thomas to John Gillmer, U.S. Consul, Bahia, 15 April 1856, in Ibid., Ex. Doc. 7, **African Slave Trade. Message from the President of the United States.**

45. B. F. Hallett to William Marcy, 5 January 1857, in Ibid., Ex. Doc. 7.

46. William Marcy to John McKeon, 3 October 1856, in Ibid., Ex. Doc. 7. In same document see Report from Charles Wise of the Royal Navy, Congo, 23 August 1858: "flagrant prostitution of the American flag to cover slave trading transactions. . . . a brig called the 'Charlotte' of New York . . . belonged to C. J. Figaniere of New York . . . then sold to Messrs. Cunha Reis of New York (the greatest slave dealer on the coast). . . . an advertisement shall appear in the New York papers to the effect that this very vessel has landed a cargo of ground nuts and oil at that port. The next case is the 'Venus' bark of 246 tons, belonging to George Butler of New Orleans," now in Congo, "a slaver"—he

was "naturalized," a "native of Hamburgh."

47. Report from Nicholas Pike, 12 March 1857, in Ibid., Ex. Doc. 7.

48. Commander Charles Wise to Sir. F. Grey, 6 August 1858, FO541/1, *Public Records Office–Kew Gardens*. See also "Register of Suspected Slavers," 1860, Cuba, FO312/30, *Public Records Office*: Many hailed from New York, New Orleans, Key West, Galveston, Boston, Philadelphia, with some traveling to Montevideo, Rio de Janeiro, Pensacola, Mobile. A typical route was "from N. Orleans for Havana . . . thence to St. Paul de Loanda." See also Edmund Gabriel, Luanda, to Lord Russell, 1 September 1859, FO541/2: "The barque 'Laura' which was dispatched from New Orleans by the firm of Pratts, Pujol & Co. in June last on a slave-trading expedition under Mexican colors" was captured; they had thought that the Mexican flag "would cover their crime in the same manner as that of the United States."

49. Richard S. Coxe, L.L.D., Counsellor at Law, Washington, D.C., "The Present State of the African Slave Trade," Washington, D.C.: Lemuel Towers, 1858, from *De Bow's Review*, November 1858, P5142, *Western Reserve Historical Society–Cleveland*.

50. Report from D. H. Hamilton, U.S. Marshal, South Carolina, 10 February 1860, Record Group 48, Roll 3, **Records of the Department of Interior,** *National Archives and Records Administration–College Park, Maryland*: "informed that a slaver . . . will be brought into that port if captured. Asks for authority to place the African in Ft. Sumner"; in same file see D. H. Hamilton to President Buchanan, 10 February 1860: if Africans arrive as "cargo . . . that instant arrangements should be made to remove them and return them to the coast of Africa—not that they will not be quite safe in my custody but because a long stay here keeps up an excitement and we have not the 'yellow fever' as a guard from the presence of idle and curious persons." On same Roll, see Letter from 48

Exchange Place, New York City, 6 March 1860: "I have just been informed . . . that during the night of the 24th February last about 1100 slaves were landed on the coast of Florida."

51. To U.S. Department of State, 22 August 1860, Record Group 48, Roll 3, **Records of the Department of Interior.** On same Roll see Moses Kelly to U.S. President, 28 February 1861: "in October last" a slaver with "694 Africans" and another with "about 616" were captured by U.S. vessels and taken to Liberia. See also Letter to "Agency for Recaptured Africans," 16 October 1860: A ship in New York City with "694 recaptured Africans on board" will be sent to Liberia, along with the "1400" on the " 'Storm King' " and " 'Erie.' " See also William C. Burke to Ralph R. Gurley, 31 August 1860, *G. W. Blunt Library–Mystic, Connecticut.*

52. Letter to "Agency for Recaptured Africans," 16 October 1860, in Ibid., Roll 3, **Records of the Department of Interior.**

53. Report, 17 July 1860, Roll 5, **Records of the Department of Interior.** See also U.S. Congress. Senate. 38th Congress, 1st Session. Ex. Doc. No. 44, **Message from the President of the United States. Relative to the Capture of the Slaver Wildfire on the Coast of Cuba, by Lieutenant Craven, of the United States Steamer Mohawk.** 19 May 1860.973.7111 B91, *Peabody Essex Museum*: This ship with 507 Negroes on board was sent to Key West. Madrid monitored these events in Florida: See Reports, circa May 1860, H1470, 0046/04, *Ministerio de Asuntos Exteriores–Madrid.*

54. Ibid., William K. Scarborough, ed., **The Diary of Edmund Ruffin, Volume 1,** 427, 10 June 1860.

55. Letter from E. E. Blackburn, U.S. Marshal, Monticello, Florida, 25 December 1858, Roll 6, **Records of the Department of Interior:** "schooner . . . has been on our coast lately selecting a suitable place to land a cargo of Africans." See also Henry Perry, River Congo, to Edmund Gabriel, Luanda, 2 May 1859, FO541/2,

Public Records Office–Kew Gardens: A U.S. ship from Jacksonville was "detained" on the South Coast of Africa then let go; "newspapers were also found on board containing accounts of indignation meetings held at Jacksonville, consequent of her detection by the authorities."

56. Report from Howell Cobb, 3 March 1858, in Ibid., Ex. Doc. 7.

57. Report from Howell Cobb, 22 May 1858, in Ibid., Ex. Doc. 7.

58. New York Times, 17 August 1860.

59. Letter from James Roosevelt, 22 August 1860, Roll 5, Records of the Department of Interior.

60. Report, 17 October 1860, Roll 3, Records of the Department of Interior.

61. Report, 31 October 1860, Roll 3, Records of the Department of Interior.

62. Ronald T. Takaki, A Pro-Slavery Crusade: The Agitation to Reopen the African Slave Trade, New York: Free Press, 1971, 219, 220.

63. Charles W. Thomas, Adventures and Observations of the West Coast of Africa and its Islands, New York: Derby & Jackson, 1860, 321.

64. Ibid., Charles W. Thomas, 324, 325. See also Journal of Thomas A. Dornin, 1860–1861, *Huntington Library.*

65. Robert Edgar Conrad, World of Sorrow: The African Slave Trade to Brazil, Baton Rouge: Louisiana State University Press, 1986, 142.

66. See Edmund Gabriel to Lord Russell, 25 February 1860, FO 541/3, *Public Records Office–Kew Gardens*:

67. Lord Lyons to Lewis Cass, 5 December 1859, in Ibid., Ex. Doc.7. In same document see also Lyons to Cass, 3 December 1859. See also Lyons to Cass, 23 May 1859.

68. Letter from Andrew Boyd Cummings, 4 October 1857, Andrew Boyd Cummings Papers, U.S. *Naval Academy–Annapolis.*

69. Letter from Andrew Boyd Cummings, circa 1857, Andrew Boyd Cummings Papers.

70. Letter from Andrew Boyd Cummings, 29 November 1858, Andrew Boyd Cummings Papers.

71. Commodore George Eugene Belknap, ed., Letters of Captain George Hamilton Perkins, USN, Concord, New Hampshire: Ira Evans, 1886, 33, 34, 39, 224–225.

72. Letter to U.S. Navy, 20 April 1857, William McBlair Collection, *Mariners' Museum–Newport News, Virginia.*

73. William McBlair to "my dear wife," 16 November 1857, William McBlair Papers.

74. Report from William McBlair, 23 September 1857, in Ibid., Ex. Doc. 7.

75. Mrs. Charles E. B. Russell, General Rigby, Zanzibar and the Slave Trade with Journals and Dispatches, London: Allen & Unwin, 1935, 196, 175.

76. Letter, 15 October 1860, Box 31, Folder 4, Kimball Family Papers, *Peabody Essex Museum.*

77. Letter, 7 September 1853, Box 27, Folder 2, Kimball Family Papers. "I have done nearly $4000 worth of trade at this place with one man about a $1000 in cash & the rest in 2 months payable in oils. He is an Italian. . . . I sold him the remaining cloth I had on hand, also the tobacco."

78. Letter, 4 September 1855, Box 27, Folder 2, Kimball Family Papers.

79. Letter, 27 November 1855, Box 27, Folder 2, Kimball Family Papers.

80. Letter, March 1856, Box 27, Folder 3, Kimball Family Papers.

81. Letter, 5 March 1859, Box 27, Folder 4, Kimball Family Papers.

82. Letter, 9 June 1859, Box 27, Folder 4, Kimball Family Papers.

83. Charles Rich to "Dear Sir," 7 May 1856, Box 1, Folder 8, Robert Brookhouse Papers, *Peabody Essex Museum.*

84. Letter from Robert Cunningham, 17 July 1859, Box 1, Folder 9, Robert Brookhouse Papers.

85. John Coker to "Friend Augusto,"22 October 1859, Box 1, Folder 9, Robert Brookhouse Papers.

86. Letter to A. E. Govea, Esq., 19 April 1860, Box 1, Folder 9, Robert Brookhouse

Papers: "I have only one American flag, therefore can not send you any."

87. Letter from Simon Stodder, 6 November 1856, Box 1, Folder 2, **Simon Stodder Papers**, *Peabody Essex Museum*.

88. Clipping, circa 1858, [translation]: Correspondence of the Mixed Commission at the Cape of Good Hope, 1853–1859, *Archivo Histórico-Diplomático, Ministério dos Negocios Estrangeiros–Lisbon*.

89. Norman Robert Bennett, "Americans in Zanzibar: 1845–1864," **Essex Institute Historical Collections**, 97 (Number 1, 1961): 31–56, 53.

90. Letter to George Abbott, 13 March 1857, Box 1, Folder 1, **Charles Ward Papers**, *Peabody Essex Museum*.

91. George Howe, "The Last Ship," 1860, Collection 503, #17, **Slave Manuscript Series**, *Tulane University–New Orleans*.

92. Arthur Lyons, Galveston, to the Earl of Malmesbury, 21 December 1858, FO701/27, *Public Records Office–Kew Gardens*.

93. Consul Thomas Miller to "My Lord," 26 July 1856, FO84/992, *Public Records Office*.

94. Report from U.K. Consul in the Azores, 12 November 1859, FO84/1082, *Public Records Office*.

95. Ibid., **General Rigby, Zanzibar and the Slave Trade**, 198.

96. "Memo on State of Affairs of the Slave Trade," 23 June 1859, FO84/1082, *Public Records Office*.

97. Joseph T. Crawford to Lord Russell, 5 February 1861, FO541/5, *Public Records Office*.

98. Joseph T. Crawford to Earl of Malmesbury, 3 September 1858, FO541/1, *Public Records Office*. See W. Edmonstone to Rear-Admiral Sir H. Keppel, Sierra Leone, 24 March 1861, FO541/5, *Public Records Office*.

99. Edmund Gabriel to Earl of Clarendon, 25 February 1858, FO541/3, *Public Records Office*.

100. Charles Wise to Fred Grey, 20 January 1859, FO541/1, *Public Records Office*. See also G. Skelton to Earl of Malmesbury, 2 March 1859, FO541/2. See also Rear Admiral Fred Grey to Secretary of Admiralty, 21 March 1859, FO541/2. See also G. Skelton to Lord Russell, 3 February 1860, FO541/2, *Public Records Office*.

101. Edmund Gabriel, Luanda, to Lord Russell, 20 September 1859, FO541/2, *Public Records Office*.

102. H. V. Huntley to Lord Russell, 18 November 1860, FO541/5, *Public Records Office*. See also Edmund Gabriel to Earl of Malmesbury, 15 April 1859, FO541/2: "The whole of this piratical trade on the African coast is now carried on under the disguise of the flag of the United States," even "Spanish vessels" were employing this banner and this had "entirely frustrated" London.

103. H. V. Huntley to Lord Russell, 5 October 1860, FO541/4, *Public Records Office*.

104. H. V. Huntley to Lord Russell, 31 October 1860, FO541/4, *Public Records Office*.

105. Letter from Luanda, 4 September 1855, Caixa de Papeis Relativos a Escravatura, *Archivo Histórico-Diplomático, Ministério dos Negocios Estrangeiros–Lisbon*: Re: a U.S. barque, the "Seamen," sailing for St. Thomas with ten enslaved Africans.

106. Letter from the Governor General of Mozambique, 12 October 1855, Caixa de Papeis Relativos a Escravatura.

107. Letter from Antonio Pedro de Carvalho, State Secretary of Foreign Affairs, 18 August 1856, Caixa de Papeis Relativos a Escravatura.

108. J. A. Thomas to John Dobbin, 20 June 1856, in Ibid., Ex. Doc. 7. In same document see also Report from Thomas Crabbe, U.S. Navy, from Porto Praya, 18 April 1856.

109. Report from John G. Willis, 9 January 1857, in Ibid., Ex. Doc. 7.

110. Report from John G. Willis, 29 January 1859, in Ibid., Ex. Doc. 7. In the

same document see Lord Lyons to Lewis Cass, 27 May 1859.

111. Ibid., **General Rigby, Zanzibar and the Slave Trade,** 197.

112. Fred Grey to Admiralty, 11 February 1858, FO541/1, *Public Records Office–Kew Gardens.*

113. Report from British Consul in Zanzibar, 4 January 1861, FO54/18, *Public Records Office.*

114. Lt. Col. Rigby to Sir C. Wood, 28 August 1860, in Ibid., **British Parliamentary Papers: Correspondence Relative to the Slave Trade, Volume 64, Number 47.**

115. Report from Joseph T. Crawford, Havana, 5 February 1859, FO541/2, *Public Records Office.*

116. Report from C. J. Helm, U.S. Consul in Cuba, 17 February 1860: "the slave trade has been for some time upon the increase on the *eastern* coast of Africa and that several large vessels under the American flag have shipped cargoes of slaves there . . . there are now indications of an intention on the part of the slave traders to resort still more extensively to the *eastern* coast. This is doubtless to be accounted for the recent reinforcement of the United States Squadron on the western coast . . . on the *eastern* coast of Africa there are no United States cruisers" [emphasis-original].

117. Charles Wise to Admiralty, 16 May 1859, FO541/2, *Public Records Office.*

118. Report of John G. Willis, 19 November 1859, in Ibid., Ex. Doc. 7.

119. Charles Wise to F. Grey, 20 July 1859, FO541/2, *Public Records Office.*

120. See Lord Lyons to Lewis Cass, 4 May 1860, in Ibid., Ex. Doc. 7: "A brig called the 'Delicia' fully equipped for the slave trade but without colors or papers to denote her nationality, was captured off [Cabinda]" by a U.S. ship. Yet ship and crew were "discharged from custody in the United States, on the ground that there is no act of Congress under which either vessel or crew can be prosecuted in the courts of law."

121. Lewis Cass to Lord Lyons, 3 April 1860, in Ibid., **British Parliamentary Papers: Correspondence Relative to the Slave Trade, Volume 64, Number 47.**

122. Ibid., Andrew C. McLaughlin, Lewis Cass, 336.

NOTES TO CHAPTER 8

1. Harral E. Landry, "Slavery and the Slave Trade in Atlantic Diplomacy, 1850–1861," **Journal of Southern History,** 27 (Number 2, May 1961): 184–207, 185, 192, 206, 207.

2. Willis D. Boyd, "The American Colonization Society and the Slave Recaptives of 1860–1861: An Early Example of United States–African Relations," **Journal of Negro History,** 47 (Number 2, April 1962): 108–126, 110. See also D. H. Hamilton to Lewis Cass, 24 November 1860, Record Group 48, Roll 3, **Records of the Department of Interior:** A "vessel was brought into the port of Charleston . . . as a slaver captured upon the coast of Africa"; "discontinue proceedings" since it was "unlawfully seized. . . . she together with her cargo should be delivered to the Spanish Consul."

3. Betty M. Kuyk, **African Voices in the African American Heritage,** Bloomington: Indiana University Press, 2003, 20, 22: "Amelia Island was such a choice location that that notorious pirate Luis Aury moved his headquarters there from Galveston, Texas in 1817. Within two months he sent 1000 Africans inland."

4. L. W. Spratt, **The Foreign Slave Trade: The Source of Political Power—of Material Progress, of Social Integrity and of Social Emancipation to the South,** Charleston: Steam Power Press, 1858, 21–22, 25, 26.

5. Cited in Joaquim Nabuco, **Abolitionism: The Brazilian Antislavery Struggle,** Urbana: University of Illinois Press, 1977, 121–122.

6. Ibid., David Eltis, **Economic Growth and the Ending of the Trans-Atlantic Slave Trade,** 210.

7. Report from Gabriel G. Tassara, Spanish Minister in Washington, circa

1860, Correspondencia entre La Capitania General de Cuba y La Primera Secretaria de Estado Sobre La Introduccion de Esclavos (1817–1873), Legajo 8048, *Archivo Historico Nacional–Madrid.*

8. Hon. J. B. Clary, "Speech on our Foreign Policy Delivered in the House of Representatives, February 7, 1859," Washington, D.C.: Lemuel Towers, 1859, F1438 C345, *New York Historical Society.*

9. Referring to the secessionist states by their chosen name is not intended to confer retrospective diplomatic recognition on this illegal breakaway formation.

10. See Dean B. Mahin, **One War at a Time: The International Dimensions of the American Civil War**, Washington, D.C.: Brassey's, 1999, 17.

11. Judah Benjamin to John Mason, 15 January 1863, in Allan Nevins, ed., **The Messages and Papers of Jefferson Davis and the Confederacy Including Diplomatic Correspondence, 1861–1865**, New York: Chelsea House, 1966, 403–404.

12. Judah P. Benjamin to L. Q. C. Lamar, 15 January 1863, in **The African Slave Trade: The Secret Purpose of the Insurgents to Revive It. . . . Judah P. Benjamin's Intercepted Instructions to L. Q. C. Lamar**, Philadelphia: C. Sherman, Son & Co. Printers, 1863, 244–322, *Huntington Library.*

13. **Proceedings and Debates of the 1864 Constitutional Convention**, Volume 0102, Volume 1, Debates 0311, *Maryland State Archives–Annapolis.*

14. Consul Robert Bunch to Lord Russell, 8 March 1861, in Ibid., British Parliamentary Papers: Correspondence Relative to the Slave Trade, Volume 64, Number 47.

15. "Folio 1," 1 January 1853, H1879, *Ministerio de Asuntos Exteriores–Madrid.*

16. See Correspondence from Spanish Consul in Charleston, 5 November 1851, 15 August 1850, 31 October 1849, 15 October 1849, 24 September 1846, H179, *Ministerio de Asuntos Exteriores–Madrid.* In same file see also "Special Report" on "Confederate States of America Treasury

Department Register's Office Richmond, Va. July 31, 1861," re: tariffs sent to Spanish Consul in Charleston.

17. A. G. McGrath to Spanish Consul, 12 February 1861, H1879, *Ministerio de Asuntos Exteriores–Madrid.*

18. See P. J. Rost to R. M. T. Hunter, 21 March 1862, Report and **New York Herald,** clipping, no date, reprinting Rost letter, H1471, 1862/1864, *Ministerio de Asuntos Exteriores–Madrid.*

19. Records Concerning the Cuban Expedition, 1850–1851, Record Group 48, Entry 142, Box 1, **Records of the Department of Interior,** *National Archives and Records Administration–College Park, Maryland.*

20. Report, 13 August 1859, [translation]: Legation of Spain in London, *Ministerio de Asuntos Exteriores–Madrid.*

21. Samuel Flagg Bemis, **John Quincy Adams and the Foundations of American Foreign Policy,** New York: Knopf, 1965, 409.

22. Report of Meeting, 1 June 1849, FO312/2, *Public Records Office–Kew Gardens.* See also **National Era,** 8 July 1852. Earlier the **National Era** of 11 September 1851, cited the **British and Foreign Anti-Slavery Reporter** to a similar effect.

23. D. Trumbull and A. R. Hamilton to Lord Palmerston, 7 July 1849, FO312/2, *Public Records Office.*

24. Ibid., Proceedings and Debates of the 1864 Constitutional Convention, Volume 0102, Volume 1, Debates 0718.

25. Ibid., J. B. Clary, 1859.

26. I. G. Collins, **Scinde & the Punjab, The Gems of India, in Respect to their Vast and Unparalleled Capabilities of Supplanting the Slave States of America in the Cotton Markets of the World: Or an Appeal to the English Nation on Behalf of its Great Cotton Interest, Threatened with Inadequate Supplies of the Raw Material,** Manchester: A. Ireland and Co., 1858, 11, 12.

27. I. G. Collins, **An Essay in Favour of the Colonization of the North and Northwest Provinces of India, with Regard to the Question of Increased Cotton Supply and**

its Bearing on the Slave Trade, London: W. H. Allen, 1858, 9; see also By an Indian Civil Servant, "Usurers and Ryots: An Answer to the Question 'Why Does Not India Produce More Cotton?'" London: Smith, Elder and Co., 1856, *British Library–London*.

28. David Brion Davis, "Impact of the French and Haitian Revolution," in David P. Geggus, ed., **The Impact of the Haitian Revolution in the Atlantic World**, Columbia: University of South Carolina Press, 2002, 3–9, 5.

29. David P. Geggus, "Epilogue," in Ibid., **The Impact of the Haitian Revolution in the Atlantic World**, 274–252, 251, 247.

30. Madrid took note of an 1843 "proclamation" from Haiti that reminded all that "'our Fathers heroically gained their liberty and country on the field of battle by making those bite the dust, who for years held them in a criminal and cruel slavery.'" See **Jamaica Despatch,** 19 April 1843, H2523/003, 1862, *Ministerio de Asuntos Exteriores–Madrid*. See also Report, 23 March 1843, Del Consulado en Jamaica al Primer Secretario, Legado H2523/003, File: "Haiti," *Ministerio de Asuntos Exteriores–Madrid*: Haiti is said to be in a state of revolution, which was of great relevance to Cuba and Puerto Rico.

31. Ibid., **Jamaica Despatch,** 13 April 1843, H2523/003, 1862.

32. John V. Lombardi, **The Decline and Abolition of Negro Slavery in Venezuela,** 1820–1854, Westport: Greenwood, 1971, 36.

33. Report from Angel Calderon de la Barca, 8 December 1836, Correspondencia entre La Capitania General de Cuba y La Primera Secretaria de Estado Sobre La Introduccion de Esclavos, 1817–1873, Legado 8036, *Archivo Historico Nacional–Madrid*. Concern was expressed here about the growth of abolitionism in the Northeast U.S. and the prospect of Cuban sugar was considered in light of the development of this crop in Florida and Louisiana.

34. Report and **New York Daily**

Tribune, 27 May 1861, H1470, 0046/04, *Ministerio de Asuntos Exteriores–Madrid*.

35. **British Packet and Argentine News,** 17 January 1857. See also **British Packet and Argentine News,** 3 August 1850. *Biblioteca Nacional de Argentina–Buenos Aires*.

36. Report from Office of the American Colonization Society, 2 September 1835, Oficios, 1862, 233/3/2, *Archivo Histórico do Itamary–Rio de Janeiro*: "The committee . . . was referred to the application of Cavalcante Albuquerque, on behalf of his government, to the American Colonization Society, deciding to know whether said society will consent to receive, protect and accommodate in Liberia, their colony in Africa, such recaptured Africans as may be taken by Brazilian cruisers from such vessels as may be unlawfully carrying them from their native land, and deliver to the society agent in Liberia." See also [translation], Manifesto of the Brazilian Anti-Slavery Society, Rio de Janeiro: Reprinted from the 'Rio News,' 1880, *New York Historical Society.*

37. See John Cell, **The Highest Stage of White Supremacy: The Origins of Segregation in South Africa and the American South,** New York: Cambridge University Press, 1982.

38. **National Era,** 23 September 1847.

39. **National Era,** 17 August 1854.

40. **National Era,** 31 August 1854.

41. **National Era,** 29 June 1854.

42. Ibid., Joaquim Nabuco, Abolitionism, 162.

43. **National Era,** 11 May 1854.

44. **New York Times,** 29 September 1865.

45. **New York Times,** 27 May 1861.

46. **New York Times,** 16 February 1858.

47. See Notes on Richard Meade meeting with the Emperor, 6 July 1861, Group 683, Series I, Box 6, Folder 87, **James Watson Webb Papers,** *Yale University.*

48. James Watson Webb to William Seward, 24 October 1861, in **Papers Relating to Foreign Affairs, Part 2, Communi-**

cated to Congress, 1 December 1862, Washington, D.C.: Government Printing Office, 1862. *National Archives and Records Administration–College Park, Maryland.*

49. Ibid., Proceedings and Debates of the 1864 Constitutional Convention, Volume 0102, Volume 1, Debates 0718.

50. Liberator, 3 February 1860.

51. De Bow's Review, 1 July 1860.

52. Illustrated London News, 22 December 1860.

53. W. D. Christie to Lord Russell, 2 June 1860, in Ibid., British Parliamentary Papers: Correspondence Relative to the Slave Trade, Volume 64, Number 47.

54. Charleston Mercury, 6 December 1861.

55. New York Times, 15 March 1862.

56. New York Times, 9 May 1862, Washington, Oficios, 1863–1864, *Archivo Historico do Itamaraty–Rio de Janeiro.*

57. Translation of Remarks, circa November 1862, in Ibid., British Parliamentary Papers: Correspondence Relative to the Slave Trade, Volume 71, Number 48.

58. Thomas Adamson to William Seward, 12 July 1862, Roll 6, Despatches from U.S. Consuls in Pernambuco, 1817–1906.

59. W. Edmonstone to Rear-Admiral Sir H. Keppel, Sierra Leone, 24 March 1861, FO541/5, *Public Records Office–Kew Gardens.*

60. Letter from Ascension Island to Rear-Admiral Sir B. Walker, 20 July 1861, FO541/5, *Public Records Office.*

61. H. V. Huntley and Edmund Gabriel to Lord Russell, 10 October 1861, FO541/5, *Public Records Office.*

62. H. V. Huntley to Lord Russell, 7 June 1861, FO541/5, *Public Records Office:* "detention of the American brigantine 'Triton' by the U.S. ship 'Constellation' . . . in the River Congo"; it had "slave fittings."

63. H. V. Huntley to Lord Russell, 9 August 1861, FO541/5, *Public Records Office.*

64. W. H. McGrath, Consul, Maranham, Brazil to William Seward, 15 September 1861, FO988I/2097, *Public Records Office.*

65. Lord Lyons to Foreign Office, 26 March 1861, in James J. Barnes and Patience P. Barnes, Private and Confidential Letters from British Ministers in Washington to the Foreign Secretaries in London, 1844–1867, Selinsgrove, Pennsylvania: Susquehanna University Press, 1993, 242.

66. Her Majesty's Commissioners to Earl Russell, 21 November 1861, in British Parliamentary Papers: Correspondence Relative to the Slave Trade, Volume 71, Number 48.

67. Commodore Edmonstone to Rear Admiral Sir B. Walker, 7 November 1861, in Ibid., British Parliamentary Papers: Correspondence Relative to the Slave Trade, Volume 71, Number 48.

68. Lewiston Journal Magazine, 11–14 May 1910, Box 3, Folder, "Slavery/Slave Trade," African Americans in Maine Collection, *Maine Historical Society–Portland.*

69. Ibid., Anne Farrow, et al., Complicity, 123.

70. Maine Sunday Telegram, 15 February 1987.

71. Ibid., Lewiston Journal Magazine, 11–14 May 1910.

72. U.S. States vs. Nathaniel Gordon, U.S. Circuit Court, Southern District, C 1-228a-229b, 1860–1861, *National Archives and Records Administration–New York City.*

73. New York Herald, 21 September 1861.

74. John R. Spears, The American Slave Trade: An Account of Its Origin, Growth and Suppression, New York: Scribner's, 1900, 221. See also New York Times, 21 February 1862; see also Ron Soodalter, Hanging Captain Gordon: The Life and Trial of an American Slave Trader, New York: Atria, 2006.

75. E. Delafield Smith to Caleb Smith, 22 November 1861, Record Group 48, Roll 4, Records of the Department of

Interior, *National Archives and Records Administration–College Park*.

76. Charles H. Jenrich, "An Error in Flag," U.S. *Naval Institute Proceedings*, January 1868, Vertical Files: Nathaniel Gordon, *U.S. Naval Academy–Annapolis*.

77. "Lincoln and the Negro," Box 3, Folder: Slavery/Slave Trade, **African Americans in Maine Collection,** *Maine Historical Society–Portland*.

78. Consul Archibald to Earl Russell, 24 February 1862, in Ibid., **British Parliamentary Papers: Correspondence Relative to the Slave Trade, Volume 71, Number 48.**

79. Ibid., John R. Spears, The American Slave Trade, 221.

80. R. F. Turing to Earl Russell, 16 January 1862, in Ibid., **British Parliamentary Papers: Correspondence Relative to the Slave Trade, Volume 71, Number 48.**

81. Consul Archibald to Earl Russell, 17 November 1862, in Ibid., **British Parliamentary Papers: Correspondence Relative to the Slave Trade, Volume 71, Number 48.**

82. E. Delafield Smith to Caleb Smith, 26 April 1862, in Ibid., **British Parliamentary Papers: Correspondence Relative to the Slave Trade, Volume 71, Number 48.** See also Letter to Caleb Smith, February 1862, Record Group 48, Roll 4, **Records of the Department of Interior:** In New Bedford a "slaver" was "seized" that was "ostensibly fitted for a whaling voyage."

83. William Seward to C. B. Smith, Secretary of Interior, 19 April 1862, Record Group 48, Roll 3, **Records of the Department of Interior.**

84. Robert Murray, U.S. Marshal, New York City, to E. Delafield Smith, 26 November 1861, Record Group 48, Roll 4, **Records of the Department of Interior.**

85. E. Delafield Smith to Caleb Smith, 4 February 1862, in Ibid., **British Parliamentary Papers: Correspondence Relative to the Slave Trade, Volume 71, Number 48.** See also **New York Daily Tribune,** 26 November 1861.

86. W. D. Christie to Earl Russell, 15 November 1862, in Ibid., **British Parlia-**

mentary Papers: Correspondence Relative to the Slave Trade, Volume 71, Number 48.

87. Rear Admiral Sir B. Walker, Simon's Bay to Secretary to the Admiralty, 15 September 1862, in Ibid., **British Parliamentary Papers: Correspondence Relative to the Slave Trade, Volume 71, Number 48.**

88. H. D. Hickley, Commander, to Vice-Admiral Sir A. Milne, 5 June 1862, in Ibid., **British Parliamentary Papers: Correspondence Relative to the Slave Trade, Volume 71, Number 48.**

89. E. Delafield Smith to Caleb Smith, 19 May 1862, Record Group 48, Roll 4, **Records of the Department of Interior.**

90. Letter from Manoel d'Oliviera Lima, 24 March 1862, Papeis Relativos a Escravatura, *Archivo Histórico-Diplomático, Ministério dos Negocios Estrangeiros–Lisbon*.

91. Letter from Arthur Magenis, 23 May 1862, Papeis Relativos a Escravatura.

92. Letter to "Monsieur Le Minister,"20 January 1862, Papeis Relativos a Escravatura.

93. Letter from "Gustav . . . Envoy Extraordinary and Minister Plenipotentiary of Portugal," 21 January 1861, [translation]: Correspondence of the Consul General in New York, 1839–1888, A28, M8, Torre 4 Piso, Ensentell 6, *Archivo Histórico-Diplomático, Ministério dos Negocios Estrangeiros–Lisbon*.

94. Letter from Robert dos Santos, 31 July 1862, Correspondence of the Consul General in New York, 1839–1888.

95. J. de Palma to A. M. da Cunha, 13 October 1865, Correspondence of the Consul General in New York, 1839–1888.

96. H. W. Slocum, Major General-U.S., to General E. D. Townsend, 25 August 1866, [translation]: Legation of Portugal in Washington, Correspondence of the U.S. Government, 1835–1869, A28, M17 Torre 4 Piso Estante 1, 15 *Archivo Histórico-Diplomático, Ministério dos Negocios Estrangeiros–Lisbon*.

97. William Seward to William Figaniere, 25 August 1866, Legation of

Portugal in Washington, Correspondence of the U.S. Government, 1835–1869.

98. Letter from A. M. da Cunha, 13 December 1864, Correspondence of the Consul General in New York, 1839–1888.

99. William Seward to William Figaniere, 26 June 1862, Legation of Portugal in Washington, Correspondence of the U.S. Government, 1835–1869.

100. William Seward to William Figaniere, 28 January 1863, Legation of Portugal in Washington, Correspondence of the U.S. Government, 1835–1869.

101. U.K. Embassy to William Figaniere, 8 November 1862, [translation]: Legation of Portugal in Washington, Correspondence of Foreign Legations and Consulates in the United States, Torre 4 Piso Estante 1, I, A28, M10, *Archivo Histórico-Diplomático, Ministério dos Negocios Estrangeiros–Lisbon.*

NOTES TO CHAPTER 9

1. B. Lindsay to James Watson Webb, January 1862, Group 683, Series I, Box 10, Folder 111, **James Watson Webb Papers,** *Yale University.*

2. J. G. Benton to "My Dear General," 28 February 1862, Group 683, Series I, Box 6, Folder 95, **James Watson Webb Papers.**

3. James Watson Webb to Luther Bradish, 10 October 1838, **Miscellaneous Mss.,** *New York Historical Society.*

4. Hannibal Hamlin to James Watson Webb, 29 November 1862, Box 9, Folder 100, **James Watson Webb Papers.**

5. Excerpt from Leonard Richard, **Gentlemen of Property and Standing,** 26–27, Box 3, **African-Americans in Maine Collection,** *Maine Historical Society.*

6. James L. Crouthamel, **James Watson Webb: A Biography,** Middletown: Wesleyan University Press, 1969, 24, 56, 57, 25–26, 22. See James Watson Webb to C. L. Lazarus, 23 February 1863, Group 683, Series I, Box 10, Folder 111, **James Watson Webb Papers:** "I appointed you acting secretary of the legation; & you presumed upon the fact to introduce into my House a German Jew Pedlar without my sanction" [emphasis-original].

7. Elise Lemire, **'Miscegenation': Making Race in America,** Philadelphia: University of Pennsylvania Press, 2002, 59.

8. Lerone Bennett, **Forced into Glory: Abraham Lincoln's White Dream,** Chicago: Johnson Publishing Company, 2000, 380.

9. Dean B. Mahin, **One War at a Time: The International Dimensions of the American Civil War,** 131, 2.

10. Clipping, circa August 1863, Washington, Oficios, 1863–1864, *Archivo Histórico do Itamaraty–Rio de Janeiro.*

11. Ibid., James L. Crouthamel, 173.

12. Ibid., Dean B. Mahin, 197.

13. Ibid., Najia Aarim-Heriot, **Chinese Immigrants, African Americans and Racial Anxiety in the United States, 1848–1882,** 65, 67, 71, 238.

14. Speech by Hon. Francis Blair of Missouri on the Acquisition of Central America; Delivered in the House of Representatives, 14 January 1858, *Kansas State Historical Society–Topeka.*

15. See [translation] Annex of Despatch Number 209 of the Spanish Legation in Washington, D.C., re: HR 576, 37th Congress, 2nd Session, House of Representatives, Report No. 148, H2523/003, *Ministerio de Asuntos Exteriores–Madrid.*

16. "Outlines of a Plan for Providing a Settlement . . ." September 1824, S10, C2, A1-3, *Archivo General de la Nación–Buenos Aires.*

17. Ibid., Robert E. May, **Manifest Destiny's Underworld,** 153.

18. Ibid., Najia Aarim-Heriot, 47.

19. Ibid., William H. Edwards, **A Voyage up the River Amazon,** 204.

20. Ibid., Lawrence Hill, **Diplomatic Relations Between the United States and Brazil,** 159–160.

21. Bridgett M. Williams, "James Monroe: Consul to Rio, 1863–1869," M.A. thesis, Youngstown State University, 1991, 15, 30, 54, 57.

22. **New York Times,** 28 December 1862.

23. James Watson Webb to William Seward, May 1862, Box 8, Folder 99, **James Watson Webb Papers.** See also N. Andrew Cleven, "Some Plans for Colonizing Liberated Negro Slaves in Hispanic America," **Journal of Negro History,** 11 (Number 1, January 1926): 35–49, 41, 43, 47.

24. "Confidential" undated document, probably from James Watson Webb, Box 8, Folder 99, **James Watson Webb Papers.**

25. Memo from Government of Brazil, circa 8 July 1862, Box 8, Folder 102, **James Watson Webb Papers.**

26. Sir F. W. C. Murdoch to Sir F. Rogers, 14 July 1862, FO5/934, *Public Records Office–Kew Gardens.*

27. Report, 12 August 1862, FO5/934, *Public Records Office.*

28. F. W. C. Murdoch to Sir F. Rogers, 19 August 1862, FO5/934, *Public Records Office.*

29. From Government House, 22 August 1862, FO5/934.

30. Letter from British Honduras, 15 October 1862, FO5/934.

31. Letter from British Honduras, 14 December 1862, FO5/934.

32. Memo, 22 September 1862, FO5/934.

33. Memo, 4 September 1862, FO5/934.

34. To "My Lord," 18 October 1862, FO5/934.

35. Report, 15 September 1862, FO5/934.

36. William Seward to "Sir," 30 September 1862, FO5/934.

37. Report, 18 October 1862, FO5/934.

38. Lord Lyons to "My Lord," 27 January 1863, FO5/934.

39. Lord Lyons to London, 26 December 1862, FO5/934.

40. Lord Lyons to "My Lord," 27 April 1863, FO5/934.

41. Letter to Lord Russell from London Legation in Washington, D.C., 28 September 1862, FO5/934.

42. **Jamaica Guardian,** 18 September 1862, 19 September 1862, FO 5/934.

43. Letter from Lord Lyons, 19 June 1863, FO5/934.

44. Report from [translation]: Consul General of Spain in Haiti, 8 April 1863, H2523/003, *Ministerio de Asuntos Exteriores–Madrid.*

45. Annual Report of President Abraham Lincoln, H1984, *Ministerio de Asuntos Exteriores–Madrid.*

46. William Seward to James Watson Webb, 21 July 1862, Box 8, Folder 103, **James Watson Webb Papers.**

47. Richard Parsons to James Watson Webb, 24 August 1862, Box 9, Folder 105, **James Watson Webb Papers.**

48. William Seward to James Watson Webb, 21 July 1862, in George Baker, ed., **The Works of William Seward: The Diplomatic History of the War for the Union,** Boston: Houghton Mifflin, 1884, 334–337.

49. Ibid., James L. Crouthamel, 174.

50. W. Vredenburg to Capt. Bythesea, 21 December 1863, in **British Parliamentary Papers: Correspondence Relative to the Slave Trade, Volume 66, Number 49.**

51. "Her Majesty's Commissioner to Earl Russell," in Ibid., **British Parliamentary Papers: Correspondence Relative to the Slave Trade, Volume 66, Number 49.**

52. E. M. Archibald, Her Majesty's Judge on the Mixed Commission to Earl Russell, 31 December 1863, in Ibid., **British Parliamentary Papers: Correspondence Relative to the Slave Trade, Volume 66, Number 49.**

53. Commodore Wilmot to Rear Admiral Sir B. Walker, 31 December 1863, in Ibid., **British Parliamentary Papers: Correspondence Relative to the Slave Trade, Volume 66, Number 49.**

54. Report, 21 February 1865, **British Parliamentary Papers: Correspondence Relative to the Slave Trade, Volume 75, Number 50.**

55. Andrew Foote to Gideon Welles, 13 June 1862, **Miscellaneous Mss.,** *New York Historical Society.*

56. "Treaty Between Her Majesty and the United States of America for the Sup-

pression of the African Slave Trade," 7
April 1862, HT1322 G7, *Louisiana State
University–Baton Rouge.*

57. Frederick J. Blue, "Oberlin's James
Monroe: Forgotten Abolitionist," **Civil
War History**, 35 (Number 4, December
1989): 285–301, 285, 286.

58. Catherine M. Rokicky, **James Mon-
roe: Oberlin's Christian Statesman &
Reformer, 1821–1898**, Kent: Kent State
University Press, 2002, 97.

59. Ibid., Bridgett M. Williams, 39.

60. Minister of Justice, Brazil, to Brazilian Legislature, 18 May 1864, in Ibid.,
British Parliamentary Papers: Correspondence Relative to the Slave Trade, Volume
71, Number 48.

61. W. G. Lettsom, U.K. Consul in
Montevideo, to Earl Russell, 22 September
1864, in Ibid., Volume 71, Number 48.

62. James Watson Webb to Marquis
d'Abrantes, 7 March 1863, in Papers
Relating to Foreign Affairs, Accompanying
the Annual Message of the President to the
First Session of the Thirty-Eighth Congress, Part I, Washington, D.C.: Government Printing Office, 1864, *National
Archives and Records Administration–
College Park, Maryland.*

63. See e.g. **Correio Mercantil**, 8
November 1861, 9 November 1861.

64. W. D. Christie to Earl Russell, 26
February 1863, in Ibid., British Parliamentary Papers: Correspondence Relative to
the Slave Trade, Volume 66, Number 49.

65. William B. Wilson to Earl Russell,
30 September 1863, in Ibid., British Parliamentary Papers: Correspondence Relative
to the Slave Trade, Volume 66, Number
49.

66. John V. Crawford, Havana, to Earl
Russell, 14 January 1863, in Ibid., British
Parliamentary Papers: Correspondence Relative to the Slave Trade, Volume 66, Number 49. In same volume see R. Edwards,
Madrid, to Maquis of Miraflores, 2 May
1863: "The 'Island Queen' was fitted out
in the United States at Havana in March
1862 with [U.S.] colors and papers and
was commanded by R. Ducham a noted

slave captain." It was on its way to
Angola. "Mr. Murray" to J. M. Brackenbury, 26 March 1863: Re: capture of a
slaver, "formerly the 'Island Queen' of
Washington" which "changed ownership
at Cadiz." J. M. Brackenbury to Earl Russell, 22 April 1864: This ship was built in
Providence, Rhode Island in 1854.

67. G. Skelton, Judge on Mixed Commission, Sierra Leone, to Earl Russell, 30
September 1863, in Ibid., British Parliamentary Papers: Correspondence Relative
to the Slave Trade, Volume 66, Number
49.

68. J. M. Brackenbury to Earl Russell, 5
February 1863, in Ibid., British Parliamentary Papers: Correspondence Relative to
the Slave Trade, Volume 66, Number 49.

69. Rear Admiral Sir B. Walker to the
Secretary of the Admiralty, 17 November
1863, in Ibid., British Parliamentary
Papers: Correspondence Relative to the
Slave Trade, Volume 66, Number 49.

70. Commander Fred Richards to Commodore Wilmost, 7 July 1864, in ibid.,
British Parliamentary Papers: Correspondence Relative to the Slave Trade, Volume
66, Number 49.

71. See e.g. Commissioner of Customs,
Thomas Freemantle and J. Goulburn to
Lords Commissioner of the Treasury, 25
July 1863, in Ibid., British Parliamentary
Papers: Correspondence Relative to the
Slave Trade, Volume 66, Number 49:
Britain captures a New York ship "Mar-
quita" near Luanda with "471 slaves on
board; the principal was "of Spanish or
Portuguese birth but is a naturalized citizen
of the United States of America and resides
in New York." He was "named Lima
Vianni or Viana."

72. Edmund Gabril and H. V. Huntley,
28 February 1862, in Ibid., British Parliamentary Papers: Correspondence Relative
to the Slave Trade, Volume 71, Number
48.

73. **New York Times**, 19 December
1863.

74. Thomas Adamson, Jr., Consul, to
William Seward, 14 November 1864,

Record Group 59, Roll 7, **Despatches from U.S. Consuls in Pernambuco.**

75. William Richard Williams to William Seward, 10 August 1862, Record Group 59, Roll 2, **Despatches from U.S. Consuls in Para.**

76. **Savannah Daily Morning News,** 10 January 1862.

77. William Seward to James Watson Webb, 13 April 1862, Box 8, Folder 97, **James Watson Webb Papers.**

78. **New York Times,** 17 November 1864.

79. Biography of Raphael Semmes, no date, Box 4, Folder 70, **Hughes-Folsom Papers,** *Georgia Historical Society–Savannah.*

80. Edward Boykin, **Ghost Ship of the Confederacy: The Story of the Alabama and her Captain,** New York: Funk & Wagnalls, 1957, 298, 299. See also Charles Robinson III, **Shark of the Confederacy: The Story of the CSS Alabama,** Annapolis: Naval Institute Press, 1995, 87.

81. Raphael Semmes, **The Cruise of the Alabama and the Sumter,** New York: Carleton, 1894, 35, 36.

82. James Tertius de Kay, **The Rebel Raiders: The Astonishing History of the Confederacy's Secret Navy,** New York: Ballantine, 2002, 169.

83. Eric Rosenthal, **Stars and Stripes in Africa: Being a History of American Achievements in Africa by Explorers, Missionaries, Pirates, Adventurers, Hunters, Miners, Merchants, Scientists, Soldiers, Showmen, Engineers, and Others with Some Account of Africans who Have Played a Part in American Affairs,** London: Routledge, 1938, 134, 140, 133. See also **South African Advertiser and Mail,** 5 August 1863. See also Alan R. Booth, "Americans in South Africa, 1784–1870," Ph.D. dissertation, Boston University, 1964.

84. John S. Wise, **The End of an Era,** Boston: Houghton Mifflin, 1899, 191.

85. Duke of Newcastle to Sir Philip E. Wodehouse, 4 November 1863, GH 1/299/141, *State Archives–Cape Town.*

86. Sir Philip E. Wodehouse to Duke of Newcastle, 19 August 1863, GH 23/29/104, *State Archives–Cape Town.*

87. Walter Graham, U.S. Consul, to London, 17 August 1863, GH 1/300/156, *State Archives–Cape Town.*

88. Elizabeth Catherine Bott, "Admiral Semmes, CN," **Louisiana State University Bulletin,** 2 (Number 2, February 1911): 1–8, 1, 2.

89. Ibid., James Tertius de Kay, 135.

90. Edna and Frank Bradlow, **Here Comes the Alabama: The Career of a Confederate Raider,** Cape Town: A. A. Balkema, 1958, 53.

91. Rafael Semmes, **Memoirs of a Service Afloat During the War Between the States,** Baltimore: Kelly, Piet & Co., 1869, 599, 602, 611, 616, 620, 638. See also Journal and Scrapbook from Civil War, Box 1, **William P. Brooks Papers,** *Georgia Historical Society–Savannah.*

92. Ibid., James Tertius de Kay, 149.

93. John McIntosh Kell, **Recollections of a Naval Life,** Washington: Neale, 1900, 219.

94. James Monroe, "Special Duties of Consuls of the United States During the Civil War," no date, Box 24, **James Monroe Papers,** *Oberlin College.* See also Statement taken by Thomas Adamson, Jr., 27 April 1863, Record Group 59, Roll 7, **Dispatches from U.S. Consuls in Pernambuco.**

95. **Savannah Daily Morning News,** 10 August 1863.

96. James Watson Webb to Brazilian Government, 10 December 1861, Box 7, Folder 92, **James Watson Webb Papers.**

97. Ibid., Dean B. Mahin, 146, 158.

98. Thomas Wilson, U.S. Consul, to William Seward, 30 May 1863, Record Group 59, Roll 3, **Despatches from U.S. Consuls in Bahia.**

99. Letter from "Palace of the Government of Bahia," 12 May 1863, Record Group 59, Roll 3, **Despatches from U.S. Consuls in Bahia.**

100. Thomas Wilson to William Seward, 14 November 1864, Record

Group 59, Roll 3, **Despatches from U.S. Consuls in Bahia.**

101. William Richard Williams to William Seward, 14 June 1862, Record Group 59, Roll 2, **Despatches from U.S. Consuls in Para.**

102. Circular from James Watson Webb, 9 October 1864, Record Group 59, Roll 2, **Despatches from U.S. Consuls in Bahia.**

103. James Monroe, "Consular Experiences in Brazil," no date, Box 24, **James Monroe Papers.**

104. Letter from Raphael Semmes, 16 June 1864, **London Times**, Mss1 Se535a, 147–170, **Raphael Semmes Papers,** *Virginia Historical Society–Richmond.*

105. "From Palace of the Government," Pernambuco, 8 May 1863, Record Group 59, Roll 7, **Despatches from U.S. Consuls in Pernambuco.**

106. Letter from João Silveira e de Souza, 9 May 1863, Record Group 59, Roll 7, **Despatches from U.S. Consuls in Pernambuco.**

107. Thomas Adamson to William Seward, 23 July 1863, Record Group 59, Roll 7, **Despatches from U.S. Consuls in Pernambuco.**

108. Thomas Wilson to James Watson Webb, 31 October 1864, Record Group 59, Roll 3, **Despatches from U.S. Consuls in Bahia.**

109. David F. Long, **Gold Braid and Foreign Relations: Diplomatic Activities of U.S. Naval Officers, 1798–1883,** Annapolis: Naval Institute Press, 1988, 328.

110. Thomas Wilson to William Seward, 14 November 1864, Record Group 59, Roll 3, **Despatches of U.S. Consuls in Bahia.**

111. **Diary of Gideon Welles, Volume 2, April 1, 1864–December 31, 1866,** Boston: Houghton Mifflin, 1911, 184–186. See also Colonel W. de Raasloff, Peruvian Navy, to John Ericsson, 24 May 1862, **John Ericsson Letters,** *New York Historical Society*: Ericsson was a Swede toiling for the Union and his correspondent offered to "construct for your Government an Armor Clad Iron Steam Vessel of war,

with revolving turret on the Monitor system. This vessel to be precisely similar to the six vessels of this class, which I am now building for the United States government. . . . for the sum of four hundred and fifty thousand dollars. . . . also willing to procure an experienced sea captain and crew to take the vessel to any port of Peru that you shall name, provided your Government agrees to pay all expenses connected with the voyage."

112. Statement by William Seward, 23 February 1865, Washington, Oficios, 1865, *Archivo Histórico do Itamaraty–Rio de Janeiro*

113. Ibid., William Seward to Government of Brazil, 26 December 1864, Washington, Oficios, 1865.

114. Frank Lawrence Osley, **King Cotton Diplomacy: Foreign Relations of the Confederate States of America,** Chicago: University of Chicago Press, 1959, 255.

115. William K. Scarborough, ed., **The Diary of Edmund Ruffin, Volume 3: A Dream Shattered, June 1863–June 1865,** Baton Rouge: Louisiana State University Press, 1972, 664, 1 December 1864.

116. C. M. Morris to President of Brazil, Box 1, Folder 3, **Confederate States of America Collection,** *Yale University.*

117. James Dwyer to C. M. Morris, 13 October 1864, Box 1, Folder 3, **Confederate States of America Collection.**

118. CSA Resolution "In Relation to the Seizure of the Confederate war-steamer Florida," 30 November 1864, **Catalogued Broadsides,** *University of Virginia–Charlottesville.* See also **Confederate Imprint 238:** "Report of the Committee on Foreign Relations," CSA, 30 November 1864, *Virginia Historical Society–Richmond.* See also "Journal of the Congress of the Confederate States of America, 1861–1865," Volume 4, 58th Congress, 2nd Session, Senate. Document No. 234, Washington, D.C.: Government Printing Office, 30 November 1864, *Huntington Library–San Marino, California.*

119. Ibid., James Monroe, "Special Duties of Consuls of the United States

During the Civil War." Ignacio de Avellar Barboza da Silva to William Seward, 22 December 1864, FO 881/2011, *Public Records Office–Kew Gardens*: This file contains a huge batch of correspondence on this incident.

NOTES TO CHAPTER 10

1. Thomas Wilson to William Seward, 14 July 1862, Record Group 59, Roll 2, **Despatches from U.S. Consuls in Bahia.**

2. William Seward to Manoel Garcia da Rosa, 15 February 1868, [translation]: Legation of Portugal in Washington, Correspondence of the U.S. Government, 1835–1869, A28, M17, Torre 4 Piso Estante 1, 15, *Archivo Histórico-Diplomático, Ministério dos Negocios Estrangeiros–Lisbon.*

3. Her Majesty's Commissioner to Lord Russell, 18 August 1865, in Ibid., **British Parliamentary Papers: Correspondence Relative to the Slave Trade, Volume 75, Number 50.**

4. Clipping, 22 July 1865, [translation]: Correspondence of Legation and Consulates of Portugal in U.S., 1852–1867, *Archivo Histórico-Diplomático, Ministério dos Negocios Estrangeiros–Lisbon.*

5. **Philadelphia Inquirer**, 13 July 1865. For more on possible Portuguese connections to the Lincoln murder, see e.g. James Harvey, U.S. Minister to Portugal, to William Seward, 1866, in **Message of the President of the United States and Accompanying Documents to the Two Houses of Congress at the Commencement of the Second Session of the Fortieth Congress, Part I, Ex. Doc., No. 1**, Washington, D.C: Government Printing Office, 1868, 686.

6. C. Vann Woodward and Elizabeth Muhlenfeld, eds., **The Private Mary Chesnut: The Unpublished Civil War Diaries**, New York: Oxford University Press, 1984, 244, 15 May 1865.

7. **New York Times**, 30 October 1864.

8. **New York Times**, 22 November 1864.

9. James Bond to U.S. Government, 15 October 1864, Record Group 59, Roll 2, **Despatches from U.S. Consuls in Para.**

10. Douglas Audenreid Grier, "Confederate Emigration to Brazil, 1865–1870," Ph.D. dissertation, University of Michigan, 1968, 53, 59.

11. Captain Frederick N. Colston, "Recollections of the Last Months in the Army of Northern Virginia," **Southern Historical Society Papers**, 37 (January-December 1910): 1–15, 12.

12. Undated Memo, **Edwin James Papers**, *University of South Carolina–Columbia*. See also Frank J. Merli, ed., "Alternatives to Appomattox: A Virginian's Vision of an Anglo-Confederate Colony on the Amazon, May 1865," **The Virginia Magazine of History and Biography**, 94 (Number 2, April 1986): 210–219.

13. Eugene C. Harter, **The Lost Colony of the Confederacy**, Jackson: University Press of Mississippi, 1985, ix. See undated clipping, Vertical Files: Immigration and Emigration, *Georgia Historical Society–Savannah*: "nearly half of the eight or ten thousand Southerners who emigrated to foreign lands after the Civil War went to Brazil." See also Alfred Jackson Hanna and Kathryn Abbey Hanna, **Confederate Exiles in Venezuela**, Tuscaloosa: Confederate Publishing Company, 1960, 13: the authors estimate a total emigration globally of about 10,000. See Ibid., Douglas Audenreid Grier, 21, 22: 4000 rebels migrate to Brazil though "some writers have put the figure as high as ten thousand." See undated Memo, **Edwin James Papers**: 4000 Southerners came to Brazil and 60 percent did not stay. See also David P. Werlich, **Admiral of the Amazon: John Randolph Tucker, His Confederate Colleagues and Peru**, Charlottesville: University Press of Virginia, 1990; Margaret Amanda Pattison, **The Emigrant's Vade-Mecum or Guide to the 'Price Grant' in Venezuelan Guyana**, London: Trubner, 1868; Robert May, **The Southern Dream of a Caribbean Empire, 1854–1861**, Baton Rouge: Louisiana State University Press,

1973; John Codman, **Ten Months in Brazil,** Boston: Lee and Shephard, 1867.

14. Letter from Henry Shipley Stevens, 17 December 1865, F2513 S844, *Western Reserve Historical Society–Cleveland.*

15. See undated Memorandum, **Edwin James Papers:** The settlements were Hastings at Santarem; Gunter on the Rio Doce; Iguape led by Ballard Dunn; Near Iguape led by Frank McMullen; Gaston's colony in Xiririca; William Norris's colony at Santa Barbara D'oeste.

16. James Monroe, "Special Duties of Consuls of the United States During the Civil War," Box 24, **James Monroe Papers,** *Oberlin College.*

17. See [translation]: Letters Received from the Legation and Consulate of Brazil in 1865 from U.S. Nationals after the Civil War, re: Emigration, 1865–1866, Washington Oficios, *Archivo Histórico do Itamaraty–Rio de Janeiro.*

18. Manuscript of "Hunting a Home in Brazil," by James Gaston, 55, *University of North Carolina–Chapel Hill.*

19. Cyrus B. Dawsey and James M. Dawsey, **The Confederados: Old South Immigrants in Brazil,** Tuscaloosa: University of Alabama Press, 1995, 174.

20. **New York Herald,** 3 September 1865.

21. Richard Maury to John Perkins, 8 July 1866, Series 1.4, Folder 19, **John Perkins Papers,** *University of North Carolina–Chapel Hill.*

22. Unclear correspondent to John Perkins, 6 June 1866, **John Perkins Papers.**

23. W. Ferguson to Edwin James, June 1984, **Edwin James Papers.**

24. Yorkville Enquirer, 2 July 1868, **Edwin James Papers.**

25. George Barnsley to Father, August 1865, **Edwin James Papers.**

26. Ibid., Lawrence Hill, **Diplomatic Relations Between the United States and Brazil,** 251.

27. David W. Blight, **Race and Reunion: The Civil War in American Memory,** Cambridge: Harvard University Press, 2001, 36–37.

28. J. D. Porter to Charles Nathan, 14 October 1867, **J. D. Porter Letters,** *University of North Carolina–Chapel Hill.*

29. J. McF. Gaston, **Hunting a Home in Brazil,** Philadelphia: King & Baird, 1867, 227.

30. **New York Times,** 25 December 1865.

31. Lawrence F. Hill, "The Confederate Exodus to Brazil," F2569, A5, H66 ("verbatim reprint from the October 1935/January–April 1936 issues of the **Southwestern Historical Quarterly**"), *Library of Virginia–Richmond.* See e.g. **Edgefield Advertiser,** 2 May 1866, re: Report on trip to Brazil by delegation of "Southern Colonization Society."

32. Ibid., Douglas Audenreid Grier, 67, 68, 69.

33. **New York Times,** 16 December 1866.

34. Edward Thornton to Earl Russell, 2 November 1865, in Ibid., **British Parliamentary Papers: Correspondence Relative to the Slave Trade, Volume 75, Number 50.**

35. Blanche Henry Clark Weaver, "Confederate Immigrants and Evangelical Churches in Brazil," **Journal of Southern History,** 18 (Number 4, November 1952): 446–468; Blanche Henry Clark Weaver, "Confederate Emigration in Brazil, **Journal of Southern History,** 27 (Number 1, February 1961): 33–53, 50: "Difficulties would arise" for Confederates, which were "accentuated by the fact that many law enforcement officers were of African descent."

36. Ibid., Eugene C. Harter, 53–54.

37. Letter from James Bond, 4 June 1868, Record Group 59, Roll 2, **Despatches from U.S. Consuls in Para.**

38. Herbert H. Smith, **Brazil: The Amazons and the Coast,** New York: Scribner's, 1879, 468.

39. Yorkville Enquirer, 23 August 1867, **Edwin James Papers.**

40. **New York Times,** 22 February 1867.

41. John Codman, **Ten Months in**

Brazil: With Notes on the Paraguayan War, New York: John Miller, 1872, 79, 132.

42. J. D. Porter to "My Dear Cousin," 5 July 1867, MSS 2P8342a1, **J. D. Porter Papers,** *Virginia Historical Society–Richmond.* This focus on Africans in South America also arose in Venezuela. See Ibid., Alfred Jackson Hanna and Kathryn Abbey Hanna, **Confederate Exiles in Venezuela,** 58, 75. See William B. Hessletine and Hazel C. Wolf, **The Blue and Gray on the Nile,** Chicago: University of Chicago Press, 1961, 62, 103, 132.

43. Alfredo Cordiviola, **Richard Burton, a Traveler in Brazil, 1865–1868,** Lewiston, Maine: Mellen, 2001, 80.

44. Whitaker to F. O. Adams, 11 November 1874, Box 2, **Adams (Israel L. and Family) Papers,** *Louisiana State University–Baton Rouge.*

45. Dr. Henry Price to Lafayette McLaws, 20 April 1866, Folder 18, **Lafayette McLaws Papers,** *University of North Carolina–Chapel Hill.* At the same site, see also Folder 204: "Latin American Projects," **Duff Green Papers.**

46. Edward Thornton to Earl of Clarendon, 6 December 1865, in Ibid., British Parliamentary Papers: Correspondence Relative to the Slave Trade, Volume 75, Number 50.

47. Robert Brent Toplin, **The Abolition of Slavery in Brazil,** New York: Atheneum, 1972, 119.

48. Ibid., Robert Edgar Conrad, ed., **Children of God's Fire: A Documentary History of Black Slavery in Brazil,** 417.

49. **Anglo-Brazilian Times,** 24 January 1866.

50. Charles Sumner to Louis Agassiz, 30 March 1865, in Beverly Wilson Palmer, **The Selected Letters of Charles Sumner,** Volume 2, Boston: Northeastern University Press, 1990, 275–276.

51. Charles Sumner to Francis Lieber, 24 December 1869 in Ibid., Beverly Wilson Palmer, 497–498.

52. Letter from Henry Shipley Stevens, 30 January 1866, *Western Reserve Historical Society.*

53. "Confidential memorandum," circa 1865, Washington, Oficios, 1865, *Archivo Histórico do Itamaraty–Rio de Janeiro.* See also Henry M. Price to Sir Frederick Bruce, 24 May 1865, FO 5/1019, *Public Records Office–Kew Gardens*: This rebel asked London to sponsor a Confederate colony in Brazil as a spearhead against the U.S. (later he organized a colony in Venezuela). Frank J. Merli, **Great Britain and the Confederate Navy, 1861–1865,** Bloomington: Indiana University Press, 1970.

54. Gary Gallagher, ed., **Fighting for the Confederacy: The Personal Recollections of General Edward Porter Alexander,** Chapel Hill: University of North Carolina Press, 1989, 547–548.

55. Undated Memorandum, **Edwin James Papers.**

56. George Barnsley to Father, August 1865, **Edwin James Papers.**

57. Matthew Fontaine Maury to "Corbin," 18 May 1861, **Matthew Fontaine Maury Papers,** *Virginia Military Institute–Lexington.*

58. Ibid., Lawrence Hill, **Diplomatic Relations Between the United States and Brazil,** 254.

59. New York Times, 15 January 1868.

60. Ibid., Manuscript by James Gaston, "Hunting a Home in Brazil," 55.

61. **New York Times,** 10 December 1865.

62. **New York Times,** 3 December 1865.

63. **Anglo-Brazilian Times,** 7 September 1865.

64. William Van Vleck Lidgerwood to William Seward, 1867, in **Papers Relating to Foreign Affairs, Accompanying the Annual Message of the President to the Second Session, Thirty-Ninth Congress, Part II,** Washington, D.C.: Government Printing Office, 1867, 300.

65. **Anglo-Brazilian Times,** 9 October 1865.

66. **New York Herald,** 22 February 1866.

67. **Anglo-Brazilian Times,** 4 November 1865.

68. New York Times, 26 February 1866.

69. Anglo-Brazilian Times, 24 November 1865.

70. Anglo-Brazilian Times, 24 December 1865.

71. Anglo-Brazilian Times, 23 June 1866.

72. Anglo-Brazilian Times, 7 February 1867.

73. Ibid., John Codman, Ten Months in Brazil, 79, 131–132, 187, 189, 195–196.

74. Matthew Fontaine Maury to "My Dear Corbin,"22 October 1860, Matthew Fontaine Maury Papers, VMI.

75. Matthew Fontaine Maury to "Corbin," 18 May 1861, Matthew Fontaine Maury Papers, VMI.

76. Hon. John Bell on "Lieut. M. F. Maury[,] Speech . . . Delivered in the Senate of the United States, April 28 and 29, 1856." "Congressional Globe, 1856," GC M45 B4.

77. "Captain Maury's Letter on American Affairs," August 1861, American Antiquarian Society.

78. Matthew Maury to Editor, 'London Times,' 22 December 1862, Scrapbook, Richard Maury Papers, Duke University.

79. Matthew Maury to Corbin, 1 May 1863, Matthew Fontaine Maury Papers, VMI.

80. Richard Maury, A Brief Sketch of Matthew Fontaine Maury During the War, 1861–1865, Richmond: Whittet & Shepperson, 1915, 30.

81. Matthew Maury to "My Dear Nannie," 7 July 1863, Matthew Fontaine Maury Papers, VMI.

82. Matthew Fontaine Maury to Captain de la Marche, Paris, 15 March 1862, Box 15, Matthew Fontaine Maury Papers, Library of Congress.

83. Ferdinand Maxmilian to Matthew Maury, 4 September 1863, Box 18, Matthew Fontaine Maury Papers, Library of Congress.

84. Matthew Maury to the Archduke, 9 October 1863, Box 18, Matthew Fontaine Maury Papers, Library of Congress.

85. The Archduke to Matthew Maury, 24 October 1863, Box 18, Matthew Fontaine Maury Papers, Library of Congress.

86. Matthew Maury to the Archduke, 10 November 1863, Box 19, Matthew Fontaine Maury Papers, Library of Congress.

87. Matthew Maury to the Archduke, 22 December 1863, Box 19, Matthew Fontaine Maury Papers, Library of Congress.

88. J. M. Maury to Matthew Maury, 12 April 1865, Box 1, Matthew Fontaine Maury Papers, Duke University.

89. Letter from Matthew Fontaine Maury, 19 May 1865, Matthew Fontaine Maury Papers, VMI.

90. Russian Minister to Matthew Fontaine Maury, 25 June 1860, Matthew Fontaine Maury Papers, VMI.

91. Russian Grand Duke to Matthew Maury, 8 August 1861, Box 14, Matthew Fontaine Maury Papers, Library of Congress.

92. Letter from Matthew Fontaine Maury, 5 September 1865, Matthew Fontaine Maury Papers, VMI. See, Ibid., David W. Blight, Race and Reunion, 78. See also "Decrees for the Encouragement of Immigration and Colonization. Office of Colonization. Mexico. November 1865." Series 1.4, Folder 16, John Perkins Papers, University of North Carolina–Chapel Hill.

93. Matthew Maury to Corbin, 31 October 1865, Matthew Fontaine Maury Papers, VMI.

94. Matthew Maury to "My Dear Wife,"27 November 1865, Matthew Fontaine Maury Papers, VMI.

95. Matthew Maury to "My Dear Sweet Brave Nannie," 7 December 1865, Matthew Fontaine Maury Papers, VMI.

96. Undated Letter from Richard Maury, Matthew Fontaine Maury Papers, VMI.

97. Matthew Maury to "My Dear Children," 1 March 1866, Matthew Fontaine Maury Papers, VMI.

98. Matthew Maury to "Corbin,"21

May 1866, **Matthew Fontaine Maury Papers,** *VMI.*

99. Matthew Maury to "Corbin," 19 May 1867, **Matthew Fontaine Maury Papers,** *VMI.*

100. Richard Maury to John Perkins, 8 July 1866, Series 1.4, Folder 19, **John Perkins Papers.**

101. Matthew Maury to Corbin, 29 January 1868, **Matthew Fontaine Maury Papers,** *VMI.*

102. Matthew Fontaine Maury to Dear Ruston, 7 September 1870, Box 1, **Matthew Fontaine Maury Papers,** *Duke University.*

103. Richard Maury to Matthew Maury, 9 September 1870, Box 1, **Matthew Fontaine Maury Papers,** *Duke University.*

104. Ibid., Richard Maury, **A Brief Sketch of Matthew Fontaine Maury,** 30.

105. F. H. Farrar to John Perkins, 21 September 1866, Series 1.4, Folder 19, **John Perkins Papers.**

NOTES TO CHAPTER 11

1. William Clark Griggs, **The Elusive Eden: Frank McMullan's Confederate Colony in Brazil,** Austin: University of Texas Press, 1987, 127.

2. Bell Wiley, "Confederate War Exiles in Brazil," **Civil War Times Illustrated,** 15 (Number 9, January 1977): 22–32, 27, 30. See also Ibid., Eugene C. Harter, **The Lost Colony of the Confederacy,** 54.

3. Ibid., Cyrus B. Dawsey and James M. Dawsey, **The Confederados,** 174.

4. "Additional Convention Between the United States and Great Britain," on the Slave Trade, "Concluded June 3, 1870," Record Group 48, Roll 3, **Records of the Department of Interior.**

5. See e.g. Ibid., Najia Aarim-Heriot, **Chinese Immigrants, African Americans and Racial Anxiety in the United States, 1848–1882.** See also "Lista Dos Navios Americanos" with "bandeira Portugeza" carrying hundreds of "coolies," 20 February 1864, "[translation]: Correspondence

of the Mixed Commission at the Cape of Good Hope, *Archivo Histórico-Diplomático, Ministério dos Negocios Estrangeiros–Lisbon.*

6. W. C. Knight, Acting Consul Cape Town, to Chevalier Duprat, 18 January 1864, [translation]: Consul of Portugal, Cape of Good Hope, 1846–1876, *Archivo Histórico-Diplomático, Ministério dos Negocios Estrangeiros–Lisbon.* In the same file see also Thomas Watson to Chevalier Duprat, 8 April 1864. See also George Frere and E. L. Layard, Cape Town, to Earl Russell, 26 January 1864, in Ibid., **British Parliamentary Papers: Correspondence Relative to the Slave Trade, Volume 66, Number 49:** "two large vessels have touched conveying coolies from Hong Kong . . . American vessels [with] Portuguese flag and papers."

7. David Birmingham, **Portugal and Africa,** Athens: Ohio University Press, 1999, 18.

8. From "Ordnance Office War Department" of U.S. to A. da Cunha, Charges d'Affaires of Portugal in U.S., 10 March 1871, [translation]: Legation of Portugal in Washington, Correspondence Received from Various Authorities and American Establishments, 1837–1888, Torre, 4 Piso, Estante 1, 17, A38, M19, *Archivo Histórico-Diplomático, Ministério dos Negocios Estrangeiros–Lisbon.* In same file, see also E. G. Wines, U.S. Commissioner to A. da Cunha, 22 May 1871, re: invitation to "International Penitentiary Congress."

9. See e.g. U.S. Congress. House. Committee on Government Reform. Subcommittee on Human Rights and Wellness. **The Ongoing Tragedy of International Slavery and Human Trafficking: An Overview: Hearing Before the Subcommittee on Human Rights and Wellness of the Committee on Government Reform,** 108th Congress, 1st Session. October 29, 2003. Washington, D.C.: Government Printing Office, 2004; Christian van den Anker, ed., **The Political Economy of New Slavery,** New York: Palgrave, 2004. Anna M.

Troubnikoff, ed., **Trafficking in Women and Children: Current Issues and Developments**, Hauppauge, New York: Nova Science Publishers, 2003.

10. Main Catalogue File, Description of "Godfrey Barnsley Papers," *Duke University.*

11. C. Berrien to Godfrey Barnsley, 22 February 1867, Box 5, **Godfrey Barnsley Papers**, *Duke University.*

12. George Barnsley to "Dear Father,"23 May 1867, Box 5, **Godfrey Barnsley Papers.**

13. F. H. Farrar to John Perkins, 21 September 1866, Series 1.4, Folder 16, **John Perkins Papers.**

14. J. D. Porter to Charles Nathan, 30 August 1867, 892-z, Folder 1, **J. D. Porter Papers**, *University of North Carolina–Chapel Hill.* For more on the rebel migration to South America, see **Missouri Republican**, 17 June 1867; **The Daily Picayune**, 19 May and 9 June 1867; **Charleston Mercury**, 17 September 1867; **New Orleans Times**, 1 December and 8 December 1867.

15. J. D. Porter to Charles Nathan, 29 November 1867, 892-z, Folder 1, **J. D. Porter Papers.**

16. "Biography of James McFadden Gaston," no date, 1469-(B)-z, Folder 1, *University of North Carolina–Chapel Hill.*

17. J. Marshall McCue to Cyrus H. McCormick, 11 April 1857, 454-z, **J. Marshall McCue Letters**, *University of North Carolina–Chapel Hill.*

18. Cyrus H. McCormick to J. Marshall McCue, 22 June 1867, **J. Marshall McCue Letters.**

19. J. Marshall McCue to Cyrus H. McCormick, 22 June 1867, **J. Marshall McCue Letters.**

20. Lucita Hardie Wait, "Memories of a Childhood Spent in Brazil," 1937, M1879, Reel 1, **Hardie Family Papers**, *University of North Carolina–Chapel Hill.*

21. Columbia [Ga.] Sun and Times, 5 February 1867.

22. **New York Times**, 15 August 1867; Montgomery Advertiser, 10 August 1867.

23. **New York Times**, 28 March 1867.

24. George Barnsley to "Father," 14 June 1867, Box 5, **Godfrey Barnsley Papers.**

25. George Barnsley to Father, 23 April 1868, Box 5, **Godfrey Barnsley Papers.**

26. George Barnsley to Father, 17 February 1872, Box 5, **Godfrey Barnsley Papers.**

27. "Our Life in Brazil," circa 1867, 1672-z, Folder 1, **Julia Louisa Hentz Keyes Papers**, *University of North Carolina–Chapel Hill.*

28. J. D. Porter to unnamed correspondent, undated, 892-z, Folder 1, **J. D. Porter Papers.**

29. Joseph Weed to "Dear Sarah," 5 August 1874, 2109-z, Folder 1, **Joseph W. Weed Letters**, *University of North Carolina–Chapel Hill.*

30. Robert S. Merriwether to "My Dear Brother," circa 1872 and Affadavit, 14 September 1872, MSS 1 D 1124a 1-42, **Dabney Family Papers**, *Virginia Historical Society.* See also Betty Antunes de Oliveira, "North American Immigration to Brazil: Tombstone Records of the 'Campo' Cemetery; Santa Barbara D'Oeste-Sao Paulo State-Brazil, 1978," F2513 O4, *Virginia Historical Society.*

31. Carolyn Smith Ward, **An American Brazilian Odyssey**, Charlotte: CSW, 1979, 35.

32. Ibid., Gary Gallagher, ed., **Fighting for the Confederacy**, 530–531. See also E. L. Jeffers, "Brazil's American Confederates: 'Once a Rebel, Twice a Rebel, Always a Rebel,'" **Virginia Country**, July-August 1986, 53–55, *Virginia Historical Society.*

33. Thomas L. Whigham, **The Paraguayan War: Causes and Early Conflict, Volume 1**, Lincoln: University of Nebraska Press, 2002, iv.

34. Vitor Izecksohn, "War, Reform and State-Building in Brazil and in the United States: Slavery, Emancipation and Decision-Making Processes in the Paraguayan and Civil Wars (1861–1870)," Ph.D. dissertation, University of New Hampshire, 2001, 181, 335, 336. See also **Savannah**

Daily Morning News, 21 November 1868: The President of Paraguay charges the U.S. Minister to Paraguay with being part of a conspiracy to assassinate him, joined by that nation's Foreign Minister. Savannah Daily Morning News, 29 October 1869: U.S. Minister to Paraguay says he is evacuating Asuncion as Brazilian troops plunder this capital, destroying and looting and ransacking archives. Savannah Daily Morning News, 29 November 1870: "Americans are said to have fought with Brazil against Paraguay. . . . one historian notes, however, that the Brazilian army court-martialed and shot two American boys for signing on as mercenaries with Paraguay."

35. New York Times, 25 November 1866.

36. Clipping, no date, Washington, Oficios, 1865, *Archivo Histórico do Itamaraty.*

37. Reverend Ballard S. Dunn, **Brazil, the Home for Southerners,** New York: George B. Richardson, 1866, 40.

38. John A. Salmond, **The Conscience of a Lawyer: Clifford J. Durr and American Civil Liberties, 1899–1975,** Tuscaloosa: University of Alabama Press, 1990, 2.

39. Dispatch from Ignacio Barboza da Silva, 22 May 1865, Washington, Oficios, 1865, *Archivo Histórico do Itamaraty.*

40. "Letter from the Provincial President of Para to the Minister of Justice," 8 July 1865, in Robert Edgar Conrad, ed., **Children of God's Fire.**

41. Ibid., **Children of God's Fire,** 232.

42. Henry Thayer Mahoney and Marjorie Locke Mahoney, **Mexico and the Confederacy, 1860–1867,** San Francisco: Austin & Winfield, 1998, 101.

43. Ibid., Reverend Ballard S. Dunn, 19.

44. Minister of Agriculture to General Wood, no date, in Ibid., **British Parliamentary Papers: Correspondence Relative to the Slave Trade, Volume 75, Number 50.**

45. New York Times, 25 July 1867.

46. Diary of James M. Gaston, 29 November 1865, 1470, Box 2, Folder 18, James M. Gaston Papers, *University of North Carolina–Chapel Hill.*

47. Ibid., "Biography of James McFadden Gaston." But see Ibid., J. McF. Gaston, **Hunting a Home in Brazil,** 123: "extractions from the Negro are greater, and the provision for his subsistence and comfort less than was experienced formerly in the United States."

48. Ibid., Gaston, **Hunting a Home in Brazil,** 228.

49. Ibid., Julia Louisa Hentz Keyes, "Our Life in Brazil."

50. "The Last Confederates Live in Brazil," 1991, **Edwin James Papers,** *University of South Carolina–Columbia.*

51. Ibid., Gaston, **Hunting a Home in Brazil,** 134.

52. **Chester Reporter,** 6 May 1906, **Edwin James Papers.**

53. Ibid., Julia Louisa Hentz Keyes, "Our Life in Brazil."

54. Undated Memorandum, **Edwin James Papers.**

55. Ibid., Lucie Hardie Wait, "Memories of a Childhood Spent in Brazil."

56. Ibid., Bridgett M. Williams, "James Monroe: Consul to Rio, 1863–1869," 90.

57. Ibid., Gaston, **Hunting a Home in Brazil,** 55.

58. Ibid., Joseph W. Weed to "Dear Sarah," 5 August 1874, **Joseph W. Weed Letters.**

59. Ibid., Diary of James M. Gaston, 29 November 1865, **James M. Gaston Papers.**

60. Ibid., Joseph W. Weed to "Dear Sarah," 5 August 1874, **Joseph W. Weed Letters.**

61. Louis and Elizabeth Agassiz, **A Journey in Brazil,** New York: Praeger, 1969, 128–129.

62. Ibid., Julia Louisa Hentz Keyes, "Our Life in Brazil."

63. Ibid., "Biography of James McFadden Gaston."

64. New York Times, 15 August 1867.

65. J. D. Porter to Charles Nathan, 29 November 1867, Folder 1, **J. D. Porter Letters.**

66. O. Whitaker to Frank Adams, 12

June 1876, Box 2, Adams (Israel L. and Family) Papers, *Louisiana State University–Baton Rouge.*

67. Ibid., Gaston, **Hunting a Home in Brazil**, 52.

68. **New York Times**, 15 August 1867.

69. **New York Times**, 25 February 1870.

70. **Anglo-Brazilian Times**, 2 July 1866.

71. Memo from A. Foster Elliott, 5 May 1866, Washington, Oficios, 1865, *Archivo Histórico do Itamaraty.*

72. **Anglo-Brazilian Times**, 23 April 1867.

73. **Anglo-Brazilian Times**, 7 August 1868.

74. **Anglo-Brazilian Times**, 8 May 1867.

75. **Anglo-Brazilian Times**, 26 April 1867.

76. Henry Sanford to U.S. Grant, 18 February [year unclear], in John Y. Simon, ed., **The Papers of Ulysses S. Grant**, Volume 24, 1873, Carbondale: Southern Illinois University Press, 2000, 375–376.

77. **New York Times**, 19 April 1876.

78. James Watson Webb to William Seward, 3 May 1867, in **Message to the President of the United States and Accompanying Documents to the Two Houses of Congress at the Commencement of the Second Session of the Fortieth Congress, Part II**, Washington, D.C.: Government Printing Office, 1868, 251–253

79. **New York Times**, 14 July 1877.

80. **New York Times**, 21 May 1871.

81. George Barnsley to Editor, **New Orleans Times**, 20 August 1871, Box 5, **Godfrey Barnsley Papers.**

82. George Barnsley to Father, 20 August 1871, Box 5, **Godfrey Barnsley Papers.**

83. George Barnsley to Father, 17 February 1872, Box 5, **Godfrey Barnsley Papers.** Barnsley's complaints were not atypical and thus are worthy of quotation at length: See e.g. George Barnsley to Father, 30 October 1870, Box 5, **Godfrey Barnsley Papers.**

84. George Barnsley to Father, 9 March 1868, Box 5, **Godfrey Barnsley Papers.**

85. James R. Partridge to Hamilton Fish, 8 September 1871, in **Papers Relating to the Foreign Relations of the United States, Transmitted to Congress with the Annual Message to the President**, December 4, 1871, Washington, D.C.: Government Printing Office, 1871, 64.

86. James R. Partridge to Hamilton Fish, 2 December 1872, in **Papers Relating to the Foreign Relations of the United States, Transmitted to Congress with the Annual Message of the President**, December 2, 1872, Washington, D.C.: Government Printing Office, 1873, 90. See also James Partridge to Hamilton Fish, 22 January 1872, in John Y. Simon, ed., **The Papers of Ulysses S. Grant, Volume 22: June 1, 1871–January 31, 1872**, Carbondale: Southern Illinois University Press, 1998, 333.

87. Report from Henry T. Blow, 5 November 1870, in Ibid., **Papers Relating to the Foreign Relations of the United States . . . 1871**, 43.

88. **Savannah Daily Morning News**, 21 November 1868.

89. **New York Times**, 31 December 1875.

NOTES TO THE EPILOGUE

1. Ibid., Eugene C. Harter, **The Lost Colony of the Confederacy**, 55.

2. Ibid., Robert Brent Toplin, **The Abolition of Slavery in Brazil**, 212–213. See also **Rio News**, 24 February 1888; **Jornal do Recife**, 21 February 1888; **Revista Illustrada**, 17 March 1888. See also **New York Times**, 16 April 1876.

3. Ibid., John Codman, **Ten Months in Brazil**, 75.

4. Isaac Myers, et al. to President Grant, April 1869, in **The Papers of Ulysses S. Grant, Volume 19**, 1995.

5. **New York Times**, 4 December 1877.

6. **New York Times**, 5 August 1877.

7. **New York Times**, 6 August 1877.

8. **New York Times**, 20 December 1880.

9. Thomas J. Jarvis to John D. Whitford, 22 September 1885, 89.2, **John D.**

Whitford Papers, *North Carolina State Archives.*

10. Thomas J. Jarvis to John D. Whitford, 3 August 1888, 89.2, **John D. Whitford Papers.**

11. Thomas J. Jarvis to William L. Saunders, 27.1, **William Laurence Saunders Papers,** *North Carolina State Archives.*

12. John C. White to Mr. Evarts, 1879, in **Papers Relating to the Foreign Relations of the United States, Transmitted to Congress, with the Annual Message of the President, December 1, 1879,** Washington, D.C.: Government Printing Office, 1879, 133–134.

13. Henry Hilliard to Mr. Evarts, 4 September 1879, in **Papers Relating to the Foreign Relations of the United States, Transmitted to Congress, with the Annual Message of the President, December 6, 1880,** Washington, D.C.: Government Printing Office, 1880, 86.

14. New York Times, 3 July 1878.

15. New York Times, 31 May 1878.

16. New York Times, 31 December 1877.

17. New York Times, 16 April 1878.

18. **Anglo-Brazilian Times, 8 March 1878.**

19. New York Times, 6 May 1878.

20. New York Times, 15 June 1886.

21. New York Times, 25 January 1888.

22. Letter from Stephen W. Hill to T. F. Bayard, 31 January 1888, in **Papers Relating to the Foreign Relations of the United States, Transmitted to Congress, with the Annual Message of the President, December 3, 1888,** Washington, D.C.: Government Printing Office, 1889, 58.

23. **Rio Daily News, 5 March 1888,** in Ibid., **Papers Relating to the Foreign Relations of the United States . . . 1888,** 59.

24. Rio Daily News, 24 March 1888, in Ibid., **Papers Relating to the Foreign Relations of the United States . . . 1888,** 62.

25. **Revista do Brasil, 15 December 1907.**

26. New York World, 1 December 1907.

27. Report from U.S. Vice Consul in Bahia, 1 December 1907, Box 12, **Richard Harding Davis Papers,** *University of Virginia–Charlottesville.*

28. Department of State to Richard Harding Davis, 19 March 1908, Box 12, **Richard Harding Davis Papers.**

29. **Baltimore Sun, 25 October 1972.**

30. **Christian Science Monitor, 3 June 1977.**

31. **New York Times, 22 April 1972.**

32. **New York Times, 3 November 1985.**

33. Interview with Elizabeth McAlpine MacKnight, 20 May 1978, Box 1, Folder 2, *Americana (Brazil) Oral History Project Collection–Emory University.*

34. Sheila S. Walker, "Africanity vs. Blackness: Race, Class and Culture in Brazil," **NACLA Report on the Americas,** 35 (Number 6, May/June 2002): 16–20, 17, 19.

35. Thomas J. Jarvis to T. F. Bayard, 14 May 1888, in Ibid., **Papers Relating to the Foreign Relations of the United States . . . 1888,** 72.

36. **New York Times, 4 July 1888.**

37. **Der Spiegel, 19 May 2002.**

38. **Estado de São Paulo, 28 April 2002;** Fernando Henrique Cardoso, The Accidental President of Brazil: A Memoir, New York: Public Affairs, 2006, 257.

39. **Los Angeles Times, 23 June 2005.**

40. **New York Amsterdam News, 22 December 2005.**

41. Louis Harlan, ed., The Booker T. Washington Papers, 1860–1889, Volume 2, Champaign-Urbana: University of Illinois Press, 1972, 237.

42. David J. Hellwig, African-American Reflections on Brazil's Racial Paradise, Philadelphia: Temple University Press, 1992.

43. Eugene Robinson, Coal to Cream: A Black Man's Journey Beyond Color to an Affirmation of Race, New York: Free Press, 1999, 184, 31–32, 145.

44. **Guardian [London], 30 December 2005.**

Index

Abbot, Joel, 62

Abbott, George, 143–144

Abolitionism: anti-abolitionist riot in New York City (1834), 172–173; Baquaqua and, 45; in Brazil, 12–13, 26, 161, 186, 199, 210, 244–245, 251; Brazil's impact on Americans' attitude toward, 105; California Gold Rush's impact on, 13, 85–88, 95–98; in Great Britain, 7, 152, 237; in Haiti, 157; hostility toward, 173; in New York, 45; Spain and, 152, 154; in Texas, 284n74; Webb and, 172–173; Wise (Henry Alexander) on, 68

Abranches, Almeida and Co., 37

D'Abrantes, Marquis, 186

Ackerman, J. L., 95

Adams, John H., 83

Adams, John Quincy: on African Slave Trade, 20–21; Brazilian slave trade, 27–28; on Portugal, 21; Ray and, 21; on search/seizure of U.S.-flagged ships, 155; support for Latin American independence, 21; Wise (Henry Alexander) and, 67

Adams, Samuel, 96

Adamson, Thomas, 194

Africa: decline in proportion of world's population, 4; nearness to Brazil, 17, 33–34; U.S. trade with, 144. *See also* East Africa; West Africa

African Americans: emigration to Argentina, 249; emigration to Brazil, 248–250

African Labor Supply Association, 130

African Methodist Episcopal (AME) Church, 248, 251

African Slave Trade, 128–149; Adams (John Quincy) on, 20–21; American

involvement in, 3, 8, 9, 10, 33–34, 53–65, 137–138, 148, 162–163, 198, 252; American Negroes involved in, 41–42; average number of slaves taken per year, 35; backers of, 16; branding of slaves, 42; Brazil in, 33–34; calls to reopen, 129–134, 151, 153; chief site of, 24; Civil War, influence on, 151–171; Civil War's ending, 15; Confederate States of America (CSA), 153, 185; decline in Africa's proportion of the world's population, 4; deportation of American Negroes to the Amazon River basin as a substitute for, 121; diplomacy in the Western hemisphere, 151, 157–158; external forces' effects on, 155, 157–158; federal laws prohibiting U.S. citizens from participating in, 3, 19, 130, 132, 134, 167, 287n48; free trade, 20; illicit trade in late 1850s, 128–149, 171; Jefferson and, 18; Maury (Matthew Fontaine) and, 114, 122; northward movement of, 146–147, 149; number of Africans shipped to Brazil, 2–3, 50, 53–54, 73; number of Africans shipped to the New World, 2, 256n3, 268n34; official closure of, 19; openness of, 38; participation by Confederate expatriates in Brazil, 205; peak period, 2–3, 8; Portugal and, 146, 223; price of slaves in Africa, 38, 129–131; profitability of, 35, 38, 46, 62, 137, 149, 273n7; prosecutions under slave trade acts, 54; provision of ships for, 3, 24, 34, 58, 79, 111, 280n34; Royal Navy's effect on, 63–64; runaways, 45–46; in 1840s, 11; secessionists and, 4, 151, 153; switching flags, 36–37, 39, 62, 221, 274n27;

trading by U. S. nationals during,
162–168, 183–187; slavery's fate, 161;
suppression of the slave trade, 163,
184–185; U.S. trade with Africa prior
to, 144. *See also* Confederate States of
America (CSA)
Clary, J. B., 152–153, 156
Clay, J. B., 46–47
Clayton-Bulwer Treaty (1850), 180
Clemson, Thomas G., 83
Cleveland, Grover, 249
Cliffe, Jose, 256n13
Clink, John Jackson, 244
Cobb, Howell, 138
Cobden, Richard, 138
Codman, John, 205, 213, 244
Coffee production in: Brazil, 8, 23, 54,
278n2; Cuba, 23; Santo Domingo (now
Dominican Republic), 23
Coggeshall, George, 91
Cohen, Joshua, 80
Cole, John, 222
Collantes, Calderon, 154
Collins, Napoleon, 194–196
Colonization of Blacks: of Africa, 172;
American Colonization Society, 306n36;
of Latin America, 6, 248–250; Lincoln
and, 173–174; political rights for
blacks, 259n34; as a remedy for slavery,
172–173. *See also* Deportation of Amer-
ican Negroes to the Amazon River basin
Colston, Frederick N., 200
"Columbia" (American frigate), 93
Columbus Wasson (later Vassão), Steve,
222
Companhia Portuguesa. *See* Portuguese
Company
Conant, Roger, 90
Confederate expatriates in Brazil ("Confederados"), 198–245; Brazilian expatriation scheme, 226; Brazilian planters'
response to, 233; Brazil's war with
Uruguay, 228–229; class origins of, 201;
conduct of, 241; conflicts with Northerners in Brazil, 205; crimes committed
by, 239, 244; desire to continue African
slavery, 201–203, 205–207, 227; disap-
pointment/disillusionment, 204, 228,
231–235, 239–240; discrediting of
slaveholders and slavery, 242; down-

ward social mobility among, 239–241;
economic and social capital of,
212–213; emigration during the Civil
War, 199; fear of being murdered in
Brazil, 227; financial ruin in U.S.,
208–209; hatred of federal government,
201–203; hatred of Yankees, 251; ill-fat-
edness of the adventure, 241–242; language barriers, 222, 226, 233, 234;
lonesomeness, 235; Lusophone culture,
241; military service in Brazil, 228;
modern-day, 252; motives for expatriation, 201–203, 204–228, 205–207;
New York Times on, 209–210, 234,
237–239; number of, 200–201, 205,
314n13; opposition to ending of slavery
in Brazil, 244–245; in Para, 199–200;
participation in slave trading, 205; pessimism about prospects for the U.S.,
205–206, 224; professionals among,
233; prohibition of importing slaves
into Brazil, 204, 231; prosperity among,
228; racial equality in Brazil, 222; racial
vs. ethnic bias among, 234; religious
issues, 222; remaining in 1876, 243;
repatriation/return to U.S., 201, 202,
221–222, 235, 240, 242–243; settlements of, 201, 240; slaveholding by,
227, 229; slaves brought by, 233; societies promoting expatriation, 203; in
20th century, 250–251, 252; as threats
to security of the U.S., 237; U.S.–British
relations, 207–209; welcome extended
to, 201, 209–212, 224
Confederate States of America (CSA): African Slave Trade, 153, 185; Brazil and,
162, 163, 190, 196–197; British ship-
building for, 192; burning of American
ships in Brazil, 192; Confederate generals and militarists serving in Mexico,
208–209; demise's effect on Brazil, 199;
detachment of Texas from, 174; diplomatic recognition of, 153, 163, 193;
existence of slavery in Brazil, 199; expatriates in Brazil (*see* Confederate expatriates in Brazil); Great Britain and,
153–154, 193; groundwork for, 159;
Maury as ambassador for, 214; Portugal
and, 171; privateers from, 162, 163,
188; slave-trading operatives, 186–187,

Confederate States of America (*continued*)
188–189; South African support for,
189–190; Spain and, 154–155; sympa-
thy in Brazil, 162, 168; sympathy in
Portugal, 168; Wise's (Henry Alexander)
role, 190
"Congo" (American schooner), 184
Conrad, Robert, 139
Convention of 1824, 20
Conway, Chaplin, 57
"Cora" (American slaver), 146
Cornwallis, Charles, 17
Costa Soares, Samuel da, 260n52, 298n4
Cotton growing in: Brazil, 11, 187–188,
209, 272n6; India, 156–157
Crampton, John, 116–117
Cratonick, Vincent, 136
Crawford, Joseph T., 147–148
Cuba: alliance/relations with the South,
14, 158; American expansionism, 123,
152; coffee production, 23; fears of
slave revolts in, 12; as a firewall protect-
ing U.S. slavery, 133; Maxwell, Wright
and Co. in, 9; price of slaves in, 145;
prosperity in, 272n6; slave trading in,
145–146, 266n25, 272n6; slavery in, 3,
34; Southern filibustering expeditions to,
155; Southern nationalists, 117; Thir-
teenth Amendment, 12
Cummings, Andrew Boyd, 49–50, 51, 140
Cunha, A. M. da, 170
Cunha, Antonio de Luis da, 41
Cunha Reis, Figaniere and Co. (aka
Figaniere, Reis & Co.), 136, 149
Cunha Reis, Manuel Bazilio da, 136
Currier, Nathaniel, 139
"Cyrus" (American ship), 64

Dahlgren, J. A., 125
Dahomey, King of, 137, 141
Davis, David Brion, 157
Davis, Jefferson: African Squadron, oppo-
sition to, 83; capture of, 230; emigra-
tion of bodyguard to Brazil, 251;
Hilliard and, 245; Louis Napoleon and,
174; Maury (Matthew Fontaine) on,
219
Davis, Margaret Lockhard, 57
De Bow, J. D. B., 83, 130
De Bow's Review (magazine), 120, 138

De Villiers, Lord, 189
"Decatur" (American ship), 62
Delany, Martin, 13
Deportation of American Negroes: to the
Amazon River basin (*see* Deportation of
American Negroes to the Amazon River
basin); to British Honduras, 179–180;
to British West Indies, 179; to Central
America, 180; Clayton-Bulwer Treaty
(1850), 180; to Guatemala, 180; to
Guyana, 179; Lincoln and, 173–174,
176–177, 180, 181–182; Radical
Republicans, 181, 182; to San Salvador,
180; Seward and, 179–181, 182–183;
Spain's view, 182
Deportation of American Negroes to the
Amazon River basin, 111–127,
172–197; American business interests,
109–110; Brazil's climate, 176, 178;
Brazil's response, 183; Chase and, 183;
Congressional support for, 175–176;
Douglass on, 124; economic boom in
the basin, 188; exclusion of France and
England from the Amazon, 122; Manifest Destiny, 116; Maury (Matthew Fon-
taine) and, 1, 4–6, 49, 68, 69, 107,
111–127, 171, 219, 222, 246–248;
precedents, 175–176; right to emigrate,
176; as a safety valve, 114, 116; as a
substitute for suppressing the African
Slave Trade, 121; Sumner and, 183;
Treaty of Union (1856), 109; U. S. foreign policy, 5–6, 111–112; Webb and, 6,
173, 176–179, 182–183, 197, 219. *See
also* Colonization of Blacks
Dewing, Sammuel, 58
District of Columbia, slave trading in, 32
"Dolphin" (American brig), 62, 277n65
Doolittle, James, 175
Douglas, Stephen, 135
Douglass, Frederick: on American
attempts to suppress the slave trade, 35;
on Brazil, 13, 103–104, 253; on depor-
tation of American Negroes to the Ama-
zon River basin, 124; Monroe and, 185;
as proposed Minister to Brazil, 245; on
Wise (Henry Alexander), 83
Dow (owner of the "Amelia"), 74
Drain, F. P., 186
Drinker, Sandwith, 61–62

About the Author

Gerald Horne is Moores Professor of History and African-American Studies at the University of Houston. His books include *Race Woman: The Lives of Shirley Graham Du Bois*; *Race War! White Supremacy and the Japanese Attack on the British Empire*; *Black and Brown: African Americans and the Mexican Revolution, 1910–1920*; *Red Seas: Ferdinand Smith and Radical Black Sailors in the United States and Jamaica*; and *The Color of Fascism: Lawrence Dennis, Racial Passing, and the Rise of Right-Wing Extremism in the United States*; all available from NYU Press.

CPSIA information can be obtained
at www.ICGtesting.com
Printed in the USA
JSHW071315071222
34428JS00001B/5